THE INFORMATION MACHINES

Also by Ben H. Bagdikian

In the Midst of Plenty: The Poor in America

THE INFORMATION MACHINES

Their Impact on Men and the Media

Ben H. Bagdikian

HARPER & ROW, PUBLISHERS

NEW YORK, EVANSTON,

SAN FRANCISCO, LONDON

1817

FIRST EDITION

STANDARD BOOK NUMBER 06-010198-9

LIBRARY OF CONGRESS CATALOG CARD NUMBER: 71-123913

Contents

Acknowledgments

The research and writing for this book were supported entirely by RAND, with constant encouragement from its president, Henry S. Rowen, and the board of trustees. While RAND does much of its work for government, no government funds were involved in any of the work for this project.

There are numerous members of the RAND research staff to whom I am indebted for stimulation and assistance, none more than Paul Baran, now of the Institute for the Future, who was a constant source of insight into computers and their social applications. Others who were particularly helpful were Fred Ikle, Herbert Goldhamer, Alexander George, Anthony Pascal, Robert Specht, Leland Johnson, and Konrad Kellen.

Research assistance was generously given by Betsy Schmidt, Eve Savage, Christine D'Arc, Barbara Quint, and Sean Duggan.

Senior consultants in field work on newspapers were Dr. William L. Rivers and Dr. James N. Rosse, both of Stanford University, and Hy Shannon, vice president for newspaper production of Field Enterprises. Their assistants were John Mayo, Daniel Garvey, Yale Braunstein, and G. Franklin Mathewson.

Special mention must be made of the unnamed proprietors, editors, and staff members of the newspapers who permitted us to observe their operations and examine their financial records.

Frank A. Philpot, of Stanford, made a useful report on news operations of radio and television stations in the San Francisco Bay area.

The Department of Journalism of the University of Michigan, working in cooperation with RAND, recorded twenty-four hours of all broadcasting heard in the Grand Rapids–Kalamazoo area, under the direction of Dr. William Porter. News portions of these recordings were transcribed and analyzed. The tapes of the full broadcasts are available for study as a joint contribution of RAND and the University of Michigan.

Invaluable help was given by John Richardson and Robert L. Stern of the National Academy of Engineering.

My wife, Elizabeth, endured mountains of paper and work with galleys.

Secretarial work on the project was done with care by Susan Turner, Phyllis Davidson, and Grace Griffin. My secretary, Molly Larsen, has my special thanks. In the final stages of the book, John Hogan of RAND was indomitable.

This book and its author benefit from insights gained in earlier research supported by the John Simon Guggenheim Foundation and the George A. and Eliza Gardner Foundation.

Despite generous contributions of those mentioned above and others not mentioned, the book itself, with whatever errors and misconceptions, is entirely the work of the author.

BEN H. BAGDIKIAN

Washington, D.C.

Introduction

In 1927 a young Mormon, Philo T. Farnsworth, working in a darkened San Francisco apartment, transmitted television images without wires. Perhaps it was symbolic that Farnsworth used the dollar sign as a test pattern and that police raided his apartment under the impression that he was distilling intoxicants. Forty years later, television was still being used primarily as a collector of advertising dollars by selling parlor entertainment.

It has taken forty years to see even dimly that this machine transformed American culture and politics, to realize that its ultimate impact is not going to be idle relaxation but active social transactions like education, community development, politics, commerce, and the direct observance of public affairs.

The invention of machines and their intelligent use are, unfortunately, two quite different human achievements. One remembers that a cousin to television, military radar for detecting distant airplanes, was practical and in service at Pearl Harbor on December 7, 1941. But it was an exotic mechanism held in such secrecy by scientists and technicians that when Private Joseph L. Lockhard noticed ominous blips on his screen at 7:02 in the morning and reported "something completely out of the ordinary," his superior told him to forget it. His superior was not stupid or disloyal. The working military professionals simply had not been told enough to build the new technique into their system of thinking. The Army had not learned how to apply radar to real-life problems. Those real-life problems did not go away, of course. Fifty-three minutes later the blips dropped bombs on a totally unprepared Pearl Harbor.

Since 1927 we have learned a little of how technology grows. We have learned less about applying it wisely. Only reluctantly do we admit that mechanical progress and pursuit of monetary profit are not by themselves beneficial to human affairs.

Since 1927 we have begun vaguely to understand something else: the profound effect on individual and social life of the distribution of information.

If men could start all over again, knowing back then what we know now, the world would be a different place. One cannot guarantee that it would be a better place: good things as well as bad happen by accident and nothing ordains that planning will be for the general good. But, if there is any justification for faith in rational humanistic thought, it is better to move with forethought.

Today we are on the threshold of a change in human communications more powerful than our innocent introduction to electronic pictures in 1927, perhaps more significant than all past changes in the technology of information. The way men deal with each other and with the distant world is about to be transformed by a combination of the computer, innovations in the transmission of signals, and new ways to feed images into this system and to take them out.

The news media—newspapers, radio, and television—are a vital part of present communications. They will continue to be, though inevitably they will change. Other informational systems also will change: education, postal service, commerce, the practice of medicine, shopping, how people live in their homes and use their leisure. All of these, including the news media, will be more intertwined with each other than they are today.

Whatever the nature of this next communications environment, something beyond the design of machines will determine how news is perceived, collected, stored, selected, and displayed. What difference will it make? Will men get more significant information or less? Will their news system permit them to understand their environment better and live in it more happily?

This book will not pretend to draw a blueprint for the future of the news. Nor will it be concerned primarily with the technology of the future, though this must be an important consideration. The focus will be on what the content of daily information will be, what form it will be delivered in, and how it will be distributed throughout the population.

This book will consider the most likely technologies that will change the way the next generation receives its news. It will look at what difference it makes in human affairs to have daily events reported rapidly, at the audience for news in the United States and some peculiarities of news in this country. It will report some of the research done for this project on the social, economic, and technological forces that shape today's news in print and in broadcasting. And, finally, it will speculate on what the new technical systems will do to the content and form of news in the United States during the remainder of this century.

Research for this book included a number of subprojects.

Data on the economics, technology, and information flow in American daily newspapers were compiled by a special field team that examined operations of a number of newspapers. Senior members of this team were Dr. William L. Rivers, of the Department of Communications, Stanford University; Dr. James N. Rosse, of the Department of Economics, Stanford University; and Hy Shannon, vice president for newspaper production of Field Enterprises, Chicago. We believe that this is the first intensive outside examination of the economics of a sample of American dailies. It was needed to overcome the lack of good economic data on American newspapers.

Patterns of news in a representative American broadcasting market were studied in a joint effort of RAND and the Department of Journalism of the University of Michigan at Ann Arbor. This project recorded the full twenty-four-hour output of all twenty-four radio and television stations heard in the Grand Rapids–Kalamazoo area. News portions were transcribed and analyzed. The entire set of tapes, believed to be unique, is available for public study as a contribution by RAND and the University of Michigan.

A third subproject was a survey by communications specialists on expectation of the nature and pace of future technological change as it affects news and public information.

This work draws upon the results of these projects as well as other sources. The most useful details from the RAND news-media project are being published in separate books and monographs. This book, while benefiting from the data and insights of these projects, is the inference of the author.

This is necessarily a work that combines objective measurement with personal values. Conflicting views of public affairs have been aggravated in the last decade as men became more conscious of the influence of the news on individual behavior and social values.

As the mass media become more pervasive, versatile, and vivid, these conflicts will become even more heated. So, before new technological systems become fixed, it may be useful to consider the choice of characteristics that lie before us, and what difference our decisions will make.

If daily news were just another household commodity, like potatoes, thinking about its future would not lead so quickly to a concern with the evolution of American society.

News as a commodity is economically interesting. Like other mass-consumption goods it is produced and disseminated through networks of men and machines, but, unlike most, each item is a handcrafted intellectual effort, making it an intriguing product of personal judgment, technology, and bureaucracy.

But the ultimate significance of the news system is not economic, technological, or organizational. It is social. News is the peripheral nervous system of the body politic, sensing the total environment and selecting which sights and sounds shall be transmitted to the public. More than any other single mechanism, it decides which of the countless billions of events in the world shall be known to the generality of men. Having done so, it alters men's perceptions of the world and of themselves: the more rapid and vivid the communication, the greater this alteration.

Inventions that increase speed and immediacy of information have always changed the nature of their world. The introduction in Europe of printing by movable type in the fifteenth century helped to produce the Renaissance and Reformation. Telegraph, railroads, and high-speed presses in the nineteenth century led to the overthrow of oligarchies and launched mass politics. Television in the 1950s crystallized the civil-rights revolution, rebellion on the campuses, and a dislocation between those who were shaped by the new machine and those who were not.

The men who control these instruments of communication have enormous power. Where once priests and kings decided what the populace would hear, the proprietors of the mass media now decide. As men gather in ever-larger interdependent masses, communications technology becomes more important and increases the power of those who control it. In an isolated village of 50 persons who meet frequently, community events are learned in face-to-face contacts more effective than any formal medium. But in a country of 200 million self-conscious human beings, the power of news systems is infinitely greater: it is a source of reality itself. For most of the people of the world, for most of the events in the world, what the news systems do not transmit did not happen. To that extent, the world and its inhabitants are what the news media say they are.

The power of news systems is great, but their task is difficult. The world is large and life is complicated. The total potential information from all places is incalculable. To observe everything everywhere is impossible. Even if possible, to transmit it all would be unimaginable. And even if all that somehow could be done, no individual could ever absorb the results.

Yet, unthinkable as total observation, transmission, and reception are, there is an imperative that pushes everyone in that direction. As the world develops modern communications in its most remote areas, the reservoir of knowable events enlarges. As the capacity for data transmission expands, more of this information reaches distant centers. And, as individuals learn how to capture information more skillfully, a wider sampling of information about the human race reaches more individuals.

Information technology has always influenced this process. In 1870, Ralph Waldo Emerson wrote, "We have the newspaper, which does its best to make every square acre of land and sea give an account of itself at your breakfast-table."

Emerson was exaggerating. Most square acres, wet or dry, are never asked for an accounting and are never heard from. During Emerson's time, whatever foreign acres were heard from in English tended to be in that part of the British Empire where there happened to be a correspondent from the London *Times*. Whatever he deemed worthy of an accounting arrived in its own good time aboard a transatlantic ship and became known among those who happened to see a paper that bothered to reprint his dispatches.

Since then, communications inventions have been attempting to convert Emerson's metaphor to reality. Continents were connected by submarine cable, the telephone was patented, radio invented, jet planes became common, communications satellites mirrored live images from opposite sides of the world, and men walking on the moon were seen and heard by a large part of the human race 1.3 seconds after the real events, as soon as the broadcast signals could travel, with the speed of light, the 240,000 miles to Earth.

It is one of the curiosities of this growth in available information that it has not quenched the thirst for knowledge, but stimulated it. As inventions bring the possibility closer to realization, more men feel compelled "to make every square acre of land and sea give an account of itself."

This impulse is not limited to leaders, whose power and responsibility give them an obvious need for instant intelligence. It is true of the majority of Americans.

Nor do they feel this extraordinary impulse only at the rare times when historic events—wars, contagions, and natural disasters—reach directly into the lives of the ordinary person. It is felt every day by most people. In fact, it is exercised a number of times throughout the day, as though men and women, immersed though they are in the distractions of modern life, were afraid that they might not be told immediately if something eventful happens anywhere in the universe. There has never been anything like it before.

The typical citizen scans his universe in a number of ways. He gets a daily printed report, usually delivered to his home, either in the morning in time for a briefing before he starts his day, or in the evening to inform him what happened while he was working. Or both.

This newspaper, while it has other advantages, is several hours late in its intelligence and this seems to make the citizen nervous.

Consequently, he also watches the news on television, sometimes in the morning, perhaps as he simultaneously eats his breakfast and reads his newspaper. More often he watches in the evening. The televised reports may be films of events that happened within the last few hours, and occasionally they are events as they are actually happening.

As though this were not enough, between his newspaper reading and television viewing, the citizen also listens to radios, in his automobile as he drives to work, or in his shop or office, or to a portable set that he takes with him to beaches, ball games, and remote summer camps.

He gets more than social and political intelligence from these activities—entertainment, relaxation, merchandising information. And it is not always clear when he is the active pursuer of information and when he is the passive target of a stream controlled by someone else. But he has the power to avoid it if he wants to, and the fact is that he takes pains to be exposed to it every day and takes particular pains to be exposed to the news.

The news system in the United States already engages a larger proportion of the population in worldwide events and does it during more hours of the individual's time than any society before has ever experienced.

In this generation, the involvement of the population in serious public information has grown enormously, thanks to rising literacy and education, and the widespread adoption of radio and television. In the coming generation, changes of this magnitude or greater will occur through fundamental inventions in the handling of information. These include the electronic computer, with its capacity for the rapid organization, storage, and retrieval of vast quantities of information, including texts, pictures, and instructions to other machines on how to handle its information and how to route it through complicated networks. There is an enormous growth in the capacity for transferring information from point to point, and this growth will reach even greater capacities. In the past fifty years the number of continental electronic-communications channels has increased from 6 to 100,000. In the next thirty years the number could easily grow to 1 billion. Devices for entering information into such a system and for taking it out are proliferating. There is an expansion of forms for the display of information—voice, moving pictures, print—and in ways for the individual to find desired data from the expanding reservoir.

The individual ingredients of this communications upheaval are still new. Semiconductors of germanium, silicon, and gallium arsenide duplicate the work of bulky glass vacuum tubes. Invention of the transistor in 1947 started the revolution that made electronic equipment cheaper, smaller, more portable, and demanding of less power.

At about the same time, the connection of electronic components by soldered wires began to be replaced by printed circuits, electrical pathways etched or stamped on insulated surfaces. This, with transistors, permitted miniaturizing of electronic equipment. In the

1960s the integrated circuit, small chips that contained both the components and the pathways between them, permitted a silicon disc the size of a twenty-five-cent piece to contain one thousand circuits that can operate simultaneously. In less than ten years, the cost of an integrated circuit dropped from $600 to $2.50.

Substitutes for paper documents also began to proliferate until by now it is possible to use microphotography to record thirty-two hundred typewritten or printed pages on a single four-by-six transparent ultramicrofiche card. It is possible to carry the equivalent of a thousand books or of sixty hundred-page newspapers in the breast pocket of a man's suit, and read them on a projector, still expensive, but already as portable as a briefcase.

Looking ahead to the uses of such inventions has obvious advantages, among them avoiding unpleasant surprises. New systems will be what men make them. To foresee developments permits consideration of their impact before narrow corporate decisions or unwise public policy or accident produces unwanted results.

This book makes some assumptions about future technology, but with trepidation.

There are many pitfalls to forecasting. Life is not completely predictable. It is more predictable than most people believe, since there is a growing body of experience with the scientific method, with the growth of technology, and with the evolution of economic and social forces. But it is not entirely predictable, for which we should be thankful.

Even the march of new machines is uncertain. Hedley Donovan, of Time Inc., put the problem succinctly during a conference held in 1966 by the American Academy of Arts and Sciences:

I could sketch a fairly orderly model of impersonal forces, factors, and trends that theoretically should have a predictable influence on the course of communications media over the next twenty or thirty years. I suspect, however, that some schoolboy, now fourteen years old, whose name I do not know, is going to conceive of an idea in 1981 that will have more influence on what communications are like in 2000 than anything I or my colleagues could logically project today.

There are other pitfalls to technological and social forecasting. One is excess conservatism. Men are inclined to see the world as basically stable or "normal" during their time and therefore stable for the future. They might be appalled or delighted with particular innovations, but these tend to be seen as aberrations that will not recur. Until the Industrial Revolution, this presumption was generally valid. Since then it has not been.

Excessive conservatism affects even men with high competence. When the first locomotives were built, some transportation experts agreed that anyone reaching the speed of thirty miles an hour would suffocate. A few months before the Wright brothers flew at Kitty Hawk, the astronomer Simon Newcomb proved scientifically that aviation was impossible. Lord Rutherford, the leading atomic scientist of his time, said that unlocking the energy of the atom could never be done. Clifford C. Furnas, a distinguished chemical engineer, in his book, *The Next Hundred Years,* published in 1936, said that atomic energy was not likely and advised readers, "Do not buy any stock in an Atomic Energy Development Company." After World War II, Dr. Furnas became president of a firm called Western New York Nuclear Research Center, Inc.

Men who are threatened by change or who are happy with the status quo tend to disbelieve in an altered future. In 1938 David Sarnoff told the Radio Manufacturers Association that "television in the home is now technically feasible." A trade magazine, *Radio Guide,* considered this hilarious. It mailed out a promotional package containing a century-plant seed with the instructions: "Plant it in a pot, water it carefully, expose it to the sunlight. When it blossoms, throw the switch on the new television cabinet that your grandson will have bought, and you may expect to see television offering program quality and network coverage comparable to that of our broadcasts today." The magazine has gone out of business.

Perception of future time is psychologically difficult. It is natural to compare a span in the future with a span of similar duration in the past, and unconsciously fill the time ahead with the same kind of events as occurred in the period just finished.

And men have not adjusted their thinking to a normal life span of seventy years: a generation is still defined obsoletely in many dictionaries and in men's minds as thirty-three years. "Next generation" implies nonexistence for this one. People who were alive in 1940 and are alive in 1970 and in the normal course of events can expect to be alive thirty years from now nevertheless still think of the year 2000 as irrelevant to them.

The most difficult predictions are not of physical artifacts but of social values and styles of life. Human expectations have changed radically in the last thirty years. In 1940 most adult Americans had barely finished grade school; today most have high-school educations or better. Most then did not own automobiles or homes; most own both today. In 1940 Hitler's Germany, Stalin's Russia, and Mussolini's Italy, together with imperial Japan, were enforcing their authoritarian domination of the world by military and civil terror. This and eleven years of an unrelieved economic depression traumatized a whole generation and made the idea of optimism, general affluence, and growth seem like fantasy.

It would have seemed incredible to an average family in 1940 with their $43-a-week income that in thirty years they would be earning four times as much, would own a $3,000 car and a $15,000 home, and that one-third of all children would have a higher education costing more than $10,000. They would not have guessed that the 1940 symbol of modern, high-speed transoceanic transportation, the *Queen Mary,* in 1970 would be a museum.

Disbelieving such changes in society, men thirty years ago would have had difficulty predicting technological innovations that became widespread.

This is not to suggest that life inevitably gets richer, fuller, and freer. Civilization itself is not inevitable. One generation, the 1910 euphoric middle classes of Britain and the United States, believed they were on a guaranteed escalator to ever-higher levels of progress and happiness. But the generation that followed them lived in a world of depression, dictatorship, and global destruction. What this does suggest is that social values of any period are subject to radical change, that these changes are the hardest of all to foresee, making it difficult to predict the physical systems these uncertain conditions will support.

If the assumption that conditions of life remain unchanged and the desire to maintain the status quo produce conservatism in predictions, the other side of the path to the future is full of pitfalls dug by uncritical optimism, wishful thinking, equating engineering with progress, reflex faith in "technological breakthroughs," theatricalism in forecasting, and the simple extension of recent change endlessly into the future.

Even if one extends into the future what seem to be absolutely certain goals for the human race, he can be wrong. In 1968 Adolf

A. Berle, Jr., noting that there is no agreement on how national money ought to be spent because personal values differ among individuals, said that nevertheless there were ten common-sense goals almost everyone would agree on. The first item on his list was "People are better alive than dead." Shortly thereafter, medical and legal specialists considering the implications of organ transplants and manipulation of human body cells raised the possibility that in the not-too-distant future a person might be kept physiologically alive forever and that this would raise the issue whether a future individual right might be "the right to die."

Nor is mechanical efficiency a reliable guide to future technology. Established human habits can frustrate the most efficient technical innovations. The standard typewriter keyboard has an artificially low maximum speed because the most common letter combinations were deliberately placed far apart so that the crude mechanisms of a century ago would not jam. Now that metallurgy and engineering have improved, and keyboards could be rearranged for the convenience of human fingers instead of metal levers, too many people have deeply ingrained typing habits to tempt any manufacturer to design a more rational keyboard. New communications technology will confront personal patterns started in childhood and ingrained by daily usage.

Technology does not necessarily change simply because it would be useful for the consumer. Men's emotions are attached to artifacts as they are to all things, and personal profit is not always on the side of the greatest good for the greatest number. Nothing ordains a change for the convenience of the users unless a producer finds his own reasons. Among the more important developments in the history of communications was the shift to parchment as a writing surface, beginning about two thousand years ago. For centuries the standard material for recording words was papyrus, formed of split reeds matted to form sheets, which, attached end to end, were stored in large rolls. Papyrus had serious disadvantages. Only one side could be written on. Scrolls had to be laboriously unrolled in order to reach any part beyond the beginning. The reading process, requiring two hands holding the partially unrolled bundle extended, was tiring and awkward. But it had high social status, being associated with priests and kings.

An alternative method used the treated hides of animals, and had substantial advantages. Though it was slightly rougher, it could be used on both sides. Because the hides were durable, their edges could be tied together or hinged, making what later became known as a book. The animal-skin pages were a quick-access storage of information, since it was as easy to turn to a middle page as it was to look at the first or last pages. It was more comfortable to use over a period of time, more compact to store, and lasted longer. But it had low status since the greatest libraries and rulers historically used papyrus.

But it was not the rational choice of technical superiority that thrust animal hides into more popular use. It was the arrogance of Eumenes II, King of Pergamum, in the second century B.C. in trying to lure the chief poet of the great library in Alexandria to his own growing collection in Asia Minor. This so enraged the poet's sponsor, the ruler of Egypt, that he forbade the shipping of papyrus to Eumenes from the Ptolemies' monopoly on the upper Nile. The King of Pergamum was forced to continue the expansion of his library by using animal skins, which took their name in the following centuries from "Pergamum" after linguistic permutations converted that word to "parchment." Ambition, greed, and the vanity of powerful men are not often charted on the graphs of technological change, but they are important and they are unpredictable.

Practicality and efficiency can even be disadvantages. In the nineteenth century as railroads pushed west across the American continent, the existence of sheltered, deep-water harbors in California was important in deciding where the railroads should terminate. San Francisco and San Diego had superb harbors. San Diego was superior because it had the added advantage of lying along the 32nd parallel, which was snow-free, unlike the route to San Francisco. But the railroad did not go to San Diego precisely because it was so good: the men who controlled the railroad, Collis Huntington, Leland Stanford, Mark Hopkins, and Charles Crocker, happened to own a great deal of land in the San Francisco Bay area and wanted no rival terminal in the south detracting from their real estate's future value. Crocker said, "We would blot San Diego out of existence if we could, but as we can't do that we shall keep it back as long as we can." In guessing the direction of technology it is wise to ask who is in the best position to profit most.

Forecasting the future of news is no exception. Communications are an enormous economic prize, underlying perhaps half of the gross national product. Existing enterprises, old and young, large and small, are in competition for favored positions. They fight to influence corporate and public policy in their direction, often with little relationship to technical efficiency or the willingness of the public to pay.

When radio news seemed to threaten newspapers in the early 1930s, newspaper interests, led by the American Newspaper Publishers Association, attempted to suppress the broadcasting of news. Using their power to deny access to the major news wire services, which at that time received almost all their income from daily papers, they forced on radio what became known to newspapers as "The Biltmore Program," because of the hotel where they met, and to broadcasters as "The Versailles Treaty," because of its harshness. It was in formal effect from 1934 to 1938. Purchasing of news from the wire services would be permitted radio only on condition that they broadcast no more than ten minutes of news a day in two five-minute segments, each news item to consist of no more than thirty words, none of it to be sponsored, and CBS and NBC to withdraw completely from the news-collection field. As broadcasting gained popular and political power, the treaty broke down.

From the start of television, entrepreneurs wished to test the idea that some viewers would be willing to pay extra for special broadcasts designed for special audiences. "Pay TV" was immediately attacked by the broadcasting and motion-picture industries, which, through their influence in Congress and state legislatures, placed FCC and statutory inhibitions on what people could pay for. Technological feasibility and consumer wishes were negligible factors; special economic power, political influence, and propagandizing through favored access to the mass media by its operators were much more important.

Even when one considers technology alone, it is difficult to know whom to ask about the future. In looking at the future of news, most of the changes seem to be coming from outside the news industry. Newspapers have had the same technology for a long time, and their traditional suppliers are the makers of typesetting machines and heavy presses. The new technology arises from computers and electronics. So those who know most about newspaper technology today are not necessarily those who know the most about newspaper technology in the future.

Broadcasting, being younger and already an electronic medium, is less tradition-bound. But it has a stake in present technology, which sends programs through the air and is organized around large national audiences. New technology could send signals in novel ways in a different pattern of distribution, changing the basic economics of broadcasting. Here, too, the leaders in commercial broadcasting, committed in corporate battle to preserving the present techniques, may not be the best to ask about the direction and pace of change.

Nevertheless, the main lines of the future seem to be clear, or as clear as a look can ever be a whole generation ahead. Somehow computers will be involved in the storage, delivery, and switching of popular communications. Somehow there will be additional capacity for the consumer in his home to receive a greater variety of information than he does now. He may be able to control the timing, content, and form of this information flow in ways not now available to him.

The timing of such developments was asked of a panel of authorities in various kinds of communications, drawing upon a forecasting technique developed at RAND. It has been shown that in general technical forecasts of a group of authorities is usually better than forecasts by any one of them. (Lord Rutherford would have been a valuable contributor to a view of the future of nuclear energy but was wrong all by himself.) A group judgment can be compiled by asking the group to meet at a conference. But this has disadvantages. The more authoritative the members of the group, the busier they are likely to be and the less able to spend time sitting around tables swapping predictions. More important, in face-to-face encounters, force of personality, articulateness, and loudness of voice may influence the results as much as technical competence and personal insight. And, once a man has stated a position in front of his peers, he may be hesitant to change his mind.

Consequently, a form of survey was developed in which authorities in a field are asked by mail for their judgment of timing and direction of innovations. They make these privately and, so far as other panelists are concerned, anonymously. The results are tabulated and the collective judgment is recirculated, with a request for comment and revised opinion, if any.

A group of about twenty-five men in fields relevant to the future of communications was asked to look ahead in the future of news. Some were academics but most were active in corporate research, typically vice presidents for research and development in leading firms involved in communications. Most had nationally recognized competence in the science and technology of communications but also in the corporate and economic factors in adoption of innovations.

The panel was asked to judge the chances of "widespread adoption" of particular innovations. "Widespread" was not defined. They were presented with a table that offered adoption of a technique in five years, ten years, and twenty-five years. Within each of these time spans they were offered a probability of adoption of zero, 20 percent, 50 percent, or 80 percent or more. They could also make written comment, which was frequently the most valuable judgment rendered. On each question about a specific technique, each panelist was asked if this was in his primary field of interest. The results were calculated on the basis of those who said yes, calling them "specialists"; on the basis of those who said no, or "nonspecialists"; and on the combined judgment of both specialists and nonspecialists.

Later, for purposes of calculating the panel responses mathematically, "widespread adoption" within any of the given periods of time was arbitrarily assumed to be when the panel agreed that there was a 50 percent or better chance.

In general, the panel was more conservative than most of the popular and technical literature on forecasts of change. But specialists usually believed devices they knew about best would be adopted sooner than did men in different (though related) fields. This can be interpreted almost as one wishes: the experts could be overenthusiastic about their own techniques, or they could be more conscious of its limitations than anyone else. But it was interesting to plot the individual responses of a few of the most distinguished men in the major fields involved. They were the least conservative of all. Thus, the more the panelist knew about a technique, the more optimistic he was inclined to be about its adoption.

Almost without exception, the panel agreed that every major step in the news process would be substantially changed between the years 1975 and 1980. They did not agree on precisely what these changes would be, though it was apparent that they expected an acceleration of present alterations in conventional techniques. More radical innovations in whole systems are expected to begin to take effect in the period after 1980, about which there is more agreement.

By 1979 they expect video programs will reach most homes through cable, special wire systems that send television direct to each home, instead of the present transmission through the air. This prediction is generally consistent with cable-industry forecasts.

Cable is basic to other home-information systems. Cable TV, or CATV (community antenna television), began in remote areas beyond the effective reach of standard television transmitters or in terrain where mountains and other massive features interfered with signals coming through the air. The CATV operator usually constructed a special antenna on the highest point available, or linked a number of these around the obstruction. From this community antenna he installed wires to individual houses, sometimes underground, but usually on telephone or electric poles on space leased from the utility. The cable to each home was connected to the consumer's television set for a monthly charge, usually $5 a month.

Originally, local and network broadcasters were delighted with the arrangement. The cable reached homes previously out of broadcast range, adding to the total audience and therefore to advertising rates the broadcasters could charge sponsors, and all at no cost to the broadcasters.

Two things changed this symbiotic joy.

Early cable had no more than three channels. The average American city has six channels available through the air. More recent cable installations have raised the number of channels for their customers from five to twelve and now forty-two, with eighty or more technically feasible. This is far more capacity than can be filled with the output of the local stations. The surplus channels began to be used for stock-market quotations, weather reports, continuous news bulletins, and television programs imported from more distant cities. Cable's extra channels began to compete with the local stations.

Then, cable moved in from the scattered rural areas where it was the sole method of TV reception, into suburban and city areas previously reached by through-the-air transmitters. In many cities, particularly ones with massive buildings, ordinary television reception is poor. The introduction of color television placed more demand on high-quality reception, and cable, for both black-and-white and for color, produces a better picture than transmissions through the air. The better-quality picture plus the increased choice of programs appealed to viewers who already received conventional transmissions.

Cable, once the compliant handmaiden to broadcasters, became a serious rival. The two are now deadly enemies and the fight continues in the courts, in Congress, in the regulatory agencies, and in the corporate trenches of a dozen industries. Broadcasters originally persuaded the FCC to put severe restrictions on cable, some of which have since been relaxed. But others remain. Telephone companies are wary, since cable ends their monopoly on wired communication into residences. As a hedge against possible triumph of cable, some of its enemies have begun entering the field themselves.

The long-range significance of cable is not its ability to duplicate existing television programs. It is the potential for two-way communications between the home and a vast array of information services: twenty-channel cable has forty thousand times more capacity than telephone wires. Such a high-capacity installation in each home, interconnected with computers, is capable of handling information far beyond voice telephone.

Outgoing signals from the home by cable already are being used for automatic reading of household utility meters and burglar- and fire-alarm systems, transmitted to a centralized location where the reading from each home can be identified. This plainly has the potential for being expanded to other more complicated messages sent directly from the home.

Future incoming programs to the home, with each receiver identifiable through its wire (like telephone), can include juvenile and adult education; video and text materials from a large number of sources, such as libraries and newspaper data banks; two-way connections with other individual sets, so that people can "speak by color television" the way they do now by telephone; and video and facsimile mail.

There are organizational and cost barriers to some of these two-way functions, such as building a switching network for high-capacity signals, but the technology for their implementation already exists.

The impact on news has already begun. Some cable systems use their excess channels to have a continuous transmission of news. One small cable system in California arranged for a local paper to supply periodic typed news stories to be put on a belt that slowly moves in front of a television camera.

Typically, the research specialists in this area were more optimistic about home cable, believing it would be widespread by 1978. Men in related fields suggested 1983.

But while the panel believed cable would be commonly installed for video service before 1980, they were not so sure that in the same time period it would carry services other than broadcasting.

A major innovation in home communications will be a reactive system, with the individual consumer having the power to order specific content and receive it immediately. There is already an elementary reactive system: it is possible to order items by telephone and get a reply by telephone. One can ask for other telephone numbers, or the right time, or airline schedules, or taped weather forecasts, and the answer comes immediately through the return electronic link of the same telephone line. A more advanced system would permit the consumer to signal out for what he wants and get an immediate televised response.

The panel believed that such a reactive system would be in normal use by 1990 (the specialists thought 1987), when the consumer would be able to get what he asked for either on his TV screen, by voice, or in a document produced in his home electronically.

The consumer will order this information, at first, by Touch-Tone telephone, the pushbutton signaling system the telephone company is introducing throughout the country. Telephone pushbuttons are faster and make fewer mistakes than circular dials. Pushbutton electronic tones, unlike dial clicks, can travel through the entire telephone switching system. They can be interpreted by a distant computer. If a number is busy, the computer can be instructed to keep trying it automatically. Or a subscriber will be able to push certain buttons that automatically transfer all incoming calls to another number.

The telephone company in the future could switch pushbutton signals to computers outside the telephone system. For example, a housewife ordering an item from a mail-order catalogue could call the mail-order computer and push the buttons representing the number code the catalogue carries for the desired item. The mail-order-house computer can send the order to its delivery department, automatically adjust the company's inventory to show the sale of that item, record the sale on the customer's sales slip and monthly statement, and then switch automatically to the computer of the housewife's bank, automatically deducting the amount of the sale from her account.

By 1979, one panelist predicted, the average home will have available to it the Bell System's Picturephone, a small television screen connected with the telephone. This is now used experimentally and industrially, and will be offered to areas of dense geographic use in the next few years (in the beginning it will be uneconomical for the company to install Picturephones in scattered locations). Perhaps by 1979 the average housewife will call the mail-order computer, which would show a series of photographs of the item she desired, each with its own code number, whose digits she could press on the telephone as she looked at the televised catalogue page.

It also means that the Picturephone could be connected with libraries and other sources of information for immediate display of texts and graphic material, though present Picturephones are limited in their size, and to black-and-white and have relatively coarse resolution.

The consumer's ability to instruct distant sources will depend on the versatility and speed of his home devices. The panel felt that by the mid-1990s Touch-Tone signaling for purposes other than telephonic connections would be superseded by more sophisticated devices. One might be a home keyboard in which messages could be typed to computers in plain language and the computer's reply typed in plain language. Or messages could be sent from a home Xerox-type machine and answers received in the same form.

In the 1980s the consumer seeing the lists or pictures of items on his television screen may be able to make selections by telephone. In the late 1990s he might be able to select them by simply placing an electronic pen or even his bare finger on the point on the TV screen where the desired item is shown. Such a signal is possible now, utilizing the energy added to the screen by the fingertip, but it is highly specialized and expensive.

When a reactive system is common, the outgoing signals will bring information back in a number of forms. The incoming information will come, the panel agreed, in the late 1980s by TV screen, and for more simple and short messages, by voice created by a computer.

Computer-created voice is already in use for simple numbers and brief, elementary words—combinations of the standard parts of sounds for letters and numbers which the computer combines on the basis of the changing stock quotations fed into the computer by tape.

Computers will someday understand normal spoken voices and create a spoken reply from their reservoir of basic sounds. But at present computers do not listen very well, though they can make simple talk (leading to an unkind male hypothesis on the gender of computers). The panel felt that computers would not understand normal spoken language even by the year 2000, but specialists in the field thought computers could create words in reply to simple questions by 1987.

By the 1990s information will be transmitted electronically to homes where facsimile machines will reproduce Xerox-like documents. By about the same date, video material that the consumer wishes to record automatically and play back at his own convenience will be possible by a version of what is now Electronic Video Recording, which is to the television set what disc records and tapes are to phonographs.

A few of the leading specialists in facsimile were optimistic about its widespread use in the home. They predicted it for the early 1980s, but the forecast for all those specializing in the field averaged 1994. Panelists in related fields were quite sure that home facsimile has a low probability (30 percent) of being widespread even at the turn of the century. Commercial facsimile that transmits and reproduces documents already is available between major cities.

There has been speculation on the existence in the average home of a large, four-by-five-foot three-dimensional color television screen. This would have the appeal of a more vivid and detailed picture, and it would also become an effective substitute for certain kinds of group meetings, since it would come close to life-size figures and whole-room perspective. The specialists in the field predicted this could be adopted by the year 2000.

The delivery of news to the home will continue to include printed information, the panel agreed, though both specialists and others felt that before 1990 whole pages of news could be displayed on TV-like screens in the home and the consumer could make documents of the particular video pages that he wished to record.

In the early 1990s news will be delivered to the home in a professionally compiled series of items, selected and displayed as editors now do it, but with the consumer able to order further information·on any of the items that interest him. The standard presentation will be updated continuously so that at any moment it may be different from earlier versions.

Within news institutions there will be changes in techniques and organizations, and a blurring of the distinctions that now exist between printed and broadcast news.

Today most community broadcast-news operations are relatively simple, a single wire-service Teletype machine which a newscaster uses as his sole source for a periodic reading of leading items. Larger television stations and network operations take more elaborate means, though still simple compared to the system for printed news. Once the news—text for reading and film for action footage—is compiled, the distribution process for broadcasting consists of transmitting it through the air.

Newspapers are very different. The major costs and most of the time in newspapers are devoted to what in the broadcasting process is cheapest and fastest—reproduction and distribution.

Newspapers categorize their serious news intake as either local or national, the national ordinarily coming from news wire services that now transmit on teletypewriters at the nominal rate of sixty words per minute. Local news is generally compiled by a local news staff, by telephone, and by person in the field. When in the field, on urgent stories under time pressure, reporters dictate by telephone to typists or other reporters, or when under somewhat less pressure, send by teletype or telegraph.

In the future, news, once written, will enter the newsroom in faster ways. Specialists on the panel felt reporters in the field before 1979 will be transmitting their stories into their local organizations either with light portable keyboards using radio or telephone connection, or portable facsimile machines. The nonspecialists disagreed, in the case of portable keyboards predicting 1988 and for portable facsimile, 1996.

The chief difference for organizations compiling the news will be the use of computers and electronic appliances for decision making. Computers are now used by newspapers in limited ways. Finished local material on typewritten manuscript is delivered to typists who retype it in order to punch continuous paper tape that the computer feeds to typesetting machines. Syndicated wire-service news comes in simultaneous typed copy and punched tape for direct use in the computer, except for changes which the local typist can superimpose on the wire-service tape. Today the typed manuscript is made by striking keys on a typewriter, and is converted to paper tape by restriking keys on another keyboard.

The panel sees a decline in the use of paper-tape technique and a steady growth in placing all news into the computer in digital form. The paper tape is awkward to handle, is relatively slow in running typesetting machines, and is limited in its ability to be edited, changed, and rearranged. The panel felt that increasingly the orignal key strokes will be used to create a magnetic tape that will put all textual material for the paper into the computer in digital form, with widespread adoption in the mid-1980s.

Placing all news material into digital form in the computer has many advantages. It can be retrieved for display in a number of ways other than on paper (such as a TV-like screen) and quickly changed by editors using electronic devices. Then, since it is already in electronic form, it can be distributed in a variety of ways, ranging from creating a printing plate in a distant plant to recreating the picture of a page on home TV. Most of the panel had low confidence in the adoption by newspapers of machines that automatically read typed copy, which is a relatively complicated process for the computer. But, using the same style of keyboard, the struck key can generate a digital signal to enter the computer directly with no intervening errors, with no need for the computer to "reread" the typed characters.

However, a few of the best-known specialists felt that, despite the duplication of effort, machine reading of typed copy would grow because it is a form of information men are used to handling. These few felt that there would be widespread machine reading of typed copy by computers in 1980. But the majority of the panel doubted that it would be widespread even thirty years from now.

Incoming wire-service news can be placed in computers in digital form at enormously increased speeds. Most newspapers now receive most of their news from teletype machines operating at less than sixty words per minute. Within a few years, computers at one news center, like a wire-service headquarters, will be able to deliver their information in digital form to a distant computer, such as a newspaper, at the rate of eighty-six thousand words a minute.

It seems inevitable that newspapers eventually will convert all their information to digital form for storage in their own computers and for interaction with data banks elsewhere.

Calling information out of a computer for reading is a slower process than putting it in, sometimes taking three times longer. But it is still faster than present handling of typewritten sheets. The Los Angeles *Times* in 1969 received a full stock-market quotation report, the equivalent of seventeen thousand words, from a computer in New York to one in Los Angeles, in thirty seconds. Once in the computer, it took three times as long for the computer to deliver a printed report. But "three times as long" was ninety seconds, a tolerable period.

As newspapers begin storing all their information in computers in digital form in the mid-1980s, their editors will begin working with something other than individual pieces of paper. The panel see editors in different parts of their buildings, or even in different cities, working at consoles like high-quality television screens, on which they can call up stories, and, discussing them in voice conferences, making changes of material on the screen. When a decision is made on the final version of the story, and the alterations are made on the screen, it is re-entered into the computer.

Also in the 1980s, a few years after the mutual electronic editing of individual stories, the panel agreed that page makeup and methods of displaying stories also would be done by editors working on the format by mutually reactive video screens.

Some panelists suggested that computers could be programmed with a large variety of page designs that the machine would automatically suggest on the basis of the length, emphasis, and style of the individual stories selected by the editor. The advantage of this would be almost instantaneous creation of the finished master page by electronic methods.

A number of panelists agreed on the technical feasibility of such electronic display editing, but questioned whether newspapers would wish to do this, using consoles that today cost $80,000. It is a relevant question.

Three or four $80,000 machines are formidable compared with the cost of paper and pencils for hand editing and free-hand dummying of pages. But even small daily newspapers spend $1 million for equipment today, a large paper more than $20 million. Most of this is spent on production—engraving, typesetting, stereotyping, and presswork. In industrial economies of this size, even the present cost of an $80,000 console would not be prohibitive if it performed advantageous work.

Once an entire paper is in a computer in digital form, alternative methods of production and distribution become possible. Today in newspapers whose total expenses range, because of size of paper, from $2.5 million to over $25 million, the cost of producing the paper, after all editing and reporting are done, is about 55 percent. This includes mechanical composing of pages, paper and ink, and presswork.

But, since all the material would be in digital form, which could be transmitted electronically, it could be reproduced electronically in the customer's home on his TV set, or in selected facsimile of items he wished to read in a document rather than on a screen.

Or a paper, instead of printing all its editions in a single downtown plant, could have smaller satellite plants throughout the area, the information sent to the satellites electronically from the computer. The panel felt this would happen by the mid-1990s. But the panel also believed that in this same period there would be direct transmission to the consumer's home of a standard inventory of news, and a few years after that, capacity for the consumer to get immediate electronic delivery of further information on any item in the standard presentation.

The prediction of both satellite newspaper plants and plant-to-home transmission reflects the feeling of other observers that there will be different patterns for large metropolitan newspapers and for smaller ones. Because of traffic problems in urban areas large metropolitan dailies will benefit most from early development of satellite plants. At present it is still cheaper to move material by truck, though it is time-consuming. But, when all material is computerized in digital form, transmission to satellites will be practical, perhaps permitting laser etching of plates on the printing press. The next step for such papers could be transmission direct to homes.

If all news will go directly to the home, it will go by cable, the panel said. Communications satellites were less likely to be used except in dispersed areas where laying cable is exorbitantly expensive.

The amount of money involved in paper-to-home direct transmission would be large. But it would begin to follow the economics of broadcasting in the sense that most of the cost of hardware would be borne by the customer. The laying of cable connections and the provision of home-receiving devices presumably would be part of a system supported by someone other than the newspaper. And this would substitute for what now constitutes most of the cost of producing a newspaper.

A small paper with annual expenses of $4 million spends almost $2 million of it on converting the completed news and advertising information into a printed package delivered to each home. A medium-sized paper with $14 million expenses spends $8 million for physical production and distribution. A large paper with $60 million annual expenses spends close to $40 million for newsprint, production, and distribution, or about $100 a year per subscriber. So, though electronic delivery to individual homes is impressive in cost, so are present costs for newspapers. When one adds the contribution made by the consumer, who presumably would buy or lease his home devices because they will also bring other benefits as well as news, the economics of mass electronic distribution and home reproduction become less forbidding.

But the total transmission of "newspapers" in video form, without a document, is unlikely. The printed word will continue to have useful characteristics compared with sound or motion pictures or texts displayed on a screen.

What is more likely is an acceleration of present trends of a gradual division of labor between audio and video presentation of some kinds of information, and printed display of others. Much of what is in newspapers—stock-market quotations, movie listings, headlines—would be satisfactory viewed on a screen only long enough for a reader to decide if further examination is desired. Other newspaper content will continue to be desirable in print—longer articles, analyses with statistics or other information requiring the ability to reread or to compare items separated in space, and items for retention in personal records.

It is not likely that any future home facsimile will produce newspapers like those now delivered by hand. The average number of pages for daily papers in the country is 53 on weekdays and 178 on Sundays. Larger newspapers have more pages than that. Each of these pages has 2.1 square feet of printed area, which would require a home reproducer to turn out over 100 square feet of printed surface every weekday and 374 square feet on Sunday.

The compact, preprinted paper delivered to the home will continue to be attractive for some time, for convenience. It will be even more attractive on the basis of cost. Newspapers produce one page per customer for about one-third to one-half a cent. Not even the optimists in home facsimile envision duplication of such low costs in the foreseeable future.

However, there are estimates of facsimile costs for smaller page sizes, such as five inches by six inches, for fractions of a cent.

And, if some of what is now printed were presented on a screen, the remaining material to be produced in document form might cost less than the full current newspaper delivered to the home.

Once all newspaper information is stored digitally in a computer, the economics of electronic transmission will begin to look tempting to counter the high costs and inconvenience of making documents in the home.

Radio and television spend most of their money in preparing the content of their programs, an almost negligible amount in distribution (the cost of physical facilities). Based on total households in the country, in 1967 the commercial television industry had property worth $661 million, or $11 per household, to distribute its programs; that same year consumers paid $3.711 billion for television sets to receive these programs, or about $47 per household.

While total newspaper production costs are not known, they seem to be about $3.7 billion a year, or, spread over all households in 1967, about $63 per household. The consumer paid subscriptions, also spread over all households, of about $24 a year. Unlike broadcasting's very small costs, newspapers spend about 55 percent of their total budget, or $35 per household, for reproduction and distribution.

As home devices evolve in the next generation, they will serve not only entertainment, home education, and live public events, but information from all kinds of organizations. Some of the costs of production and distribution now borne exclusively by newspapers will begin to shift to the consumer, as they already have for broadcasting.

For newspapers this will be tempting because it will reduce their original investment in heavy printing equipment. It will also reduce the time lag in printing and distribution that is increasingly bothersome, especially for evening papers. Already, evening papers that are not on suburban doorsteps by 5:30 P.M. are considered lost to television. But, because of complicated press runs, fatter papers, and problems in distribution, the delay between completion of editorial matter and its delivery is growing. It is not unusual on a metropolitan evening paper to have a seven-hour delay between the last news deadline and final delivery of a paper, at a time when the portable transistor radio, the car radio, and home television produce accelerating news distribution.

An important qualification must be made of the panel's forecasts. Members of the panel were asked to predict when each technique would achieve "widespread adoption." After they responded to that, a somewhat arbitrary value was assumed in which "widespread" was equated with 50 percent or more probability of adoption. An innovation can have a significant impact on society long before it has a 50-50 chance of "widespread" use or before it is used by half of all the population. The airplane, for example, materially changed domestic and international transportation even though in so affluent a country as the United States 80 percent of the population had never flown in an airplane. It was not until the 1940s that telephones had been installed in half of American homes, but long before that telephones had altered communications.

Similarly, over the next thirty years, many of the innovations the panel judged would become widespread by a certain date might make a noticeable impact before that date. Many new home devices, for example, will be installed by those who have a professional use for them, just as teletypewriters connected to computers are already being used in the homes of some computer programmers and analysts. From there, use of the new device expands to additional specialists until general familiarity and reduced cost in its manufacture lead to popular adoption.

Some innovations can be important to a minority of news organizations long before they spread to the majority. For example, offset printing, using photographic instead of cast-metal techniques, is used by only about 25 percent of American daily papers. These are the smaller ones, for which offset, at the moment, is peculiarly effective. But the technique has already had an important social effect in making it significantly cheaper to enter the weekly-newspaper and other small-edition publishing field. And portable facsimile senders for reporters, though not predicted for widespread use until 1979, are already being used by a few large newspapers in 1970.

Large newspapers have different problems and ecomomics than small ones. Unlike small dailies, very large ones handle massive quantities of information, spend millions of dollars on cumbersome production techniques, suffer critical difficulties in producing multiple editions for different zones of their urban complex and have growing obstacles to distributing the papers from central printing plants. It is conceivable that the largest papers will adopt some new techniques before small ones, and this could influence the way millions of people get their news long before the date the panel guessed this would be "widespread."

The panel was not asked its opinion of this kind of selective growth. So the events they predicted may be important long before the date forecast for "widespread adoption." Years prior to that date news institutions might already have started a basic transformation.

If newspapers begin to make part of their computerized news and advertising available to the home by electronic means, the distinction between newspapers and broadcasters will begin to fade. And if this news is offered in a variety of forms and with a growing choice by the consumer of what and when he can receive, the relationship of news organizations to the news audience will undergo significant change.

What the future holds for all news organizations is a vast increase in the scope of their news gathering, in the quantity and speed of their intake of information, radically new methods of storing and selecting from this expanded reservoir, and increasing versatility in presenting it to the consumer. For the consumer there will be more control over what information he receives and over the timing and form of its arrival in his home.

THE INFORMATION MACHINES

Information Machines
and Political Man

It has taken two hundred years of the Industrial Revolution for men to realize that they are not very good at predicting the consequences of their inventions: to the surprise of almost everyone, automobiles changed sex habits. Information devices are no exception: machines for mass communications produce unexpected changes in the relationship of the individual to his society.

It is not clear what the ultimate effect will be of introducing electronic techniques to news and other information services. But communications inventions of the past have produced patterns of change that are useful guides to the future.

Knowledge has always been a key to power. Traditionally, political information has been restricted to the highest levels of leadership and only later has trickled down to lower echelons, helping to preserve hierarchical authority.

When leaders and their constituents begin to receive information at the same time, important things change in their relationship.

First, social reaction time is accelerated, speeding the pace of developments for both leadership and electorate.

Second, the dependence of lower echelons on higher ones is decreased and power based exclusively on initial possession of information is destroyed.

Third, leadership may find itself at a disadvantage in responding to demands for action. Where incoming messages stimulate fast reactions, and both leadership and constituencies get the information at the same time, large institutions are by nature less volatile than small organizations, and will usually react more slowly.

For these and other reasons, authorities will always attempt to control information for the public good as they see it. One method of control is release of deceptive material. Leaders have special access to mass channels of communication and they can use this to inundate the audience. In a sense, the drowning of the individual in carefully designed self-serving information is the counterpart of the ignorance of mass audiences in times past. It is worse to the degree that it provides an illusion of full knowledge.

But so far even the most skilled authorities at information control have been unable to exercise mastery over all popular information over long enough periods to prevent nonestablishment knowledge from having a significant impact.

Discerning segments of the audience, though surrounded by the noise of propaganda, are able to extract relevant information, either because they have enough background knowledge to judge official declarations, or because the realities of their life situation are at convincing odds with the establishmentarian flood.

This is a dilemma for all institutions. Instant and universal communication disrupts traditional patterns, tempting leaders to restrain the trend. But the needs of a dynamic system make sequestering of information dangerous for other reasons. In a complicated and interdependent society the general population must comprehend the environment. If leadership takes action without the earlier diffusion of fundamental knowledge, an ignorant constituency may be panicked or unresponsive.

It is a myth of our time that unfettered dissemination of critical knowledge produces shocks peculiar to open societies, and that when open societies compete with authoritarian ones, democratic populations must deny themselves normal access to official information. Free information is most hazardous for an authoritarian regime. Interchange of information within the population, including between government and its public, is the origin of vigor and creativity in policy, increasing the store of available ideas and testing their relevance. So not only are democratic societies better conditioned to the impact of new information and therefore more stable in the face of it, but their system of government is dependent on it.

A population that requires insulation from uncontrolled information is living in the wrong era; for the last few centuries this insulation has become increasingly porous, and regimes that have used it for social control have lived precarious existences. There have been massive tragedies associated with authoritarian regimes and the dictatorships that marked the early stages of newer nations. But it has gone almost unnoticed that among modern, centralized governments, the regimes with the greatest longevity have been democratic, not authoritarian. There are not many monarchies left; the dictatorships mutate or die. Freedom of information is not a small part of this evolution.

Consequently, introduction of mechanical devices like the transistor and television halfway through the twentieth century had powerful influences on social change. These devices either energized previously inert populations or they rapidly changed the perceptions of those already engaged in the political process.

The spasms of change in American society in the mid-1960s are attributable in large part to new methods of communication. It is interesting that a similar wave of change more than one hundred years earlier, in 1848, was the aftermath of the same kind of fundamental alteration in human communication.

In January, 1848, there was an insurrection in Sicily, followed by an astonishing succession of rebellions and revolutions during the next twelve months that shook every regime in Europe except Russia, Spain, and the Scandinavian countries. The basic causes involved the Industrial Revolution and urbanization, with the consequent growth of nationalism and individualism. New communications accelerated the change and in so doing caused events to happen differently. It was the kind of thing Napoleon had in mind when he said, "Cannon killed the feudal system, ink will kill the modern social organization."

Under the new urban conditions of the 1840s, ideas that had lain dormant for generations, like democracy and doubts about the divine right of kings, gained new urgency, spread by new ways of transmitting information and expressing opinion. The new communications were not only freer because they were novel but because they, like the new cities, escaped the thinking of traditional leaders. The new channels of communication had such vastly enlarged capacities that even had older leaders appreciated their significance they could not have controlled them without basic changes in governing structures, which was precisely what leadership regarded as intolerable. But once the innovations were established, men used them. Channels of communication abhor a vacuum. New channels are no exception.

What were the new channels? In the years between 1820 and 1848 the steamship, railroad, new printing techniques, and the telegraph produced stunning changes in the way individuals saw themselves and their positions in society.

Particularly important was the change from animal transportation to abstract communication. From prehistoric times to the nineteenth century, messages of substance could travel no faster than a man or horse could run, a pigeon could fly, or a boat could sail.

For centuries there had been an urge to exceed these limits. But speed-of-sound and speed-of-light transmissions were crude, expensive, and unreliable. Pre-Columbians had a system of hilltop signals from the southern tip of South America to Central America, but these carried one-signal ceremonial messages. American Indians used smoke signals. Armies had long used hand signals, guns, and drums and bugles, but these were effective only over short distances for a small inventory of messages.

Semaphores were highly developed in Europe in the eighteenth and early nineteenth centuries, but they suffered from the same crude vocabulary and dependency on fair weather. Their speed was about one signal a minute. It took eleven minutes for Lord Nelson to display the flags at Trafalgar that read, "England expects every man to do his duty."

The opening of the Erie Canal in 1825 was memorialized by a series of cannon, each 8 miles apart, with the signal traveling 364 miles in one hour. At about the same time, a syndicate of stockbrokers set up hillside semaphores between the markets of New York and Philadelphia, sending priority quotations in prearranged order with ten-digit signals over the 100 miles in half an hour. But when words became necessary, or the order of messages required change, or clouds intervened, the system failed. Like radio aerial navigation in the early days of World War II, it was least effective when it was most needed.

The slowness of ground travel forced messages into the air. Carrier pigeons were increasingly used in the early nineteenth century. One operator used a five-hundred-pigeon flock to deliver news to East Coast American newspapers. But the training of flocks was long and elaborate, their top speed sixty miles an hour in good weather. Most pigeons could learn one route with a maximum range of two hundred miles. Only exceptionally talented birds were omnidirectional. They were faster than horses, but they were also more succulent: the eighteenth-century pigeon is more convincing than Marshall McLuhan that the medium can be the message.

For all practical purposes, the running horse was the only reliable fast communications medium for centuries up to the two decades before 1848. Over short distances it could achieve fifteen miles an hour. Over longer distances the speed diminished and travel time had to be measured in days. The fastest overland transmission with a capacity to carry involved messages was probably the American Pony Express, which required 190 stations, 500 horses, and 80 riders to achieve an average speed between St. Joseph, Missouri, and Sacramento, California, of five miles an hour, or a total elapsed time of ten days. The alternative, stagecoach, took months. The Pony Express charged $5 a message, later reduced to $1 per half ounce, and when the company expired in 1861 it had a net loss of $200,000.

Transoceanic travel had remained static for centuries. Except for the slight advantage of American clipper ships, long-distance water speeds did not change much between Columbus and Robert Fulton. The first completely steam crossing of the Atlantic was in 1832, the first scheduled run in 1838. Samuel Cunard founded his all-steam line in 1840.

These were also the decades of the railroad. Between 1828 and 1848 national railway systems were inaugurated in Belgium, Denmark, France, Germany, Hungary, Ireland, the Netherlands, Poland, and Spain. In the United States there were twenty-three miles of railroad in 1830 and nine thousand miles in 1850.

Large-scale personal travel has always been a formidable mass medium of communication. Armies—like those of China, Persia, Greece, Rome, Britain, and the United States—have usually produced more lasting cultural than military change. Military invasion has often been unwittingly a two-way communication. The Roman Army created the English and Romance languages by speaking pidgin Latin with the provincial rustics. The Crusaders never accomplished their military mission, but their return traffic changed Europe with Islamic scholarship. Any massive change in personal travel is a significant event in communications, and the new modes of long-distance travel in the 1830s and 1840s were no exception.

But the most spectacular leap in communications came when

message transmission was separated from transportation. The telegraph, sending messages with the speed of light, had a social, economic, and cultural impact comparable to that of television a century later.

Samuel Morse patented his telegraph in the United States in 1837, but others in this country and Europe had produced working devices well before that. In Europe there were operating systems before 1840. A submarine cable was laid between England and France in 1850.

Communications links quickly created new institutions for disseminating information. The nerve ends of telegraph in the United States spread southward and westward from Boston, New York, Philadelphia, and Washington. In the decade after the telegraph reached Illinois, in 1845, for example, thirty newspapers were started. The pattern was duplicated in Europe.

In both Europe and the United States the telegraph did more than simply raise the quantity of information. It placed knowledge in new places under changed conditions. It bypassed traditional systems for controlling information.

Well into the nineteenth century, the written word was regarded by many authorities as a privileged communication. The ability to write was restricted, and from the fourth century to about the seventeenth it actually diminished in incidence among urban populations, when compared with ancient Athens, Alexandria, and Rome. Plain written language was, in effect, a secure code.

The limitation in written and printed messages reflected the existing technology. Portable writing surfaces were scarce and scribes even more so. For a long time after the fourth century a distinction was made between writers, who became extremely few in number, and readers, of whom there were more. The invention of movable type in the 1450s intensified this difference, since the typesetter and printer could duplicate the written word without more writers. This perpetuated some control of information since only a few specialists made written symbols. Among upper-class eighteenth-century ladies it was still considered genteel to read but gauche to write.

The growth of printed information worried the new mercantile class as it had earlier worried the Church. This is a common attitude of established power toward new systems of communications. New channels appear threatening to an establishment, as popular literacy did to the Church during the Middle Ages. Governing groups almost inevitably become involved with control of information. Usually, the instability of new knowledge continues until the established order not only drops its objection but adopts the new mode to preserve whatever remains of its influence, changing from an enemy to a champion of the new communication.

Before the Reformation and the Napoleonic Wars, the Church restricted the spread of written messages, both in the training of specialists in writing and in approval of new works. But thereafter the Church, faced with the new power of entrepreneurs, turned to popular education and literacy as a way to prevent complete dominance over young minds by the new mercantilism. At this point it was the mercantile class that objected to the Church's teaching literacy. An English writer in 1763 criticized the religious schools that taught reading since working-class students would refuse "those drudgeries for which they were born." Men like James Mill and Adam Smith argued unsuccessfully that the new capitalists should support public education. The mercantilists ignored the pleas. But by the mid-nineteenth century the new industrialists were so alarmed by growing urban riots that they reversed their position and supported general education and literacy as a measure to allow the working classes to "govern and repress their passions."

In the late eighteenth century South Carolina and most other Southern states passed laws making it a crime to teach a Negro to read. By the mid-twentieth century instruction for competent literacy was considered therapy against ghetto violence.

Control of nineteenth-century printed matter depended on the availability of materials. For one thing, portable writing surfaces were expensive and hard to produce, for centuries limited to the skins of animals. The finest carrier of a message was vellum, the hides of new-born animals, and the most exquisite of vellums the uterine tissues of stillborn lambs. Control over such a limited system was relatively simple.

By the time of Gutenberg, paper made from rags began to replace parchment, increasing availability of printed matter and reducing the price. Costs dropped even more in the 1840s when boiled wood chips began to replace cloth as a common ingredient of paper.

At about the turn of the century the Foudrinier machine ended the traditional technique of making one sheet of paper at a time in favor of continuous production. In the United States, newspapers used 3,000 tons of paper in 1810 and 78,000 in 1849. Population during this period increased more than 300 percent and newsprint use 2,600 percent, and since papers remained about the same size, it is evident that a large new segment of the population was being exposed to the printed word.

The price of the printed word dropped drastically. The usual cost of a newspaper in the United States in 1810 was six cents. The first penny paper was *The Cent* in 1830; the first successful one was Benjamin Day's New York *Sun* in 1833, followed by James Gordon Bennett's *Herald* in 1835 and Horace Greeley's *Tribune* in 1841. The new channels of information were not simply expansions of the old but created different styles and content. In the United States there had been 235 individual newspapers in 1800; there were 2,300 in 1850.

These technological and economic developments came ten to twenty years earlier in Europe, but there another practice inhibited expansion. There was a "tax on knowledge," a stamp for every published piece of paper. In 1815 in Britain this came to fourpence on every copy of a newspaper, an exorbitant levy that came close to suppression. In 1828 the tax alone cost the *Times* of London £68,000. It tended to make for content that pleased the authorities.

Despite prosecution for newspaper-tax evasion, underground papers in Europe proliferated and made tax collection ineffective. In 1836 the English tax was reduced to a penny and finally abolished in 1855. Despite the tax even the legitimate press grew, from 39 million individual copies printed in 1836 to 122 million in 1854.

In France the same kind of growth occurred, from 28 million legally taxed papers in 1828 to 79 million in 1846. This trend was duplicated in most European countries. (One of the first acts of the monarchies after their restoration in 1849 was attempted suppression of the popular press.)

The years before 1848 also saw radical changes in the mechanics of printing. The printing machine of Gutenberg was a wooden winepress modified to push his assembled metal letters onto parchment. This remained the basic design, and the material still wood, until a Saxon printer, Friedrich Koenig, invented a metal rotary press in

1813 and the next year ran it with steam. During the 360 years between Gutenberg and Koenig, the standard speed for printing was six hundred impressions (three hundred pages, both sides) a day. In 1814 the *Times* of London, using Koenig's press, turned out eleven hundred impressions an hour. By the middle of the century British and American presses were turning out twenty thousand impressions an hour.

The content of newspapers changed as their technology and cost changed. They had been for centuries establishmentarian. Their content had been heavily laden with theology and official edicts. The establishment press continued in the new era; but a large number of the new papers expressed new ideas from a previously inert or silent part of the population.

With limited communications, the propagation of printed news was almost entirely through officially approved channels. Papers printed in the major capitals became the source of printed news everywhere. In the early 1800s, incoming ships from Europe would be met in the outer harbors of American ports by sloops operated by American newspapers rushing to pick up the British papers. Selected stories from London were reprinted in the major papers of the largest Eastern cities. The Eastern papers would then go by mail to outlying communities, which would, in turn, select from the papers of the Eastern cities. A postal provision of 1792 was that every publisher could "send one paper to every other printer of newspapers within the United States, free of postage." Papers exchanged by printers formed an arterial system for international political information but their basic information was limited to selections from a few established newspapers in major capitals. Any editing along the way was necessarily a diminishing of original information that was already quasi-official.

The telegraph freed provincial printers from the role of passive consumer of weeks-old information from established sources. Original information could be received direct.

With telegraph, all papers, large and small, big-city and provincial, were closer to an equal access to sources of information. Telegraphy marked the beginning of the transformation of the local purveyor of news from printer, a mechanical conduit of remotely processed material, to an editor, an individualistic interpreter with access to his own information. It was a process that would reverse itself seventy-five years later when publishers had to become industrialists again.

The same dissipation of social controls took place with books and helped to create a new intellectual and social climate. Large-scale printing made it easier to create large-scale changes in social attitudes. In the centuries before Gutenberg there had been approximately 30,000 new titles and editions of books produced in Europe. In the 150 years after Gutenberg, up to about the year 1600, there were 40,000 new titles. From 1600 to 1700 there were 1.25 million new titles; from 1700 to 1800 there were 2 million. From 1800 to 1900 there were 8 million new titles. Exponential growth of recorded knowledge has been with us ever since.

The content of books from the fall of Rome to the seventeenth century remained theological and philosophical. The French copyright law of 1793 freed publishers from official monopolies and much of the content control, increasing the flow of ideas. Napoleon reimposed controls that lasted well into the nineteenth century, but once the printers were freed, they were hard to suppress, especially with the new personal mobility of the period. They moved to the Netherlands and Belgium, where they turned out massive quantities of the works of Molière, Voltaire, and Rousseau, and others whose writing had a subversive impact on absolute monarchy. The output of these printers spread to the United States and the rest of Europe. They created a large and lively French underground distribution. Generations after their deaths, writers began to have widespread social impact thanks to the relevance they seemed to have for an audience that discovered them through the new technology.

The spread of information, the broadening of the range of ideas, and the consciousness of mutual knowledge propagated the political epidemics of 1848. New kinds of communications had become the pacemakers of change. It was a phenomenon repeated electronically a hundred years later. Electronics suddenly short-circuited the ancient linkage of literacy and abstract intellectuality.

Literacy and its supporting technology were the basis for political activism after the Industrial Revolution. Literacy is still considered the major remedy among primitive societies for such cultural backwardness as headhunting, poor sanitation, relaxed nakedness, and optimum blood pressure. But it has always been a relatively slow process. In general, the conversion of an essentially illiterate society to an essentially literate one takes a minimum of from fifty to a hundred years, long enough to provide some degree of continuity and time for adjustment. For example, it has been estimated that in the early years of the United States less than 200,000 of the 4,000,000 population were literate. By 1840 60 percent were literate, by 1950 about 97 percent (though this overstates literacy in terms of effective skills for contemporary occupations). The change occurred over a long period of time, roughly concurrent with the growth of industrialization and urbanization.

Global illiteracy is still massive. In 1950, according to UNESCO, 44 percent of adults in the world were illiterate.

But, both in the United States and the world in general, literacy is not distributed evenly and since literacy traditionally has been a measure of social and political involvement, the unevenness can have serious consequences.

For example, in the United States illiteracy is said to be 3 percent, but it is 2 percent among whites and 11 percent among nonwhites. If routine access to current printed material is added to personal illiteracy, the proportion of the American population that does not regularly absorb printed information is closer to 20 percent. (The poor typically lack routine reading material.) Global illiteracy is even more uneven.

It is for this reason that electronic communications can have profound effects on events. As long as men could not travel easily and had no other way to perceive those in distant places, there was a tendency toward stability despite great disparities in conditions of life. When this isolation ends it brings drastic reaction.

Printed information used to be the main instrument of this penetration and its required development time permitted periods of adjustment for political systems sensitive enough to respond. But the rapid growth of radio and television telescopes this time and presents societies with fast reactions they have not had to cope with in the past.

Within the United States there are significant differences in social use of various kinds of communications. There is some reason to believe that the educated population is using more communications-grade paper (26 pounds per capita in 1900; 80 in 1925; 140 in

1955; and 196 in 1965) but that this is not extending to the uneducated. At least ˙20 percent of the population, for example, do not regularly buy a daily newspaper. Noncommercial message transactions on paper are either diminishing in number or rising only slowly.

Between 1955 and 1965 the percentage change in per-capita use has been:

Telegrams sent	(−43%)
Daily newspapers bought	(− 8%)
First class and air mail sent	+14%
Average daily phone calls	+47%
Radio sets owned	+48%
TV sets owned	+64%
Average daily hours TV sets are turned on	+84%

There are important class differentials in the distribution of these communications and probably in their impact.

Differences in television viewing by class is striking. Watching declines as social class rises. Harold M. Hodges, Jr., in his book *Social Stratification* (1964), reports that "lower-lower" class respondents watched television one hundred eighty minutes a night, while persons labeled "upper" class watched sixteen minutes.

The reasons for this class difference probably include fewer recreation alternatives for the poor; larger families and more crowded housing for the poor, so less opportunity for privacy, including from television; the relative inexpensiveness of television compared with other entertainment; and a lower level of skepticism about remote subjects among the lower-income groups because of fewer competing sources of information.

Quite aside from the larger quantity of exposure, the less educated may be more energized by each hour of exposure. One obvious reason is the different relationship between their own lives and those they see on the screen. The other is the familiar hypothesis that the less political knowledge a man has the more he will be affected by a new piece of knowledge. The educated and sophisticated individual can match new information against a large inventory of previously absorbed conceptions. The innocent observer cannot. Probably it is the manifestation of this that causes established groups initially to fight new communications channels but later reverse themselves and encourage use of the new channels in order to diminish radicalism initially stimulated by the same channels.

This is not to say that the educated viewer cannot be conditioned by mass-media programming. But there is evidence that the more sophisticated the viewer in the subject at hand, the less susceptible he is to manipulation by the isolated fact. This is confirmed by studies on voting behavior, of individual judgment of the news, and of the influence of consumer advertising. The most volatile voters in general are the least experienced. Most surveys of attitudes toward news show a much higher regard for news in general than for news about a subject on which the respondent has some knowledge. Advertising campaigns can produce large-scale sales of commodities that are marginal to the viewer or simply favor one of a class of goods already in his thinking; advertising is much less persuasive in changing central concerns.

It is interesting to apply to the impoverished American television viewer the observation of Neil P. Hurley, S.J., of the Department of Sociology of the University of Notre Dame, and director of the Instituto de Comunicaciones Sociales in Santiago de Chile. He wrote of impoverished foreign audiences:

Even a James Bond movie, a doctors' or a nurses' TV serial, a space-exploration adventure, or a private-eye mystery inculcate the values and attitudes that reinforce the Western model of man as a shaper of his own destiny, as one free of environmental determinism and the heavy hand of the past, as a person capable of innovation and choice. Willy-nilly then, American commercial media are promoters of change since they impart a sense of activism to passive peoples, an unmistakable conviction that the individual is a maker of history, and that men are engaged in an on-going process of moral struggle and irreversible choices. The "drop-ins" who are exposed to a stream of such messages receive the definite impression that today is not like yesterday and therefore tomorrow need not be like today. It is no small achievement, this erosion of a fatalistic view of life with its monotonous symbol of the masses as pawns on life's checkerboard of days and nights.

One must add to this the prevailing use of violence for attention getting, which teaches ritual murder to each child from his earliest years of learning, and implants the assumption that human differences are inevitably resolved by physical violence. Here again there may be a class difference in impact. To the middle-class child this televised lesson remains fantasy, diluted or negated by his personal experience at home, in the neighborhood, and at school, and by a fairly early intake of printed material of a humanistic nature. For the impoverished child the lesson of violence does not necessarily remain fantasy but seems confirmed by his life experience.

The persistent and ingenious consumer advertising of American television has cultural effects all the more powerful among the deprived. Programming is filled with the imperative to buy and consume, implying that this is a measure of normalcy and propriety.

The growth of broadcast information in this country has had social effects paralleling those that preceded the 1848 revolutions in Europe.

The acceleration of social reaction time is obvious. Within hours of the assassination of Martin Luther King there were riots and near-riots in over one hundred American cities. Police had no more advance warning than potential demonstrators.

In 1796 when George Washington announced his decision not to run for re-election he called in a sympathetic editor, D. C. Claypoole, on a Thursday and said he would deliver a message the next day. Claypoole spent the weekend setting the "Farewell" in type and printing his *Daily Advertiser*. The political leadership in Philadelphia saw it Monday morning and, presumably, began making plans and marshaling forces toward a succession. The *Advertiser* went by horseback to New York and Baltimore, reaching there late Monday night. From there it went by mail coach to outlying communities, where, after a week to ten days, it arrived and was either clipped and reprinted by a local paper or posted in a coffeehouse. If there was a local reaction and if it was reported in the local paper, this news went in the reverse direction by mail coach, arriving in the major Eastern cities in a week or ten days, and then to Philadelphia where the newspapers in the capital took note of general reaction around the country. The political leadership had a three- to six-week head start in policy formation.

In 1968 when Lyndon Johnson announced his decision not to run for re-election, with insignificant exceptions every American learned of this at the same time. Leader, subleader, and thousands of local political units all began on the same starting line of change. And they all knew that they all knew.

Another characteristic of communications innovations, seen in mid-nineteenth as well as mid-twentieth century, is the lack of control over new channels.

This does not mean that there are not attempts at control even in the United States. Authorities complain bitterly over uninhibited dissemination of information, and about criticism of official acts and declarations. Fear of riots has led many authorities to ask for censorship of news about disorders since this knowledge may stimulate similar reactions elsewhere.

But inevitably the consequences are ambivalent. Political leaders have a bias in favor of television, in which they are in control of their own message without interruption and, during their appearance may be able to exclude interpretation, refutation, or opposition. This control over a planned television appearance is probably a major source of the recurrent attacks on journalists who disturb carefully prepared television images with interpretations and editing.

In 1964, Charles de Gaulle, then President of France, referring to his political opposition, said, "They have the press. I have the RTF and I intend to keep it." (Office of Radiodiffusion-Television Française is the state broadcasting system, which had become the instrument of the regime in power.)

In 1962 when Richard Nixon lost a campaign for the governorship of California and bitterly denounced the printed press for its reportage of his campaign, he added, "I can only thank God for television and radio for keeping the newspapers a little more honest."

If television permits total control during a leader's speech, it has the possibility of criticism at a later time. Furthermore, centralized mass-media systems are not the only electronic devices used in social and political events. Access to electronic equipment by the civilian population is analogous to the spread of literature after printing technology became widespread.

Authorities often ask broadcasters and newspapers to quarantine news of civil disturbances, but for $10 anyone can buy a receiver that intercepts police calls, which may tell more than an ordinary newscast. Similarly, observers of a scene that is blacked out in the news have at hand their own telephones.

In early 1968 a youth group held a demonstration in Grand Central Station. When police attempted to break it up there followed a chaotic scene which no one participant could encompass. But in the crowd there were observed individual participants with transistor radios to their ears as they marshaled those immediately around them. They were listening to a rock-'n'-roll station that had a reporter making live broadcasts from a balcony of Grand Central Station describing the overall scene, giving individuals in the crowd a better strategic picture than many battlefield commanders have. Electronic equipment is cheap and easily obtained, and devices like walkie-talkies are available to almost everyone.

Even where authorities control all formal systems of communications, national boundaries are becoming increasingly porous. The world level of communications expertise and equipment is rising so rapidly that outside information is penetrating closed societies that had successfully insulated themselves for centuries.

The Soviet Union is reached routinely by hundreds of outside radio broadcasts a week and no longer even tries to interfere with most of them. Even in China, travelers become conduits for information going into that insulated country and coming out of it. International broadcasting is heard all over the great Chinese land mass.

The passive rebellion in Czechoslovakia in 1968 against the intrusion of Soviet-bloc troops was organized and sustained by clandestine use of radio and television transmitters and underground newspapers.

During most of his regime in the 1960s, Charles de Gaulle's political opponents could not get significant air time, and anti-Gaullist news was censored. However, when the disturbances of spring 1968 occurred, the vulnerability of this control was evident.

First, strikers "captured" the broadcasting system. Frenchmen were astonished to hear anti-regime speeches and to see protest demonstrations that they were unprepared for.

But quite beyond that—for eventually the authorities regained control of state broadcasting—detailed coverage of the tumult in France was being provided by stations outside the country's borders, like Europe Number One in the Saar, Radio Luxembourg, Radio Monte Carlo, and Radio Andorra.

Within the United States a third significant factor has had an impact: communication with populations not ordinarily reached by printed information.

Part of the past stability of Negro oppression in the South was due to strict local control of information. The typical pattern was that local newspapers, radio stations, libraries, and schools did not give out information that would disturb existing racial patterns. The only Negro news that was printed in most places was of Negro crime, stimulating white fears to keep tight social and political control. Pretelevision radio was not a serious disruption of existing patterns. For one thing, race relations were not a major item in national news and even when they were they could easily be censored out: production of local radio programs was relatively inexpensive. The result was not only a preservation of the status quo but a conditioning of both whites and Negroes either to believe the moral and social justification for the status quo or to discourage any hope of changing it.

National television was more difficult to control locally. By the time of mass TV ownership, race relations had become a dominant theme in the news, especially after the Supreme Court school decision of 1954 (which was not routinely reported in all Southern papers). For another, local creation of television programming was extremely expensive, compared with the cost of taking network material. And, lastly, television transmitted a more complicated message than the printed word or radio. The professional operating the camera, especially on live broadcasts, could not control or predict the consequences of every piece of information being sent. The background could often tell more than the foreground to which the editor was focused. A rich medium has many novel effects, many of them unintended.

In pretelevision radio, professional boxing was a popular program, typified by manic verbal descriptions of mayhem inside the ring. In the early days of television the same announcers were used and continued the staccato reporting of apocalyptic struggle, but the camera revealed a scene in which apathetic partners made lackadaisical probes of the empty air. It was the end of boxing as a regular broadcast sport. Boxing was replaced by a new kind of deception, visual rather than audible, professional wrestling, which was designed for the new medium. Rotund actors wearing garments that visually symbolized arrogance, or effeminacy, or masculinity, or virtue pretended to torture each other and to produce irreversible physical damage. Yet even this new art form palled as the children of television noted that each week they saw the defeated villain lying near death but seven days later viewed the cripple renewed in health, granted television immortality.

But the impact of a new medium is powerful in larger human concerns than muscular dramatics.

The rebellion of American blacks against the racial caste system, though rooted in deep social and economic trends, was profoundly influenced by a novel medium of communications whose newness was important in its impact. The mobilization of Negro rejection of their three-hundred-year status, and the comprehension of this by the white majority, is attributable in significant part to the failure of traditional social controls over news media that used to be typical of the American South.

The basic effect was to accelerate social change. In the past, blacks who became skilled in literacy tended to leave for other regions of the country, in a dispersion that prevented accumulation of black activists in the South. Most of the black population in rural areas were semiliterate or physically isolated or both. Presumably, functional literacy would have reached them in the usual decades required for such a cultural change. The slowness of this process was made even more sluggish by lack of schooling and, for those who could read, censorship of anything that would encourage racial change. "Contraband" literature—outside newspapers, activist pamphlets, etc.—existed but it had to be physically transported and its effectiveness required its preservation, which meant that it was also dangerous evidence of violation of local taboos. At best these printed messages were usable by only a small portion of the population.

Television changed this. In the mid- and late 1950s millions of Deep South blacks received direct and unfiltered racial news for the first time. The most illiterate Negroes developed detailed knowledge of the civil-rights movement in a short time. In conversation with those they trusted they confessed to knowledge of court decisions, government actions, and organizational activity on behalf of Negroes as seen "on the Huntley-Brinkley," the two most popular national newscasters of the period, whose hyphenated name among the isolated blacks became a generic term for television in general and for televised civil-rights news in particular.

Segregationists were aware of the dangers to them of the penetration of television. In 1956, for example, a bill was introduced in the

Louisiana legislature that would have made it a felony to transmit or receive any television program that portrayed Negroes and whites together in a sympathetic setting. At the time the main concern was with an entertainment show, the Arthur Godfrey program, which featured a black singer, and with the Brooklyn Dodgers baseball team, which had a black star, Jackie Robinson. But Louisiana had to abandon the attempt as technically unfeasible. Controls that might have been effective with printed pieces of paper would not work with electromagnetic waves.

There were, and are, more sophisticated controls. Many stations refused to carry network programs devoted explicitly to race relations, and the rejection of such programs by local outlets is still significant in the South.

Censorship of local programs is far more effective. There was widespread exclusion of any local news of the black community that could portray Negroes as normal citizens. Black organizations did not have equal claim to public-service programming, and black political candidates had such severe problems buying conventional television time that a prolonged legal battle was necessary to establish the right of black candidates to equal access with whites to local political advertising.

But, long before the courts ordered the end of denial of television time to black candidates, television had made a powerful impact on the racial perceptions of the black and white population. This early impact and its escape from usual social controls arose from the relative richness of television compared with print and audio. Included in a moving-picture scene are vast quantities of signals, some peripheral and in the background. Different viewers focus on different signals. What seems marginal to some may be central to others, producing differing impressions from the same scene. What looks "bad" to some people will look "good" to others. A television news item of a United Nations proceeding might include five seconds of an African diplomat speaking in French, a brief episode that might be casual to most whites but astonishing to rural Negroes and whites who had never before seen a culturally sophisticated black speaking to multiracial dignitaries. Some of television is broadcast live as events unfold in real time, so is not predictable or subject to prior review. A white baseball player hugging a black teammate after a winning play may occur faster than a local station operator can obliterate the scene, even though it might have startling effects in regions where this would be forbidden.

In the case of the simpler media, like print, messages are easier to predict because they are less complicated. But television was new and full of simultaneous images, producing effects that often surprised those who thought they were controlling it.

The stimulus of this powerful new medium accelerated social evolution and produced severe stresses typical of rapid change. Fortunately, the same channels make possible, though they do not guarantee, resolution of these stresses.

This same impact will reach enormous dimensions when applied to global populations. New communications are penetrating all parts of the world but the problems these will create, unlike those in the United States, will not be so easy to remedy. The American economy, if it wishes, can absorb the demands created by political activism of previously inert portions of its population. But there is no foreseeable time when the global economy could do the same thing for the economically depressed populations of the world.

Nevertheless, the same activation by communication is spreading to the underdeveloped populations of the world, as it did twenty years ago within the United States.

In absolute numbers, the United States still has the largest increase in civil broadcasting. But electronic media are leapfrogging the growth of the printed word all over the world. The truly radical changes are likely to come from the present rise of nonprinted communication in underdeveloped countries.

In 1950 in North America there was 3 percent illiteracy, in Europe 8 percent. But in Latin America it was 42 percent, in Asia 63 percent, and in Africa 84 percent. By 1960 the figures had not changed drastically: down 8 percent in Latin America, 8 percent in Asia, and 2 percent in Africa. Between 1950 and 1960, because of population growth, the absolute number of illiterate adults in the world increased from 700 million to 740 million.

The use of printed materials follows the same pattern, except that it is even more accentuated in the highly literate societies. The sale of books sold in the United States in current dollars rose 60 percent from 1958 to 1963. New titles produced in North America rose 40 percent. But in Latin America, Asia, and Africa the numbers remained almost constant.

There is another characteristic that follows this same malapportionment: national incomes. The gap in national and median personal incomes between the developed and the underdeveloped nations is increasing and, combined with population growth, is the most ominous trend in global history.

Electronic techniques are bypassing print, rapidly eliminating the traditional fifty-to-one-hundred-year cushion of time that used to be given emerging countries teaching their citizens to read.

Percentage Increase in Communications Use 1958–1965

	United States	Rest of the World
Telegrams	(−31)	14
Letters sent	21	25
Newspaper circulation	3	41
Telephones	40	82
Radio receivers	49	84
Television receivers	40	156

While the absolute numbers remain largest for North America and Europe, the percentage changes in other places, though based on extremely small beginnings, raise the likelihood of more radical response.

Based on the *UNESCO Statistical Yearbook,* the percentage increase in numbers of radio receivers per thousand population from 1950 to 1964 was:

	1950–1964 Percentage Increase	Actual Numbers per 1,000 1950–1964
North America	75	427 to 744
Europe	83	134 to 245
South America	130	64 to 148
Asia	220	9 to 29
USSR	415	61 to 315
Africa	430	7 to 37

The bypassing of the printed word will have the usual social impact of novel communications with novel content on an unlettered population, and this has special meaning for the less-developed countries.

There is, for example, the rapid increase in numbers of transistor radio receivers. Until their invention in 1948, radios were still relatively expensive and relatively nonportable. They needed conventional wired electric systems, or else cumbersome batteries. The receivers were large and noticeable. The sets required upkeep for vulnerable parts like vacuum tubes and were sensitive to physical abuse.

Transistors are cheap, sturdy, and portable, and need no wired power source. They are small, easily hidden, and listened to in remote primitive places like bedrooms of American adolescents and small villages in Celebes.

American factory sales of consumer-product transistors went from 198,000 units in 1954 to 75 million in 1960 to 550 million in 1966. The Japanese produced 20 million in 1963 and 79 million in 1966.

Another factor in diminished control of communications is the sharp decrease in numbers of "wired" radio receivers. These are the loudspeakers connected to master receivers which usually have been tuned to the voice of authority. The individual listener has had no choice of wavelength or, often, of listening or not listening.

In 1950 at least 7 percent of all receivers in the world were wired, in 1964 only 1 percent. The change was mostly in the Soviet Union, which in 1950 had 88 percent of all its radio receivers wired, with officialdom in charge of the wavelength. In 1964 only 48 percent of Soviet receivers were wired. During this time receivers per 1,000 in the Soviet Union went from 61 to 315, or 11 million to 72 million sets. This meant an increase in "free receivers" in the USSR from 1.3 million in 1950 to 37 million in 1964.

In 1966, according to *Newsweek* magazine, the Pentagon's Advanced Research Projects Agency determined that there are 15,000 to 20,000 Russian shortwave radio operators, many of whom converse with other operators all over the world.

The rising number of individual television sets is a familiar trend. In 1953 there were 31 million sets in the world, of which North America had 90 percent and Europe 9.7 percent. The remaining $\frac{3}{10}$ of 1 percent was operating in Russia with 200,000 sets, South America with 100,000, and Asia with 10,000 sets.

By 1964 the number of television receivers in the world had grown to 164 million, of which North America had 45 percent and Europe 31 percent. Africa had 490,000 sets (1.6 per 1,000 population), Latin America 5.1 million sets (31 per 1,000), and Asia 18 million (10 per 1,000). The Soviet Union had 13 million sets (57 per 1,000).

Community viewing of television in some places has become formalized in clubs and commercialized audience collecting, expanding the impact per individual receiver.

A common social activity in some countries was described by Oscar Lewis in *Five Families*. In a Mexican neighborhood on weekends families would pay 25 centavos to watch the television set in a more affluent home. As ownership of sets increased, owners competed for audiences, offering free potato chips and candy to the *telespectadores* and enlarging the viewing period to the late shows. Lewis noted that since the advent of television, people stayed up later at night, listened less to radio, bought more on the installment plan, and girls dressed with noticeably more style.

The social impact is evident in a number of other places.

In Saudi Arabia the government, more or less subtly opposing religious fundamentalists, since 1965 has expanded the government television network into areas of religious conservatism and high illiteracy. Though movies, dancing, and alcohol are banned in the country, the network shows, along with twenty-minute readings of the Koran, *Peyton Place, The Fugitive, Combat, Voyage Beneath the Sea,* and American Westerns. Films are altered so that when a Western soundtrack has the outlaw slamming a silver dollar on a bar and demanding, "Gimme a slug of whiskey," the Arabic subtitle or dub may have him say, "Give me a glass of orange juice." When boy and girl approach to kiss, the film fades out (though Mickey and Minnie Mouse in the cartoons, once edited short of an embrace, are now allowed to kiss).

In Buenos Aires television had expanded rapidly in the slums. Of five channels received, four are nongovernment and carry a heavy schedule of American films, with commercials. Father Juan P. Pruden, who heads an Argentinian social agency, said that "television is giving them an intimate picture of life in a middle-class house. It's sparking aspirations for something better."

Here, as elsewhere, there are television-viewing clubs and other formal audience collections, so that all 500,000 slum dwellers of Buenos Aires probably see television at one time or another.

The attempts of authorities to preserve the communications status quo have been predictable and they have, as usual, ultimately been frustrated. Licensing and control of receivers was the usual method for radio. This has generally been ineffective, since radio is an efficient means of communication for a developing country, and inhibiting its use penalizes growth of education and commerce. Silencing rapid communications and preserving ignorance has too high a cost for any regime that needs the outside world or has ambitions for its own economy.

In the attempt to keep communications predictable, Russia once interfered with the most disruptive outside transmissions, notably the Voice of America and the British Broadcasting Company. But this, too, was made ineffectual by the spread of technology. Not only receivers proliferated, but transmitters. Any country in the world is now surrounded by more transmitters than it can jam. In 1952 there were 6,500 radio transmitters in the world. In 1964 there were 16,000. Russia stopped jamming most outside broadcasts in 1963.

Television transmitters also have grown in number, but their control is easier, since television, unlike most radio, is transmitted by line of sight, its range measured in tens of miles, while radio can go thousands. In 1955, there were 677 in the world, only 146 of them outside North America. In 1964 there were 5,100, of which 4,100 were outside North America. This makes for additional international viewing, some of it not particularly welcome to the host nation. Canadian television stations carry programs often taboo on American ones and are heard along the northern border of the United States. Conversely, Canadian authorities are not always happy with American programs seen in Canada. The American Broadcasting Company has stations just across the border in Mexico, thus evading the jurisdiction of the Federal Communications Commission but reaching an American audience. In Europe alien populations live near each other and can often get foreign telecasts.

But even this relatively minor escape from central control could change radically with space satellites, which may soon have the capacity for direct transmission to individual receivers.

Father Hurley, commenting on the individualism and urge to

improvement that many American commercial programs propagate among foreign television viewers, adds:

Interlarded with these values, however, are others that are not in the central tradition of the classical Western view of man. One discerns such dubious philosophies as nationalism (America *über alles*), materialism (blind faith in an escalator standard of living), doctrinaire conservatism (social conformity and resistance to change), liberal progressivism ("things get better all the time"), and social Darwinism (survival of the fittest and might makes right).

Since not many Americans are aware of the impact which advertising-supported media have outside the U.S., the power of the American business creed, so sensitive to certain freedoms and so indifferent to others, is underestimated. What has not been thoroughly investigated as yet is the impact of such a creed on simpler, less advanced societies with other types of strain and pressures. For one thing, media messages which reinforce the status quo are ill-fitted to societies which need drastic democratic and social reforms.

Not all new communication is destructive. But it is all disruptive. This suggests that Orwellian programming and isolation of total populations will fail, at least in any global application. Admittedly, it is an optimistic assumption, since there exist formidable instruments of conditioning and coercion. The accelerated social reaction time created by new modes of communication could be harnessed to obliterate opposition by overwhelming individual response with the hysteria of mass conformity. Hitler is the most fearsome model; the example of Stalin does not stimulate optimism. The ultimate impact of television on American political campaigns is yet unknown.

But there are reasons to believe that the new methods of communication will make thought control by authorities harder, not easier. In almost every country where there is any degree of industrialization and occupational sophistication, there has grown a significant degree of skepticism about official dogma. In countries like the Soviet Union and its Eastern European satellites this skepticism has been fed by communications channels the authorities have been unable to control.

Personal travel, necessary for scientific, industrial, and commercial growth, is no less a factor in social change than it was when railroads made their impact in 1848. The richest and most effective communications medium in the world, the hundred billion cells of the individual human brain, increasingly crosses cultural, regional, and national borders with unpredictable consequences.

It is significant that the rebellion of Czechs against conservative Moscow leadership in 1968 was mobilized and sustained through the use of radio and other media, but was preceded in 1967 by the travel of 300,000 Czechs outside their own country.

The jet airplane may do what the railroad did a century ago, becoming a medium for exchanging values among otherwise isolated cultures. International air passenger-miles flown, in millions of miles, have been:

1940	100
1950	2,214
1955	4,499
1960	8,306
1965	16,789

Unless there is an effective international cartel on mass information, the growing ease with which any society can communicate with individuals in any other society will make normal the intrusion of new and disruptive knowledge from outside.

This is already true for radio. It may become true for television. Already it has been demonstrated that circling airplanes can make effective telecasts to thousands of square miles below. There is already being planned a "pirate" television station aboard an airplane that will circle just off the British coast and reach British television sets, escaping all regulation for transmission or content. International communications satellites will become common in the 1970s, and while it is not clear what agreements will regulate their use there is no doubt that they will increase cross-national and cross-cultural communications within the human race.

The idea of thought control is abhorrent to the free mind. In a period of proliferating channels of communication and of social interdependence it may not even be possible. The history of new modes of communication has been that new information reaching new audiences ultimately alters the status quo and broadens the participation of individuals in the social process. It is not tolerable to accept unified control of the mass media or their use exclusively for commercial purposes. In the future expansion of communications, the lesson of the past would seem to be not increased rigidity in a futile attempt to force new channels into old practices but to create social and political institutions appropriate for a world in which all populations will begin to have access to the total knowledge of mankind.

How Good Is Fast?

2

Augustus John Foster was a supercilious young Englishman who felt that most men were beneath him, especially Americans and most particularly those who dwelt in their crude national capital, Washington.

But on his last day in the city, on June 23, 1812, he felt an uncharacteristic sense of personal failure. As British minister to the United States he had hoped to avoid war with the former colony. For ten years the United States, a neutral in the wars between England and France, had protested that France closed her ports to any American ship that first put in at England, while Britain, in her hated Orders in Council, said she would treat American merchant ships as enemy vessels if they first touched at French ports.

On May 22, the vessel *Hornet* arrived from England with word that the Orders in Council had not yet been repealed. On April 3 President Madison wrote to Thomas Jefferson, "It appears that . . . they prefer war with us to a repeal of their Orders in Council." In early June Congress voted for war. On June 19 Foster was called to the Department of State and informed that a state of war existed.

The next Tuesday, on his last visit to the American President, Foster asked a final question: if the Orders in Council had been repealed, might it have prevented war? President Madison said it might have.

Neither the President nor the departing British minister knew that as they spoke the Orders in Council no longer existed. Congress declared war not knowing that two days earlier the British Foreign Office announced in London that the Orders would be repealed. On June 23, the day of Foster's last visit to the White House, the British Cabinet issued a formal proclamation revoking the Orders. A difference of time zones between London and Washington meant that hours before Minister Foster entered the White House for his last diplomatic contact before war, the immediate cause of war had been officially removed.

The President of the United States, the British representative in Washington, the Secretary of State, and the Congress all acted as though the Orders in Council existed. History subsequently moved as though they existed. The difference between reality and men's perception of reality is not a small thing in the fate of nations.

It is arguable whether rapid communications would have prevented the War of 1812. There were other issues. And after years of frustration, the momentum toward war might have been irreversible. But the momentum gained power because it fed on ignorance of changing conditions.

The fact was unknown in Washington, but English industrialists and their newspapers that had been treating their former colony with casual condescension were suddenly expressing alarm. The United States was urgently needed to supply raw material and markets for the idle mills in Nottingham, Leeds, and Birmingham, where unemployed English laborers were rioting. But the English riots of April and May were unknown to the men in Washington, who assumed in May and June that England remained inflexible.

Slow communications caused even more bizarre results in the War of 1812. The most spectacular event was the Battle of New Orleans, which changed the shape of the United States, but which, in the void of messages, was fought two weeks after a peace treaty had been concluded.

Peace feelers from both sides started almost as soon as hostilities. Direct negotiations began in Ghent in August of 1814. For the Americans the outlook was grim. The United States Navy consisted of sixteen vessels, the British of six hundred, and despite a few spectacular American exploits the American Navy was bottled up or captured. The only American counterstrategy, an invasion of Canada, had failed. The British finally defeated Napoleon, their serious enemy, so in April, 1814, they dispatched three large land forces from Europe to America. The United States was close to bankruptcy and the New England states were threatening secession over a war they hated.

For the British negotiating team at Ghent, their superiors in London were only three days away by stagecoach and sailing vessel across the English Channel, which was fortunate for them since they were clumsy and needed correction. It took the Americans from two to three months to send a message to Washington and get a reply. Luckily, the American negotiators were extraordinarily competent. It was just as well for the Americans that neither they nor the British knew that, at one point when the Americans were demanding a concession, Washington, D.C., was in the hands of the British Army and public buildings in the capital were in flames. Not knowing this, the American negotiators insisted on their point, and, similarly ignorant, the British conceded it.

The British Prime Minister had other things on his mind. He was preparing for the Congress of Vienna to settle the power structure of Europe. Englishmen at home were tiring of the war in America. He told his negotiators at Ghent to make peace.

So in London and Ghent the word was clear: there will be a peace treaty. In Washington the feeling was the opposite: the war would now become deeper and more desperate.

In the American Senate on December 24 there was a debate on how many more men to call to arms from the states and territories. At that moment at Ghent the two sides were celebrating the peace treaty they had just signed. (The Americans toasted the King and stood at attention while the band played "God Save the King"; then the British toasted the President and stood at attention while the band played "Yankee Doodle," the words to "The Star-Spangled Banner" having been written only fourteen weeks earlier, unknown to both the British and American dignitaries in Ghent.)

Two weeks later the Senate deliberated on a resolution from the House of Representatives called "An Act to Prohibit Intercourse with the Enemy," though there was, at least on paper, no longer an enemy.

But there was an enemy beyond the reach of paper. A powerful British force had reached the mouth of the Mississippi River, where it was under months-old orders to attack the American troops of Major General Andrew Jackson. The British commander, General Sir Edward Pakenham, and Jackson, of course, did not know the war was over. They prepared for one of the largest land battles of their time, with ten thousand men on each side. The British were confident. The natives of New Orleans disliked the Americans. General Jackson had a bad leg, dyspepsia, and diarrhea. But by nightfall of January 8 the British had suffered a stunning defeat—two thousand casualties, including three dead generals, one of them General Pakenham. The Americans had suffered only seventy-one casualties.

Word of the victory at New Orleans reached Washington on February 4 and celebrations spread all over the country. A new and impoverished nation had been filled with self-doubt and internal divisions, believing itself threatened with extinction at the hands of the most powerful empire in the world. But its homely backwoodsmen defeated the professional veterans of the Napoleonic Wars. Every city and town in the new nation rejoiced. Ten days later word arrived from Europe that the Treaty of Ghent had been signed.

Eventually, of course, it became clear to officialdom that the peace had been concluded on December 24 and that the Battle of New Orleans, fought on January 8, was therefore militarily superfluous. But psychologically most Americans equated the end of the war with the victory at New Orleans. They had, after all, celebrated the military victory first and then, ten days later, the peace. It was a hard sequence to erase. Among other things, the spectacular military victory at New Orleans helped obscure the fact that the peace treaty did not resolve a single issue for which both countries had gone to war.

The disjointedness in communications produced confusion that had a deep effect on the future of the country. The belief in the importance of the Battle of New Orleans diminished the internal divisions within the country. It took the sting out of the fact that America had achieved none of the goals for which it had gone to war and that it won not because of military power or competence but because its enemy's mind was on something else.

What would have happened if the military as well as diplomatic peace had come before the Battle of New Orleans? A huge British force would have been on location at the mouth of the Mississippi, its veterans led by a respected and skilled commander, facing a relatively unknown American general who, had he been like most of the American military leaders in the same war, could be assumed to be incompetent and ineffective. In fact, a British envoy had been dispatched to the United States with a number of postwar contingency plans for future pressures on the United States, one of which assumed the poised threat of the Pakenham troops. The Battle of New Orleans solidified the vast Louisiana Purchase into the American territory; otherwise the United States today might end at the Mississippi. It strengthened the dubious national belief, persistent to this day, that simple backwoodsmen are always better than educated men. It sent Andrew Jackson into the White House.

The lessons of this bizarre episode in communications are not simple ones. They imply the advantage of illusion over reality, of not knowing the war was over so that one could fight and win the Battle of New Orleans. Because the American nation emerged stronger and more confident, it seems to say that quick news has its disadvantages. And indeed it has.

We have come a long way from the six-week crossings of the Atlantic in sailing vessels and the five-day stagecoach messages from New York to Washington. And it is not an unmixed blessing.

For example, in the early-morning hours of August 3, 1961, a Continental Airlines Boeing 707 took off from Phoenix, Arizona, with seventy-three people aboard, headed for its next stop, El Paso. Shortly after 3 A.M., a passenger woke from his dozing in time to look through the passage to the cockpit and see two men point their pistols at the head of the pilot.

The first word the ground heard of this event was a radio call from the plane's pilot, Captain B. D. Rickards, to the El Paso tower requesting ground crews to prepare to put on sufficient fuel to take the plane to Havana, Cuba. This information was quickly sent to law-enforcement agencies, the Federal Aviation Agency and the Federal Bureau of Investigation. Tension between the United States and Fidel Castro in Cuba had been mounting steadily. Seven months earlier the two countries had severed diplomatic relations. Less than four months before that, the American-planned Bay of Pigs invasion of Cuba had ended in humiliation for the United States. Two weeks later an American airliner, a National Airlines Convair, had been seized in flight by a Cuban sympathizer and forced to fly to Havana. Just nine days before the episode in El Paso a second plane, an Eastern Airlines Electra, had been similarly seized and flown to Cuba.

At 3:19 A.M. the Boeing 707 landed at El Paso, where crews

pretended elaborate activity in order to provide time for protracted negotiations with the armed hijackers. At 8:30 the President of the United States, John Kennedy, was notified that the hijackers were attempting to force the plane to fly to Cuba. The President called J. Edgar Hoover, Director of the FBI, and Najeeb B. Halaby, Administrator of the Federal Aviation Agency. After consulting with them over the telephone the President sent word direct to federal agents in El Paso: do not let the plane take off for Cuba.

By this time there were two hundred law-enforcement agents on the field at El Paso. The hijackers had permitted sixty-one of the passengers to leave the plane. Some of the released passengers were hysterical. Word quickly spread to the general public.

In Odessa, Texas, 250 miles away, William Payette, a regional manager for the United Press International news service, was on a tour of the area with a local correspondent. When they woke up in their Odessa motel they turned on the morning television news and heard of the plane in El Paso waiting for take-off to Cuba. The two newsmen immediately flew to El Paso and arrived in time to see some of the passengers being released. First the released passengers and then FAA officials told newsmen that four Cubans were holding the plane and trying to hijack it to Havana. The newsmen put the information into the national news system at once.

Because of the difference in time zones, the still-incomplete episode was unfolding as East Coast afternoon papers went to press. In Washington, the *Daily News* was on the street with banner headlines declaring that four men were hijacking a plane, its story saying, "The hijackers, all believed to be ardent followers of Cuban Premier Fidel Castro, seized the plane," and quoted passengers who said they saw two Cubans entering the cockpit with guns.

The wire-service stories continued to send bulletins as Congress convened at noon. Behind the dais of both the House and the Senate there are two Teletype machines, carrying bulletins from the two major American news services, Associated Press and United Press International. Shortly after the two chambers convened for business on August 3, the Teletypes sent out bulletins about the El Paso incident, including such statements as "It was the second hijacking of an American plane by Castro supporters in nine days. . . ."

Senator Styles Bridges of New Hampshire took the floor of the Senate:

"Mr. President, for the second time in nine days a commercial airliner, manned by American crew members, and transporting American citizens, has been hijacked by armed Cubans . . . while over the soil of the United States . . . the plane which was hijacked by Cubans was not flying over international waters nor over the soil of Cuba. The plane was still in the United States."

Senator Engle of California asked for the floor: "If Cubans who engage in such actions act on a conspiratorial basis, with aid by the Cuban government, and thus take action against the people of the United States, that amounts to an act of war, does it not?"

Mr. Bridges: "It certainly does."

Mr. Engle: "I hope prompt action will be taken to ascertain whether this series of events—first near Miami, and now at El Paso—constitutes an act of war and should be dealt with accordingly."

Senator Kenneth Keating of New York said, "I wish to associate myself completely with the remarks of the senior Senator from New Hampshire and with the observations made by the Senator from California."

Senator Miller of Iowa urged the imposition of a blockade of Cuba.

In the House of Representatives, Congressmen also were shuttling between their wire-service machines and the floor. Representative Steven Derounian said, "I am shocked over the hijacking of a Continental 707 just out of El Paso, Texas. I call for instant action to recover what little remains of the guts of American foreign policy. The world must know that Castro is not stronger than the will of our government. . . . The picture of a few paltry men defying the armed might of the United States must be reversed, and instantly."

Congressman Alger agreed. He said that the El Paso attempt "was a well-organized effort indicating the support of the Cuban government behind these acts of piracy. . . . There is only one course of action open to us and that is to use the full might of American military forces."

Mr. Alger proposed issuance of an ultimatum to Castro and "failure to act on his part at the expiration of today's deadline should call for immediate occupation of Cuba to guarantee the return of freedom to that unhappy island."

Representative Dante Fascell of Florida rose to say that the country should take "whatever economic or military action may be necessary."

Representative Williams of Mississippi said that the President should "issue an ultimatum to Castro demanding, first, that he order these hoodlums at El Paso to release the passengers, crew and aircraft immediately." He said if the ultimatum to order the El Paso hijackers to surrender was not obeyed, the United States should take action "even to the extent to using the armed forces. . . ."

Congressman MacGregor agreed. "If Castro will not immediately order his agents at El Paso to surrender, and will not honor a demand from President Kennedy . . . I feel the American people would support steps [to] establish a free government within Cuba . . . with governmental leaders transported to Cuba by parachute, surface ship or submarine, and . . . give it the military assistance it needs to eliminate communism and restore freedom to Cuba."

Congressman Emanuel Celler joined the call for immediate action against the hijacking. "They are Castro inspired," he said. "What is the answer? I would quarantine Cuba. I would throw a naval and aerial blockade around Cuba."

Congressman John Lindsay of Manhattan agreed with his Brooklyn colleague. "These hijackings by fanatic Castro sympathizers and crazed gunmen have endangered the lives of many Americans. . . . Today's incident at El Paso should not be allowed to occur again."

The hijackers, of course, were not Cubans, but native-born Anglo-Saxon Americans. There were not four, but two. Payette of UPI had interviewed federal and other law-enforcement officials as they surrounded the plane in El Paso, and they all referred to the two men holding the remaining crew and passengers as hostages as "Cubans." When the plane moved to take off, federal agents shot out its tires and two agents who had sneaked into the plane during the transfer of passengers subdued the gunmen. As "the Cubans" were pulled from the disabled plane, Payette yelled to the older one, asking his name. The captive said, "Leon Bearden." Payette asked where he was from. "Chandler, Arizona." Payette ran to a phone and called in this latest information. He then called the wire service's Phoenix bureau and found that Bearden was a used-car salesman from Arizona who had been convicted of forgery and theft and had once been in a mental hospital. The other "Cuban hijacker" was his sixteen-year-old son.

There is a complicated moral to this episode. Part of it is that communications systems are amoral—they transmit lies, errors and paranoia with the same serene efficiency with which they transmit truth, accuracy, and reality. For a crucial period of time, the people in El Paso were certain that the hijackers of the airplane were Cubans and that they were part of a Castroite conspiracy to humiliate the United States. And, thanks to rapid communications, this assumption was shared by the President of the United States, the Director of the FBI, the most vocal part of the United States Congress, and much of the public at large.

In a time of intercontinental missiles, of supersonic aircraft, and other swift implements of national power, some of the constitutional stewards of the authority to declare war were insisting on warfare. Their opportunities for catastrophic error were fed by a beautifully efficient system of communications.

But another part of the moral is that the correction of the error was similarly spread with efficiency. Correspondent Payette, yelling across a barrier to the Arizonan, probably sent out corrective word faster than any official machinery could. It is worth noting that his wire-service agency the next week advertised in a trade magazine, "On the El Paso jetliner hijack story—UPI was first by 25 minutes on the spot news break . . ." without adding that it was first with incorrect information (the competing wire agency was second with incorrect information, and both obtained it as quickly as possible from authorities on the scene who were incorrect to begin with).

These events, together with such lucky outcomes of the misconceptions of the Americans in the War of 1812, encourage the view that rapid communications are a threat to reason and wise decision making. There are real disadvantages to the swiftness and pervasiveness of modern communications. They encourage reaction to minor, immediate events rather than major trends. Long lapses between the receiving of information permit study and contemplation. When diplomats went to conferences on slow boats or stagecoach, their preparatory thoughts were undoubtedly more cohesive and integrated, undisturbed by constantly inserted new bits and pieces of information. It must have been easier to consider long-term consequences of acts and to review in the mind what, once announced to others, would later be hard to reverse. As the communications net becomes more widespread and efficient, men seem forced to withdraw from it periodically to consider what all its insistent signals mean. Today the country is spotted with intellectual retreats where men must go if they wish to think and talk without interruption.

But the rapid communications network will not go away. And no arbitrary paralysis of the system is likely to succeed.

For one thing, it has not been proven that diplomats in sailing vessels and lonely kings made better decisions than envoys in jet airplanes or presidents with telephones. If the shrewd American negotiators at Ghent, cut off as they were from Washington by weeks of sailing time across the Atlantic, could use their native wit and perception to win points for their country, the incompetent British negotiators in the same place had their errors quickly corrected by the faster communications with London. Splendid isolation does not help a stupid or uninformed leader become wise; there is much in rapid communication to dilute his errors. Believers in elitist decision making protected from public intrusion seem unimpressed with the long history of disasters produced by uninhibited leaders. From the earliest times, public powerlessness has supported irrelevance, charlatanism, and error.

The state of mind of large populations sooner or later influences events. This state of mind is created partly by artificial communications, but not entirely, despite the conventional wisdom that popular beliefs and acts are completely created by the mass media. The workingmen who rioted in Leeds and Nottingham in 1814 were reacting to the real conditions of their lives, not to distant messages. But understanding of the state of mind of distant men is dependent on rapid and efficient communications, and societies have failed for lack of it. The British in 1812 failed to understand how incapable President Madison was to prevent a declaration of war. The Americans of 1814 had no idea that British public opinion was reversing the direction of the war. The failure to know reality as it exists at the moment, and blindness to the force of public values, require continuous sheer good luck to prevent disaster. Without reliable and perceptive communications, men and nations deal with each other in fantasy, each seeing the world differently, like characters in a Pirandello play, the result beyond calculation, reason, or prediction. Yet there persists a notion of the superiority of conducting relations among societies divorced from public opinion and cut off from news that provides some understanding of contemporary developments among distant populations. John Foster Dulles once said, "If I so much as took into account what people in other countries are thinking or feeling, I would be derelict in my duty as Secretary of State." A few years later, the United States suffered a humiliation in its invasion of Cuba at the Bay of Pigs because it depended entirely on a willingness of Cubans to rebel against their leader, Fidel Castro, when a public-opinion poll taken earlier by an American research organization showed 86 percent of Cubans supported Castro and this support was rising. Social and political decisions made in isolation require a degree of sheer luck that most sane men will not accept.

It is a pleasantry that most people can make better decisions on the toss of a coin than their leaders make on the basis of complicated information. In reality, no society will survive very long if it accepts a 50 percent chance of making the wrong move at every decision point. It must have information to which it applies reason and value judgments. It must have communications with the environment to which decisions will apply.

Fast and accurate news is important to develop a fundamental understanding of the causes and effects of human events. If Americans thought that the Treaty of Ghent was concluded because they had beaten the British at New Orleans, it may have served a useful psychological need at the moment, but it was a defective view of how men and nations act. Bad chronology makes for bad analysis. Unless the real sequence of events is known, it is almost impossible to perceive cause and effect. When communications are slow and confused, filled with gaps, or manipulated to cause delays with some events and speed with others, the basic view of reality is damaged, and it becomes easier for reasonable men to reach false conclusions.

But, if the rapid and reliable transmission of news about public events is necessary for democratic survival and for an accurate view of reality, there are dangers in this efficiency, dangers that will increase with technological developments in the next thirty years.

Even under the best of circumstances, news of some events will produce intense reactions, among both leaders and the general public. The conclusions voiced on the floor of the Senate and House the afternoon of the El Paso plane incident were wild and misguided but they were based on a reasonable deduction. There had been two airplanes hijacked earlier by Cuban sympathizers and Castro had used possession of the planes to force concessions from the United States. Almost everyone assumed that the third incident was similar. What is there that prevents the kind of intemperate reactions expressed in Congress that afternoon from producing a massive public reaction of even worse dimensions?

There is some protection today because of a peculiarity in the news-and-communications network. The news media are extremely efficient in spreading information outward to the public. It can implant a fact, an idea, an emotion in the minds of almost every American in a matter of minutes. A study of how people learned of the shooting of President Kennedy in Dallas showed that 44 percent of the people knew it within fifteen minutes, 62 percent within thirty minutes, 80 percent within forty-five minutes, and 90 percent within an hour. When one considers the vast range of locations and circumstances of the whole population during the daylight hours, this is remarkable. About half the people heard about the shooting from radio or television and they notified the rest either in person or by telephone.

Knowledge of an event like the hijacking of an airplane or the assassination of a public figure is spread so efficiently that practically the whole population is stimulated at the same moment. It is like a massive dose of adrenalin into the public bloodstream.

At present when this happens, the reflex action confronts a peculiarity of the present mass-communications system: it is extraordinarily effective at carrying messages outward to the population, but it is almost useless in transmitting return messages in the opposite direction. Newspapers daily go out to 86 percent of the population, after which they are a passive collection of paper, their readers without significant capacity to reciprocate a signal. Radio and television go out to about 98 percent of the population, but they, too, are one-way media, and whatever the citizen's reaction to his radio and television sets may be, the broadcasting system does not immediately know it.

There are some return links from the recipients of news. A tiny fraction of the consumers have personal access to proprietors and professionals within the mass media and can call on the phone or write a personal letter that will be read, but this is a negligible percentage of the audience. On dramatic events or when appeals are made for a response, there are telegrams and letters sent, but at most these, too, represent only a small percentage of the total audience, and the occasions of their use are few.

There are public-opinion polls of various kinds, a consequence of the one-way character of the mass media. The demands of modern, interlocked economic and social systems require some mechanism for testing the effects of outwardly transmitted signals, sometimes merely to test mechanical efficiency of media systems, like advertising, but also for more serious purposes like testing acceptance and effectiveness of public policy and programs. But these take time, running from days to months. And they depend on sampling a small fraction of the public, 1,600 or 35,000 people out of 200 million. Their impact is limited by the lapse in time between the outward signal being tested and the calculation of the sample's reaction, continuing public skepticism about the validity of sampling, and the knowledge that many polls are biased in design or use.

Furthermore, the method of testing reaction is one that moderates emotion. There is a passage of time between the public's learning of an event and its being asked for an opinion. Presumably this passage of time permits conscious and subconscious reflection and places the event more in perspective.

The method used in expressing a reaction also tends to moderate initial emotion. The act of composing a telegram or writing a letter, or answering questions for a stranger at the door or over the telephone, is of a different quality from the first inner emotion on learning of a dramatic event. Finally, most of these polls have no legal standing. They are interesting and often significant but they are open to any interpretation anyone wishes to make of them.

Most decisive in the American system is the return message from the public embodied in elections. Here the public votes for candidates and sometimes on issues. This involves a substantial percentage of the population and the results are legally binding. But the moderating effects in this method are even deeper than with informal poll taking. The elections occur infrequently, with lapses of as much as six years, in the case of United States Senators, placing immediate events in perspective. The casting of ballots is usually preceded by public debate and mutual interaction with some opportunity for exposure to different points of view. And the final act of placing a mark on a legal ballot has enough symbolic power in the public mind to support the theory that many voters who express fierce opinions beforehand nevertheless, when confronted with this almost reverent act in democratic society, draw back from rash impulse.

But what will happen if forecasts of the future mass-communications system are correct, if the citizen in his home will be able to send out an instantaneous signal of his opinion? What if this signal will be identified as his on the basis of his wire connection with a computer (as telephone-company computers now identify his personal telephone on long-distance calls), and if the total reaction from all households can be tabulated by the computers in minutes?

If the El Paso airplane incident happened at such a time, would the general public act the way the more vocal members of Congress did? If the initial reports were wrong, as they sometimes are, would this reaction not only have been dangerously ill-considered, but also based on false premises? If this reaction were the definite and provable sentiment of the large majority of the citizenry, would it be possible for more cautious leaders to resist such an instant mandate?

A picture of 100 million American adults expressing instant and precisely recorded emotion is awesome. It is even more so when this act is extended to all societies around the globe.

There is no reason to expect that mass-communications systems of the future will become less efficient in spreading information to the public. Those in control of these systems, or having special access to them, will be able to use them in attempts to produce results they desire. There is reason to believe that future systems will permit the receiver of these messages to express his reaction instantly, in continuous referenda or even legal votes. A yes-no button on every home console allows no time for reflection or correction of error.

There are mechanical problems in achieving such a system, but none that are insuperable. Certainly, cable connections to the home and their interconnection with computers will permit recording of home-generated signals. Secure identification of each "voter" is a problem, but it is one that the contemporary credit-card system struggles with and, despite its problems, copes with. Counterfeiting of identity cards and other fraud will be problems, but the same problems exist with conventional balloting. Turning the individual credit card or voter-registration card into an electronic identification for insertion into a slot of the home console is not a difficult task and already is possible in some forms. Computer security to prevent electronic manipulation of results also is a problem, but there are practical solutions available now if the computer industry and the government wish to adopt them.

Such a future system raises fears that the public will react rashly and irreversibly to real events or to contrived ones. One of the episodes most often quoted to show how the American public can be stimulated into mass hysteria is the radio drama produced October 30, 1938, by Orson Welles, when his Mercury Theater broadcast a version of H. G. Wells's novel *The War of the Worlds*. The novel was rewritten to present a realistic set of radio announcements, including interruptions of conventional-sounding programs to give bulletins of the landing of Martians in New Jersey. Newspaper and police-department switchboards were clogged with calls from alarmed citizens who believed that there had been an invasion by strange creatures (the broadcast, coming one month after Hitler's diplomatic triumph in Munich, was during a period of imminent war). There were traffic jams between Philadelphia and New York as motorists either drove to the mythical place of the New Jersey landing or drove to escape. Some people went to church and prayed.

The Orson Welles program was a media trauma that still haunts those who see the possibility of producing mass hysteria by the electronic distribution of seemingly real information. It is well to be haunted by it. But it is also well to remember that only a small minority of listeners believed in the reality of the "invasion." The great majority, despite a remarkable imitation of reality by the program, recognized it as fiction, or at least did not act as though they believed it to be true.

The same is true of more systematic reactions to election and other kinds of mass-media campaigns: those who are influenced purely by the mass-media output are a small minority who are characterized by a low level of basic information on the subject at hand. It is the unsophisticated voter who is most easily changed in his behavior, and the consumer making an unimportant choice between similar products who is vulnerable to mass advertising.

The most persistent, omnipresent, vivid, and talented demagoguery today is television advertising, which inundates a mass audience hourly. It has obvious effects in causing consumer decisions on relatively minor matters, and it probably has deeper effects in producing national values for material possession and uniformity of style. But there are no commercials of consequence for buying homes and higher education for children, yet American families make such major decisions despite the hourly barrage to spend their money on other things. The point is not that advertising is without effect, because plainly it has influence. But it does not often pre-empt critical judgment on matters that are of deep personal concern to the audience.

The centralized efficiency of television in election campaigns is cause for concern. Political candidates in a few carefully contrived appearances are able to reach millions of minds. And, while there is a distressing body of evidence that false images projected through television have been successful on many occasions, it is often overlooked that not only do the manipulators of a new medium become more sophisticated in its use, but so do its audiences. It is not yet clear what the final nature of this equilibrium will be. But skilled exploiters of television for political purposes have been voted down on enough occasions to sustain hope. The "television generation" of the 1960s is characterized by a degree of skepticism about television campaigning bordering on the cynical.

Rapid and widespread communications have already produced moderating effects on demagoguery, though this is seldom noted by those most fearful of television. Demagoguery was at least as common when candidates actually spoke in the presence of the audience if the texts and descriptions of nineteenth-century stump speakers are any measure. The stampeding of voters, most of whom were in total ignorance of the outside world, was easier then.

Today when the flamboyant legislator makes melodramatic speeches and threatens catastrophic action he is fairly certain that no one will put him to the test on what he says. Efficient outward communications, added to efficient recording of public opinion, will tempt demagoguery and undoubtedly produce new forms not yet seen. But they will also dampen it, since there will be rapid test of wild suggestion. For one thing, when demagogic leaders now call for rash behavior, the usual reaction of more responsible political peers is silence, since they know that in most cases such talk disappears and is forgotten. But when such talk appears in danger of effectiveness, countermoves are made—by the President, by officialdom, by differing colleagues in Congress, by members of the public who seriously disagree. If rapid two-way communications gives demagogues greater power, it will give antidemagogues similarly increased efficiency. If error is spread as rapidly as truth, it is well to remember that it is equal speed, not superior. The clumsy British negotiators at Ghent had their mistakes corrected by what was for that period fast communications.

Throughout history, there has been fear of the consequences of extending power to the total population. There is similar fear of extending two-way mass communications to the total population, since this is a form of political power. The prediction has been of mass ignorance and mass hysteria. But mass hysteria has happened more often, it has lasted longer, and it has had more disastrous consequences in times when there were no mass communications. Whole generations became hysterical and committed to self-destructive acts because there was no system to provide communications among those who perceived the error. The Crusades, which Sir Steven Runciman called "a long act of intolerance in the name of God," lasted two centuries and consistently produced the reverse of their goals. It consumed uncounted hundreds of thousands of lives, destroyed more Christians than Moslems, and produced more Moslem influence in Europe than Christian influence in the Middle East. It might have been different had there been a mass-media system to traverse cultural boundaries and a mechanism for recording the perceptions of those undergoing the experience, to have sent convincing word back to the source that an entrancing theory was a catastrophe.

Thus far, civilization has adjusted to the acceleration and spread of information. It has done so by maintaining an equilibrium in exchange of knowledge that matched stimulus and response. Panic, irrationality, and demagoguery are not more virulent today than they were in past eras.

Societies in the past had to cope with the radical effects of the telegraph, penny press, telephone, and radio, all of which redesigned the nervous system of politics. The coming generation of computers and electronic channels represents that kind of change, but with a larger leap in potential communications power than has ever happened before. Not only will a single man, or a small group, be able to mobilize the simultaneous attention of hundreds of millions of human beings, but it will be possible to obtain from whole populations an almost instantaneous response. This will be to politics what nuclear fission was to physical weapons, an increase in power so great that it constitutes a new condition for mankind. The new communications will permit the accumulation of a critical mass of human attention and impulse that up to now has been inconceivable.

The ultimate effect of these new techniques will, like nuclear fission, depend not on any inherent evil or virtue in the physical process itself, but on the morality of men who use it and the comprehension of its power by those most affected by it. Like nuclear weapons, it will test the ultimate humanism of civilization.

The Audience for News

3

An early enthusiast of progressive technology is said to have informed Henry David Thoreau that the newly invented telegraph would permit "Maine to speak to Texas," to which Thoreau replied, "But what if Maine has nothing to say to Texas?"

In the last third of the twentieth century new technology will be capable of disseminating more daily information to more people than ever before in world history. It is worth asking the obverse of Thoreau's question: Who will be listening?

Today there is already an ever-rising amount of news being spread around the globe. How big is the audience for this information? How big will it be in the future? Is the enlargement of mass communications only a mindless multiplication of words and pictures directed at a supersaturated audience? Or is there some reason to expect that in the next thirty years men will want more news than they get today?

News as it is thought of today—information about distant events transmitted speedily to a popular audience—is a novelty in history. In the thousands of years of organized societies on earth, men have survived more than 99 percent of their time without it. Once it was the ruling medicine men, priests, and kings who, like the Lowells, spoke only to themselves or to God about the regulation of society. Over the centuries this tiny circle was expanded only minutely. The idea that large segments of the population have a legitimate claim to being told what is going on is a new one. The notion that the total population is entitled to such information is newer still. Leaders have always understood that knowledge is power and that to share current political and social news is to share the power to govern, which is why full public information and democracy are inseparable partners.

The most dramatic demonstration of this novel thesis was the formation of the United States. The Declaration of Independence said that "governments are instituted among Men, deriving their just Powers from the Consent of the Governed." Supporting this was the assumption of the First Amendment of the Constitution that the consent of the governed is meaningless unless it is based on a continuously informed population.

But even the basic documents of the American experiment did not reflect the United States when the nation was founded. The Republic initially governed 4 million people, of whom the great majority were forbidden by law to participate in their own governance: black slaves, black and white indentured servants, all women, men who did not own property, and men who could not read or write. Less than 10 percent of the population was permitted to grant or withhold "the Consent of the Governed." Even a generation later, in the first election with anything like an accurately counted presidential vote, only 356,000 persons, 24 percent of the group eligible by age, took part in the election of the common man's candidate, Andrew Jackson.

The politically engaged audience today is much expanded, in absolute numbers and in proportion of the population. There are only vestigial pockets of arbitrary ineligibility for voting. Of those eligible to vote, about 70 percent do in fact cast ballots in presidential elections, and when those who have recently died or recently changed residence are taken into account, the percentage is even higher. This voting audience in 1968 was 76 million.

There is more than a casual relationship between political engagement and the audience for news. The characteristics of those most likely to vote are almost precisely those most likely to absorb daily news. Among other things, this suggests that use of the news media is important to the political process and that the future of news has something to do with the future of society. Radical change in the audience for news has more implications than just commercial possibilities for the newspaper and broadcasting industries.

Until the last three generations, the direct audience for printed news was small and simple to measure: those who could read. There was a secondary audience, since the literate could read out loud or paraphrase for those who were illiterate. But the necessity for oral translation inhibited the spread of printed news and gave special power to the literate middlemen.

During parts of the last century, a majority of European and United States adults could not read. Industrialization and urbanization led to general education and literacy, greatly enlarging the audience for printed news. By mid-twentieth century this potential audience was well above 90 percent of the adult population.

The regular use of print has always been influenced by the availability of printed materials. Before the fifteenth century, the limitations were severe. Handwriting was the medium of remote communication, and it was practiced by a very small number of specialists in the religious community who wrote on relatively rare animal skins. Reproduction of texts was slow and expensive, sometimes measured in years for one reproduction, and once done it was usable by a group that was not much larger, those who could read. For centuries, even royalty depended on reading and writing specialists for written communication.

With the invention of movable type in the fifteenth century and the production of paper from rags, a revolutionary change began. The new specialist, the printer, reproduced someone else's words at a radically accelerated rate and at relatively low costs.

One result of this leap in the duplication of ideas was the growth of nonprivate, nonprivileged forms of communication, among them the newspaper. Official fear that the new process would jeopardize tightly held political power repressed growth of newspapers for about 150 years. But in the seventeenth century printed news began to grow. By 1960 throughout the world there were 8,000 daily newspapers with about 290 million circulation. One-fifth of all individual papers and of total circulation was in the United States.

Even in the United States the audience for daily news remained small until mid-nineteenth century. By 1850 there were 750,000 newspapers sold a day, by 1900 the number was 16 million, by 1950 it was 54 million, and by 1968 it was 62.5 million. This has been a spectacular growth measured over the whole previous century, even taking into account the simple growth of population. In 1850 one daily paper was sold for every 30 persons in the country, while today it is one paper sold per 3 persons, or a 10-fold increase.

Even this may be understated. It is traditional for most newspapers to exaggerate their circulation for reasons of prestige and advertising revenues, which are generally scaled to the number of papers purchased. By 1914 advertising in the United States had become suf ficiently important to stimulate the creation of the Audit Bureau of Circulation, which since then has established strict standards for measuring newspaper sales, confirmed by direct audits. Since that time statistics on daily newspaper sales have been precise. If pre-1914 figures had been as conservative, the growth of newspaper reading would look even more spectacular.

Who is most likely to buy a newspaper? Knowing the answer to that may suggest changes in the future audience for news.

Not every person or every family buys a daily newspaper in the United States. The total audited figures for circulation are not very helpful in identifying who buys a paper and who does not, since these are simple aggregate numbers. There are many claims by publications, all subject to skepticism because of the temptation to attract more prestige and advertising revenues by claiming readership by the most profitable consumers.

In 1959, the Bureau of the Census conducted a survey of households subscribing to daily newspapers. This did not count newspapers sold by vendors on the street, which could change the statistics. But street sales are of diminishing importance in the United States, though still substantial in the large cities. And there is some basis for accepting those who receive home deliveries—62 percent of all households —as generally representative of all people who buy newspapers.

The most likely buyers of newspapers are the best educated; those in skilled professional, technical, and managerial white-collar jobs; the wealthiest; those who live in urban areas; those who are married; and people between the ages of thirty and fifty-four.

Occupation and years of education are about even as the leading factors in newspaper buying.

Educational Attainment of Household Head	Percent of Households with Daily Delivery
No years of school	20.3
Elementary	
1 to 7 years	45.0
8 years	61.4
High school	
1 to 3 years	65.7
4 years	73.7
College	
1 to 3 years	76.6
4 years or more	79.9

Characteristic	Percent of Households with Daily Delivery
All households	62.0
Labor Force Status of Household Head	
Labor force	63.9
Employed	64.6
Professional, technical, and kindred workers	75.2
Farmers and farm managers	54.5
Managers, officials, and proprietors, exc. farm	77.4
Clerical and kindred workers	64.9
Sales workers	73.4
Craftsmen, foremen, and kindred workers	70.9
Operatives and kindred workers	59.8
Private household workers	31.5
Service workers, exc. private household	53.2
Farm laborers and foremen	22.8
Laborers, exc. farm and mine	44.7
Unemployed	45.3
Not in the labor force	54.5

Other characteristics of newspaper buyers are:

Family Income	Percent of Households with Daily Delivery
All income levels	68.0
Under $3,000	57.5
$3,000 to $5,999	67.8
$6,000 to $9,999	80.4
$10,000 and over	84.1

Age of Household Head	Percent of Households with Daily Delivery
Under 25 years	44.8
25 to 29 years	56.1
30 to 34 years	63.4
35 to 39 years	67.3
40 to 44 years	66.9
45 to 49 years	65.8
50 to 54 years	63.6
55 to 59 years	61.7
60 to 64 years	62.3
65 to 69 years	61.6
70 to 74 years	58.4
75 years and over	58.5

Marital Status and Sex of Household Head	Percent of Households with Daily Delivery
Male	64.6
Married, spouse present	67.2
Married, spouse absent	21.9
Widowed and divorced	42.9
Never married	35.8
Female	50.2
Married, spouse absent	40.3
Widowed and divorced	52.5
Never married	51.3

Television Status of Household	Percent of Households with Daily Delivery
With television	67.3
Without television	30.8

Tenure and Residence of Household	Percent of Households with Daily Delivery
Owner-occupied	72.3
Urban	77.2
Rural nonfarm	69.5
Rural farm	56.2
Renter-occupied	45.7
Urban	46.8
Rural nonfarm	47.6
Rural farm	31.8

Tables from *Current Population Reports, Population Characteristics,* June 3, 1960, Series P-20, No. 102, "Household Delivery of Daily and Sunday Newspapers: 1959."

The highest newspaper-buying category is people with four years or more of college, 79.9 percent; the lowest, those with no years of school, 20.3 percent, or a difference of 59.6 percent. This is similar to the difference of 54.6, between the biggest buyers of newspapers—managers, officials and proprietors—and the lowest—farm laborers.

These statistics tell the characteristics of the heads of households that get a newspaper delivered daily, but they do not describe those who ultimately read the paper. It is probable (but not certain) that the head of the household reads the paper. But it is not obvious who else reads this same paper which is important in thinking about who in the future will be interested in daily news.

There has been a national sample of actual reading of newspapers. It was paid for by seven Canadian newsprint companies, developed and implemented by the Opinion Research Corporation of Princeton, and designed by the Bureau of Advertising of the American Newspaper Publishers Association. These are sources interested in proving the advertising potential of print, though the Bureau of Advertising has a better record of social-science discipline than most other trade groups.

This 1966 study was made of 2,470 individuals drawn from a national probability sample. Instead of asking people how they received their news, they were shown particular items that came from various media and asked which were familiar. This avoided answers about "news," a word that may mean different things to different people.

Eighty percent of those interviewed had read a daily paper the day before. Exposure to the news in a newspaper the day before was answered this way:

Age

21–34	75%
35–49	79
50–64	83
65 and over	74

These numbers for readership are much higher than the data for household heads subscribing to a paper. And the peak subscribing age was forty to forty-four years, while the peak reading years were fifty to sixty-four.

Education

Grade school or less	62%
Some high school	75
High-school graduate	85
Some college	87
College graduate	90

Here, too, all the numbers for reading seem higher, though not very different. Peak subscribing was 80 percent for college graduates, while peak reading for the same category was at 90 percent.

Annual Income	
Under $3,000	59%
$3,000–4,999	70
$5,000–7,999	79
$8,000–9,999	88
$10,000 and over	89

Here the agreement with subscribing is fairly close. The range for subscribers was 57.5 percent of those under $3,000 annual income to 84 percent for those $10,000 and over.

Occupation	
Professional	88%
Manager	91
Clerical-sales	85
Craftsman	80
Manual	71
Farmer	70
Not employed	68

Tables from "When People Want to Know, Where Do They Go to Find Out," Newsprint Information Committee, undated, p. 93.

Here, too, the rank order for readers is the same as for subscribers.

The statistical evidence is that as people get more education, move into white-collar jobs, earn more money, reach the twenty-five-to-fifty-four age bracket, and settle in urban areas, they develop a greater appetite for news. And these characteristics have been the historic trend in the American population.

All the factors that make for news absorption have been rising steadily and substantially since World War II. Median grade attainment from 1947 to 1967 went from nine years to twelve. In 1950 there were 22 million white-collar workers, who constituted 40 percent of the work force, and in 1967 this number had grown to 34 million or almost 50 percent of the work force. Disposable family income rose from $3,200 in 1945 to $8,700 in 1967, which, despite inflation, more than doubled real purchasing power. The number of people who voted went from 49 million to 71 million. Americans living in urban areas in just the decade 1950–1960 increased from 97 to 125 million.

All this would suggest that families would buy more newspapers than ever. But they didn't.

	Newspaper Circulation Per Family Daily
1945	1.28
1950	1.23
1955	1.16
1960	1.12
1964	1.07
1965	1.05
1966	1.06
1967 (prel.)	1.05

Statistical Abstract of the United States, 1968, p. 505, Table 744.

During precisely the period of enlarged audience for news, daily paper sales per family dropped 18 percent.

Imbedded in the numbers already cited there is a hint. As the high-readership characteristics approach the top—in education and income, for example—the rise in news absorption either levels off or goes down.

One possible answer is that newspapers contain a great deal of entertainment, merchandising, and other material that is not serious daily political and social information. Perhaps this is why most people buy newspapers. But serious studies show that absorption of serious news follows the same pattern as reading of whole newspapers. The same decrease in reading of serious news occurs among the most educated people one would expect to see reading more.

For example, in 1949 a survey by Wilbur Schramm and David M. White showed that in readership of public-affairs content, the essence of serious news, there was this pattern of readership:

Grade-school education	23%
High school	39
College	36

Journalism Quarterly, Vol. 26, pp. 149–159.

One explanation is the end of a once-common practice by many families of buying more than one newspaper a day, either two or more editions at different times of day of the same paper, or two or more competing papers in the same city. After World War II many newspaper-reading families moved to the suburbs, where, typically, there is no locally based newspaper. Families once interested in central-city schools, taxes, highways, and policing and offered papers dealing with those subjects, moved to areas that lacked even one paper primarily concerned with them, let alone two or more papers.

Another factor in the drop of newspapers sold per family was the end of competition among newspapers. It has always been true that, where two or more papers were published in one locality, a significant number of families bought all the competing papers. When competition dies, duplicate buying ends. And, while the total number of dailies has remained remarkably stable in the last twenty-five years (1,749 in 1945 and 1,749 in 1967), the types of papers have changed. Some very large competitive papers died. Generally they were replaced by small monopolies in other places. In one year, 1963, for example, about the same number of dailies died or were merged—twenty—as were born—twenty-one. But the average daily circulation of the new papers, even three years after their birth, was less than eight thousand, while the average of those that died was more than seventy thousand.

There was yet another change: broadcasting.

The first direct competition for the news audience was from radio. At first, it seemed not to make serious inroads. In the early 1930s about 40 percent of American families owned radios, but during that decade newspaper sales seemed to respond more to fluctuations in the sick economy than they did to broadcasting. By 1949 there was near saturation of American households with radio. In the next several years, newspaper sales per family began their steady downward slide, even though radio ownership remained about the same, and television was just beginning its appearance on the scene.

Radio, it is clear, did not displace the newspaper as an institution. But it did begin the atrophy of that part of printed news that depended entirely on the initial announcement of melodramatic events.

It is normal for most medium-sized and large papers to issue more than one edition a day. Most of these editions are different from each other mainly because they are directed at different geographic zones within the paper's distribution area. But some are different mainly because of the time of day. Big-city afternoon papers, for example, often have an edition around noontime for sale to the central-city business-district lunchtime crowds and another late-afternoon edition for the same crowds going home and wanting late sports scores or stock-market returns or dramatic or dramatic-sounding events that occurred between the noontime and the late-afternoon editions.

Before the war there was still another category of multiple edition, the "extra." This was a special issue of a daily paper inserted into the normal printing schedule on the basis of a single dramatic event whose importance and salability seemed to justify interruption of regular printing schedules. Assorted urchins would be gathered hastily and handed bundles of the extra to hawk in the streets of the central city.

Radio began the slow decline of the late editions of daily papers. As portable radio sets became common in offices, shops, factories, automobiles, and attached to the ears of teen-agers, late-breaking news became known long before the hours it took to produce and distribute printed news.

Radio killed the extra. Even so spectacular an event as the start of World War II for the United States, the surprise bombing of Pearl Harbor, produced relatively few extras because by the afternoon of Sunday, December 7, 1941, almost everyone in the country knew the knowable facts through radio. "We interrupt this program . . ." became an assurance that genuinely dramatic news would be heard first through broadcasting and removed an important factor in the multiple sales of newspapers.

The end of extra editions was hastened by the rising cost of newspaper production and distribution, and the move to the suburbs. Even if an unscheduled edition were printed, it would require organizing a fleet of trucks already committed to normal deliveries, and recruiting of suburban juveniles whose affluence limits their eagerness to miss meals, playtime, or homework for a minor one-time monetary reward. The traditional area for heavy sales of unscheduled editions, the central city, has become either nonresidential or a poverty neighborhood. Besides, the sound of a newsboy crying, "Extra!" in the streets would not necessarily induce heavy buying; householders would more likely turn on radio and television sets in the expectation that anything genuinely spectacular would be broadcast at once and with later information than would be available in print.

Radio comes close to being the universally-present communications medium. Of the 300 million sets in working order as of January 1, 1969, about 216 million were in homes, or an average of almost four per home. Less than 2 percent of households are without a radio. There were 74 million radios in automobiles and 10 million in public places like restaurants and garages.

An audience survey by the National Broadcasting Company in 1965 was announced as showing that on any one day 92 million people were listening to radio, or 75 percent of the population 18 years old and older. The same survey showed that during a week 111 million people, or 91 percent of the adult population, listened to the radio at some time.

The trends begun modestly by radio have been intensified by television. In the five-year period of radio saturation before the appearance of television, newspaper sales per family dropped 4 percent. In the 1960–1965 period, when television as well as radio approached saturation, the decline in newspaper sales per family was 6 percent, although this was a period of rapid increase in the incidence of high education and income that usually stimulates interest in the news.

Television ownership advanced rapidly, from 12 percent of households in 1950 to three-quarters of all households five years later, until today when 98 percent of all houses wired for electricity have at least one television set, or 97 percent of all American homes, if one excludes Alaska and Hawaii.

What is the audience for television? One clue is, of course, the possessors of television sets, 97 percent of the population. This is a significant difference from the basic data on newspaper sales, with a maximum of 80 percent of households, and on newspaper readership, about 86 percent. This difference is deepened by the fact that newspapers require literacy and, unlike television, eliminate functionally illiterate adults and all very young children.

The television audience was calculated in 1965 to be 81 million on any one day, or 66 percent of the population 18 years old or over, and 107 million, or 87 percent of the adults who watched at some time during any given week. Most of this watching is during prime-time evening hours, 7:30 to 11 P.M., when at least 63 percent of all sets are turned on and have an audience said to consist of 31 percent men, 40 percent women, 11 percent teenagers, and 18 percent children twelve and under.

Ownership of television sets tells something of potential exposure to broadcast news and public affairs. Heads of households lacking television are those under age twenty-five (of whom 11 percent have no set) and those over sixty-five (of whom 10 percent have no set).

Ownership of two or more sets suggests intensity of interest in the family and desire for selectivity. Here the pattern is the same. Highest multiple ownership, 35 percent, is among households headed by someone between the ages of thirty-five and forty-nine. Nonowners of sets follow a familiar pattern: low in education, income, occupational status, and urbanization. Owners of two or more sets have the opposite characteristics.

The same people who tend to buy newspapers tend also to buy television sets. The most reliable study of newspaper delivery, the 1959 survey by the Bureau of the Census, showed that only 31 percent of nontelevision owners subscribed to a daily paper, compared to 67 percent of television owners.

Data from the A. C. Nielsen Company, which surveys the extent of television viewing, show that the average number of hours a day that an American television set was turned on in 1968 was six hours and thirty-eight minutes and that with only slight fluctuations this has been rising from four hours and fifty-four minutes in 1955.

If this is true, then it constitutes a number of important factors in the future of news. For one thing, it would mean that the American home is in continuous active contact with a news-disseminating source for more than six hours of every day. While the set may be tuned to nonnews programs, it means that should urgent news develop it would be heard at once or very soon without any effort by the householder. This not only reduces the need for extra-edition newspapers, but also diminishes dependency on newspapers to announce all high-priority news.

It means something else important. If all sets turned on are being watched actively, then this pre-empts six hours and thirty-eight minutes of the waking hours of every person paying attention to television.

But sets turned on, even if accurately counted, are not the same as sets watched. Another television-industry document, issued by the Television Information Office, citing surveys made by Roper Research Associates, shows median hours of viewing by individuals reached by the survey rose from two hours and seventeen minutes in 1961 to two hours and forty-seven minutes in 1968.

The systematic watching of television news and its relation to all news is not obvious but there are some indicators.

Ratings released by the Television Information Office show that network evening news during the winter months is viewed by approximately 78 percent of all television homes, or by an audience of about forty-three million homes. In the summer months the audience drops to about twenty-seven million homes, but of these about the same percent, 77, listen to the evening news broadcasts of the three networks.

Special public-affairs programs that are not live public events have a substantial, though smaller, audience. Network programs on the history of Hitler's Third Reich were watched by nineteen million homes, and a program on the Warren Report of the Kennedy assassination was seen by twenty-two million households.

The audience for melodramatic public events is enormous. In total size and in the proportion of the population it is a social phenomenon without precedent in history.

The 1968 Democratic convention was seen by fifty million households, 88 percent, even though one of the networks offered conventional entertainment programs. The Robert Kennedy assassination and funeral were seen by fifty-three million households, 95 percent of the households with television at that time. The moon flight of Apollo 11 was seen by fifty-four million homes, or 94 percent, and each of these watched an average of fifteen hours. The John Kennedy assassination and funeral were seen by 96 percent of all television homes, who watched an average of thirty-one hours and thirty-eight minutes.

No entertainment program has ever reached more households than these events.

When people are asked, "Where do you usually get most of your news about what's going on in the world today?", they have answered as follows:

Source of Most News	12/59 %	11/61 %	11/63 %	11/64 %	1/67 %	11/68 %
Television	51	52	55	58	64	59
Newspapers	57	57	53	56	55	49
Radio	34	34	29	26	28	25
Magazines	8	9	6	8	7	7
People	4	5	4	5	4	5
Don't know or no answer	1	3	3	3	2	3
Total mentions	154	157	147	153	158	145

"A Ten-Year View of Public Attitudes Toward Television and Other Mass Media, 1959–1968," a report by Roper Research Associates issued by Television Information Office, p. 2.

In the intense competition between electronic and print media for advertising dollars, surveys of consumers are used as promotional weapons, employing variations in survey design and wording to produce favorable results. So it is not surprising that there are differences of audience size, depending on who makes the study. The newsprint industry designed its own survey in 1966. Asked to identify actual news items that the respondents could have received on only one medium, their replies within a year of the television-sponsored survey, differed in this way:

Source of Most News	Television-Industry Sponsored Survey, 1967	Newsprint-Industry Sponsored Survey, 1966
Television	64%	29%
Newspapers	55	59
Radio	28	4
Magazines	7	8

Television industry data from "A Ten-Year View of Public Attitudes Toward Television and Other Mass Media, 1959–1968," a report by Roper Research Associates issued by Television Information Office, p. 2. Newspaper industry data from "When People Want to Know, Where Do They Go to Find Out," Newsprint Information Committee, undated, Table 1, p. 40. Totals may exceed 100 percent because respondents often cited more than one source.

Perhaps the most remarkable finding in these surveys is the durability of newspapers as a source even under television-sponsored surveys.

The study sponsored by the newspaper industry showed 78 percent reading a newspaper the day before, 60 percent watching one or more television newscasts, and 55 percent hearing one or more radio newscasts.

One significant difference in the television survey may be the phrase "news about what's going on in the world today" as a measure of "news," associating "world" with "news." With few exceptions, broadcast news has been minimally oriented toward local news, and therefore is associated mostly with national and world news.

The newspaper-industry survey based "best way to find out about news and editorial items" on listing particular news items of which four items were specifically identified as "local." On all of those items—as well as some others—newspapers were regarded as the "best way" by a large margin over television, an average of twenty-five percentage points. On "foreign politics," "national politics," "business," and "science-space," television led by an average of ten points.

Even conflicting and competing surveys make clear that there has been no large-scale pre-emption of one medium by another, that each is used for a different set of reasons. Certain kinds of news continue to be dominant in print, other kinds in radio and television. In most kinds of news the media seem to reinforce each other—more and more people use both—rather than cancel each other out.

In this generation, for the first time in the history of any large nation, the potential audience for news had become almost the total population. The audience for printed news is limited by age and literacy. Broadcast news is limited by age alone, and that is not a severe one. It takes about ten years to achieve reading competence, starting from instruction at age four or five. Significant absorption of television and radio information begins even before age four. Certain televised public events—riots, disasters, military combat—and a large amount of secondary reporting with visual reinforcement are seen by preschool children who cannot read.

The ratings of listenerships on dramatic public events seem to cover almost all the population. Television and the ubiquitous car and transistor radios, plus the telephone to provide quick second-hand reporting, means that for the first time in history something approaching the total population of a society is in instantaneous contact with urgent global—and extra-global—developments.

Since the absorption of news seems to go up with certain characteristics of population, what is the prospect for the future audience for news? The audience by the year 2000 will be larger in simple numbers. Predictions of total United States population range from about 318 million to 361 million. If it is halfway between these it will mean an increase of 70 percent in the population. The number of households, now 60 million, may reach over 100 million. People who absorb news at a high rate will proliferate. Urbanization, which now places 70 percent of the population in or near a large central city, will increase. Half the future American population will probably live in three great concentrations, along the northeastern seaboard between Boston and Washington, along the northern-central tier between Chicago and Pittsburgh, and along the southwestern Pacific seacoast from San Diego to San Francisco.

Today there are about 70 million Americans in the 25–54 years of peak news absorption, or 36 percent of the population. In 1990 there will be 127 million, or 42 percent of the total population.

Income also will rise. In 1965 the average family income was $8,380, a level at which there is about 93 percent newspaper readership by the head of the household, 97.5 percent ownership of television, and about 100 percent ownership of radio. By the year 2000, average family income measured in dollars of present purchasing power has been predicted to range from $21,000 to $25,000.

The lowest purchasing rate of newspapers and for ownership of television and radio is among families with less than $3,000 annual income. In 1965 there were about ten million of these families, about 16 percent of all. By 2000 it is predicted that despite the total growth of households, there will be less than six million of such families, and they will constitute only 6 percent of all households.

Occupations in the United States (and in all developed countries) are moving rapidly in the direction of professional, managerial, and technical white-collar jobs, which constitute the peak market for news. The jobs with lowest news usage—farm laborers, unskilled manual labor, and rural farmers—are being eliminated by automation and other social changes.

Perhaps the most relevant intellectual measure of information appetite is education. And this has been increasing at a very rapid rate. In 1965 the adult population had completed an average of 10.3 years of schooling, but the 25-to-29 age group—who would be over

65 in the year 2000—had averaged 12.1 years. There is reason to believe—because of job requirements and income levels—that increases in average levels of education will continue. By the year 2000 more than half the population will have had two or more years of college. "By the year 2000," say Scammon and Wattenberg, "perhaps graduate degrees will be as common as college degrees today and college degrees as normal as high school diplomas."

By the most simple extension of present trends, the audience for news in the next thirty years should increase enormously. This would be in absolute size, which is important since it constitutes an expansion of the number of consumers to support future systems, but also in the amount of money each individual will have to spend.

It will be even more important in the proportion of the population that has an intense interest in the news, since the larger a part of the total country a news-hungry segment constitutes, the more influential they will be in establishing national standards of a mass system.

But two major problems arise in this otherwise euphoric projection of the future news audience.

One is that the amount of time available in waking hours for the absorption of information has rather rigid limits. There are limits even if one theorizes radical notions like insertion of information into the brain during sleeping hours—which is not likely in the next generation. No matter how many hours one sets aside for learning, there seems to be an absolute minimum time required for the human brain to receive and register a bit of information. So, whatever new devices are foreseen in this century and whatever novel shorthand methods may be created to control the speed of presentation, the nervous system and the brain apparently cannot be pushed beyond a given limit.

New techniques permit an enormous increase in data speeds. Present transmission of most news to newspapers and broadcasting stations is at a rate of less than sixty words a minute. A rate of twenty-four hundred words a minute is already used in some places from computer to a documentary version for human reading.

If human reading speeds should be heightened to an average of a thousand words per minute, a man spending all his waking hours reading without interruption could absorb a maximum of a million words. But no sane person would do such a thing. Two hours a day spent on news and newslike information is very high and would mean a maximum absorption of 120,000 words of print a day. Major newspapers already present readers with that every day.

The absorption of words from radio and television will be even less, since a rapid speaking rate of about two hundred words a minute cannot be doubled without approaching levels of unintelligibility. Pictorial and other sensory impressions can be made richer and faster, but these, too, cannot be accelerated much beyond present speeds.

So, whatever the expansion in the mass appetite for news in the future, there are limits to waking hours that can be spent absorbing information. Speeding the rates of mechanical word transmission is not a measure of what human beings will be able or willing to receive.

There is another problem in assuming that the quantity of news absorbed will go up in proportion to the technical capacity of information machines.

Most surveys of news consumption show a steady increase in actual use of these media according to education, income, and the other familiar characteristics. But these surveys are carried out with varying degrees of care and scientific objectivity. Usually they are publicized by an industry trying to prove a very large audience in order to capture part of the $17 billion spent each year for advertising. Consequently, all media-sponsored surveys of audience are suspect. If the studies should be well designed and carried out but produce results harmful in the competition for advertising, they are not publicized. So it is a safe assumption that some unscientific selection process has always been a factor—at the very least a veto over publishing results—in any measurement of audience by a news corporation.

This makes particularly interesting surveys by academic and other nonindustrial investigators without a stake in the news industry.

One of these is a survey by Harold Hodges, Jr., of San Jose State College, California. He interviewed in depth a random sample of more than three thousand heads of households in three counties of the San Francisco Bay area. He did it over a period of six years in the late 1950s and early 1960s when television ownership was in the 85–90 percent range. Since ownership of television progressed generally from upper-income families to lower-, viewing by upper-income households is not likely to be understated for reason o nonownership. Television watching could be understated on grounds that some upper-educated persons might deny watching television when in fact they do, but the figures cited by Hodges are so overwhelming that even a fairly large margin of dishonest replies will not change the overall trend.

Hodges classified respondents by class, using the conventional measures of income, education, and occupation but adding certain attitudes toward society. He divided the lower class into lower-lower and upper-lower, the middle class into lower-middle and upper-middle and called the fifth category simply "upper." He found an enormous difference in television watching by class, from three hours a day for the lower-lowers to sixteen minutes for the uppers.

Social-Class Level and Television Viewing

Class Level	Minutes Watching TV per Weeknight	Percentage Who "Never Watch"
Upper	16	33
Upper-middle	31	30
Lower-middle	63	18
Upper-lower	100	9
Lower-lower	180	0

Social Stratification: Class in America, by Harold M. Hodges, Jr., Table VII, p. 161.

Hodges concludes that " 'the' television audience is a fanciful entity—that the audience is, in fact, many audiences, each of them stratified by age, sex, and ethnic differences, by personality needs, by degrees of urbanity and sophistication, and above all else by social-class membership."

Hodge's drastic drop in viewing by upper-level consumers is not reflected in surveys by the television industry which would be loath to publicize so large a loss of affluent viewers. But other studies, including some by the media industries show a curious, if smaller, loss of consumers at the highest income and educational levels.

For example, the Bureau of the Census survey of newspaper subscribers shows a steady increase as occupations become more highly trained, but at the very top level, "professionals," the rate drops from "managers." The same is true for the industry-sponsored survey of readers, where 88 percent of professionals read a paper but 91 percent of managers. The academic study by Schramm and White of readers of public-affairs content showed an increase with more education, but a drop from 39 percent for high school graduates to 36 percent for college graduates. In a survey distributed by the television industry, college-educated people watched television half an hour less than the median for all people, and upper-income people twenty-three minutes less a day.

This decline at upper levels of education, income, and occupation becomes important in judging the future audience for news. There is a powerful trend toward increasing numbers and proportions of Americans in the upper levels. Does this mean that as the population achieves the highest levels of education and income, its appetite for news will diminish?

Perhaps the man with a college degree and a high income and a highly professionalized job is so refined in his taste and has access to such rich sources of information that he is bored by the diluted material in mass news. In addition, his relative sophistication would tell him that important historic developments are best detected at longer range than by daily bits and pieces, turning him more to books, periodicals, and lecture-seminars.

It would be odd if this interpretation did not have some validity. News systems in the United States are for all practical purposes one-class productions. They are constantly under pressure to reach the largest possible single audience, which means including enough of the specialized and analytical information to interest the more sophisticated but not so much that it bores the more casual citizen. The decline in news absorption at lower levels may come from the fact that the poor don't own as many television sets or subscribe to as many newspapers. The decline at the upper end of the scale can't be explained by economics, so it could be boredom.

The survey by Hodges confirms some of the boredom thesis: ". . . the truly significant differences are more intricate in nature, for the same study discloses that viewers in each class level differ quite radically in their appetites for specific shows, generic types of programs, and television in general . . . the upper-middle levels were becoming increasingly weary of television programming and commercials."

Whatever strength there is to the theory of boredom and dissatisfaction with the news media among the upper classes, they presumably could be overcome by changes in mass programming or—significant for technology—more specialized alternatives for the many different audiences.

But there is an additional explanation for the slight upper-level decline in newspaper reading and the marked decline in television viewing.

For one thing, political engagement as measured by voting does not show the same rate of decline with education, income, urbanization, and occupation. At the same levels where there are downturns in the use of the news media, voting participation continues upward at a steep climb. Much of the information needed for intelligent participation in political affairs is contained in the news media. Analyses in books and periodicals are useful historically and for basic comprehension, but they are less helpful in reaching immediate decisions on current voting issues especially local and regional ones. If the upper level of the population is not less intelligent in its voting behavior, then it is dependent on the daily news.

As men and women reach higher levels of education and move into occupations with enlarged responsibilities, and therefore of higher income, their patterns of daily life change. They tend to cease being governed by a simple and predictable work day and work week. Working lunches, working dinners, evening meetings, after-meal reading of professional or commercial literature, participation in civic, professional, or intense social groups becomes more common. Such people less often are available to watch television during its prime hours. The forty-hour week with the steady nine-to-five hours that provide the basic assumptions of news-media production schedules is more typical of the factory worker, store clerk, and carpenter than it is of the doctor, senior engineer, sales manager, and professor. Ironically, professionalization of occupations with its high income rewards has not produced a simple expansion of daily leisure time but an increasing intrusion of career into almost every available segment of waking hours.

If it is true that men and women in the more intellectualized occupations have added interest in daily social and political developments, this comes into conflict with the difficulty of precisely this category of person to be free at the times when such information is being presented to the general public.

Control of the reception time of news then becomes important.

The evening paper can be saved until the busy consumer has time to read it. And, in fact, the drop-off for newspapers of high-education-and-income persons is less than for television. The upper-level decline for newspapers is 3 percent for professionals, 18 percent for "college-educated" persons. In the Hodges data, the television drop-off for the "uppers" compared with the "lower-middles" is 25 percent.

At present the main television news is at fixed times in the day, usually around 7 A.M., 6 P.M., and 11 P.M. There is no inexpensive way at present to record and preserve a television program for viewing in the home at a time of the consumer's choosing. This may not always be the case. When that happens, technology may change absorption of news by class. Both boredom and unorthodox daily schedules can be overcome by future technology.

What the future audience for news seems to be—barring military or civil catastrophe—is a vastly enlarged number of people interested in the news and able to pay at least three times as much for it as they do today. But this does not seem to mean a simple expansion of time per person available for news and public information.

What the trends both of technology and the characteristics of the American audience seem to foretell is a news system with a richer variety of information, a rapid way to detect what is available, easy pursuit of subjects of maximum interest to the individual beyond the standard presentation, and control over the time the information is presented.

Some Peculiarities of American News

4

Among world news systems, America's is peculiar.

In other countries there are national newspapers issued in one or two important urban centers and distributed as the primary serious journals throughout the country. Local papers are marginal and parochial, classified geographically and culturally as "the provincial press."

In most countries radio and television also are centralized, with few local originating facilities. Programs typically emanate from a central studio owned and controlled by a government monopoly.

In the United States, the typical American consumer receives all his daily printed and broadcast news from a local private enterprise. There are historical reasons for this unique pattern in the United States and social reasons why it should continue. Though there are contemporary trends diminishing local independence, compared to world systems the American news continues to be rooted in the local community.

The American news is even at odds with its own technological and corporate environment. It transmits most of its information through national monopolies, the telephone and telegraph systems. Its major suppliers of national and world news are two highly centralized national services, the Associated Press and United Press International. The newspaper industry as a whole is one of the country's largest and as such operates in an economic environment of corporate giantism and oligopoly. Yet the news itself continues to be dispensed through a highly fragmented collection of local firms.

In the United States no national newspaper is readily available in all parts of the country at its time of publication. The *New York Times* comes closest to being a national newspaper, but it is printed only in New York City and despite its considerable influence does not displace a significant portion of national newspaper reading.

The *Wall Street Journal* is published simultaneously in six different locations and is readily available in more cities than any other daily, but specializes in business and finance. The *Christian Science Monitor* of Boston is distributed nationally but its countrywide circulation is small.

Broadcasting in the United States also operates through local firms; national networks dominate prime-time television and are important in national broadcast news. But even the networks and their affiliates operate exclusively through local outlets.

No other country approaches this degree of localism in news institutions. In Russia, for example, metropolitan Moscow has less than 3 percent of total U.S.S.R. population, but Moscow-based dailies have 87 percent of all Russian daily circulation. In Japan, metropolitan Tokyo has 11 percent of national population, but Tokyo-based dailies have 70 percent of national circulation. In Britain, metropolitan London has 14 percent of population, but its dailies have 70 percent of national circulation.

In contrast, metropolitan New York and Washington, D.C., together have 6.6 percent of national population and together their daily papers supply only 9.6 percent of daily papers throughout the country.

Technical innovations in the coming years could change the fundamental pattern of public information distribution in the United States, and it is logical to ask whether the unique localism in the United States can or should be preserved. This question is worth asking because prevailing explanations for the absence of national news media in the United States seldom touch on its profound social basis.

The usual explanation for the lack of national newspapers is that the United States is so large geographically that it has been impossible to transport a paper speedily from its city of origin to all other cities. This has been one influence. But if it were the controlling factor, it would be predictable that new technology would quickly eliminate the pattern of local newspapers, since remote reproduction of large quantities of documents will become increasingly fast and inexpensive. One need not even wait for future developments. Present technology permits effective centralized control of newspaper production over great distances. Russia is two and a half times larger than the United States but manages to control most of its papers from Moscow.

Still another explanation usually offered is national affluence that can support many papers. This, like geographical size, is a factor but not a controlling one. A number of countries have a higher rate of per-capita newspaper buying but support fewer individual papers.

Country	Daily papers sold per 1000 population	Number of individual daily papers
Sweden	501	117
Britain	488	106
Japan	465	174
New Zealand	380	41
Australia	370	60
Denmark	347	67
Switzerland	344	126
West Germany	332	416
Unitod States	312	1754

Data from *Statistical Abstract of the United States, 1968,* Table 1272, p. 862.

Note, for example, that Japan, with about half the population of the United States, sells about 50 percent more papers per capita, but has only one-tenth as many individual dailies.

The American broadcasting news system follows somewhat the same pattern, with a large number of individual radio and television stations spread throughout the country. This is primarily the result of governmental regulatory policy rather than market mechanisms that govern placement of newspapers. But it is significant that government policy places a high value on localized radio and television stations. Governments of other industrialized countries favor centralized systems.

Centralizing radio broadcasting would be technically simple. Commercial radio signals ricochet between the surface of the earth and layers of the atmosphere during the evening, propelling themselves over very long distances in every direction. Thus, it would not be difficult to produce nighttime coverage of the entire continental

United States from a single transmitter. As a matter of fact, this was done from 1934 to 1938 when WLW in Cincinnati was permitted to operate at 500,000 watts.

Daytime radio signals fade more quickly, but with easily achieved power and selected frequencies a single station can still be heard within ranges of several hundreds of miles, so that a few stations could easily cover the entire United States.

Despite this technical feasibility of a few stations covering the entire country, there are 6,200 commerical AM and FM radio stations operating in 2,672 separate American communities. The largest number of radio stations in a single area is 34.

If the only desired end in the distribution of radio stations were diversity on a national scale, this could be achieved more easily, economically, and with greater variety than the present scattered locations. It would be possible, for example, to have 100 powerful radio transmitters that could reach every radio in the United States, rather than 6200 weaker ones reaching only their own locales. And the 100 centralized ones would provide more choice for the average listener, whose present maximum local stations are 34, with most communities able to receive far fewer. But the 100 centralized stations would not conform to the special force of localism in the United States.

Television cannot be so easily propagated from a few national transmitters because its carrier wave has a range less than a hundred miles and is even more disturbed than radio by intervening masses. But if national coverage with several channels were desired, it could be produced by several centralized studios whose programs would be relayed to each locality by relatively simple translator stations that are automatic. Instead, there are 639 commercial television transmitters in operation in 285 metropolitan areas, each with facilities for originating its own programs, rather than merely relaying national ones.

The fundamental reason for this persistent localism in American news institutions is a peculiarity in American political organization and the prevailing pattern of family money spending.

More governmental functions are left to the local level in the United States than in other developed countries. Schools, property taxes, land use, public health, large areas of business regulation, and many other political and social activities are controlled by locally elected and locally controlled bodies in the United States, while in other countries many of these are controlled by national governments or administered by national bureaucracies.

These locally controlled policies have maximum immediate impact on family life, such as schooling for children, design and location of homes, routes of local highways, and rates of personal property taxes. Such decisions are made by a complicated but highly localized set of political bodies. There are 18,000 municipalities and 17,000 townships. Within these are 500,000 local government units of one kind or another directly elected by local residents, 100,000 of these being directly elected local school boards, and 70,000 of the local jurisdictions possessing the power to impose taxes on their constituents.

No national newspaper or national broadcast news program can tell the local citizen what he needs or wants to know about these local activities that affect his family life. Furthermore, what is relevant to one local jurisdiction is only minimally significant for the next, since school systems, property taxes, and similar matters follow strictly local lines and cease to apply across the local boundary. Continuing information from relatively small districts is a unique imperative of the American social system.

Another powerful force for localism in the mass media is the large amount of local money spending by the average family. Mass purchasing power requires enough spending decisions to support advertising as a major economic activity.

American family income has been rising rapidly. From 1929 to 1962 average family personal income, measured in constant 1954 dollars, rose 70 percent. This, and the demands of modern urban and occupational life, have made necessities of some consumer goods that previously had been luxuries or nonexistent—refrigerators, cleaning compounds, formal city clothes. And, as national styles of work and social life evolved, other consumer goods became essential for coping efficiently with the environment—telephones, a family car, and electrical appliances like vacuum cleaners, radio and television sets. So, even at the lowest levels of income, the pressure for large-scale consumer purchasing became significant.

The great majority of this family money spending is done locally among competing enterprises. There are 1,700,000 retail stores in the

United States. The average American family spends $5,000 a year in them. Many of these stores advertise in competition for this disposable family income, and most of their advertising is in the general locality of their stores, in the mass media of the region.

Thus, there is both a political and an economic base for the localized pattern of American news media.

But there are conflicting forces at work, some in the direction of the traditional fragmentation of news firms, and some in the direction of a more homogenized, national pattern of a few organizations dominating the country. At present, there seems to be a tenuous equilibrium between the forces, with a surprising degree of stability among small journalism units despite the national trend toward large national corporations. The nature of new technology and the way it is organized could be crucial to the fate of this equilibrium.

The stability and profit of small, local journalism firms are remarkable, considering their rarity in other countries. In the daily-newspaper business, for example, there is a common pattern of a few large firms controlling a disproportionate share of the total market. In the United States, 8 percent of the largest papers have over half of all circulation. The smaller papers, those under twenty-five thousand circulation, constitute 70 percent of all daily newspaper firms but they have less than 20 percent of national circulation.

Circulation of Papers	Number of Papers of this Size	Percentage of all Papers	Percentage of Total Market
500,001 and over	11	0.6	14.0
250,001 to 500,000	28	1.6	15.6
100,001 to 250,000	93	5.3	24.4
50,001 to 100,000	112	6.4	12.3
25,001 to 50,000	255	14.5	14.6
10,001 to 25,000	462	26.3	11.8
5,001 to 10,000	467	26.7	5.3
Less than 5,000	324	18.5	1.9
Total Papers	1,752	100.0	100.0

Editor and Publisher Yearbook, 1969, p. 17. Percentages of papers and of total market added.

In the usual corporate trend, where in a field of 1,752 firms the top 2 percent have 30 percent of all the business, consolidation would proceed until most smaller operations would be absorbed by the giants. There is, in fact, a strong trend in the newspaper business toward consolidations, mergers, and chains, though these do not take the conventional form of centralized production, planning, and sales and do not seem to enjoy the usual economies of scale. But, while consolidation grows, the distribution of the market among smaller papers remains fairly stable, thanks to the emphasis on local self-government and local merchandising.

Location of broadcasting stations is decided by the Federal Communications Commission, and though these decisions are influenced by market demand, they are more influenced by limitations of positions on the dial. And, since there is no simple measure of "customers" for broadcasting because the consumer does not pay directly for his broadcast, determining how stations share their market is somewhat blurred. But, of the 2,624 AM and AM-FM stations reporting profits to the Federal Communications Commission in 1967, the distribution of profitable stations by size of their community looked like this:

Population Category of Community where Station Is Located	Number of Stations in Communities of this Size	Average Percent Profit on Gross per Station Before Federal Tax
2,000,000 or more	146	28%
1,000,000 to 2,000,000	106	27
500,000 to 1,000,000	217	19
250,000 to 500,000	241	15
200,000 to 250,000	58	15
150,000 to 200,000	89	13
100,000 to 150,000	116	13
50,000 to 100,000	71	11
25,000 to 50,000	239	13
10,000 to 25,000	465	11
5,000 to 10,000	457	13
2,500 to 5,000	294	12
Less than 2,500	125	12

From *AM-FM Broadcast Data, 1967,* F.C.C. Document 27306, February 7, 1969-B, Table 8. Percentages of profit added.

Here, as with newspapers, one sees advantages with domination of larger markets, but relative stability in the smaller ones.

The pattern of economic activity of television stations by size is more difficult to discern in official data, since the Federal Communications Commission does not issue comparable information for television. There are fewer television stations nationally, and fewer per market. There are over two hundred television markets; the top ten markets have more than a third of all TV households in the country and the top forty markets have two-thirds. Since there is a narrow limit to the number of television stations in any market because of the frequency shortage in the air—seven is the VHF maximum—there is a poor fit between available audience and available stations. Pittsburgh, for example, has $23 million a year in advertising revenues for its three television stations. The New York market has $130 million in television advertising revenues, or 5.6 times as much, which presumably would support 5.6 times as many stations, which would be sixteen or seventeen stations. But in New York there are only seven stations. Thus, the physical limitations of electromagnetic space in broadcasting through the air distorts any tendency to let television broadcasting adjust itself to potential audience or demand for advertising.

The news media from the start were carriers of local merchandising information. The newspaper in the United States began as a printed extension of bulletin boards of taverns and coffeehouses, its content mainly of ship arrivals and their offerings of cargo. These papers sold for six cents each, a very high price in the eighteenth century, designed for the affluent in the local population. The nonadvertising content consisted largely of reprinted stories from the English papers which arrived on the same ship as the merchandise. Until the Revolution, the most common name for American newspapers was *Advertiser*.

This pattern was enhanced by the absence of very large cities in the eighteenth-century North American continent. When the first dailies were established, the two largest cities, New York and Philadelphia, each had twenty-five thousand population.

Most of these early papers were published either by the local postmaster or by a local printer. Colonial postal service was crude and unreliable, a private monopoly granted by the Crown, and operating in only three cities. The population was a dispersed agricultural one, kept deliberately unindustrialized by the mother country, lacking the urbanization that might have encouraged a different press pattern.

As the country grew it developed a different demographic pattern from Europe, which already had its population clustered around large cities. The American frontier expanded and its population kept proliferating outward to virgin territory. A lively apprentice system produced many printers who had a reputation for itchy feet and parched throats, drifting drinkers who fell out of one job to another just beyond their reputation, but leaving behind the idea of a locally printed sheet.

Other factors helped create many small papers instead of a few large ones. One was the absence of a tax on papers. The European attempt to control the press through stamp taxes was so burdensome in many countries that it inhibited new papers. This concentrated circulation in the few papers that were rich and stable enough to pay the heavy duty on individual editions, and that tended to be very establishmentarian.

In the United States there was both constitutional and statutory encouragement for a free and growing press. Congress was forbidden to make any law abridging the freedom of the press. And the new postal system set up by Benjamin Franklin, an ex-printer, and William Hunter favored local printers. Each subscriber to a newspaper was charged nine pence sterling a year for every fifty miles the paper had to be carried by the postal system. On the other hand, papers sent from one printer to another went free. Thus, the individual subscriber was penalized by distance while his local printer was not; this encouraged printers to clip and paste other papers from distant cities and reprint locally.

In 1833, the largest American daily, the New York *Courier and Enquirer,* had a circulation of forty-five hundred, and that probably exaggerated, and most other American papers had less than a thousand circulation. The same year, the London *Times* and at least two Paris papers had circulations of more than fifteen thousand each.

The most spectacular burgeoning of the press came in mid-nineteenth century, largely because of new communications technology, like paper production from wood, high-speed presses, railroads, and the telegraph. The prices of many papers dropped. It became possible to buy a daily paper for a penny. In 1800, there had been 235 individual newspapers in the country, by 1850, 2,300. By 1860, there were more than three times as many papers in the United States as in

England and France. Always local merchandising and local government stimulated indigenous papers, and the number of dailies rose to a peak of 2,461 in 1916.

But with World War I the number of newspapers in the country began to decline and has continued to decline until today there are 1,750 papers, a drop of 30 percent. And since that time there has been a rise in strictly national news media, separate or nearly separate from the local papers and broadcast stations. The rise was slow until the last twenty years, during which it has become marked.

Since 1940, total daily newspaper circulation in the United States has risen about 50 percent, roughly the same as population. But the carriers of daily national news have outpaced this. The *Wall Street Journal*'s circulation in its home state increased 2,100 percent, but outside New York it went up 4,700 percent. The *New York Times*'s circulation in greater New York rose 30 percent, outside its own city, 165 percent. The *Christian Science Monitor*'s circulation in its home city, Boston, actually dropped slightly, but elsewhere in the country it rose 26 percent.

National news magazines, an invention of the period, have gained even more rapidly. In the 1940–1968 period, *Time, Newsweek,* and *U.S. News and World Report* increased their circulation 585 percent.

Responding to the same growing appetite for national news, new special supplementary news services for daily papers concentrated on serious Washington and world reportage and analysis. The New York Times Service was going to 16 North American papers in 1956 and to 211 in 1969. The Los Angeles Times/Washington Post News Service started in 1962 with 21 papers and in 1969 had 189. *Congressional Quarterly,* a relatively sophisticated summary and statistical analysis of legislative activity in Washington was subscribed to by 1 paper in 12 in 1955, but in 1968 by 1 paper in 6, even though it had a rival in a new service, Center for Political Research.

But, during the same period of marked growth of national news media, there was growth in strictly local ones. Hundreds of specialized papers, many classed as "underground," sprang up, with a circulation estimated at 4 million. "Establishmentarian" weeklies, mostly serving small areas, also grew. During the decade 1958–1967, daily newspaper circulation rose 5 percent, but circulation of standard commercial weeklies rose 51 percent. Some operators forecast even more spectacular growth. John E. Tilton, of Suburban Papers, Inc., of Minneapolis, said, "In the next 20 years, someone will start another 2000 suburban newspapers."

Nevertheless, commercial pressures for ever wider jurisdictions, made all the more tempting by easier and cheaper long-distance transmission of information, raise the possibility of increasing separation between local media and national.

Two factors push in this direction. One is the growth in popular consciousness of national and world affairs, the result both of increased cosmopolitanism and education and the enlargement of the role of the national government and world events in the life of the average family.

The other factor is the trend in contemporary advertising and merchandising reversing the historic role of rooting the local media to their immediate communities.

In the late nineteenth century, newspapers for the first time took seriously the possibility that at least one newspaper could be sold to each household each day. By then it was technically possible to manufacture enough papers for this kind of saturation. Advertising was becoming an important national economic activity and assuming an ever larger share of the newspaper's revenues. In 1867 $50 million a year was spent on ads; in 1900 this had gone up ten times, by 1950 a hundred times.

Merchants generally buy space or broadcasting time on the basis of the cost of exposing their advertising to a thousand persons, or cost-per-thousand. As individual newspaper production plants developed the capacity to print one complete newspaper for every house in the community, and advertisers clearly became indirect subsidizers of these plants, the working of the marketplace made it inevitable that it would be less expensive for the advertisers to support one plant in a community instead of two or three or a dozen. Even with the increased advertising rates that a local monopoly could charge, the cost-per-thousand was cheaper than advertising in two or more competing papers.

Since World War I the number of individual newspapers has declined, though the surviving papers have become fatter and devote a larger percentage of their space to advertisements. Since World War II advertising content in daily papers has gone from 52 percent to 61 percent, the size of papers from twenty-two pages a day, of which eleven were ads, to fifty pages in 1965 for the average daily, of which thirty were ads.

Fatter papers meant larger plants, more presses, more typesetting machines, and larger work forces. Processing of advertising is more demanding and expensive than that of news matter. Costs rose. But, once plates were on the presses, labor costs remained relatively level and the cost of added circulation was largely the cost of paper and ink. And, since advertising was placed more on the basis of cost-per-thousand than any other single factor, it was advantageous for a paper to increase its production, even if it meant extending its sales beyond the limits of its immediate city.

Conversion of newspapers into substantial manufacturing plants inhibited growth of new papers in new communities. Surviving papers gained monopolies in their own communities and pushed beyond the city limits to nearby communities. Consequently, the cost of starting new papers in the new communities at the edges of the metropolises was unattractive, since the established nearby papers were always prepared to produce papers for the new communities at small incremental cost. The country created more and more communities, and served them with fewer and fewer newspapers.

Year	Daily Papers	Cities with Dailies	% of Daily Cities with Competing Papers	% of Urban Places with Own Dailies
1880	850	389	61	90
1910	2202	1207	57	53
1920	2042	1295	43	48
1930	1942	1402	21	44
1940	1878	1426	13	41
1945	1744	1396	8	—
1961	1763	1461	4	29
1968	1749	1500	3	—

From *Subcommittee on Antitrust and Monopoly,* "The Failing Newspaper Act," Part 6, p. 2842, Table 1, "Trends in Ownership of English-Language Dailies of General Circulation and Content in the United States, 1880–1968," percentage of daily cities with competing papers added. Number of urban places from *Historical Statistics of the United States,* p. 14, and *Statistical Abstract of the United States,* p. 16.

The consequences of this reversal of the traditional American tendency for each community to serve its self-governing functions with its own news medium are difficult to measure. But the change from 90 percent of urban places with their own daily paper to less than 30 percent is a radical one, and it may have radical consequences. It could be a contributing factor to the growing inability of municipalities to control their social and political affairs, to the psychological loss of community identity characteristic of newer towns and cities, and to the sluggishness with which urban governments responded to postwar social pathologies and the slowness with which this pathology, once felt, came to national attention.

The need for systematic community communication in the United States is self-evident from the number of important functions left to local decision. Jack Lyle, in his book *The News in Megalopolis,* notes that the local press is usually thought of as a watchdog over local government, and while this is true, there is a positive function as well: ". . . officials want to get information to the public . . . because of the proliferation of public agencies, such bodies are actually competing for the attention of the individual citizen and for coverage within the news media."

Lyle's research showed that community communications depend more than anything else on the presence of a locally based printed news medium. When he asked local officials how frequently their activities were covered by news media, both city-government and school-district activities showed coverage in this way:

Local weeklies	53%
Local dailies	53
Metropolitan dailies	17
Radio and TV	0

Banfield and Wilson in *City Politics* note that a city like Chicago has 341 different officials with identifiable authority in city and county matters and "in most cases there is no formal mechanism by which all these governments can be brought together."

The growing number of radio and television stations has not relieved this trend because broadcasting pays little attention to systematic local reportage. Robert Paul Boynton and Deil S. Wright, in a study of council managers in cities of over 100,000 population, found that "Local news is the base of a newspaper's operation. A high percentage of its total space is allotted to community concerns. Radio and television have other primary interests."

Boynton and Wright polled city managers on their judgment of mass-media influence on municipal affairs, with these results:

Degree of Influence	Newspapers	Television	Radio
Highly influential	51%	8%	2%
Moderately influential	42	50	33
Limited influence	7	23	49
No apparent influence	0	20	16

"Communication Gap: Is Anybody Up There Listening?" by Robert Paul Boynton and Deil S. Wright, *Public Management*, March, 1968, p. 2.

This parallels a survey by the Bureau of Advertising of the ANPA which, in 1966, polled a cross-section of readers on the "best way" to find out about local affairs, to which 48 percent cited newspapers, 13 percent television, and 15 percent radio. Both the newsmakers and the news consumers depend on the local printed newspaper for important community information.

The basic causes for present community malaise in the United States can hardly be laid at the door of absent or delinquent news media. Even with ideal local attention to civic affairs, it would be difficult to cope with the bewildering maze of governmental and quasi-governmental units, often uncoordinated and frequently at cross-purposes. But apathy or frustration produced by this random agglomeration of civic functions is deepened by the lack of locally based news media that even try to follow and publicize systematically the more important developments. In a country of 100,000 autonomous school districts and 400,000 other local governmental units, it is significant that fewer than 30 percent of the communities in whose boundaries they lie has any locally based news medium.

This poor fit between community units and news media comes largely because newspapers and radio and television stations, even though they carry a place name in their identification, do not arrange their output by civic boundaries but instead by merchandising territories. As the automobile determines the range for shopping, merchandising territories increasingly ignore civic boundaries. And, as these shopping territories enlarge, the growing production power of the mass media follows them through communities whose civic affairs they largely ignore.

The effective boundary line of most newspapers is a territory called "retail trade zone," which varies in definition from place to place but commonly ends in neighborhoods where the paper's daily sales fall to between 5 and 20 percent of the total households.

Broadcasting stations occupy territories called "markets," which are usually the area of the effective range of their broadcast signal.

About 400 markets are calculated for daily newspapers and about 230 markets for broadcasting stations. Within these are most of the 500,000 units of local government. Given the total space for serious local news in newspapers, and the total time devoted in typical broadcasting stations, it would be impossible to give systematic reportage of all the important public-affairs developments in each of the significant public bodies within the market areas of individual news media.

In 1969 a majority of the FCC raised questions about the transfer in ownership of the only television station in Hutchinson, Kansas, KTVH, Channel 12. The Commission was concerned with concentration of ownerships, but KTVH is typical of other television stations in its jurisdiction, which represents problems regardless of ownership.

KTVH covers about 18,000 square miles with its strongest signal, with average penetration of 90 percent of the 344,000 homes. If the 23 counties for which KTVH is the primary station have their share of all local governmental units in Kansas, they contain over 800 different governmental bodies, including 210 municipalities and 110 school boards. About 350 of them levy taxes.

If the station devotes typical TV time to local news (not including sports), and if each of the governmental bodies in its area made only one newsworthy decision a month, and if the station happened to cover this decision, and if the station devoted all of its local newscasts exclusively to the deliberations of these public bodies, each would have reportage of thirty seconds a month.

KTVH is part of the Kansas Broadcasting System for the purpose of selling commercials. This network of television stations advertises itself as "a 93 county major television market of 403,400 television homes, 1.3 million people in a five state area with a consumer spendable income of over $3.5 billion. . . ."

For merchandisers, such a network is effective. As reporters of events within their boundaries, it reduces each civic function to a fraction of a minute per month.

Yet the merchandising function continues to favor ever larger geographical territories, so that the cost of reaching each consumer will drop. This is impelled not only by the larger shopping ranges made possible by the automobile, but also by the growth of unified national brands, commonly available "at your local" (anonymous) drug, department, or grocery store. Standard-brand cosmetics, food, and cigarettes do not need to specify particular stores or addresses in order to stimulate sales by wide-area broadcasting or newspaper advertising.

Among newspapers, two categories of standardized retail goods make up 42 percent of all newspaper advertising: automobiles with 28 percent, and foods with 14 percent. In television, in 1970, four categories of nationally standard brands made up almost 60 percent of all television advertising: foods with 19 percent; toiletries, 17 percent; tobacco, 12 percent; and drugs, 11 percent.

The retail outlets for these standardized items are also becoming regionally and nationally standardized by a relatively small number of recognizable and dominant firms. The combination of near-universal recognition of both store names and brand names means that broad, homogenized advertising becomes more effective, and the small medium with a special audience less competitive.

Especially with broadcasting, whose entertainment and news also are increasingly produced in a national source, the financial rewards lie with enlargement of area and of gross population, even to the deliberate exclusion of a station's immediate home base.

The Federal Communications Commission recently took note of this tendency. "We have . . . noted that there is a tendency on the part of stations in suburban communities in metropolitan areas, to identify themselves with the entire metropolitan area rather than with the particular needs of their communities." The FCC intervened when the only full-time radio station in Camden, New Jersey, was about to be sold to a Texas corporation which intended to eliminate all local programming serving the 117,000 population of Camden in order to attract advertising for programming designed for the metropolitan Philadelphia area across the Delaware River, although Philadelphia already had twenty-eight of its own radio stations.

Technology helped eliminate the idea of every community with a news medium of its own. But even broadcasting once started as a local service. When the British Broadcasting Corporation started in 1922, there was no practical network system in existence. Consequently it established twenty strictly local stations with only ¼ kw power (American communities now have stations with many times that power). When communications technology improved, the BBC became a centralized operation out of London. Frank Gillard, managing director of radio for the BBC, says that the result has been that the former development of local talent in discussion, entertainment, and culture atrophied as only the highly professionalized work of London reached the air, and that "democracy in the country breaks down at the local level."

If England, which depends far less on local decision making for the health of its basic institutions than the United States, is apprehensive about a breakdown at the local level for lack of local media, the United States has cause for concern. Although the United States has far more local media than any other country, it is far more dependent on such media than any other country. And these local media are expanding their territories, largely at the expense of neighborhood, community, and city information and programming. The commercial imperative is not news but to reach the largest possible undifferentiated gross numbers of audience for purposes of national and regional advertising. And this advertising is less and less tied to particular communities.

One illustration of the difficulties this produces in civic affairs is the state of Delaware, which has no commercial television station within its borders, although it has at least 170 governmental units in it, including 50 self-governing school boards. (The state has three daily newspapers, two of them published by the Du Pont interests who thereby control 88 percent of daily circulation in Delaware.) If a state or local official wishes to reach his constituency by television, or a candidate for United States Senator wishes to campaign among the citizens of Delaware, he has no single television transmitter that reaches all the state with the most favorable, Grade A, signal. The best the senatorial candidate can do, if he wishes to use a VHF station that is received by 50 percent or more of the homes in the state, is to purchase time in two stations, each in a different state.

One, in Philadelphia, reaches the two northern counties of Delaware, which have 121,000 television homes. But for this he must pay $1,150 for five minutes of time, because the Philadelphia station also reaches a potential of 2,279,000 homes, mostly in Pennsylvania and New Jersey. To reach the southern county of Delaware he must then go to a Baltimore television station that reaches the 22,000 TV homes of Sussex County, Delaware. But, because the Baltimore station also goes to 1,600,000 TV homes, most of them in Maryland and Virginia, he pays $500 for five minutes. Thus, he pays $1,650 for five minutes of communication with an audience 96 percent of whom he does not wish to speak with because they live in four other states. As a matter of fact, a television station resists any programming, even if paid for, that has appeal for only 4 percent of its audience, since it will diminish the audience for subsequent programs.

So the fit between advertising jurisdictions that tend to fix the limits of news media, and the local units by which most people live and work becomes ever more maladjusted. It could change if new technology permits local media without much advertising. Or if new technology permits delivery of messages to special audiences while retaining broader distribution for regional messages.

The ability of a community to keep in touch with itself began to deteriorate when populations became so large that it was no longer possible for all voters to fit in the same hall. Community identity, self-knowledge, and cohesion have been worsening ever since.

The technical innovations of the next generation could evolve in a way that would make local self-government more chaotic and community identity more damaged, leaving ever more communities lost to the world of modern communications. The further homogenizing of mass communications could produce deeper pathology in neighborhood life and community government, with little information on how national ideas can be applied at the local level.

On the other hand, future technology could provide a restoration of community communications resembling the New England town meeting. New methods have the capacity, the low cost-per-channel, and the ability to limit particular programs to small areas like neighborhoods. But if they are to do this they will have to be driven by something different from the present commercial mass-market mechanisms. For all practical purposes, "the audience" for the news media today is first a collection of people with money to spend and only second a specific collection of citizens with private and public problems to solve. New techniques of communications can reverse that order but this will require basic changes in public and corporate policies that shape the distribution of information.

The Printed News System

It is impossible to calculate the potential number of events in the world that on any given day might interest some consumer of news. No news system can conduct a continuous survey of all the interrelations of the 3.5 billion human beings on earth and their 167 governments. Even in the communications-conscious United States, there is only a microscopic portion reported of the events of some public impact that occur among merely the conventional organizational sources of news, like the 10,000 national associations, 91,000 governmental units, 121,000 schools and colleges, 320,000 churches, and 2,500,000 business firms.

There will never be enough professional reporters to record all potential news, since theoretically it would require one observer for every participant in human events. If this unpleasant ratio of half the world reporting the activities of the other half should come about, there would not be enough communications capacity for all the reports to be transmitted. If all the reports could be transmitted, they could not be printed. If they could be printed, the reader would never have the time to look at the results.

Yet, unachievable though it is, this is what the news system attempts every day, condemned to a state of perpetual restlessness because it is committed to an impossible mission. It assigns such observers as it has to the places it thinks most likely to produce noteworthy occurrences, and prints what it can of the results. In the United States this is done mainly through the systems of the printed press: the two major news agencies, Associated Press and United

Press International; a number of supplementary services that provide specialized journalism; and the contribution of daily papers feeding selections from their own staffs into the national nets. Broadcasting adds significant and vivid items but in terms of original reporting it is a minor part of the total.

The professional at the local hub of this network is a crucial, if obscure, figure, the local newspaper subeditor who stands between the results of the whole reporting system and the reader. He has different titles in different places, perhaps "managing editor" in a small paper, or "news editor" in a slightly larger one. Or "telegraph editor" originating a generation or two ago when distant news came by Morse code into local newspaper offices. Or "wire editor" because today most news comes into the office on teletype machines leased from the national news distribution agencies that are known in the trade as "wire services." Social scientists have decided to call him "gatekeeper" because he controls which stories will be printed and which go to the wastebasket.

He is an obscure man both to the public and within his own trade. Reporters and correspondents have the glamour of being on the scene and having their names attached to accounts of events. Executive editors and publishers are respected or feared by public figures because they control the organizations that decide which men will remain in the public eye.

The gatekeeper does not attract similar attention, but in some ways he has more unofficial power than reporters and publishers. He decides which of the routine stories that arrive on his desk each day will be seen by the public. And by making these decisions he notifies all others in the system which stories in the future are likely to get printed and which ones it is pointless for them to report.

He is not all-powerful. Decisions on major stories are usually, but not always, made by others. If his decisions are noticeably contrary to the news policy of his editorial or corporate supervisors, he hears about it and usually, but not always, conforms. If his decisions are seen later to be drastically different from those on other papers or broadcasting stations that his organization takes seriously, he may alter his standards. Or he may not.

But the daily avalanche of information that flows into a daily newspaper is so great, and decisions are made so rapidly, that most news stories are committed to print quietly and irreversibly by the gatekeeper acting alone.

RAND field studies show that typically the gatekeeper receives five stories for every one he puts into the paper. In general, the larger the circulation of the paper, the greater the percentage of stories thrown away, since the larger papers, though they have more space, have even more sources of news. The Washington *Post,* for example, with 500,000 daily circulation, is listed as subscribing to the Associated Press, the United Press International, the Los Angeles Times/ Washington Post News Service, Chicago Tribune–New York Daily News Service, Chicago Daily News Service, London Sunday Times Service, Dow-Jones Service, and Reuters News Service. For each of its services, it has one or more teletype machines bringing in news more or less continuously. Most smaller papers subscribe to only one service, either AP or UPI, whose output is received on three or fewer teletype machines.

On most papers studied, the gatekeeper daily scans five times more words and five times more individual stories than he can use. But on larger metropolitan dailies (over 350,000 circulation) he may see ten times more words and seven times more stories than the reader ever sees. What the gatekeeper throws away is generally never knowable to the reader. It is as though the events reported in 80 percent of the stories that arrive in local newsrooms never happened. This is inevitable but it is awesome.

What follows is not a description of the total information intake of a whole newspaper, but only that minority but paramount category known as "straight news." In most of the papers studied, this consti-tuted about 27 percent of the total paper. Advertisements took 54 to 67 percent of the total paper. Of the nonadvertising space, news took from 62 to 86 percent of space, the remainder being sports, financial, and non-news features.

There are other gatekeepers on the paper. Those who handle the flow of advertising into the daily editions are important because, among other things, they determine how much space will be left for news. On almost all papers the advertising department determines total pages to be printed and only after this does news receive its allocation.

The conversion of volume of advertisements into total pages for the day is not simple. Presses print varying combinations of pages. Papers are always issued with an even number of total pages since sheets are printed on both sides. But, because of complications in multiple printing, cutting, and folding that vary from paper to paper, paper size may be increased by jumps of two pages, in others by four pages, in others by six. Part of this calculation is mechanical, but part of it is financial, since it may not be profitable to increase the size of the paper for a small surplus of advertising. The final decision on number of pages for the day is held off as long as possible in order to print a maximum of ads. Thus, early in the editing cycle the gate-keeper may be told that he has a certain amount of space for his news, but as the final deadline approaches this may be changed.

The individual who makes the calculations on paper size is even more obscure than the gatekeeper of news. It is frequently an elderly retainer, seldom extravagantly paid, who over the years had divined the paper's philosophy on page changes and shown an aptitude for remembering the numerical permutations of how many ads convert to how many additional pages at which levels of total number of pages. Sometimes called a dispatcher, this person is frequently unknown by name or function to the news gatekeeper whose daily work he so seriously affects. Usually the dispatcher's decisions are final and irreversible. On some papers on some occasions, these decisions may so drastically limit space for dramatic news that the top editors may object, but this usually requires a last-minute appeal to the publisher or owner.

For the news gatekeeper this standard procedure creates a condition of continuing chaos.

Ideally, the man selecting news for his community would gather before him the entire collection of news items harvested that day, study them comparatively, and then make his selection of which item is most important, which is of second importance, which is of third, and so forth. Having made those decisions, he would observe the total to see if, aside from the individual value of each story, there is something in the total daily report that relates individual stories to each other. Finally, he would, of course, give special weight to the mostly recently arrived news since, almost by definition, later news should have a better chance of getting into the paper than earlier news. Then it would all be placed quickly before the reader.

That is not what happens. The editor never sees all the stories before he makes his decisions. At the start of his deciding, he does not know what the total news report will look like, so he cannot pre-select items that will give cohesion to the final paper. And the latest news, far from having the greatest chance of getting into the paper, has the least. And after he has made the bulk of his decisions it could be ten hours before most of the readers see the results.

To reverse this, two technological developments would be necessary. First, the full news report from which the local editor makes his selection would have to be available to him at the time that he begins to commit his stories to print. This does not happen today because, among other reasons, the machines that transmit news into his office do it slowly and piecemeal.

But, even if the full report were instantly available, the manufacturing process that converts this to print is even slower. The newspaper printing system is a lugubrious, expensive, intricate mechanical beast that, like an ulcer patient, must be fed slowly and steadily throughout the day.

Two mechanical systems are used by daily papers in the United States.

Letterpress, the traditional process, is still used by a majority of papers and all large ones. Its basis is the casting of each individual letter into metal, the revolution in printing that began in Western Europe in about 1450. Johann Gutenberg designed individual metal letters and a way to hold them properly to form sentences. Inked and pressed on paper, they produced the printed page. Gutenberg set type by placing each metal letter by hand in its proper place at the rate of one line a minute. So did everyone else for 430-odd years thereafter.

In 1886 in Baltimore Ottmar Mergenthaler produced a large, ungainly machine to do it faster. As an operator pressed a letter on a keyboard, a mold for the letter fell into place, and when molds for the letters and spaces reached the end of the line, melted hot lead was shot through them to form a casting of the completed line. The cast metal lines, arranged in columns, were carried by hand to a table where they were arranged to form the total page. Mergenthaler's Linotype machine cast at the rate of 4.9 lines a minute.

In 1932 the Teletypesetter was invented to operate the linecasting machine not by hand but by a perforated paper tape which actuated the keyboard. Before this, when human beings operated the keyboard, they varied in speed, and even the best of them would have to pause from time to time, to scratch their heads, sneeze, or to decipher the typewritten or handwritten words they were casting. And while they paused the expensive machine was idle. If instead the operator's keyboard created paper tape bearing instructions for the Linotype, his pauses kept only the simple tape-punching mechanism idle, and after he made all his corrections on the tape, the tape could drive the machine steadily at its optimum rate. This raised speeds to 5.6 lines a minute.

In 1960 the computer was put to work removing some of the human judgment in making the paper tape, like deciding when to end a line and how to hyphenate a word. This raised typesetting to fourteen lines a minute.

In five hundred years the speed of setting type had risen from one to fourteen lines a minute, and in many newspaper shops this was considered the end of a typographical upheaval.

For photographs, there is a different but similarly complicated process by which the negative is projected onto a photosensitized metal plate and the image treated with acid to pit the areas selectively so that dark areas have many ink-bearing dots and white areas none.

When the cast letters and photoengraved plates are completed they are assembled to form the printed page. For most of the history of printing, this became the printing surface, successively inked and pressed on sheets of paper. For longer use, the original type and engraving were used as a master, and a papier-mâché form was pressed on the raised metallic letters to form a negative. Laid on its back, this mat was filled with hot lead to make a duplicate printing surface. Attached to a flat plate and daubed with ink, it was pressed down on the sheet of paper, which was then pulled out, folded by hand, and became a newspaper.

For 350 years the device for making the inked impression on paper was basically the same as the one used by Gutenberg, which was a converted wine press that instead of pushing grape against grape was made to push inked type against paper, and gave the institution of "the press" its name. This produced about one hundred impressions an hour. In 1810 it was attached to a steam engine, which raised the rate to two hundred impressions an hour: a four-page paper with five hundred subscribers would take ten hours to be printed. In England in the early 1800s Friedrich Koenig invented a rotary press, and after his first machine was demolished by an angry crowd consisting of both management and labor, it was successfully installed in the *Times* of London and produced twenty-four hundred impressions an hour. The four-page paper that formerly took ten hours to be printed could be produced in fifty minutes.

This rotary press required a curved printing surface. This was made by placing the mat in a semicylindrical form, from which a lead casting was made and placed on the rotary press. The process, called stereotyping, could produce identical duplicate plates for multiple impressions of the same page.

This is still the process used on most papers. It still takes from seven to ten hours, reverting to the time lag of 160 years ago, though, of course, producing modern American papers of many more pages and in very large numbers.

A different process, offset, was adopted after World War II and is in use in about a quarter of American dailies, all smaller ones. Instead of using cast metal letters and engravings, a photograph is made of the completed page and printed on a thin photosensitive sheet of metal or plastic-coated paper. The process leaves the dark areas of the plate—letters, punctuation, dark parts of photographs— with a slightly greasy surface. Attached to the printing press, the thin, flexible plate is first rotated against a water roller, which moistens the white areas but is repelled by the greasy dark ones. Next it is rotated against an ink roller. The watery white areas reject the grease-based ink, but the dark areas retain it, leaving an inked impression of the page. The printing plate is next rolled against a rubberized cylinder on which it deposits (or offsets) its inked impression of the page, and the rubberized cylinder is rolled against the moving web of paper on which it makes the final transfer of the inked page impression.

Offset produced higher-quality printing, with more positive dark areas. But its chief advantage is its natural partnership with the most important invention in typesetting since Gutenberg.

A new device, instead of casting hot lead to make individual metal letters, uses optics and electronics to project at great speed an image of each letter onto photosensitized paper. It can project these letters in many sizes or style and for any line length desired, changing each character electronically or through lenses rather than physical movement. In some cases it projects each letter precisely on the page where it will appear in final form. In 1964 the Photon and Mergenthaler companies introduced such a machine that cast eighty lines a minute. In 1966 an RCA device cast eighteen hundred lines a minute. In 1967, a CBS-Mergenthaler Linotron, usable for the moment only for specialized publications, was bought by the U.S. Government Printing Office; it casts fifteen thousand lines a minute.

Suddenly, the newspaper business, which thought it had experienced a radical change in 1960, found its technology in danger of total obsolescence. If it was slow to respond it was partly because it was experiencing for the first time what other industries had discovered: each basic invention, like rabbits and people, bears the seeds of a multiplication of yet more and faster new creations. The history of converting the written word into print looked like this:

Date of Introduction	Lines Cast per Minute	Years Required for Birth of New Technique
1454	1.0	
1886	4.9	432
1932	5.6	46
1960	14.0	28
1964	80.0	4
1966	1,800.0	2
1967	15,000.0	1

The Bible, whose letters took Gutenberg five years to set, could now be produced by the Government Printing Office in seventy-seven minutes—once the programmers had created a magnetic tape to instruct the computer how to project the letters onto the page.

Even after the creation of words on photosensitive paper, letterpress systems must make an engraving of the images in order to achieve a raised metal printing surface. But offset, which prints with a photographic plate instead of cast metal, can use its original photocomposed pages, eliminating most of the cumbersome and expensive intervening steps of hot metal linecasting, photoengraving, and stereotyping.

The linkage of computers and photocomposition will revolutionize production of all images, whether on the printed page or on the electronic screen. Newspapers will be no exception. But the conversion will not be simple and quick.

For one thing, cumbersome and expensive though they are, the present newspaper procedures are reliable and tested, and in an industry where total mechanical failure is unthinkable this makes for understandable caution.

Offset, which most efficiently uses photocomposition, is not yet perfected for very large papers. A large metropolitan paper must have duplicate plates for simultaneous printing of many pages in large daily editions, and this requires it to manufacture about sixteen hundred heavy metal printing plates during each publishing cycle. Each of these plates can be cast in about twenty seconds. If offset were used, each photoplate would take about two hundred seconds, or ten times longer. Even when plates are completed, offset presses are slower than letterpress, at present too slow for a large paper.

Furthermore, newspapers have a great deal of money invested in their old machinery, as much as $1 million worth for a small daily and more than $25 million worth for a large one. Newspapers are even more loath than most businesses to discard machines that still work, even if they have been largely written off in tax depreciation. It is a conservatism compounded of many elements: local leadership that finds it difficult to believe that the family business might someday do without the traditional clank of typesetting machines and roar of the presses, fear of difficulty with unions whose membership might feel threatened, and complacency that comes from monopoly.

So as papers become larger they become slower. There grows a widening separation in print between the word "new" ("having existed, or having been made, but a short time") and the word "news" ("a report of recent events"), not growing out of a desire for more time to reflect but because in the ultimate technological irony of the news profession, the demands of machines rob men of time to think. From the moment the gatekeeper arrives at his desk, sometimes fourteen hours before his work will be read, he must begin to feed the cumbersome mechanisms that convert news into print. Because each story he sends out reduces the remaining space, any succeeding story of the same importance has less of a chance of being seen. The machines of the news system are biased in favor of old news.

A 1961 study of twenty-three Wisconsin afternon dailies' use of

Associated Press wire copy showed that the most important single factor in use of stories was their time of delivery. Of all stories received before 8 A.M., 49 percent were used; between 8 and 10 A.M., 44 percent; between 10 and 11:30 A.M., 30 percent; after 11:30 A.M., 13 percent. When stories were filed in fragments over a period of time, the later fragments presumably reporting later developments, were more often discarded than those received earlier.

There are other nonnews factors that influence what the reader will see. Space for news varies from day to day not on the basis of news events but on when American families plan their weekly shopping. Those are the days when department stores, used-car dealers and supermarkets do their maximum advertising. Since quantity of advertising determines quantity of news, there is minimum news space on Saturdays, Mondays, and Tuesdays, and maximum space on Wednesdays, Thursdays and Fridays.

But the maximum news space on maximum advertising days does not help much to increase the quota of late news. Mechanical departments producing a twenty-four-page paper, as they might on a Saturday, reserve their last hour for the few pages, like page one, that are prime news display spaces and receive news until the last minute. When the same staff put out a ninety-six-page paper, as they might on a Thursday, they require the same time for these last late-news pages. So they must work even faster in the early hours of the publishing cycle to process the larger number of total pages. On such a day, the gatekeeper must send out masses of news very early in the editing cycle, to fill up the added pages. Very early stories tend to have no time relevance and often no other kind except that they are available and fill space.

This process is raised to a level of exquisite frustration by the fact that the gatekeeper may be informed in the middle of his day that his available news space has changed.

In all of this, the gatekeeper is haunted by two opposite perils. One is failing to send out enough copy to fill his allotted space. If this happens, there are empty columns and the paper cannot go to press on time, a psychic trauma on a newspaper. It is also a logistic one: fleets of delivery trucks are on minute-by-minute schedules, bundles of papers have to make trains and planes, and networks of newsboys must get their papers on time or else will, on a morning paper, abandon their paper routes for school. An evening paper's trucks will get stalled in rush-hour traffic and the paper will be delivered to the home after 5:30 P.M., by which time most papers assume they have lost the reader to the evening meal and television.

On the other hand, if the gatekeeper sends out too much news, he will get a report each day on how much this has cost the paper. Excess news that has been set in type but not used costs hundreds of dollars and the daily amount of wastage is a figure most managements take pains to circulate to those responsible.

The calculations of all those involved in this process are usually done by a combination of mental arithmetic and running totals kept on a pad of paper, all juggled while they do other things.

So decisions on what news goes into a daily paper and what stays out are not made in serenity with full knowledge of alternatives. Each story is not judged solely on the basis of its importance compared to all other stories available that day. Instead it is compared to stories already committed to print and to stories not yet seen. The editor must also consider how much time and space remain, and how much money and time it will cost to reverse earlier decisions on the basis of later and better information.

A basic indicator of available news is the incoming information from wire services. The hourly product of just one teletype machine in a local newsroom, an iron technological constraint on the creation of a daily newspaper, is shown below.

Papers of varying sizes have varying numbers of such machines.

Time Period	Words Received on One AP "A" Wire Teletype
10 to 11 A.M.	2,600
11 to 12 noon	2,800
12 to 1 P.M.	2,800
1 to 2 P.M.	2,600
2 to 3 P.M.	2,600
3 to 4 P.M.	2,500
4 to 5 P.M.	2,900
5 to 6 P.M.	3,300
6 to 7 P.M.	2,900
8 to 9 P.M.	1,900
9 to 10 P.M.	3,000

One metropolitan paper studied had twenty-two, most of them producing information at the rate of the single machine above, some of them handling specialized information that came in spasmodically.

It may be a measure of the vague conventional wisdom that dominates newspaper technology that it is often assumed that each teletype machine delivers either sixty-six words a minute for more recent machines or sixty words a minute for the more common ones. Editors assume that these theoretical maximum speeds are the effective rate. The RAND study which counted the intake on different papers in different parts of the country found a consistent average of forty-five words a minute. In a trade in which transmission of information is crucial, a near-universal error of 25 to 47 percent is interesting. The error is not operationally serious since wire services and local editors have adjusted to the real rates of the machines, regardless of what the number may be. But it is revealing of the traditional lack of systematic study of the flow of information in an industry that is based on it.

The slowness of the wire complicates the problem of corrections and additions. The first versions of stories are transmitted as they come along, even if they are not yet complete. The wire services insist that they have a deadline every minute. The steady demands of broadcasting throughout the day and the deadlines for multiple editions of daily papers in many different time zones around the world mean that even the fragmentary, first visible evidence of an event will be wanted by some client about to broadcast or go to press. Thus, in one seven-hour editing cycle, one wire-service teletype machine carried eighty-three items, about twelve per hour, which consisted of fifteen complete stories, fifty-four parts of stories (including corrections and additions), and fourteen messages (mostly notices to editors of major stories expected in the near future).

On one suburban evening paper of less than fifty thousand circulation, with three wire-service machines, most of the copy was handled by the news editor, who was the main gatekeeper, with the help of two assistants. The original yes-no decision on each story was made by the news editor. Only then might he hand the story to his assistants for cutting or other changes. If he decided against a story, as he did with 80 percent of them, he personally put it aside.

The news editor arrives at 6 A.M. to find an overnight accumulation of fifty thousand words, most of it regional and national news from the wire services, some of it from the paper's reporters in outlying bureaus, who transmitted it by teletype the night before.

In addition to making decisions on incoming wire stories, this particular news editor makes decisions on local stories handed him by the city editor and the state editor. He also is handed the output of two wirephoto machines that during the day produce ninety-six photographs, from which he selects sixteen. He must commit his photographs much earlier than his texts since mechanical processing of pictures is time consuming. Though the presses are not scheduled to roll until 1 P.M., most photos must be selected by 8 A.M.

Unlike wire-service news, most of which is discarded, almost all information originated by the local staff is used. This is mainly because the basic decision on the value of the story was made when the reporter was originally assigned to it. It is partially because, having invested its own manpower, the paper is prejudiced in favor of using the story. The wire service, having to estimate the interests and tastes of hundreds of news clients, presents a surplus of stories, making the local selection more stringent.

Time	Words Received	Words Selected
6 to 7 A.M.	50,000	500
7 to 8 A.M.	10,000	2,500
8 to 9 A.M.	10,000	8,000
9 to 10 A.M.	8,000	4,000
10 to 11 A.M.	10,000	3,500
11 to 12 noon	10,000	3,500
12 to 1 P.M.	10,000	400

During the seven-hour editing cycle, the news editor looks at and makes the initial decision on the following volume of news from the three wire machines and local staff.

During this same period he receives and sends out for processing five thousand words of local staff-originated news; joins in the selection of photographs received by wire; is consulted on assignment of stories by the city editor during the morning hours; designs and redesigns page one as the news changes; and carries on conversations, drinks coffee, and remarks informally upon the news.

In his first hour, in addition to going through the accumulated fifty thousand words, he also makes a rough dummy of page one, drawing in the stories as he predicts them at that moment. His decisions on which stories will go on page one are frequently influenced by whether there are good photographs to accompany them. But photo decisions have to be completed four hours before the last text decisions.

At 8:30 A.M. a secretary hands the news editor mailed press releases which he looks through for five minutes. Then the news editor is offered a local story but after consulting a pad on his desk announces that he already has too many stories for the available space. Shortly afterward the secretary hands him a second batch of mailed press releases, but having just determined that he is running out of available space, the news editor throws away the releases unopened.

At 10 A.M. a new page-one dummy is drawn. At 11:30 it is re-drawn and the original story that was going to lead the paper is pushed to the inside. At 11:40 the news editor discovers that he miscalculated on available space and instead of being oversupplied is undersupplied. He quickly sends out earlier stories that were rejected. Twenty minutes later, the city editor shows him page one of the first edition of a paper in a nearby metropolis and the news editor changes his headline to conform with a more interesting emphasis made by the big-city paper. Fifteen minutes after that, a wire service sends a completely new story on the same subject, and he throws out the entire previous story and uses the new one, which requires changing the metal plates for page one which had already been cast. This decision increases the amount of daily type he has ordered but will not use. And it misses the printing deadline slightly, which is not so serious since this is a one-edition paper with a relatively simple dis-tribution system.

Thus, during seven hours, the staff, headed by the gatekeeper, who made almost all the initial decisions, processed about 110,000 words, or the equivalent of a book. And did a number of other demanding tasks at the same time. A book-publishing house normally takes from six months to a year to process a book with the same quantity of information. The content of a newspaper is very different from that of the average book, but the difference in their technology and working styles is striking.

Morning papers which, in the United States, constitute 18 percent of all dailies with 41 percent of all circulation, are less hurried than evening papers. Most public events occur during the day, so a morning paper can make its decisions after most of the business of the nation has been completed and the number of unpredicted new items falls off. A morning paper's production and distribution are completed while its customers are asleep and are not being informed by radio, television, telephone, and word-of-mouth of all the latest developments. While the most important working hours for editors who produce afternoon papers are from 6 A.M. to noon, those for morning papers are 3 P.M. to midnight. A dramatic event at 11 A.M. must be reported without delay by an afternoon paper whose printing may be only an hour away. A dramatic event at 5 P.M. gives a morning paper three to five hours before printing in which to confirm, add details, provide background and interpretation. Ironically, afternoon papers are the ones whose headline news has been pre-empted by broadcasting and which therefore are under the greatest pressure to provide confirmation, details, background, and interpretation. A cumbersome technology, aided in this case by the fact that within domestic time zones most newsmakers and news consumers sleep at night, reverses the factors that would make for the most rational distribution of speedy public information.

On a metropolitan afternoon paper there is a very large gross intake of words and stories, for just the regional and national news, of over 400,000 words and 2,500 different news items, coming from 22 teletype machines, most of which operate 24 hours a day. The paper used 40,000 words in 300 items. This is not counting information coming in for special departments like sports and financial.

From 6 P.M., after the last edition of this large afternoon paper has gone to press, to 1 A.M. there is a skeleton staff reading and processing incoming stories for the next day's paper, sending from two to five stories an hour for typesetting. There is an increase in numbers of stories selected between 1 and 2 A.M., which is after most morning papers have gone to press, thus making post-one-o'clock news usuable for afternoon papers, even though these papers will not be delivered to suburban homes until thirteen hours later. There is another peak in numbers of stories sent for processing between 6 and 7 A.M., when the full-time staff begins its day, and another peak between 10 and 11 A.M., when the latest possible news is pushed into the paper.

The initial yes-no decision on the 2,500 stories with 400,000 words is made by three men, one in charge of nonpolitical national news, one of other national news, and the other of regional news. The latter two simultaneously direct their staffs. But there is a difference in the nature of the handling on the larger paper. Almost every story selected for insertion in this metropolitan paper, once the gatekeeper had taken the usual seconds to make his decision, was then handed to a reporter or rewrite man to read, check, compare with other stories on the same subject, and, usually, to rewrite.

So, while the gatekeepers on the large paper each handled twice the wordage of the gatekeeper on a small paper, the stories they selected were subject to relatively careful and individualistic treatment. Yet they discarded 90 percent of incoming stories and for the most part their decisions on the discards were irreversible.

On the basis of observations during the RAND study, the typical gatekeeper of news makes his decisions with remarkable speed. Discarded stories took from one to two seconds of reading each. The time taken for the initial decision on stories destined to go into the paper was somewhat longer, but not a great deal on the average. On stories selected for use, the gatekeeper usually seemed to scan the entire story, judging from the movement of his eyes but also from the fact that he occasionally caught a typographical error and compulsively corrected it in the latter part of the story.

One very fast gatekeeper took an average of four seconds to handle (read, decide to use it, and indicate the changes he wanted made) a story of 225 words. Shorter items used would take two seconds, longer ones ten seconds at a maximum. The average for observed gatekeepers was about six seconds per story selected for use.

This is a virtuoso performance of decision making. Judgment is exercised almost instantly without time for reflection or references. Whatever values the gatekeeper brings to these decisions he brings by reflex.

What is the basis for these reflex decisions on what becomes American public affairs?

It would be naïve to think that only some abstract professional standard determines whether stories will be printed. The editor who assigns a reporter has his personal values involved, and so does the reporter who decides which facts to report in what context; so does the gatekeeper who winnows the finished items destined to be printed, and so does the owner of the journalism corporation who employs them all. These personal values are in shifting equilibrium with professional standards of fairness and proof. One gatekeeper observed in the RAND study remarked to no one in particular as he scanned a story about the pacifist-pediatrician Benjamin Spock, "Dr. Spock is a kook." But a fairly straightforward wire-service story on Dr. Spock was used in the paper.

In a study by David Manning White twenty years ago, a gatekeeper was asked if he had any built-in prejudices that influenced his decisions:

> I have a few prejudices, built-in or otherwise, and there is little I can do about them. I dislike Truman's economics, daylight saving time, and warm beer, but I go ahead using stories on them and other matters if I feel there is nothing more important to give space to. I am also prejudiced against a publicity-seeking minority with headquarters in Rome, and I don't help them a lot. As far as prejudices go, I go for human interest stories in a big way. My other preferences are for stories well-wrapped up and tailored to suit our needs (or ones slanted to conform to our editorial policies).

Nor would it be realistic to think that the gatekeeper is completely insulated from official policy on the paper. In a benchmark study of contemporary journalism, Warren Breed's "Social Control in the Newsroom," the author describes the unstated but pervasive presence of publishers' values in the decisions of working journalists, including the gatekeepers.

Official news policy is usually vague and almost never spelled out to any individual journalist because of the taboo in the trade against tampering with facts. Newspapers, especially monopoly newspapers, are expected to be objective in the sense that they provide equitable access to the news columns and fair treatment of topics and individuals. Cases in which owners or executives order the suppression of stories or their insertion for "policy" reasons are met with disapproval in the trade.

Nevertheless, policy is exerted in effective ways. Editorial executives control the assignment of stories, which is the most crucial decision in journalism. They decide whether the finished story will be used or not, and if used, with what emphasis and length, and whether or not the reporter's name will appear on it. Rewards and punishments for reporters are almost never explicitly on the basis of adherence to official policy, but on most papers it is clear to the staff that stories of a certain kind receive rewards and in many papers these are stories that please the proprietor. Since newspaper staffs have a minimum of bureaucracy, tasks are carried out in an informal, highly personal atmosphere of professional camaraderie, so there is a tendency to avoid acrimony, which can mean pleasing supervisors.

On the other hand, the reporter has considerable control over the recounting of facts. If he insists on a particular description of a situation, it is unusual for a superior to overrule him on grounds of policy: unless a story can be attacked on grounds of accuracy, significance, or reasoning, even a disapproving superior will feel obligated to print it. There is hesitation to fire a journalist for reportorial nonconformity to a paper's economic or social policy, since this is regarded in the trade as unethical behavior by management; where there is a reporters' union it is forbidden by contract. There is far less hesitation to fire the reporter's superior for failure to conform to a publisher's ideas. In this ambiguity, social rather than direct pressures are the dominant mechanism for encouraging conformity to the political and social policy of the journalistic corporation.

A number of factors inhibit these pressures, though they do not eliminate them. Primary is the almost universal contempt among professional journalists for anyone who deliberately distorts information. Subtle mutations may be difficult to prove or even recognize but there are individuals and organizations that habitually make gross distortions for ideological and other reasons. Nevertheless, even the most hardened manipulators are defensive when exposed.

Professionalism is increasing. Reporters and correspondents are better educated and more independent than in the past. The qualities of a good journalist—disciplined observation with an ability to write clearly—are in such demand in other occupations that the competition for the best journalists has enhanced their standing in their own trade and strengthened professionalism within news corporations.

Readers are more sophisticated and better informed than before. The proliferation of alternative sources of information has made the audience more critical and able to compare accounts. Many events are seen directly on television in their original form, or listened to on radio, ending the exclusive power of second-hand printed reports. The growth of national media, like radio, television, and news magazines, permits comparisons with the local newspaper version of national events. Much of the population has received some grounding in high school and college in the social sciences and other disciplines relating to public affairs, diminishing their innocence toward fragments out of context.

So the gatekeeper, though he seems to perform like one, is not a valueless machine operating in a social vacuum. His decisions, resulting in the printing of most stories seen by the public, reflect his personal as well as his professional values, and all the surrounding pressures that converge on him.

The RAND study watched 45 key men at work on the 8 papers studied. The papers were not intended to be an accurate cross-section. For one thing, 8 out of 1,752 is a very small section. Nor were they selected on a random basis. The fact that they agreed to what is probably the first economic and operational study by an outside organization not in their employ makes them unusual papers. They are probably among the better papers, a judgment based partly on reputation and partly on the supposition that the least-secure and worst-run papers would be least likely to agree to this examination. On the other hand, the papers were not selected for any reason other than the likelihood of their agreeing to cooperate and their representing, if not a cross-section of all papers, a cross-section of different types of papers. In the sample were papers from every geographic region and major type: a small weekly, a small-city monopoly, a medium-city monopoly, a big-city competitor, morning papers, evening papers, independent papers, and chain papers.

All of the men observed and interviewed were either gatekeepers or the gatekeepers' immediate superiors and subordinates. They constituted the group whose interactions make practically all the daily decisions on the news that appears in their communities.

Their median age was forty-four; half were between forty and fifty, and the ages ranged between twenty-five and sixty-eight. Newspapers are no different from other social institutions in the age relationship of their leaders to the general population. The median age of the

American population is about twenty-seven. Only two of the gate-keeping editors were less than thirty. For a mass medium, this raises questions of mutual perception between audience and producer, though age of the population and age of editors could hardly match. Infants at the age of one day do not become eligible candidates for editorships; effective institutional leadership requires learning and experience that result in leaders who are older than many whom they serve. Peak age range for buying newspapers is thirty to fifty-four years, which makes the gatekeepers representative of those customers who pay for the subscriptions. The median age for buying newspapers is forty-two and the median age of gatekeepers of the news is forty-four. (A major factor in newspaper reading is the amount of time habitually spent inside the home. In general, the rate of newspaper reading is high for teen-age children, drops from age eighteen to about twenty-four as they are away at college or in military service, or newly married with both partners working and out of the house, then rises sharply as the first baby is born, and remains fairly consistent until retirement age, when reading goes up again.)

The gatekeepers are upwardly mobile, with more education and higher status jobs than their fathers. Their fathers averaged eleven years of education, the gatekeepers sixteen. Twenty-five percent of fathers were farmers or laborers; 57 percent were in nonprofessional white-collar jobs. Most journalists live in a tribal world of egalitarian informality, where even the title "journalist" is considered preten-tious, and their business is referred to as a trade. But in recent years the term "profession" has been conferred on them and received without complaint. Only 18 percent of their fathers were in a pro-fession.

The past anti-intellectualism of daily journalists in the United States is disappearing, though it remains strong among older men. Of the forty-five gatekeepers, seven had no college degree, thirty-seven had A.B.s, and six had master's degrees, a radical change from fifty years ago, when most newspapermen had no college education. Of those with college degrees, 60 percent majored in a conventional discipline, and 40 percent in journalism.

The party politics of gatekeepers reflect the conflicting outlooks of the working professional and the corporate chieftain. Most newspaper proprietors, like other kinds of proprietors, are Republicans. Most working journalists are Democrats; 73 percent of the gatekeepers in the RAND study said they were Democrats (60 percent said their fathers were Democrats). Since 1930 most Americans have voted Democratic and party registrations heavily favor the Democrats. Newspaper reading and voting are highly correlated, so presumably there is greater political rapport between working journalists and their readers than between journalism proprietors and readers.

The cultural habits of gatekeepers influence their perceptions and news decisions. Like most professionals, the gatekeepers say they do not spend much time before their television sets, only forty-six minutes a day. Though newspaper gatekeepers generally are sensitive to broadcast news, 22 percent said they almost never watched television.

They are more diligent about reading newspapers. They all read their own paper and all others published in their city, if it was a city with local competition, or any adjacent paper with significant penetration into their own territory.

Of the prestige papers, the leading one read regularly by the 46 gatekeepers was the *New York Times* (16), followed by the *Wall Street Journal* (10), the Los Angeles *Times* (6), and the Washington *Post* (5). One or two said they regularly read the Louisville *Courier-Journal,* St. Louis *Post-Dispatch,* Kansas City *Star,* the London *Times* and the London *Mirror.*

The magazines most often read regularly by the gatekeepers were *Life* (21), *Time* (19), *Newsweek* (18), *Editor & Publisher* (14), *Harper's* (12), *Look* (11), *Saturday Review* (9), *The New Yorker* (8), *The Atlantic* (7), *Esquire* (6), and *Columbia Journalism Review* (6).

Readership of more serious magazines was reported by a small number of the men: *Trans-Action* (3), *Scientific American* (3), and *Atlas* (3).

The disparities in reading are not flattering to the idea of a crucial selector of news keeping in touch with the world of ideas and social development. Fewer than half of the gatekeepers regularly read the *New York Times,* and these are generally the same minority who also read the *Wall Street Journal* and the Washington *Post.* The heaviest readers of the quality magazines tend to be the same minority Among the magazines listed once as being regularly read are *Daeda-*

lus, Journal of Modern History, New Statesman, and *London Times Literary Supplement*—but they were all read by the same man who shortly after the RAND study left his editing job to become a college professor.

The heaviest reading of serious books was done by the minority of gatekeepers who also read the *New York Times* and *Harper's.*

Of the forty-five in the gatekeeper group, eleven actually made the initial decisions on the bulk of stories. (There were eleven in eight papers because some papers published separate morning and evening editions.) The others were either immediate assistants or superiors who would participate in discussions of borderline cases. But, with the execption of the few leading stories of the day on page one and a few special stories, the initial and final decision was made by the eleven prime gatekeepers.

In general, the eleven prime gatekeepers compared with the total editing group were younger (average age, thirty-five); had the average education (four years of college); were more inclined to be Republicans (37 percent); spent less time looking at television (thirty-eight minutes a day); did not regularly read a nationally oriented newspaper (72 percent did not regularly read the daily *New York Times*); did not regularly read a quality magazine (64 percent did not); and like the others about half did not read more than one book a month (though the other half reported a very large number of books).

The prime gatekeepers on the smaller papers were usually older, since they were the No. 1 or No. 2 editor, who also governed the entire news operation. The prime gatekeepers on larger papers were younger, probably because of specialization in larger organizations, and because senior editors spend most of their time directing the staff and fashioning policy rather than making story-by-story decisions.

With some individual exceptions, the most serious reading of newspapers, magazines, and books was done by the gatekeepers of the papers with reputations for quality and by those in the largest cities.

The gatekeepers have dual—and sometimes conflicting—cultural pressures. On the one hand, they should have knowledge and perspective superior to most of their community. They exercise an important educational function for the entire population, deciding what is important for the community to know about social and political events in the world. In this they are making decisions for, among others, college graduates in their area, 90 percent of whom read the newspaper, more than any other educational group. (Of the gate-keepers in the study, 82 percent had college degrees.) In this role, the gatekeeper is saying, "This is what I think you ought to know." In this role, presumably the gatekeeper is aided by some insight into serious developments, as seen in his heavier reading of magazines and books. *Trans-Action* and *Foreign Affairs* would help.

But the gatekeeper is also engaged in popular communication. There are commercial pressures for him to attract the attention of as many people as possible, and in a democracy there is a parallel social need to engage as large a part as possible of the total population in public information. Furthermore, the public is not just a passive recipient of news, but a source of it, and the gatekeeper as a profes-sional in mass communications must know his audience both to understand it and to speak to it. In addition to "This is what I think you ought to know," he also says, "This is what I think will interest you." They are not always the same thing. And for this it is relevant to know that half the adult American population never went to college, and that while college graduates and high-income people are the most consistent readers of newspapers, almost 60 percent of those who earn less than $3,000 a year and 45 percent of manual laborers also read newspapers.

In the light of this, it is interesting that in general the gatekeepers' knowledge of their community makeup was vague. Most guessed fairly accurately the percentage of nonwhites in their circulation area, but they were less accurate with average income and educational level for the whole community, or for the most significant minorities in the community. About 90 percent were first asked these questions in face-to-face interviews, and later were asked to fill out a questionnaire asking some of the same questions. In the later written response, a few had the precise data, obviously having looked it up. A few more had precise data for some of the questions but not for others. But most gave no accurate figures. The failure to fill in accurate figures probably reflected a disinclination to look up the statistics, but in some cases it could have been lack of knowledge of where to find them. After the study, one editor, disturbed at how little demographic information his key group had about their readers, decided that thereafter the entire staff would be instructed on the characteristics of the audience.

And so the printed news system is like a funnel with five times more material pouring into the top than can come out of the bottom, with a few crucial men controlling the valve that passes one story for every four that is rejected. By far the greatest volume poured into the funnel comes from outside the city, on teletype machines that now produce news at the rate of 45 words a minute. Selecting the few stories that will fit into the paper and be comprehensible to readers is now a process that seems to reach the limits of human speed and judgment. Yet there are replacements for the present teletype machines that in the near future will deliver 1,050 words a minute, still another design that will deliver 2,400 words a minute, and finally one that will transfer a full news report from a central computer into a local newspaper computer at the rate of 86,000 words a minute. These are, respectively, 23 times, 53 times, and 1,900 times faster than the machines that present news to local editors today. Such speeds make clear the obsolescence of even recent methods of converting words into print: 5.6 lines a minute cast in 1932, 14 lines in 1960, 1,800 lines in 1966, 15,000 lines in 1967. The rapid reception of information and its rapid conversion into a printed form presentable to a mass audience will mean that men and procedures now used to produce the daily news will undergo fundamental change and with that will come a change in the nature of the news itself.

Among other reasons, this will change the news because gatekeepers, who now must compose the day's news in disjointed fragments, will begin to approach a total view of the news before they make their main decisions. The ability to place 86,000 words a minute into a newspaper's computer means that the total present intake of even the largest papers can be delayed until late in the editing cycle and then transmitted in a few minutes. It cannot all be printed out or read by a human being in a few minutes, but it can be indexed and abstracted by the computer so that the 110,000 words for the small paper and the 400,000 for the large one need not be scanned in the original.

Seeing index lines or abstracts for a few hundred or a few thousand stories would also take time, but these are looked at now in a very short time in the bulky total stories. Having the short reference lines alone would speed scanning. It would not permit the gatekeeper to judge the quality and detail of the total story. However, since the total file would be in his computer and since this could be connected to a video screen console, he could instantly call up, by story number or indexed words, the total text of any particular story, read it and make editing changes or give marginal instructions by "writing" on the proper place on the video screen. He might do this by himself and then send the story back into the computer. Or he could have other editors and reporters simultaneously looking at the same story on their consoles and talking to each other over their audio circuits, deciding jointly whether to use the story and, if they did, whether to change it. After each man had suggested or "written" in his changes, they could all see it in final form on their screens and, agreeing on it, send it back into the computer, or on to a reporter or rewrite man who would further alter it on the basis of their recommendations. Or else the reporter or a staff specialist would look at the story on his console—possibly in another city—and make his recommendations to the editors as they all viewed the story.

There would still be a need for continuous updating of many stories as they actually unfold during the day and as numerous journalistic sources develop background and interpretations for earlier stories. These updated additions and insertions could come in directly to the paper's computer, adjusting each story as it rests in storage, so that without human intervention and decision making each story when called up by the editor would be in its latest form.

Plainly, the 45-words-a-minute rate per machine is not going to be raised to a continuous stream of 86,000 words a minute, since in the 12-hour cycle that would place an appalling 62 million words inside the newspaper each day. Instead, there would be bursts of transmission that would periodically introduce new batches of information. Nevertheless, it would be strange if the added capacity did not radically enlarge the number of total stories available to each local editor each day, either in total routine deposits into his computer, or in a menu of story titles from which he would make his selection.

Consequently, the selection process that now has the gatekeeper selecting 100 items out of 500, or, on a large metropolitan paper 300 items out of 2,500, may in the future force him to select the same number of items from a much larger total. The editing process already crucial since it is the step that eliminates 80 to 90 percent of all incoming matter from reader consideration, will become even more powerful and demanding. Editors will become increasingly important and their personal values more influential.

How rapidly information is edited and after what degree of comprehensive accumulation will depend on how the manufacturing stages of a newspaper can be accelerated. If they remain as they are today, the increased reception and editing of news will have minimal effect, since the editors will still have to feed the production machine slowly and continuously throughout the day. The greatest delays in printed news are not in the compiling of news but in its conversion to print.

If, however, the manufacturing process is shortened, it will permit full and up-to-date review of the total report of the day before final decisions are made and the results placed massively into the production stages. Photocomposition holds this possibility since photographic films of final pages can be created from computerized information. The editing of stories and of photographs and their graphical arrangement placed back in the computer can be converted electronically into plates for printing or for home display without further manual transactions.

If, in addition to that, later home systems permit display of a standard news package in the home, with the consumer able to order additional material, the editing process will change even more. In that case, the 80 or 90 or 99 percent of all stories eliminated by the editor or the standard package can remain in the computer, for callup by consumers. The consumer on his video screen might, for example, see an index of the total available stories, just as the editor did in selecting the standard package, and, like the editor, the consumer will be able to select which stories and how much of any story he wishes to see. The citizen in his home will see the editor's selections of leading items based on his professional judgment, a service most consumers will want for a very long time. Most people will continue to be busy with careers, education, family affairs, and outside activities and be unwilling and unable to edit their own newspaper each day. But they may no longer have to accept as final the decision of the gatekeeper. After viewing his selections, they can pursue stories in more depth or call up stories the editor did not include in the standard package. This will not only give greater diversity in news based on individual desires, but the computer, recording what is called for, will make it clear what the range and intensity of citizen interest is.

It is likely that the average citizen, like the average scientist, scholar, and professional, will learn to scan his literature by abstracts and indexes, and that news organizations will increasingly offer him such a rapid daily inventory. It is also probable that a standard display of news will continue to be presented, in printed form delivered to the home and, much later, transmitted electronically. But there will probably be available either on continuous special channels or on the basis of orders sent out from the consumer's home console, added depth and breadth of news that will make each citizen his own editor. This will end the finality of the gatekeeper decision, and wisely so since the gathering of news spreads wider and its intensity and detail get deeper as the years pass. But until some way is found to give the citizen greater access to this enlarged reservoir, the decisions of even the wisest gatekeepers will become increasingly difficult.

Printed News
as a Corporate Enterprise

⑥

News is an intellectual artifact fashioned under a code of professional ethics and received as a cultural experience.

But it is also the product of a bureaucracy with employees, unions, and stockholders, processed in a manufacturing plant that has some of the same characteristics as its sister factories that produce hubcaps and monkey wrenches.

In the United States the role of the press is assumed to be an independent monitor of the environment, and since it cannot be an instrument of government, it has evolved as a private enterprise. This means that the press can survive only if it shows a profit, which influences its behavior and is a force shaping its future.

Profit making creates conflicts between the news as an educational institution and the news as a godless corporation. It also forces a view into the future when the technical and organizational structure of news will change, with different economic constraints than the ones that shape the news today.

Printed and broadcast news corporations differ in their patterns, though both are private enterprises and produce the same class of product.

"Newspapers" technically refer to all publications carrying information on newsprint sheets for a general audience, issued daily, Sundays, or weekly. There are slightly over 10,000 newspapers by this definition, but this book is concerned mainly with daily papers, of which there are about 1,750. There are about 8,000 weekly papers. In strictly financial and industrial terms—though less so in social and political ones—daily newspapers represent the substance of all newspaper operations, with more than 90 percent of all revenues and manpower.

Newspaper publishing is not a minor activity in American corporate life. It is the fifth-largest United States manufacturing industry in employment (360,000), tenth-largest in value of shipments ($6 billion), and is one of the ten fastest-growing industries in the country (70 percent growth, 1958–1968).

But, despite its aggregate size, because of the localism inherent in American news, printed news is issued through local private enterprises.

The American emphasis on local roots for news influences not only its content but the nature of its ownership. Usually started as a local operation, expressing the viewpoint of a man who owned a small press, a newspaper tends to be owned by a private family or a small, closely held corporation. In recent years a number of major papers and chains have become public corporations, but the total number is still small. In 1969 there were 15 companies engaged in daily journalism which offered their stock to the public; these companies controlled 123 newspapers (7 percent of all dailies) that have 14 percent of total circulation. Even when papers offer their stock to the general public, operating control usually resides with relatives or corporate heirs of the earlier owners. The managerial and technological revolutions that have transformed control of policy making in other large American industries have largely bypassed journalism corporations. In the United States, newspaper publishing continues to be an inherited privilege.

For example, the *New York Times* and the Los Angeles *Times* are both parts of publicly held corporations, but they are headed, formally and operationally, by relatives of their founders of three generations ago. Other major dailies, like the Washington *Post,* the Boston *Globe,* the Washington *Evening Star,* and members of the Hearst chain are still governed and operated by relatives of their founders or most important previous owners.

The maintenance of printed news as a family enterprise holds a special place in the mythology of the trade. There continues to be a legend of a crusading proprietor whose main interest is civic betterment and for whom personal profit is so unimportant as to tempt him to perpetual bankruptcy for the sake of journalistic virtue. Whatever occasional truth this may have in reality is moderated by the fact that many heirs to newspapers are indifferent publishers, and in the late 1960s profits for "average" papers as reported by trade magazines ran to 20 percent of gross before taxes.

But, aside from legendry, personal leadership and family participation in newspaper ownership have been important for at least two reasons.

Much of an American newspaper's function is reporting and pursuing local issues. Absentee ownership of a conventional corporate kind is less likely to detect local problems and make a serious commitment of corporate energies. There are many cases of negligent local owners and conscientious absentee ones, but on the whole absentee owners are less sensitive to local nuances. A locally rooted family or a personal operator whose family is part of the community is more susceptible to the social and informational needs of the paper's surroundings.

Secondly, newspapers have enormous latitude in their news efforts. They are publications with multiple appeals, containing daily television schedules, prices of goods in local shops, sports, comics, and hundreds of other varieties of information. Serious news is only one of many functions. A paper may have the most casual handling of low-cost national news and negligent treatment of more expensive local news and still be bought regularly for other reasons by a large enough number of people to make the paper profitable for many years.

So if added effort is put into the quality of its journalism, there is no simple measure of its economic profit. Over a short period it diminishes profits. There probably is economic punishment for journalistic negligence in monopoly newspapers, but it is very slow to appear. Consequently, some force other than conventional corporate ambition usually moves a newspaper's leader to achieve professional excellence. This force is usually personal pride and family association with the paper. Unfortunately, uninhibited personal direction of a newspaper also permits perpetuation of incompetent or irresponsible leadership, for which the community has no remedy. The tradition of the personally involved owner is strong and, while it produces numerous cases of entrenched morbidity, it also is the most important single factor in papers of excellence.

This is the opposite of the situation in most modern corporate organizations. As described by John Kenneth Galbraith, "modern economic society can only be understood as an effort, wholly successful, to synthesize by organization a group personality far superior *for its purposes* to a natural person with the added advantage of immortality." The group personality, Galbraith adds, is necessary because in "modern industry a large number of decisions, and all that are important, draw on information possessed by more than one man."

Modern corporate pressures are beginning to erode the tradition of personal direction and family control of newspapers.

The ethic that permeates daily journalism has its origins in the idea of the printer-journalist who controls both his intellectual and manufacturing product by writing, typesetting, printing, and selling his paper, either all by himself or with a few employees, with no bureaucratic barriers between his desire to say something and its embodiment in a printed paper.

In 1810 the average circulation of all American daily papers was 550, composed letter by letter by hand out of the type box, each paper individually printed on a single, hand-operated flatbed press, folded by hand, and placed on sale, in some cases, all by the same man, who may have put the type together as he thought of what he wanted to say, without even first writing it out on paper. In 1900, average circulation per issue of an American paper was about 7,000, by now written by a professional reporter, its type cast by a complicated Linotype machine, produced on a power-driven rotary press, and sold by a system of newsboys. Today average daily circulation per paper is 36,000 (dividing the average daily circulation of all papers, 62,500,000, by the 1,752 individual papers).

A paper of about 36,000 circulation in 1970 is a substantial local enterprise, given the size of community such a paper finds itself in. *Average Medium Daily* happens to be in a size class that is "average" in a statistical way—the 255 papers in the 25,000-to-50,000 circulation category constitute 15 percent of all papers and have 15 percent of all circulation. Below their size, there are larger numbers of papers, but each category of the smaller-size papers has less than a proportional share of total circulation. On the other hand, as papers get larger in size, they diminish in total numbers, and their share of the total market goes up rapidly until the 39 papers of more than 250,000 daily circulation, which is 2 percent of all papers, have 30 percent of all circulation. Thus, compared to the papers that are read by most Americans, the 36,000-circulation paper is very small. Even so, *Average Medium Daily* is a substantial business enterprise. And it has grown in so short a time that its inherited management is not fully aware of just how complex it is.

In 1940 *Average Medium Daily* had total assets of about $100,000 and annual revenues of about $100,000. After taxes it showed a slight loss.

Today *Average Medium Daily* has total assets of $4 million and revenues of about $4 million, with an annual profit, after taxes, of slightly more than $300,000. It has two hundred employees, to whom it pays $1.5 million a year, of whom seventy-three are in mechanical production, forty-three are engaged in selling and processing advertising copy, forty are in editorial operations, thirty in circulation, and fourteen in general administration.

The industrial operations of *Average Medium Daily* plainly absorb most of the paper's energies. It prints over half a billion individual pages a year. As on all dailies, more than half the employees are engaged in mechanical production and distribution. Even though it is a paper of only 36,000 circulation, it spent a third of a million dollars on its typesetting equipment and $1.25 million on its presses. It pays $250,000 a year in taxes, which is not very different from its profit after taxes, so there is a lively interest in tax rates and government spending among the second generation of the three owning families, some of whom also draw salaries as well as dividends.

Even so, *Average Medium Daily* is very different from large papers. A majority of Americans read papers of a size above 100,000 circulation. The largest American daily is the New York *Daily News* with 2.1 million circulation, but circulation size quickly drops to the *Wall Street Journal,* which sells a million copies a day in six regional editions, then to the Los Angeles *Times* with 856,000 and the *New York Times* with 840,000. A rough median of paper size seen by most urban readers is 400,000 circulation, issued by *Big City Daily,* which is owned by a company with other financial interests—including a sister publication of similar size in the same city—newspapers constituting only 30 percent of the corporation's interests. *Big City Daily*'s newspaper subsidiary grosses about $70 million a year, with assets worth $35 million. *Big City* has 2,800 employees, of whom 2,000 work in mechanical production and distribution.

Smaller papers are smaller in three ways: in numbers of pages per issue, in total papers printed per day, and in the number of different editions issued each day.

The smaller paper is in a smaller community with fewer local advertisers and attracts fewer national advertisers. Since the volume of advertising determines the number of pages in American papers, small advertising volume results in a low number of pages. There are fewer papers printed daily because its community has fewer households that might buy the paper. And it issues fewer editions because the area of its coverage has fewer neighborhood and governmental units, so that it is possible to provide their news and advertising information in one standard edition a day.

The area covered by a larger paper encompasses massive retail establishments typical of a metropolis and so needs more pages to carry ads. The same area is densely populated, with thousands of governmental units and citizen organizations. Suburbs at one edge of the city will have little interest in news from suburbs at the opposite edge, so each will receive its own area edition.

For both large and small newspapers, inherited and home-grown personal leadership faces dilemmas in the growing size and complexity of present newspaper corporations. These stresses are especially severe in planning the future.

There is, first of all, the genetic roulette every community is forced to play with its local paper. If the heir of the publisher, or his son-in-law, happens to be an intelligent and effective journalistic leader, the community receives a good daily paper. But if the heir happens to be incompetent or becomes more interested in breeding bulls, the community will receive an indifferent paper.

Or if the publisher has a number of heirs who cannot decide which shall take the leadership and allocate the profits, the paper fragments under Malthusian subdivision of dividends and control until it is drained and thrown aside.

Even if an owning family is fortunate in heirs, and their newspaper continues to have both quality and growth, inheritance taxes on such a substantial personal property eventually make it difficult to retain family control. Tax laws permit assignment of such a property to children without taxes, which means that a family-owned newspaper can be left by its first owner to his heirs, often with an intervening set of trustees. But when it finally inherits control, the third generation faces very large taxes. The United States is now in the third generation of its most important large daily papers.

To avoid the inheritance taxes and at the same time retain family control, newspapers may redistribute their ownership through public sales of stock, retaining within the family or a family trust a voting bloc large enough to control policy but not large enough to pay high death duties. Or they may form a tax-free foundation to own most of the stock and retain enough voting shares to exercise family control.

Beneficial though this family control may be in local concerns and pride of product, it presents serious problems in coping with technological change.

Contrary to conventional wisdom, multi-million-dollar corporations with rapidly changing technology are not often coped with successfully by a single individual acting intuitively. Modern cost accounting, systems analysis, operational research, and adaptation of a complicated product to a changing society require integrated, trained staffs of specialists.

The Economist Intelligence Unit, after a painstaking examination of London daily newspapers, said: "Possibly the industry's greatest problem is its dominance by a small number of highly individualistic proprietors, with their own personal interests and philosophy of management."

Yet distinguished journalism requires strong individual leadership with intuitive powers: the demands of corporate efficiency and of journalism are often at odds.

The fragmentation of management in the newspaper industry is matched by fragmentation in its work force and labor unions.

As one of the first industries to be unionized, newspapers have strong craft unions, each process manned by a different union, which may also control the training, hiring, and work patterns for that process. In an industry in which there must be 100 percent reliability of daily production, this produces complicated stresses, since unions are frequently at odds with each other, as well as with management.

Unionization of American newspapers is not consistent. There are some plants, usually small, that have no unions, and some large ones that have only one or two. But most papers of any size have a spectrum of unions.

One metropolitan daily, for example, deals with fourteen unions that have seventeen operating units. The American Newspaper Guild, AFL-CIO, is the reporters' union, which in some places also includes clerical and custodial workers. When finished news copy and photographs leave the newsroom, the text is set in metallic type, which is under the jurisdiction of the International Typographical Union, the oldest and most powerful of all newspaper unions. Photographs are converted to metal engravings, which is under the Lithographers and Photoengravers Union.

Once the text, headlines, and illustrations have been cast into metal, and composed into pages, they are used as master forms for making mats, cardboardlike negative impressions, which are then placed in stereotyping machines that pour hot metal into the curved mats to produce the semicylindrical plates that are attached to the printing presses. This process comes under the Stereotypers Union.

The stereotype plates then go to the presses. The printing of a newspaper is done by feeding large rolls of paper, the "web," through the presses at high speed. Handling of the unprinted paper is under control of the Paperhandlers' Union. The presses themselves and the paper while it is being printed are under the jurisdiction of the Web Printing Pressmen's Union. A subunit of the Pressmen's Union is the Press Wipers, with control of cleaning the press exterior and substructure.

As the printed and folded papers come out of the presses, they must be counted and tied in bundles for various newsstands and truck routes. This is under the jurisdiction of the Mailers' Union.

Once placed on the trucks, the bundles come under the jurisdiction of the Drivers' Union. Maintenance of the trucks comes under the Mechanics' Union.

The Machinists' Union maintains machinery in the plant other than in the composing room, where the machinery remains under the jurisdiction of the Typographical Union. The Electrical Union controls electrical maintenance, the Painters' Union painting of walls and equipment, the Building Cleaning Union the cleaning of offices, corridors, and office washrooms. The Operating Engineers cover building maintenance related to plumbing, steamfitting, and heating, but not equipment installation. Subunits of the Operating Engineers' Union are the Elevator Operators, who run all manual elevators; the Carpenters, who do carpentry; and the Janitors' Union, whose members clean and maintain washrooms in production areas, unlike the members of the Building Cleaning Union, who clean the business and news offices.

In many papers, contracts with each union are negotiated separately, but if one union goes on strike, all respect the picket line, which usually means suspension of printing. In cities with competing dailies, there is usually an agreement among publishers to close down operations if one paper is struck, and usually an unwritten agreement that outside papers will be restrained from moving in to fill the void.

Not only do individual unions compete with each other for wage rates and jurisdiction, but as the manufacturing process for newspaper publishing changes, the need for specialists changes, threatening some unions with extinction, which puts their rivalry on a life-or-death basis.

Most major American manufacturing industries have an industrial-union pattern, one big union with jurisdiction over the entire production process. Thus, any change in production and manpower requirements can be negotiated with a single union, and reduced needs for men in one step of the process can be handled by attrition and by transferring them to other parts of the plant. But the newspaper industry continues to have craft unions in which no unit takes responsibility for any other step in the process and generally will not accept into membership members of other unions in the plant who may not be needed in obsolete crafts.

Unions and management both have been reluctant to change this fragmented pattern. Each union wishes to maintain its own existence and bargaining power. Management fears that one big union, while more rational and flexible, would provide union leaders with more centralized power.

As a result, the newspaper industry, while not the most unionized, has the most chaotic manpower arrangement of any major industry facing technological change.

The future promises even more severe stresses from this Byzantine arrangement. The computer, for example, is sometimes used to accept news stories and arrange the lines in the proper length for the column width of the paper, which means inserting proper hyphenation when a word has to be divided at the end of a line. The American Newspaper Guild, whose members include reporters and copy editors, insists that the handling of copy, plus the predictable future use of the computer to do other editing and formulating of news stories, properly made this a reporting and editing function, which is true. The International Typographical Union insists that the computer is converting text to tapes that control automated typesetting machines, which is a process that falls into the jurisdiction of the Typographers, which also is true. This kind of struggle continues, moderated only by the desire of each union to retain the cooperation of all other unions in the event of strikes.

It is worth speculating on the problems involved should future news media take one suggested form: all incoming information placed in a computer, edited and formated by electronic consoles in the newsroom, and then transmitted direct by cable into the home, to be viewed on a screen or reproduced in document form by facsimile. Under present arrangements only one contemporary union, the American Newspaper Guild, would retain any jurisdiction over the journalistic process. A possible exception would be building maintenance and janitorial services, but even they would be minimal since in present operations the editorial function of newspapers requires a minority of space and staff. Should news in the future be transmitted into the home electronically, the manufacturing function of newspapers would disappear. The fourteen unions now involved in the industrial and distribution functions of newspapers will not view this future with equanimity.

The *ITU Review,* house organ of the typographical union, said in 1967: "It is imperative that, right now, ITU members in all branches of the trade start planning to learn the intricacies of electronics and of the various devices powered by electronics. It is the members' own security that is at stake as well as that of their families and their union. Progress refuses to be sidetracked."

Both management and union make philosophical statements on the future but behave differently in their immediate handling of present innovations. Shortly before his death, the former president of the ITU, Elmer Brown, said that it was inevitable that there would be electronic transmission of all news, "probably first into satellite plants of papers, then into neighborhood centers and finally into the home directly."

Asked what would happen to the present fourteen unions in that event, he said, "Oh, there will be one big union that covers the whole process." Asked which union that would be, he smiled broadly, as unspoken confirmation of his union's primacy in strength among all newspaper unions.

However, at the community level, where union contracts are negotiated, the view has been less cosmic, influenced by local personalities on both sides of the bargaining table.

On the basis of the RAND studies, it appears that the traditional management complaint that the peculiarities of newspaper union patterns causes exorbitant costs is an oversimplification. Except for the very largest paper studied, productivity of editorial workers was constant regardless of unionization. The high cost for the largest paper was due almost entirely to the intense editorial effort put into each inch of printed editorial matter, partly because of local competition and partly because of multiple editions throughout the day.

In mechanical departments, pay per worker responds more to size of paper and number of pages printed per day than to unionization. Where pay scales differ, they reflect local standards of pay in other industries more than degree of unionization within the paper.

Productivity per mechanical worker does not vary significantly between union and nonunion shops. Modernization of equipment and effective management policies show a greater impact.

It is sometimes asserted that the high degree of unionization in mechanical departments of newspapers and the relatively low level in editorial departments has resulted in manual workers getting paid more than professionals in the newspaper business. The studies show that in some places manual workers are paid more, but unionization does not seem to be the explanation. Of seven dailies, the editorial workers of four were paid more than the mechanical staff; only one of the four papers had a reporters' union and all four had mechanical unions. In three of the papers, manual workers received higher pay than editorial workers; of these three, two had no mechanical unions.

Unionization has raised wage rates in the newspaper industry as a whole, as it has for the entire economy. Nor can there be any doubt that rapid changes in technology are inhibited by the fear of technological unemployment by workers able to implement their fear through organized labor, and that this is compounded by inter-union rivalries. But the pay and productivity data in this study show that these matters are highly oversimplified in trade publications and conventional wisdom of the industry, and that modernized plants with effective managements can produce more profitably with unions than some plants without unions.

A powerful underlying reason for the relative insensitivity to impending technological changes in the newspaper industry is the widespread belief at the local level, of both management and labor, that no radical changes will occur in this generation. Union members in isolated crafts find the idea of radical changes almost intolerable since these imply not only loss of a particular job but the extinction of the entire craft to which the individual has committed his career. This has been a common reaction in other industries where modernization and automation have wiped out whole classes of occupations, making some men useless in mid- or late-career. The human and the social stresses of such radical technological changes have been reduced in industries like automobiles, telecommunications and meat packing by joint planning on future change between management and labor, and by agreements that men with seniority whose trades have been abolished would be retrained and transferred to other jobs. In the newspaper industry this has not happened because both the unions and management are fragmented, the unions by specialized trades sealed off from each other, management by the fact that it operates in relatively small local units whose leadership, compared with that of large national corporations, is unsophisticated in modern methods of planning, in long-range predictions, and in navigating of radical change.

For example, most owners and publishers queried about the future predicted only minor changes in present production techniques. Typical was the prediction that in the next decade the most radical change in his paper would be a change in page design from eight columns to six. Others tended to see an increase in mechanical efficiency that is insignificant on the scale most technologists expect. There is some reason to believe that since the RAND field work in spring and summer of 1968 there has been a significant change in the perception of the future among newspaper publishers. One indication is the appearance of radical innovations in other fields of printing. Another is the proliferation of technologically sophisticated trade publications that bypass the traditionalistic newspaper organs. New suppliers in electronics and graphics have convinced some previously unimpressed publishers that newspaper production will not be immune to basic change.

Nevertheless, there is a degree of technological backwardness that is remarkable for one of the country's major industries, and one that is in a field—information—being subjected to spectacular new developments. This traditionalism is a reflection of the pattern of family proprietorships, but it is also consistent with the overwhelming business pattern of American newspapers—local monopoly operation.

By coincidence, the achievement of stable monopolies among newspapers has occurred just at the time when their technological base is beginning to erode.

Competing newspapers began to disappear as newspaper industrial operations became complex and mass advertising rewarded the dominant publication. The high cost of a newspaper industrial plant whose production is limited to its immediate geographic area does not encourage new entrants to challenge an established company. Advertisers are primarily interested in getting their message before the largest possible audience at the smallest cost per thousand, and it is cheaper for them to support one newspaper plant reaching all consumers than two plants in which each reaches half.

Sixty years ago there were 1,200 cities in the United States with daily papers, and 689, or 57 percent, had daily papers operated by competing managements.

Today there are 1,589 cities with daily papers. Of these, only 45, or 3 percent, have competing managements, and half of these are semi-merged in the sense that they combine their profits, advertising, sales, production, and distribution functions. Less than a dozen cities have face-to-face competition in which papers issued by different managements are issued at the same time of day.

Local monopoly in printed news raises serious questions of diversity of information and opinion. What a local newspaper does not print about local affairs does not see general print at all. And, having the power to take initiative in reporting and enunciation of opinions, it has extraordinary power to set the atmosphere and determine the terms of local consideration of public issues.

Corporate concerns also enter the picture. As a high-investment monopoly, a newspaper has little reason to fear successful new competition. Besides, if consumers of news are dissatisfied, the conventional remedy of new enterprises to meet unfilled needs does not apply: the primary *economic* product of the newspaper is advertising and this is not often the cause of consumer dissatisfaction. Where there is dissatisfaction with the news or political values of the paper, there is no way to produce a competitor of like magnitude without access to advertisers who prefer a single, one-factory producer. This is true even though advertising prices of monopoly newspapers, when corrected for differences of size and other variables, are significantly higher than for competing papers.

There is a significant difference in the news content between monopoly and competing newspapers. A study in *Journalism Quarterly* for autumn of 1966, reported on an area that had a monopoly paper, was then confronted with a new competitor of equal strength, and then had the competitor approach failure, with these results:

The original monopoly devoted 40.8 percent of its nonadvertising space to local news, which is the most expensive to generate. When a competitor appeared, local news was increased to 50.6, or a 24 percent increase. When the community reverted back to a monopoly, local news dropped back to 43.3 percent. The RAND study shows that local news, inch for inch, costs 90 percent more to generate than national news.

Another result was that under competition there was a marked increase in quick-reward items (dramatic news, sensation, crimes, physical disasters), and when competition diminished there was more delayed-reward news (long-range developments and articles in depth).

Thus, monopoly has been a mixed phenomenon for the reader, diminishing the opportunities for diversity and tempting papers to choose less expensive news, but at the same time permitting a less sensationalist handling of information.

Though the typical newspaper corporation operates a monopoly in its locality, it finds itself in a corporate dilemma that is unusual for a growth industry. It has usually saturated its community so that there is little room for large-scale expansion. If the practical maximum newspaper sales in an area is about 80 percent of households and a local monopoly already sells its papers to 80 percent of households.

there are no grand new fields to conquer, beyond rising economic growth in the community and the professional pride of improving the quality of the existing product.

But, because profits can be high, and with them taxes, the investing impulse is strong, and it has expressed itself in two ways: chains and conglomerates.

There has been growth in the formation of newspaper chains (though in trade literature the word "chain" is unpopular and the euphemism "group" is preferred). A newspaper chain is two or more papers in different locations owned by the same business management. Their expansion in recent years has been phenomenal. In 1910—considered a time of national newspaper giants like Hearst and Scripps—there were 13 chains that owned 62 papers, or fewer than 3 percent of the 2,400 daily papers of that era. In 1968 there were 159 chains that owned 828 papers, or 47 percent of all papers. The largest number of papers controlled by a chain belonged to the British Lord Thomson, who controlled 36 American dailies (and said his aim was to own 100), followed by Gannett with 29 papers, Scripps League with 28, and Newhouse with 23. Because chain operators are not attracted to the smallest papers, they own the larger papers that control a majority of all daily circulation. The largest 35 of the 159 chains controlled 63 percent of all papers sold each day in the United States. The largest controllers of circulation were the Chicago Tribune group, over 3.6 million daily circulation; Newhouse group, over 3.1 million; Scripps-Howard group, over 2.5 million; and Hearst newspapers, over 2 million.

The informational significance of this is to extend centralization of control of news beyond the local monopoly that already exists in 97 percent of American cities. Given the tendency for one-man direction of newspaper enterprises, at least in theory American newspaper readers have their daily printed news and opinion determined by fewer than 1,700 men, including one in each of the 1,545 cities that have only one newspaper management. Chains increase this informational centralization: 63 percent of all daily newspaper readers— members of 39.5 million households—theoretically have their printed diet controlled by 35 chains or, possibly, 35 men.

The pejorative implications of the word "chain" go back to the public discovery at the turn of the century of the unique economic and political power of all trusts and monopolies. They go back to the days of Hearst, who regularly placed a standard message in every one of his papers with a single order from his headquarters. They carry over from the first impact of entrepreneurs in the newspaper business who recognized that profits could be made in buying, merging, and liquidating newspapers the way profits can be made liquidating textile mills.

Frank Munsey was an impersonal trader in newspaper properties, seeing this as a natural extension of his success in buying, merging, and liquidating grocery stores. It was an activity that brought almost universal condemnation from traditional newspaper operators of that day. When Munsey died in 1925, the late William Allen White, owner of the Emporia (Kansas) *Gazette,* wrote in his paper: "Frank Munsey, the great publisher, is dead. Frank Munsey contributed to the journalism of his day the great talent of a meat packer, the morals of a money changer, and the manners of an undertaker. He and his kind have about succeeded in transforming a once noble profession into an eight percent security. May he rest in trust."

It is not the kind of epitaph any contemporary daily publisher is likely to print about any other publisher. Chains are now respectable, and the power of the press is sufficient to create and maintain tax and other laws leading to further economic concentration in the mass media. Official spokesmen and publications for trade organizations in both newspaper publishing and broadcasting, for example, consistently oppose any limitation on owners of one medium buying control of another.

As a practical matter, the structured conformity of all newspaper chains is exaggerated. Many chains give their local outlets considerable autonomy. Adaptation to local conventions is important to increase acceptance and revenue. On the other hand, the lively trading of newspapers is not bringing new ideas into daily print. In most cases, when a newspaper owner sells his paper, he looks for a buyer who will perpetuate the same political values. When the Orlando *Sentinel and Star* in Florida was sold to the Chicago *Tribune,* the chief executive of the *Sentinel-Star* announced, "There isn't another newspaper organization with whom I would have entertained negotiations. . . . Our basic philosophy on government . . . for community progress and civic upbringing is almost identical." When the Du Pont interests speculated on selling their monopoly news-papers in Wilmington, Delaware, the leading suggestion was, "Out-right sale to an outside newspaper organization whose political and economic views closely parallel those of the present ownership. . . . To avoid having the papers fall into unfriendly hands through a second sale, the sales agreement should give Christiana or its suc-cessors the first opportunity to purchase the papers if they should be again put up for sale."

Newspaper chains have formed rapidly despite the fact that chains do not enjoy the conventional centralization that cuts down produc-tion costs. Economies of size might occur if all papers of the same organization were produced in the same place, in which case building, overhead, editorial staffs, and expensive production equipment could be used at greater capacity. But since newspapers are locally rooted, acquisition of an added newspaper usually means operation of a separate plant in a different community. There are some economies of scale possible in bargaining for editorial features and slight ones for newsprint, but these savings are insignificant.

The chief force today in chain formation is corporate affluence among daily papers and tax laws that favor investing the profits elsewhere. Newspapers today make 12 to 15 percent profit on assets after taxes, which is quite respectable. When a newspaper proprietor is chief of a closely held corporation, he is not under the conventional pressure to make maximum distribution of earnings to the stock-holders who are frequently relatives and friends. Tax regulations permit accumulation of undistributed earnings free of the usual tax on undistributed earnings of 38 1/2 percent for amounts over $100,000—if the accumulation is for buying another property of the same type. Thus, accumulated newspaper profits tend to be used to buy other papers in other places. The most harmful effect of chain formation may be that profits made in a community paper are not re-invested in that paper. The community daily has become a source of capital to be invested elsewhere.

Newspaper editorial and industrial operations are complex and unstandardized. If an entrepreneur is fortunate enough to gather a team of specialists skilled in managing the enterprise, the limitations of a strictly local operation tempt him to spread the expertise to other papers in other places.

An interesting secondary reason has been given by some chain operators for their acquisition of additional newspapers.

Newspapers are extraordinarily secretive about their operational and economic information, to the point of self-damage. More than any other industry of comparable size, the daily newspaper industry in the United States has insisted that it not be studied by economists (unlike, for example, the daily newspaper industry in England, which subsidized the Economist Intelligence Unit to do a thorough operational and economic study of the London newspapers and paid for its publication). This withdrawal from detached analysis stems from the industry's origins as personal family businesses, its insistence that it should be exempted from many standard business laws, and its historic fear of governmental monitoring. These impulses are enforced by the press's special access to public opinion and its consequent influence over public policy.

In the standard industrial data for the United States there are important categories that do not list newspapers. For example, the *Statistical Abstract of the United States, 1968,* in its table of "Manufacturing Establishments—Gross Book Value of Depreciable Assets and Rental Payments" lists such industries as "tobacco manufactures" with $713 million in assets, and "leather and leather products" with $581 million, but has no category for newspaper publishing, whose physical assets are many times more (in the period 1958–1968 papers invested $1.75 billion in new equipment alone).

The *Statistical Abstract* table "Largest Industrial Corporations—Selected Financial Items, by Industry: 1966" lists such corporations as "apparel" with $13,092 sales per employee, and office machinery and computers with $14,713 sales per employee, but not the newspaper industry, which has $16,000 sales per employee (this table gives return on invested capital, which is the newspaper industry's most sacred secret). The American Newspaper Publishers Association insists it has no data and no estimate for the value of the physical assets of the American daily newspaper industry, even though this is a crucial figure for any industry that has to make decisions on future technology and corporate health.

In the annual Economic Report of the President, February, 1968, as printed in the *Statistical Abstract,* the table "Manufacturing Corporations—Relation of Profits After Taxes to Stockholders'

Equity and to Sales, 1960 to 1967," out of twenty-two categories of industry, the tenth-largest industry in the country is omitted with the notation, "Printing and publishing, except newspapers." Another table on sales and profits of industries is headed by the note, "Excludes newspapers."

In 1968, Paul Rand Dixon, then chairman of the Federal Trade Commission, told a Senate antitrust hearing, "I do not know how profitable this industry is. I have no idea." Reminded that a 1947 law ordered the FTC to issue quarterly reports on basic data, including profits, for whole industries (not individual firms), he replied that when he was first asked about newspaper data, "I swear I thought they were included. I went and looked and they were not there." Asked why there should be this unique omission in a standard report on the national economy, he concluded, "I kind of suspect nobody wanted the newspapers mad at them . . . this is the only answer I get."

The Securities and Exchange Commission also issues periodic reports on industry, and these also omit newspapers. When William Farson, of the American Newspaper Guild, inquired of the SEC why newspapers were omitted, the SEC referred such questions to the United States Bureau of the Budget, which administers the reporting system. Farson told a Senate committee in 1967 that his staff was told, "The Bureau of the Budget considered 'the fourth estate untouchable.' "

Newspapers studied by RAND offer some insight into newspaper profits, though its sample was small. All manufacturing corporations (a category that would include newspapers if their profits were not systematically omitted) had 5.0 percent profit on sales after taxes in 1967. For the largest industrial corporations in 1966, there was a 5.6 percent return on sales, with individual industries ranging from 12.1 percent for mining, to 3.2 percent for food and beverages.

In the RAND study, for daily newspapers whose data permitted uniform calculations, the average profit on sales after taxes was 6.5 percent, with a range from a high of 10.7 percent to a low of 3.5 percent. This was a very small number of papers, compared to the total of dailies. But their financial data were compared with one of the better collections of newspaper finances covering a large portion of papers, and on the basis of their comparative profits before taxes, the papers in the RAND study had profits that were 73.9 percent of the average for all papers in their revenue class. On that basis, the profit after taxes of daily newspapers in the United States would average 8.8 percent, or 76 percent higher than the national average for all industries. It is important to note that this figure is heavily weighted toward the medium-sized dailies, ranging from 30,000 circulation to over 200,000. But these dailies represent the middle 50 percent of all daily circulation.

Average profit on equity for papers in the RAND study was 11.4 percent. These, too, are 73.9 percent lower than for most papers; the more common figure is 15.5 percent on equity. The average for all manufacturing corporations in the country for 1967 was 11.7 percent.

There is irony in newspaper secretiveness about corporate affairs. Total or average or large-sample data about the newspaper industry would be minimally revealing about individual firms because there are so many firms, 1,750 dailies and 8,000 weeklies, owned and operated by about 8,000 different newspaper companies. There are much more revealing data for automobile firms, for example, of which there are only four. Over 90 percent of all daily newspaper firms operate local monopolies, so they are under less competitive pressure than most industries whose statistics are publicly disclosed.

It is ironic, too, that newspaper publishers have so consistently refused to give some items of standard industrial data needed to produce a useful picture of the national economy, though they operate an industry that insists on disclosure by others whose affairs bear upon the public welfare.

The final irony is that newspaper secretiveness has damaged newspapers. Lack of precise and consistent data has prevented independent economic and operational analysis common in other industries. This has been a major barrier to achieving greater efficiency in newspapers, and is a serious barrier to intelligent decisions about future technology.

The more perceptive newspaper owners know that they lack enough precise data from their own trade association or from disciplined external analysis. One way they make up for this void is by purchasing interests in other newspapers or buying whole newspapers outright, giving them an opportunity to examine a larger quantity of operating accounts. A chain owner has the advantage of more realistic and precise data than men who own merely a single newspaper.

Group ownership also permits more versatile capital formation. A large organization can pool its investment money more efficiently than a small one. Furthermore, budgets can be kept momentarily low (since revenue is not quickly responsive to high journalistic quality), by way of concentrating the chain's money on modernizing or expanding its other papers. Or, where it has competition, a chain can subsidize its fight with profits from its noncompetitive papers. In 1967 the Department of Justice obtained a consent decree from the Lindsay-Schaub newspaper chain, then owners of six papers. The government said the chain had taken an intentional $3 million loss between 1956 and 1963 while trying to overcome a competitor in Champaign-Urbana, Illinois, making up the loss from other papers in its chain, just one of which, a paper in Decatur, Illinois, with sixty-five thousand circulation, made a profit of $5 million during the same period.

The American newspaper is peculiarly and importantly a local institution. It has been remarkably secure in its recent stage of local monopoly. Yet tax laws discourage the strengthening of this local institution by its own profits. Proprietorships and family ownerships permit unusual latitude in using these profits however the owner wishes. The result has been that profits from one paper are often used to buy other papers, or even to invest in stocks and bonds, since capital-gains taxes are lower than conventional corporate taxes. During the time of stability and profits in the 1960s, most daily papers have failed to use their freedom to use profits for maximum reinvestment to strengthen the paper in quality of content or even in preparation for a new technology.

In the 1970s, daily newspapers will find themselves in a new corporate and technological world. They began as a craft, the one-man printer. They evolved into an editorial profession, the community spokesman who had something to report and entered the printing trade only as a means to that end. They began the twentieth century as an important local family business. But reluctantly and not without losses for the consumer of news, they are now entering the impersonal world of modern corporate finance and empire building.

They enter this uncertain world partly because of a new competitor, broadcasting. From the start, newspapers and broadcasters have had a love-hate relationship, brutal infighting alternating with profitable marriages of convenience. New technology hints that in the not-too-distant future, newspapers and broadcasters, like some old married couples, may end up looking remarkably alike.

The Broadcast News System

7

Most Americans have no choice in their local printed news: in 97 percent of all cities with daily newspapers, one company prints the only news in town. It is a continuing theme of concern in a society that places a high value on diversity and on a maximum flow of information.

So it is not surprising that the basic communications law governing broadcasting in the United States should insist that radio and television be local institutions in sufficient numbers to provide maximum choice for the citizen. Consequently, today there are 7,586 radio and television stations in the United States, each one designed and organized to create its own local material, providing most Americans with a choice of over twenty different broadcast outlets in their own metropolis.

The localized broadcast system, it was hoped, would achieve two objectives. It would meet the ideal of the Founding Fathers of multiple outlets for ideas and information in each locality, an ideal that the economics of newspaper publishing made impossible for printed news in the twentieth century. And it would create a separate and independent system for the collection, compilation, and distribution of political and social intelligence, acting as a contrast and a balance to the older printed news establishment.

This has not happened.

Broadcast news is fast and continuous throughout the day. It is vivid in its direct transmission of public events. And it offers a useful summary and repetition throughout the day of the leading national news items.

But it does not take advantage of its many local outlets to produce variety and choice for the listener. Its duplication of timing robs the citizen of a reasonable choice of when to hear the news, and duplication of content makes much of the choice of timing meaningless. Half of broadcast news is heard during less than 10 percent of possible times of transmission. Because so many stations broadcast their news at the same time, and because when they offer alternative times so much of their content is a repetition of news from other channels, in most American cities over 80 percent of the stations could stop broadcasting news without a net loss to the public of news or of choice of times to hear it.

And, instead of creating a comprehensive news system that offers a service independent of the printed news networks, broadcasting uses the product of the printed news—either through the use of standard wire services that are fed almost entirely by newspapers and newspaper-controlled agencies, or else by simply reading headlines from the local newspaper. Instead of creating a separate news voice, broadcasting, with very few exceptions, follows the lead of the printed news and siphons off the results in a few short items that it then broadcasts in stereotyped fashion in massive duplication.

What emerges is a pattern of news that follows the pattern of all broadcast content: regardless of the number of outlets in any community, stations concentrate around a few standard types of programming, and within each type there is substantial duplication among all the stations in that category. With few exceptions, the initial intent of translating maximum local stations into maximum choice of content and timing has largely failed.

Even in the largest broadcasting markets, with as many as thirty to forty stations within range of a household radio set, a maximum of seven types of stations are standard almost everywhere throughout the country: continuous news, country-Western music, rock-'n'-roll music, popular music, classical music, rhythm-and-blues music, and educational stations. Within each of these categories, with the exception of "educational," content is essentially the same. The listener is offered a choice in timing, in the sense that if he has five rock-'n'-roll stations available, they will all play substantially the same songs, drawing from the "top forty" in current popularity, but in a different order.

In broadcasting, news is a minor by-product of a local staff.

In the average newspaper, the reporting and editing of news is a major operation, even though manufacturing absorbs greater energy. Though it has an audience of less than forty thousand, this average paper will have about forty full-time employees specializing in reporting and editing, and will spend over $400,000 a year for its news operations. Some of its staff will spend full time covering either outlying communities, or else specialized activities within the central community, like City Hall, the courts, and welfare.

Broadcasting is a striking contrast. The national networks maintain some specialists who cover the White House, the State Department, Congress, and space exploration and science, but after a few major national and international categories of that kind, routine and consistent reporting becomes insignificant. Local broadcasting stations, even among the larger and more professional staffs, seldom are assigned to systematic coverage of a special area in a way that originates new information. Instead, broadcasting uses the printed news or publicity notices to dispatch a crew to make a record of a predictable event. The average and smaller broadcasting stations do even less.

The *Average Medium Daily* newspaper described above lies almost exactly at the halfway point among American newspapers in size and news budgets. Station XYZ, a real station in the Western half of the United States, is probably among the top 30 percent of AM radio stations in news budgets and efforts. Unlike the majority of AM stations, XYZ does not depend entirely on a disc jockey or announcer merely to read the top items from the agency teletypewriter in its studio or to read the headlines from the most recently purchased local paper. XYZ has a two-man staff. The first man begins work at 6 A.M., which gives him twenty minutes to make selections from the accumulated offerings of his United Press International teletype news service and from the local daily paper. For each of the first three hours of the broadcast day, there are two newscasts of four minutes each. The first one the newscaster fills 80 percent with verbatim items from the UPI teletype and 20 percent with headlines he rewrites from page one of the local morning newspaper. For the second newscast he uses about the same ratio of wire-story and local news, except this time his local stories consist of the rewritten first paragraphs of some of the same newspaper stories.

Between the morning newscasts, he receives a telephone call from another station fifty miles away asking him to read a story over the telephone that can be recorded and used on the distant station. It is about an event in XYZ's town. Both stations happen to be using precisely the same sources of news, the UPI teletype and the local morning paper in XYZ's town. The XYZ man reads his own rewriting of these sources, giving the impression that the station fifty miles away has a special reporter on the scene collecting original information. Stations often exchange such voice services, though each party already has the same information.

Mechanical rewording of the same item is done for the station by its wire service. The wire-service agencies feed their teletype circuits for broadcasting stations from the main newspaper wire, cutting down total words and revising the wording for broadcast purposes. The broadcast wire constantly repackages leading items throughout the day, in nineteen five-minute summaries in each twenty-four-hour period. So at any moment the local announcer need not select or rewrite news items. The agency editor rewrites previous items, usually without additional information. On XYZ, one story is used six times without additional information but reworded five times.

In the newsroom of XYZ there are a teletype machine, an ordinary telephone, and an intercommunications line to the station manager and sales department. The only specialized news communication other than the teletype is a telephone from the county communications center, which takes the initiative to notify the station if there are traffic accidents, fires, or other law-enforcement events. It is the source of the heavy portion of crime and accidents on XYZ and carries only what county officials decide to call into the studio.

By the fifth newscast of the day, the UPI wire has supplied two versions of each story, so that they may be rotated in adjacent newscasts using different words, without the need for local rewriting.

The sixth newscast on XYZ is a verbatim repetition of the fifth.

By the seventh newscast, the announcer has collected from the wire-service machine three different wordings for each story, and these are used in alternating sequence in successive airings throughout the remainder of the first half of the broadcast day, without further insertion of new information or rewriting.

The day Station XYZ was observed, the UPI moved a bulletin announcing that the Supreme Court nomination of Judge Clement

Haynsworth of South Carolina had been rejected by the Senate. The announcer decides not to break into the music program, but wait until the next regular newscast. Earlier, when the county had called in two nonfatal accidents, he had broken into regular programming with "latest bulletin" announcements.

On the ninth newscast for the day on XYZ, the only two items different from the first newscast are the Haynsworth item and one other.

Thus, the effective editors for XYZ are not in the studio. They are the wire-service-agency editor in a nearby city who makes selections for the nineteen five-minute summaries for all broadcasters and the newspaper editor who decides which stories to put on page one of the local paper (which has no corporate connection with Station XYZ), and which the XYZ newscaster rewrites.

For XYZ, there was no reporting in the traditional sense. The station had no one in the field. At no time during the observed day did anyone in the radio studio initiate a telephone call in order to check or collect news. The station has a radio-equipped automobile with its call letters and the word NEWS painted in large letters on the side, but it is there largely for advertising purposes.

Most radio stations make less effort on news than XYZ, but larger stations, particularly larger television stations, do have a professional staff. The top 5 percent of television stations in local news exceed *Average Medium Daily*'s $400,000 annual news budget, and some are in the millions. But the entertainment emphasis in broadcasting is symbolized by the fact that each of the top 50 percent of newspapers spend more money on news operations than each of the top 5 percent of broadcasting stations. One network-owned-and-operated television station in the Western United States, PQR-TV, is a major station in its metropolis. It has about thirty employees in the news department, producing four newscasts a day. Two five-minute newscasts are not very different from XYZ's—a reporter reads brief news items from the wire agency teletype.

The major effort of the staff is directed toward the one-hour program of local news. The fourth newscast is a reduced version of this one-hour effort.

The station subscribes to six news wires, using both Associated Press and United Press International. In addition, the network offers filmed news and commentary on a special coaxial connection that permits the local producer to order videotaped portions he wants later in the day. His decision is made on the basis of a teletyped description of the video material, which is used automatically unless there are technical deficiencies in the recording, like fuzzy sound or lack of synchronization between sounds and the movement of lips.

PQR-TV has about five reporters available each day, who are, like all television reporters outside of New York and Washington, general-assignment reporters. They follow orders of the assignment editor of the station, whose strategy has to take into account that each assignment must have a high probability of producing usable news, with filmed scenes, which on television usually means interesting action or sound.

Television reporters in small cities are also their own cameramen. In larger cities, like the one PQR-TV serves, union contracts require a separate cameraman. In still larger cities, a separate sound-recording man is required. In New York City each news event covered by television requires a reporter, a cameraman, a sound man, and a separate automobile driver. The two-man teams at PQR-TV can record, at most, two events a day. This gives the station a maximum of ten original items each day. Local television reporters cannot cover any single story or theme for any length of time. They must make their film quickly in order to get to their next assignment and get it all back in time to process the film for the evening newscast.

There are two main sources of cues for the assignment editor. One is the newspapers of the region, which are used as leads in deciding where to send camera crews. A wire service also lists events scheduled for the region for each day. Press conferences are of considerable interest, since they have a precise time, which avoids idleness by the reporter-and-cameraman crew and permits planning for processing of film.

One possibility on this day is a dramatic but peaceful demonstration that has been going on for a week, producing almost daily news. PQR-TV sent a crew to cover the demonstration for a newscast several days earlier. Some of the film made at that time was not used on the air. The decision is made to use this surplus footage. A station reporter calls the demonstrating group on the telephone to record the interview. The reporter's telephone call cannot reach any of the demonstrators so he speaks with the wife of the caretaker of the grounds where the intruding demonstrators are living. The surplus footage from several days earlier is used on the evening news, with the voice over it of the reporter talking to the caretaker's wife, giving the impression of a fresh on-the-scene report.

A major conference is covered, a day-long series of sessions that brings to the city some of the world's leading experts on pollution. PQR-TV covers the conference by sending a camera crew to a press conference and recording forty-five seconds of an interview with a television personality present in the pressroom. No PQR-TV reporter or cameraman attends any of the sessions or talks to any of the world experts. In the newscast that night, sponsorship of the conference is given incorrectly.

Four hours before the big newscast of the day, the first edition of a local paper is brought in with a page one feature on spectacularly bad construction on a local public building. A crew is quickly assigned to the public building but comes back to report that the building is locked. Since there is little time to arrange to see the defects, the story is eliminated.

(It is common in larger cities that television stations have a courier outside the pressrooms of major newspapers to rush early editions to the television station, since the two media live in fear that a major story in one medium will be missed by its own audience. On the other hand, the news decisions of many newspaper editors are significantly conditioned by their watching of late-night and early-morning television news and what they hear on their car radios as they drive to work.)

That night the major newscast of the day has ten local items, seven of them based on press conferences. Following a full hour, counting commercials and station promotions, there is a half hour of national news from network headquarters.

Thus, in both the small radio and the large television station, the national news is substantially the leading items in the standard wire-service menu for the day—a headline service. Local news is a re-action to the initiative of others: free information from official sources, press conferences called by those wishing publicity, or plagiarizing headlines and first paragraphs of a local paper. With the exception of some network news, and a few outstanding radio and television stations in the larger cities, local broadcast news does not perform original or systematic coverage of major local affairs but instead is a passive repository for efforts initiated by others.

Even where there is a total lack of professional reportorial and editorial initiative, which is to say in the great majority of markets, the headline-reading service is still an addition to public information. It provides widespread dissemination of news that would otherwise be limited to those readers of newspapers who happened to read a particular item. The severe limitation of broadcasting, the inability of any station to say more than one thing at a time, extends the audience for news: those who are waiting for something else, like music or sports or entertainment, will listen to some news rather than take the effort to shut off the set. And because most markets have many stations, and newscasts are not all at the same time of day, those who are primarily interested in the news have a choice of time in which to hear what they believe is the latest news.

But a study of the pattern of news in an American market shows that, while more of the public hears the leading items of news because of radio and television, the duplication of effort in urban areas is wasteful and stereotyped. The news from a few stations provides most of the information and choice of times to hear it; the additional contribution of the remaining majority of stations is insignificant.

In a cooperative effort by the Department of Journalism of the University of Michigan and RAND, the news of a representative broadcasting market was recorded and transcribed as actually broadcast. The University of Michigan group recorded a full day's broadcasting by all the stations heard in the Grand Rapids–Kalamazoo, Michigan, area, and transcribed all the news given by the twenty-four stations. The stations included three television stations, eight FM radio stations, and thirteen AM radio stations (two of them located in Chicago but heard in enough Grand Rapids–Kalamazoo homes to constitute a commercially significant audience). The recording was done noon-to-noon, June 2 and 3, 1969.

Analysis of the transcriptions and the conclusions given here were done at RAND.

Grand Rapids–Kalamazoo was not selected for any preconceived characteristics except that it is in the middle range of important broadcasting markets, and is convenient to one of the country's leading university departments of journalism. Located in mid-America, Grand Rapids–Kalamazoo lies between the thirty-fifth and fortieth largest broadcasting markets in the country. The forty largest markets contain almost two-thirds of the American population. Television's best signal reaches 390,000 homes in the area, radio far more.

It is a profitable television market, though for radio it is financially rewarding only for the leading stations. The three television stations in 1967 had revenues of $8,991,000, with profits before taxes of $3,376,000. The sixteen AM and FM stations for which the FCC has issued aggregate financial figures grossed $3,865,000 in 1967, with profits before taxes of only $64,000.

The study shows the speed of broadcasting over newspapers. The leading items of national news were available hours in advance of the two local papers, both evening dailies, one each in Grand Rapids and Kalamazoo. In fact, the leading national news item during the period was known to the broadcast audience almost twenty-four hours ahead of the first mention in the local papers, thanks to the breaking of the story just after the local papers had gone to press. This, in itself, is a clear demonstration of one superiority of broadcasting: speed.

Another superiority is the diversity of times in which some news is available. There were no all-news stations in Grand Rapids–Kalamazoo. But the average time devoted to actual news was almost 8 percent of all programming, with individual stations ranging from 3 percent (a television station) to 17 percent (an FM radio station). The average for all three television stations was 5 percent, for all AM's was 10 percent, and all FM's was 8 percent. The average quantity and quality of AM radio news was superior to average TV and FM.

The FCC tends to query stations at license-renewal times if their newscasts fall below 1 percent of total programming. The Grand Rapids–Kalamazoo stations are well above that and even higher than the average given for most markets, since the percentages here are for time actually spent in giving news, and not for commercials and promotions during newscasts. A minor item that emerged from the study is that a "five-minute" newscast is usually three minutes and twenty seconds, and a "fifteen-minute" newscast twelve to thirteen minutes of actual news.

The news was distributed over twenty-four stations that collectively broadcast at 439 time periods during the twenty-four hours. Plainly, there was some news available at more times throughout the day and night than would be possible with existing print sources.

One striking—if ambiguous—service of broadcast news is its brevity. The average broadcast news item had sixty-four words. Some stations gave each item fuller treatment. The leading television station for news, WOOD-TV, gave a full hour and twenty-nine minutes for actual newscasting, with more than double the items of other television stations, yet averaged a relatively high 102 words per item. Aside from simple numbers, its summaries were carefully compiled with retention of all essential information. (This study ignores the added dimension of the video portion of television news, though it, too, is plainly an added communication.)

But broadcast news viewed as a whole in a single community is extremely wasteful.

Though all the stations were on the air with most national news before the local papers, some were lackadaisical about important news and didn't bother to update with substantial new information. The leading news story for the day was the collision at sea between the Australian carrier *Melbourne* and the American destroyer *Evans*. First news of the accident was put on wire-service teletypes in the area between 5:45 and 6:15 P.M. Eight stations in the area had broadcasts after 6:15, ranging from 6:30 to 7:15, without reporting it. They might have felt that the news was not important, but that is not likely, since the wire services handled it as a bulletin item considered urgent, and most of these same stations later put the item in top position. More likely, their news is hastily clipped together by a busy announcer or disc jockey an hour or two before the newscast, and afterward he is so busy doing commercials or other work in the studio that he cannot change newscasts. One station went off the air at nightfall, after the accident, but without a newscast, so its listeners did not hear about the collision until the next morning, when it did use the item but gave it inaccurately.

And though there were 439 newscasts by the 24 stations, 75 percent of these were useless to the listener because they occurred in duplicated timing. Assuming that the listener tunes in one channel at a time, he has 108 unduplicated newscast times a day in the 24 stations. This is a useful number, but a small proportion of the total.

Even the 108 unduplicated times of news are diminished by the rush of broadcasters to match each other in competition for attention. Half of these newscasts are concentrated in three periods of the day, noon to 2 P.M., 5 to 7 P.M., and 7 to 9 A.M. In two favorite times, noon to 12:15 P.M., and 6 to 6:15 P.M., there were sixteen stations on the air with news. At the third most favored time, 5 to 5:15 P.M., there were fourteen stations newscasting. At 8 to 8:15 A.M., thirteen stations were newscasting.

Neither in the amount of news heard nor in the choice of times to hear it is this duplication rational as an exercise in public information, though it may be profitable as a marketing device to retain attention.

During the twenty-four-hour period recorded in Grand Rapids–Kalamazoo, 381 separate items of news were heard, if one listened to every station all the time and counted each unique news item. If all of these items were aired not over twenty-four stations but on only one, using the fastest broadcast announcing speeds, they would require two hours and forty-three minutes of newscasting. One station, WLAV-AM, in fact, had three hours of newscasting.

However, many of these 381 items were repeated by the same station at subsequent newscasts, which is a service to the listener, letting him increase his chances of hearing a particular piece of news even if he missed it at the original airing. The average item was used 2.3 times. So to broadcast the total news heard that day with the same degree of repetition would take 2.3 times the 2 hours and 43 minutes, or 6 hours and 15 minutes. Thus, the listeners of Grand Rapids–Kalamazoo could hear all the news with the same number of repetitions they heard on June 2 and 3, 1969, if one station devoted 375 minutes, or 6 hours and 15 minutes, of its time throughout the day to these news items and their repetition. If it were a 24-hour station, as some were, this would still leave it 17 hours and 45 minutes, or almost three-quarters of its time on the air for some other kind of programming.

Eighty-three percent of all newscasting, an aggregate of 2,287 minutes, or 38 hours and 7 minutes, was wasted, offering the listener no additional information or usable choice of times to hear it. Using average news time for each of the 24 stations, 95 minutes of actual news a day, four stations could give all the news with the same degree of repetition. So far as news is concerned, the other 20 stations are superfluous.

Whatever advantage there is to news repetition among stations is diminished by two factors. One is that there is no assurance that the listener who wants minimal news will find it on the station that gives him his favorite programming.

Secondly, it is generally the case that the stations that give the least news also give the least accurate news. On the leading item in the twenty-four-hour period recorded, for example, one FM station among the lowest in amount of news given also had a high instance of carelessness or lateness, not bothering to add important new facts to leading stories even though the new information was received hours earlier in its studios. An AM station, also among the lowest in total amount of news given throughout the day, continued to give incorrect information on the leading news item of the day for twelve hours after other stations had it correct. Two hours later when it finally corrected the information, it devoted only twenty words to the entire item.

One conceivably could justify such wide differences in the quantity and frequency of newscasts on the basis of serving varying tastes in news. But if a station gives only minimal news on grounds of serving an audience that wants only the briefest summaries, then it is all the more important that this small amount be as accurate as possible. If in addition to the portions of the daily news being small, they are also inaccurate, it raises the question whether no news would be better.

There is a short half-life in broadcast news for all but the most spectacular stories. The morning the wire services reported a Supreme Court decision affecting military trials, it was considered sufficiently important so that twenty-three of the twenty-four stations used the item at one time or another. But more than half of these twelve stations, broadcast it in one time period, between noon and 12:15 P.M. Four used it for the first time between 12:30 and 12:45 P.M., two of them between 5 and 5:15 P.M., and one did not use it for the first time until 6:45 P.M. Thus, 50 percent of the original airings of this item were at the same time of day on twelve different stations.

Most news, no matter at what time given on what station, is in almost identical language. The exceptions are a few major stations and highly localized items. Local items consist mostly of police reports of accidents, fires, and crimes, often used as received from the authorities, or else paraphrased headlines from the local paper, or publicity releases that may or may not be rewritten.

National news items are, with very few exceptions, read as they are received from the wire services, so that report after report appears on the transcriptions with identical language, sometimes broadcast at the same time. At one period, for example, there were three stations on the air with newscasts. All three used fifteen items in common. Two of the stations had thirty items in common. It was possible in one fifteen-minute segment to hear twelve stations reading the same item with essentially the same words.

In a number of instances, five-minute (that is, three-minute-twenty-second) newscasts were repeated at later intervals with identical items and words being used. Given the large amount of arbitrary rewriting by some stations merely to give old information an appearance of freshness, verbatim repetition is better service since it eliminates an opportunity for errors in rewriting, which appeared to occur regularly. A Supreme Court decision that is described in the Associated Press wire service received in the studio as saying that certain cases involving military men "may" be tried in civilian courts, came out as rewritten in the local studio "must" be tried. Again, this kind of error is found mostly on the stations that give brief and infrequent news.

How did the radio and television stations compare with their two local newspapers as purveyors of news?

Broadcasters were, of course, faster on national news and spread their news over longer periods of time.

But the two papers themselves varied considerably. The Grand Rapids *Press* is an evening paper with 134,000 daily circulation. The Kalamazoo *Gazette* is an evening paper with 58,000 circulation. The two cities are about fifty miles apart. Because of the range of broadcasting signals, both cities are in the same broadcasting market while each newspaper concentrates on its own city.

The *Press* had a total of 83 breaking news items, in a different mix than the radio and television stations. There were 297 stories on the air that were not in the *Press,* but since this includes 24 stations that covered a far larger area than the *Press,* the difference is diminished. The *Press* had 41 items that appeared on none of the 24 broadcasts of news. It had about 23,000 words of breaking news, none of the items repeated, of course. This was more news than given on any one station, and more than four times as much as the average station. It gave more local news than any broadcasting station.

The *Gazette* had 153 breaking stories. The 24 broadcasting stations collectively had 228 stories not in the *Gazette,* but like the *Press* the *Gazette* covers a more constricted geographical area than the broadcast market. The *Gazette* had 99 stories that were not on the air. Its 36,000 words were more than three times more than any one station's unrepeated words of news.

What is permitted the newspapers, of course, is depth of individual stories, and the average length of stories shows this. The *Press* averaged 275 words a story, the *Gazette,* 236, while the newscasts averaged 63 words an item. The longest item on any broadcasting station was 780 words, while six of the newspaper stories were longer. The *Gazette* had one story with 2,500 words, which, on the air, would take longer than 16 minutes, or more than most total newscasts. Averaging the longest single news item for each broadcasting station gives 300 words, so what was normal length of average items for the two newspapers was the extreme limit for broadcast news.

However, where there was care by newscasters, on the leading story of the day it was possible for the best stations collectively to include practically all of the essential facts about that one story that appeared in the two dailies. But this was true only of those few stations that compressed information thoughtfully and of the limited proportion of news items in which hard facts are easily counted. On the collision of *Melbourne* and the *Evans,* it would have been necessary to listen to five different broadcasting stations in ten different broadcasts to equal the information given in any one of the two local newspapers on the same story.

The two papers used identical stories from the wire services but rearranged paragraphs. The only additional information in the papers on the collision that did not appear in the ten best broadcasts was the background item that the carrier had been attacked by Japanese planes during World War II and that an Australian rear admiral was aboard the carrier at the time.

The many newscasts about the *Melbourne-Evans* collision throughout the day reported a varying number of fatalities, starting high, about seventy, dropping down to fifty-six in later newscasts, and finally reaching seventy-six, as more accurate counts came from the scene. The newspapers, coming out late with their account, had the more accurate, single figure. Had the paper gone to press earlier, of course, it would have had the fragmentary, incorrect figure on fatalities. But what this makes clear is that the advantage of broadcast news of giving numerous late notices as they arrive is also a disadvantage for the listener who cannot listen throughout the day: the one report he hears may be too early to have the complete and confirmed facts. It is a useful notification service of an event. But because most broadcast listeners are spasmodic ones, it is possible that they collect more incomplete fragments about the characteristics of the event. The collision on one station had killed twenty men while others were saying seventy; at a later time most were saying fifty-six; and later still they were saying seventy-six. One's view of the severity of the incident depended on which station one heard and, even if he combed all stations, at what time of day he heard the news.

There was one noticeable difference between broadcast and printed news of the collision story: all the facts that were in the papers, which are usually delivered to subscribers by about 5 P.M., had been broadcast at least five hours earlier, and some facts twenty-three hours earlier. The newspapers go to press around noon; when subscribers turned on their evening news (on most stations) they heard about an accident that was not in the newspaper already inside their homes, and would not be in print in their homes until almost twenty-four hours later.

On the other hand, only the most obsessive listener to all channels would have been able to hear all the earlier news over the air that he received much later in his newspaper. And to do this he would have had to listen to one Chicago AM station heard in the area, one Grand Rapids FM station, and three AM stations. And he would have had to comb through these stations over a period of several hours.

It is no surprise that broadcast news is briefer and carries less detail, and will continue to in the near future, for two fundamental reasons. One is that it is impossible for radio and television to present more than one item at a time to the listener. So if it wishes to retain the interest of those who may be uninterested in the first story but may be in a later item, the station dares not dwell too long on the first story. Another reason is that broadcast news offers, more than anything else, speed of delivery, and quite aside from holding the attention of its maximum audience by shifting subjects quickly, it loses its advantage of speed as it develops individual subjects in depth.

The newspapers in Grand Rapids and Kalamazoo, neither of them among the more distinguished papers in the country, could present their readers with a total of 236 hard news stories with a combined total of almost 40,000 words. It would have taken four hours and thirty minutes of continuous radio talking to deliver that same quantity of news in broadcasting, and if the usual newscast ratios of interruptions for commercials, station breaks and promotions were added, it would be closer to eight uninterrupted hours of talking.

Furthermore, if a broadcasting station pursued a single story in depth, as the *Gazette* did with a feature on a new regional airport, it would take seventeen minutes of continuous talking, during which the station might lose every listener who was not particularly interested in a new airport near Galesburg. An eleven-hundred-word story in the *Gazette* on the Kalamazoo city commission on police and community relations would have taken seven minutes of continuous talking on a radio newscast and during this time would have lost many of its listeners. The story pursued a subject of interest mainly in Kalamazoo, which is only one of the many communities covered by the stations' signals.

The newspapers could present all of this "simultaneously." It was all printed in the same package which the reader could scan in less than the time it takes for the standard newscast, instantly rejecting stories he is uninterested in and going on to something he cares about. Within a given long story, he can skip those parts that bore him and run through the remaining portions with his eye, something denied his ear with radio and his eye with television, which must receive the broadcast news at the standard speed of the stations with no way to scan, skip, and dwell.

There is another important advantage to newspapers, particularly the newspaper in small and medium cities like Grand Rapids (population, about 228,000) and Kalamazoo (population, about 90,000). The two cities are only fifty miles apart and nearby cities of the same general size also have daily newspapers. This means that each paper concentrates on its own city and county affairs without fear of boring readers in other places. And, while neither of these papers is unusual in local coverage, their local stories go well beyond the police reports and press releases that constitute so much of broadcast local news. Both the Grand Rapids and the Kalamazoo papers have most of their circulation (84 percent) concentrated in their own counties.

But the broadcasting stations cover a far greater geographical area, and do it with a far smaller journalistic apparatus. The three television stations alone have a signal area that covers over 17,000 square miles and 24 different counties. The radio stations collectively cover an even larger area, especially at night. Two of the radio stations heard in the area are in Chicago, 125 miles and 2 states away, and while these provided a slight increase in numbers of news items heard in the Grand Rapids–Kalamazoo area, even this small addition was only for national news since local Chicago news was of minimal interest in Michigan.

The average of 95 minutes a day of broadcast news per station overstates the extent of local affairs handled on the air. Broadcast news repeats many of its items. In the test day, all the stations averaged 36 percent repetition. This brings original news down to about 60 minutes a day. Forty-three percent of this was local news, some taken from the local papers (and therefore not useful as a faster service than printed news) or else routine law-enforcement news originated by the law-enforcement agencies. The average station had 26 minutes of local news a day. All 24 stations cover more than 24 counties. If these 24 counties have their proportionate share of all Michigan governmental units, then the average broadcasting station heard in Grand Rapids–Kalamazoo has 26 minutes a day in which to report the news from 150 municipalities, 230 townships and 310 school districts. The average Grand Rapids–Kalamazoo station has 18 newscasts a day, which is less than 90 seconds per newscast for local news items. Since the average item is repeated 1.3 times in order to give the listener added opportunities to hear a given piece of news, all local news—that is, news from 150 municipalities, 230 townships, and 310 school districts—has 40 seconds to get on any one newscast.

Only a few stations conduct any independent news reportage, and even that mostly as a reaction to printed news and preannounced press conferences. But, even if there were intensive efforts by all stations to do systematic coverage of their areas, they could not possibly cover the public affairs of their communities without a massive change in the system of licensing stations, in the allocation of frequencies and geographical locations, and in their programming and economics. The combination of wide-area broadcasting, the economic competition for maximum general audiences, and the inherent characteristics of sound and sight transmission of information make it impossible for the present broadcasting system to do adequate local reporting in the United States. Some stations do outstanding work, given these limitations, but under the best of conditions routine and continuing coverage of specific areas of local American life is almost impossible on the air.

Newspapers, almost by nature, can do a better job of this, and of presenting detail in national news. This is not because they are more virtuous and civic-minded (though the traditions in printed journalism define civic duty more rigorously than broadcasting traditions). But, because they are a nonephemeral medium, they are more tightly focused in a particular area, and they can present masses of information that the citizen can scan, reject, or absorb at will.

The price the citizen pays for this advantage of newspapers is that he gets his news later, as much as a whole day later in the case of communities with a single daily. And while he reads his newspaper he cannot do anything else. He can listen to radio or to the audio of television while doing other tasks that do not pre-empt his eardrums.

Most listeners have a choice of times and channels. But duplication of timing and of content severely reduces these alternatives. And, since broadcasting generally does not pursue local public issues in depth, its content is bland and usually undistinguishable from one station to another, diminishing the diversity that might come from numbers.

What no newspaper can match is the vividness and richness of those public affairs that radio and television transmit directly. This, by itself, is an advantage of broadcasting that is worth the existence of the medium in public affairs. Permitting the average citizen to see the President of the United States answering questions at press conferences, or to hear the greatest public events with their own sounds unfiltered, even with all the risks of propagating fraud and contrivance, is still a stimulus to public engagement in political affairs of a magnitude that no printed medium can match.

Though broadcasting is capable of transmitting a fuller appreciation of public affairs, it has failed to do this at the local level. The Federal Communications Commission requires stations to justify their being allotted a space in the public airwaves by serving their communities, and a nominal measure of this service is 1 percent news and 5 percent public-service programming. News is displayed wastefully. Public-affairs programming is not much better. What passes for local broadcast initiative in public service may be a corporation publicity film shown on television at 8 A.M. of a Sunday morning, or a tape-recorded evangelist (tape provided by the subject) at 1 A.M. on radio. There are stations that do creative and effective original local work, but they are a small percentage of the seventy-five hundred broadcasting stations in the country.

On the other hand, it is difficult to know precisely what seventy-five thousand broadcasting stations produce every day. The broadcast frequencies of the United States are a badly used national resource, but it is not easy to prove it comprehensively about fifty million hours of programming a year. An analysis merely of the quantity of news in only one market, Grand Rapids–Kalamazoo, for only one day, was formidable enough. Making an analysis for all programming for three hundred times more stations seems impossible.

Yet there is a law that commands the FCC to grant broadcasting licenses only to those corporations that operate in the public interest with standards of community service that stations are supposed to meet.

Broadcasting licenses come up for renewal every three years, whole states at a time. If the FCC agrees that each station has lived up to its service requirements, it grants a three-year license to each radio station for $75 and to each television station for $150. There is considerable exchange of paper in this process, but it is largely meaningless. For one thing, there is one important question the FCC has never answered. For another, the method used by the FCC to judge performance is one of the more futile in regulatory history.

The unanswered question is whether each station is supposed to perform as though it were the only station in town. Or can community service be shared, so that what one station does adequately does not have to be repeated by others? If there are twenty stations in a market, does each one have to have news that assumes that no one else is broadcasting? Or if it can be proven that there is sufficient access to news from other stations, can it devote all its time to music, or lectures, or talk shows, or market quotations? If the news output of Grand Rapids–Kalamazoo includes an enormous waste of time by men whose minds are really on something else, why not let a few stations concentrate on serious coverage of the news, and relieve the dozens of announcers and disc jockeys of the burden of pretending that they are editors of political and social information?

One reason this question has never been resolved lies with the method used by the FCC to judge performance at license-renewal time. Each broadcasting station is required to keep a minute-by-minute log at its transmitter. Each new program is supposed to be noted in times to a fraction of a minute. When there is a thirty-second commercial, that, too, is indicated. And when the announcer comes back with a station identification, that is recorded. At the end of the broadcast day, the log may contain for each broadcast item eight entries: the station identification time, the time on for that item, the time off, the title of the program, the duration of that item, the type of item ("commercial," "public-service announcement," "editorials," "news," "entertainment"), whether it is live or recorded, and what category of FCC programming it comes under ("religious," "educational," etc.).

At the end of the day, there may be four hundred entries, sometimes handwritten, in a thirteen-page log.

As the three-year license renewal time approaches, the FCC sends to each station a request for a random selection of its logs over the last three years, specifying, for example, a Tuesday in May, a Wednesday in September, a Thursday in June. The result for each station is a "representative week log" which is then sent to Washington as one basis for the commission's decision whether to renew the license. If there are 400 entries per day, there would be 2,800 entries per week. About 2,500 station licenses come up for renewal each year. This makes about 250,000 pages of logs—7 million entries to be checked each year. The Renewal Branch of the Broadcast Bureau of the FCC has one accountant and three broadcast analysts to process these logs along with other application materials. Four civil servants, even of the most diligent kind, cannot read and judge 250,000 pages and 7 million entries each year.

The logs are poor measures of performance both because their information is too vague, and because, even if it were precise, four human beings cannot analyze 7 million entries.

One answer is to make the logs more informative by ending the arbitrary classifications stations now report. Their chief distinguishing entries have to do with public affairs, now vaguely lumped under such headings as "agriculture" and "religious" and "educational," which serve as umbrellas for quantities of promotional and self-serving material paid for by others. All public-service programming should indicate whether it originated in the station's own broadcast area, whether it was live or recorded by the station, or recorded by someone else. All public-service materials paid for or recorded by someone else should be identified by the source. Public-service log items should be kept separately and available on more than a "representative week log" basis. The FCC should ask for perhaps thirty whole weeks selected at random throughout the three-year license period.

Then the representative-week logs plus the public-service logs, after their random dates have been selected by the FCC, should be typed so that they can be read by a computer, not a difficult or expensive process. The logs for all stations in a particular market or metropolis should be handled together. The computer, in addition to selecting out the summaries for each station, can be programmed to print out graphs and tables that also show the comparative patterns of each station in a given market, and show clearly and easily what all the stations in a market produce for that market. This way the FCC can see what the citizen in his community has available to him from the total of all his stations, which is how the citizen looks at it, rather than merely what each station does by itself. It would permit station specialization if this contributes to a full span of program choice in the community.

If the emerging community profile of broadcast services shows massive duplication in some areas and serious omissions in others, the FCC at license-renewal time could issue its findings to the stations applying for renewal and invite them to propose a rearrangement of programming to fill the unmet need and at the same time invite new applicants for licenses who will be able to fill the omission if the existing stations do not. This would change the present tendency for all stations to imitate the most successful ones and would reward those that move in new directions.

This kind of computation would also reveal the morbidity of present local public-service programming: most of it is now promotional material publicizing a few organizational activities to which stations grant vast amounts of free time, so long as the organization pays for the material. A survey for the United Church of Christ in Western states shows that the overwhelming "public-service" programming is from right-wing evangelists and other sources that send the stations their taped material free.

The handling of news would also be judged by the total available to the community from all stations rather than looking for a fixed percentage of news from each station. The pressure to have minimal news does not produce useful information. Instead, it results in a large army of local disc jockeys and announcers pasting together a few items of news, often inaccurately, almost always duplicating in both time and content what other stations do better, and maintaining the pretense that an expert player of records or a man valuable to the station mainly because of the timbre of his voice, is a competent editor of serious news.

Even under the best of conditions—practical detailed logs with meaningful categories—there will be a limit to what the FCC or any other government agency can do about broadcast content. The gross violations of fairness and other conditions of license holding are not difficult to judge or control. But subtle or indifferent programming is beyond easy judgment. After one eliminates massive unfairness, the analysis of detailed content begins to place the government in the role of censor. Just as difficult is the decision of how much a small station can afford of certain kinds of programming. The commercial motive has limits in support of socially needed but small-audience programs. When one minute of the best commercial air time is worth $65,000, a competition results that is suited to mass marketing but not to national values and culture. What is needed in addition to commercial stations is a larger number of noncommercial stations. Financing must be large enough to support vigorous programs but free of annual appropriations by Congress that would merely replace FCC control of content with congressional control.

The Corporation for Public Broadcasting is a semipublic body designed to support local noncommercial activities. Its meager funds at present originate from Congress. Many individual members of Congress are themselves owners of broadcasting properties or are indirectly involved through their law firms' representation of commercial broadcasting firms. Thus, one-third of the members have a financial stake in commercial broadcasting. All members have their political fates closely tied to their local broadcasters, whose sympathy is crucial during election campaigns. When these facts are added to the formidable political power of existing broadcasters in their Washington lobby, it is clear that there will always be serious resistance to fragmenting the commercial audience by supporting vigorous noncommercial programming.

The extent of this resistance can be seen in the position of noncommercial operations at the end of the 1960s. There were 687 commercial television stations and 182 noncommercial ones in the United States. A great many television markets had no noncommercial station. Furthermore, noncommercial stations lived in perpetual poverty, unable to pay for the technical and creative program origination that commercial television takes for granted. Each commercial station spends an average of $3 million a year for station operation. The Corporation for Public Broadcasting asked Congress for a total of $20 million in 1969, or the equivalent of less than seven commercial station budgets, but the White House recommended only $5 million, which, spread over the 182 noncommercial stations, would be less than the money that two average commercial stations spend.

There is an urgent need for substantial, nonpolitical financing of noncommercial broadcasting in the United States. The selling of deodorants and detergents should not be the primary goal of the most powerful communications instrument in American society. The Ford Foundation has suggested that the new communications satellites be, in a sense, "owned" by noncommercial broadcasting so that a portion of annual satellite revenues will go automatically to educational stations. This, of course, requires an act of Congress, but once Congress makes the decision, there would not be the annual pressures on content that the Congress has exhibited in other areas where it appropriates money for cultural and educational activities.

Britain and Japan support substantial noncommercial television by allocating funds from the tax the government charges every owner of a television and radio receiving set. The United States has no such tax on home sets. The government does levy an excise tax on automobiles and other consumer items, and if the Ford Foundation satellite plan fails, consideration might be given to such an excise on new radio and television receiving sets.

An ultimate alternative with present through-the-air broadcasting will be to exploit the fact that the FCC broadcasting license is a piece of paper of enormous commercial value. A three-year television-station license costs $150. Yet, the average market value of a television station in the top 50 markets is $20 million. Once an applicant gets his $150 piece of paper from the FCC he can, in effect, sell it for $20 million. License trading is a lively activity in commercial broadcasting for a variety of reasons. A 50 percent tax on the purchase price of traded stations would reduce the traffic in licenses and if allocated to noncommercial broadcasting would begin to return to public service the frequencies that are so wasted today.

Within this decade, the present technology of broadcasting will be transformed from transmission through the air to delivery by cable. This, in itself, can change the nature of programming. But if the new systems follow conventional market pressures they will fail to use the new technology for community services, repeating the failure of present broadcasting technology. In the next ten years cable and satellites will have an opportunity to recover from the disappointing history of commercial broadcasting's first forty years.

Broadcast News as
a Corporate Enterprise

The first advertising commercial was broadcast on August 28, 1922, when the American Telephone & Telegraph Company advertised itself over its own station in New York City. But the idea was offensive to almost everyone, including AT&T, which forbade any other station to broadcast any commercials on pain of losing AT&T telephone and wire services. The Secretary of Commerce, Herbert Hoover, foresightedly predicted the future communications potential of broadcasting but had a euphoric view of what was "inconceivable": "It is inconceivable that we should allow so great a possibility for service, for news, for entertainment, for education and for vital commercial purposes to be drowned in advertising chatter."

Even the National Association of Broadcasters for years insisted that advertising should be limited to daylight hours, leaving the evening "family hours" uncontaminated by crass commercialism.

The growth of radio as a corporate activity was also inhibited by innocence about electronic regulation and by the domination by newspaper corporations of the field of news and of mass advertising.

In the mid-twenties legal uncertainties about the right of the government to tell anyone which frequencies he could use led to a chaos of sounds in the air as stations went on and off the air without licenses, interfered with other stations, wandered over the dial, and increased their power in attempts to outblast stations already on the same frequency. By the time Congress granted the federal government power to regulate broadcasting with the Radio Act of 1927, one of every five existing stations had to be shut down because there was no space on the dial. In 1934 the Radio Act was amended by the Communications Act, that established the electromagnetic spectrum in the air as a national resource to be allocated and regulated by the federal government through the Federal Communications Commission. The FCC was ordered to grant "temporary" monopolies (licenses for three years) to those companies it decided were most likely to operate their stations "in the public interest, convenience or necessity."

Once radio broadcasting was stabilized by the Radio Act, there was serious attention to making it show a profit. Earlier suggestions that the new medium be operated by foundations, or a government trust fund, were rejected, with commercial broadcasters promising to devote a quarter of their programming to educational purposes as part of their obligation for being granted a temporary monopoly in the public airwaves. The alternative to public financing was advertising subsidies, but this met immediate and full-scale resistance from newspapers. The dailies, through their control of news agencies, forced radio to limit itself to negligible traces of news. They also left the impression with major advertisers that if the advertisers insisted on flirting with the new medium at the edge of town, they might find themselves locked out of their big newspapers house on the hill. For years, radio was insignificant as an advertising carrier.

Forced to woo advertisers away from newspapers, radio offered a relatively simple inducement. National advertisers in newspapers had to deal with each local paper individually, which was expensive and cumbersome. Radio offered to form a single network contract, with the network doing all the paper and contract work with individual stations. Thus, advertising inducements shaped broadcasting into a national medium, which it has tended to remain ever since.

Radio established itself in the American culture in the 1930s, as an entertainment and advertising medium through such popular national programs as *Amos 'n' Andy,* as a news medium with the international broadcasts from Europe during the growth of Nazism and the start of World War II, and as a public-affairs carrier with the Fireside Chats of Franklin Roosevelt during the Depression. Its revenues grew and its share of total advertising increased.

(This demonstrates a factor that is almost but not quite self-evident: whether it be papyrus scrolls or cable television, the immediate cause of widespread adoption of a communications medium is its content, not technical feasibility or price or promises of future utility. *Amos 'n' Andy* and FDR's Fireside Chats impelled Americans to buy radio sets in the 1930s, Howdy Doody, Milton Berle, and national political conventions sold initial television sets in the 1940s. FCC regulations, national networks, and improved receivers helped, but they only made possible the programming that convinced consumers to participate.)

Television after World War II made it clear that radio would become a secondary communications system. It was feared radio might even fade into obscurity, but this did not happen. The number of stations has increased steadily until today there are 4,200 commercial AM stations on the air, 2,000 FM stations, and 400 educational FM stations. The number of receivers has also grown until today there are 300 million, or one and a half for every man, woman, and child in the country. Nevertheless, there are still about 25 million people who live in areas that are not within range of any local night broadcasting, in such sparsely settled places that they are unattractive for local advertising purposes, and therefore devoid of the broadcasting services normal for the rest of the country.

The corporate leadership of radio differs dramatically from that of newspapers. The mythic emotion attached to printed journalism goes back centuries. Its heroes are part of the basic philosophic struggles of Western civilization—freedom of speech, of the press, of political activity. John Locke, Daniel Defoe, Jonathan Swift, John Milton, Voltaire, John Stuart Mill all fought in the borderline of political philosophy and journalism on which an independent press was founded. In the United States, John Peter Zenger, Thomas Paine, Elijah Lovejoy and William Allen White are accepted models of printing and publishing heroism, while editorial-corporate giants like Horace Greeley, James Gordon Bennett, Joseph Pulitzer, William Randolph Hearst, E. W. Scripps, and Adolph Ochs are standard names in the history books. The press, by name and by iron tradition, is enshrined in the First Amendment of the United States Constitution. The local roots of the American newspaper give it power, status, and high visibility in its own community. And while traditionally the architecture of the typical newspaper building is in a class with that of shoe factories, it is usually a factory in the center of the city with the air of a major institution. Publishers tend to identify themselves with the centuries of tradition and with the journalistic and corporate giants who preceded them.

Radio broadcasting is less than fifty years old. Its status in the First Amendment is still a matter of argument. It has its heroes but they are few and not generally operators of the medium in the way that Greeley and Pulitzer were. Instead they are employees like Edward R. Murrow and H. V. Kaltenborn, who, partly because they express themselves on an ephemeral medium that leaves historians no convenient record, are forgotten after their generation. The corporate leaders of radio, like William Paley and David Sarnoff, are not seen as very different from the corporate chiefs who manufacture automobiles and girdles. Their leadership has more to do with finance than with philosophy.

And, while newspapers began primarily as a medium for serious information, radio is primarily a medium of entertainment, which makes for greater popularity but not high status. Owners of radio stations, unlike publishers of newspapers, are not asked to speak at leading community affairs or granted honorary degrees, nor do they enjoy the other perquisites that attach more than a financial aura to corporate ownership.

Consequently, broadcasting properties are not heirlooms like newspapers, but financial investments that are used for profits and traded more or less like any other property.

Like newspapers, radio stations have owners and stockholders but they preside over a very different kind of production unit. The average circulation of a daily newspaper is 36,000 and such a paper requires about $4 million in physical equipment before it begins operations. The average radio station requires an investment in tangible assets of $162,000, mainly a studio with microphones, taping and other electronic and office equipment, plus a tower and transmitter.

The daily newspaper of average circulation has two hundred full-time employees. The average radio station has eleven full-time employees.

Thus, the average radio station is a small enterprise in terms of investment in tangible property and in full-time employees. Its expenses follow a different pattern from those of newspapers. Of radio stations reporting time sales of $25,000 or more a year, the largest single expense, 37 percent of the total average annual expenses of $195,000, goes to "general and administrative," making it a largely commercial rather than editorial and manufacturing process. Of the remainder, 32 percent goes to costs of programming content, 20 percent to selling of advertising, and 11 percent to technical and engineering costs.

There are a substantial number of monopoly radio stations but they are not the largest money makers nor do they approach the 97 percent of monopoly in newspaper cities. In 1967 there were 2,152 places with radio stations, 230 of them metropolitan areas. Of these, 1,544, or 72, percent had only one radio station. Fourteen percent of communities have two stations, 5 percent have three stations and so on, until nine metropolitan areas have 20 or more stations each.

The dependence of a community on a monopoly radio station is lessened by two factors: the monopoly status is based on the station's physical presence in the community, and in most places the station's signal can be heard in other nearby communities whose own monopoly stations reciprocally can be heard; and at night radio signals go much farther and clear channels covering large areas of the country are then heard in places with only one local station.

The social effect of a monopoly radio is further lessened by the fact that broadcasting has until now been only slightly concerned with original reporting and commentary on local issues, so dependence on a monopoly station is still largely a matter of dependence for music and other entertainment.

Revenues and profits of stations depend largely on the size of their communities. For example, average radio-station profit before federal income taxes in 1967 was $48,000, but the average for the 146 stations in metropolitan areas of 2 million population or more was $327,000.

Of 3,976 stations reporting to the FCC, 2,654 showed a profit and 1,322 showed a loss in 1967. But having a monopoly, or near-monopoly, even though it is in a small town, helps. The average loss of all radio stations that were in the red (33 percent) was $30,000. Of the 1,482 stations in one- and two-station communities, only 417, or 26 percent, reported losses and their average loss was $10,000.

Underlying traditional thinking about both printed and electronic media is the idea of an independent local organization providing daily information for its own community. This is moderated by nonlocal forces in both newspapers and broadcasting. In radio it is altered by networks, chains, and conglomerates.

Networking—the interconnection of a number of local stations to produce standardized programming with central control—developed early in radio. As soon as wire connections permitted local transmitters to be tied in to national studios, the economies of size immediately asserted themselves in both news and entertainment.

News of national and international events plainly was not going to be covered by the average local station with its eleven employees and its annual budget of $195,000. This was handled in the beginning as it was with newspapers, by buying at a relatively low cost a wire-service teletypewriter that sent national news into the local studio, to be read by a local announcer. This is still the technique used by most radio stations.

As radio developed it became clear that, to a greater extent than was true with newspapers, the personality of the announcer had an effect on the listener. A familiar voice and style, plus some personal interpretation of the news, was more appealing than an anonymous voice reading standard wire-service bulletins. The early news reporters and commentators on radio gave the medium whatever reputation it gained for original news dissemination: Kaltenborn, Murrow, William L. Shirer, Edgar Ansel Mowrer, Robert Trout, Dorothy Thompson, Quincy Howe, Raymond Swing. And, even though these pioneers in radio news commentary were not lavishly paid (while Kaltenborn was covering the Spanish Civil War he had to pay his own travel and living expenses and got $50 a broadcast from CBS), they were plainly more expensive than any local station would pay.

The need for spreading costs was even stronger in entertainment, where the salaries were high. Local stations could not begin to afford talent of their own that would compete with Eddie Cantor, Ed Wynn, and Jack Benny.

But the supreme imperative for networking was advertising. Newspapers pre-empted local retail advertising, not only by tradition and community power, but because they were a printed medium with illustrations and prices that could be compared visually. But there were no national newspapers, and the idea of millions of people listening to their favorite radio program was obviously one to attract advertisers. Since radio, in its early struggle against newspapers, offered to reach this audience with one program and one billing, and network and advertising headquarters were both in New York City, the network arrangement for radio was further speeded.

Today there are four national radio networks that own 19 stations outright (network ownership of local outlets is limited by the FCC) and have varying affiliations and contracts with other local stations. The network revenue in 1967 was $40 million, or only 5 percent of the total revenues of all 4,000 stations. This reflects the decline of the influence of networks in radio since the rise of television. In 1937 networks accounted for 48 percent of all radio income.

Radio chains, like newspaper chains, have been growing rapidly and for some of the same reasons. In 1939 there were 39 radio chains, 14 percent of all radio stations. In 1967 there were 373 chains that owned 31 percent of all stations. This growth is despite the FCC 7-7-7 rule that forbids common ownership of more than 7 AM stations, 7 FM, and 7 TV. Most radio-station trading is among chain owners, and each year shows a net increase in the number of stations owned by groups and an increase in the average number of stations per chain. A majority of the most powerful stations are chain-owned.

Networking, which began with a desire to control hardware and patents and then to attract advertising, has now grown into a major cultural force in the world. The dominant popular culture in the United States is produced by radio and TV networks and their contractors, and then exported to other countries.

Chain Ownership of Commercial AM Radio Stations, 1939–1967

Year	Number of Chains	Chain-Owned Stations	Total Number of Stations	Percent Chain-Owned
1939[1]	39	109	764	14.3
1951[2]	63	253	2,232	11.3
1960[2]	185	765	3,398	22.5
1964[2]	215	900	3,937	22.9
1967[3]	373	1,297	4,130	31.4

Table from *The First Freedom*, by Bryce W. Rucker, Southern Illinois Press, 1968, p. 189.
[1] Warren K. Agee, "Cross-Channel Ownership of Communications Media," *Journalism Quarterly*, December, 1949, p. 414.
[2] Data for years 1951, 1960, 1964, is from *Activities of Regulatory and Enforcement Agencies Relating to Small Business*, Part I, p. 88.
[3] Data for 1967 is from FCC records, *Broadcasting Yearbook*, 1967, and information released when broadcasting property sales were approved by the FCC.

The advantages of centralized production of radio programs are far greater than for newspaper material. Local advertisements and news play a much more important part in newspapers than in broadcasting. And whether or not the newspaper material is locally or nationally originated, the process of manufacturing the printed paper and distributing it takes most of the paper's manpower and production facilities. Broadcasting has almost automatic "production and distribution." Once the material is received in the local studio, its dissemination to the audience is a matter of electronic transmission from its tower. Thus, a program sent by wire from New York to a local station is sent to the home receiver almost automatically. The cost of producing the New York program is fixed, so the greater the number of local stations that share in its distribution, the greater the overall profit.

Another advantage of networking is program promotion. Newspapers tend to go into each home on schedule, to be read by subscribers in a reliable habit that makes certain that major items will always be seen. Broadcasting offers several alternative channels in most communities, and there is no fixed time for the audience to absorb any particular channel. Thus, an ingrained habit of weekly or daily programming, fixed by a highly popular or well-known personality, is important to guarantee a large audience. The alternative is notification of special programs through program listing, advertisements in newspapers, on billboards, and on the broadcast channel itself. Here, too, a unified national system of promotion is cheaper than a strictly local production that must be promoted in each town at a different time.

Thus, economies of size work toward giantism and national networks with more force in broadcasting than with newspapers.

Radio Corporation of America, for example, was originally formed in 1919 as a consortium of General Electric, Westinghouse, and Western Electric, the manufacturing arm of AT&T. Their purpose was to form an American cartel that would wrest dominance in American communications from the British-based Marconi operations. They would share in the resulting radio and other communications patents, and divide the profits. General Electric and Westinghouse were given the exclusive right to manufacture radio sets and RCA was to sell them. AT&T was granted the monopoly in the manufacture, lease, and sale of transmitters.

AT&T apparently was the first to appreciate the profit in linking stations together. It owned WEAF in New York City and in 1923 added a station in Boston, then one in Washington, D.C. By 1924 AT&T had a twenty-three-station national network. When RCA decided to do the same thing, AT&T blocked it by threatening to deny any RCA network use of AT&T telephone lines, which were, of course, needed to make a network. By 1926 AT&T and RCA had reached an agreement: in return for letting RCA go into the radio network business, AT&T would be given exclusive right to supply radio stations with communications lines. Once that division of labor was made, Westinghouse and General Electric also went into the network business.

In September, 1926, RCA formed the National Broadcasting Company as its broadcasting subsidiary, with a twenty-one-station network. On November 15, 1926, it made a continuous four-hour broadcast from a central studio to all twenty-one NBC stations plus four independent stations that had agreed to carry portions of the network program.

By 1927 the NBC network had bifurcated into the Red network and the Blue network. Where NBC could not buy powerful local stations outright it made contracts of affiliation in which the station contracted to carry certain network programs in return for some of the resulting revenues. In 1943, NBC so dominated national radio that the FCC forced it to divest itself of one of its networks and the NBC Blue network was sold to a firm that called itself the American Broadcasting Company.

After NBC's original success, independent stations tried to compete by a number of devices to pool their markets and programming, the result finally being formation of the Columbia Broadcasting System. It was bought in 1928 by William Paley. Six years later the Mutual Broadcasting System was formed by a number of powerful radio stations.

Over a twenty-year period radio moved onto the center stage of American mass communications, sharing attention with newspapers until it, too, was moved aside to make way for a new medium, television.

Television had been broadcast experimentally in England in 1927 and in the United States in 1928. RCA began experiments in 1936 and had seventeen experimental stations by 1937. The New York

World's Fair in 1939 was probably the first significant impact television made on public consciousness. The first FCC license for commercial television was granted July 1, 1941, to an RCA station. Ten stations followed on the air but World War II intervened and during the war only six stations broadcast. There were not quite five thousand home receiving sets in existence at the end of World War II.

Corporate developments in television grew out of radio. Sophistication with electronic media in the previous twenty-five years produced both good and bad effects for the public. RCA, which had the firmest foothold in the new medium, argued for restricting television transmission to the limited airwaves called Very High Frequencies, which would permit only twelve channels throughout the country. CBS wanted the government to use the less crowded and spacious Ultra High Frequencies. RCA won and this preordained commercial television to a limited number of outlets whose programming would be controlled by a few national organizations: in the scarcity of channels only the highest bidders would be able to compete for entry into the consumer's home.

By 1948 the 5,000 home sets had increased to a million; four years later there were 17 million. By now there are one or more sets in 60 million homes. These are served by 506 VHF commercial stations on the air, 177 commercial UHF stations, 77 VHF and 103 UHF educational stations.

Television followed some of the same corporate patterns as radio, except that it rapidly became a much bigger business controlled by fewer operators. The year financial statistics began to be significant for television, 1948, it had $9 million in advertising sales and radio had $416 million. In 1954 radio revenues took their first downturn since the Depression, to $451 million; television that year had $538 million. In 1968 radio had $1 billion, television $2 billion.

Television lies between newspapers and radio in the size of individual corporations. Where the average daily paper has an investment of $4 million in tangible assets, and the average radio station $162,000, the average television station has $1.93 million in original costs for physical assets. This is a substantially higher level of financing than for radio, but it has substantially higher potential profits. In 1967, not a particularly good year for television, the average station revenues were $3.76 million and expenses $3 million. This cash flow does not require a large establishment either in physical space or in manpower. Where the average daily newspaper employs two hundred, and the average radio station eleven, the average television station has sixty-five employees. In the budget of the average television station, 10 percent was for technical production costs, 63 percent for the cost of programs, 8 percent for selling advertising, and 19 percent general and administrative costs.

Profits of television corporations follow a clear pattern: network ownership or affiliation is most profitable, independent operation less; big-city profits are higher, small-city, lower.

Of all stations reporting to the FCC in 1967, 83 percent showed a profit, but 84 percent of network affiliates were profitable, compared with 72 percent of independent stations.

Of stations with profits exceeding $5 million, 16 were network affiliated and 1 an independent; profits between $3 and $5 million were reported by 16 network affiliates, no independents.

A curious pattern of profits appears when stations in markets of only one or two television stations show an average profits of only $91,000, but stations in markets that have three or more stations show an average profit of $820,000. Monopoly or near-monopoly does not pay in television, but that is because of the "artificial" shortage of channels in large cities. The "artificial" shortage is in economic terms: there is no balance achievable between the demand for buying advertising time on television and the number of channels available to meet that demand. The crowding of the popular VHF spectrum, that permits only seven effective channels regardless of the population density, means that rates and profits increase from this shortage. It is not surprising that the market value of stations in the top markets range between $100 million and $550 million dollars, even though their tangible assets are a minute percentage of this and their basic license to operate costs $150.

Given the relative shortage of effective television channels in metropolitan areas it is not surprising that networking of centrally controlled content for television is far greater than for radio and newspapers. Local live programming represents about 13 percent of all TV content. A former FCC chairman, E. William Henry, said that for the remaining 87 percent of the time local stations "throw the network switch, or open a syndicated film package as they would a can of beans." The percentage of nationally controlled content during the prime-time hours of seven to eleven is 95 percent.

Nor is there any doubt of the economic advantage of one large system over many small ones. The three television networks and their 15 wholly-owned stations in 1967 earned $11,000 per employee and had annual profits before federal taxes of 108 percent of the depreciated value of their assets. The 604 other television stations earned $8,100 per employee and had profits of 50 percent of the depreciated value of their assets.

But this economic advantage is at the cost of local community needs in diversity of programming and availability of content for special audiences. This is particularly important in the consideration of news, which is especially sensitive to localism and to diversity of outlets.

Despite the location of stations and the allocation of frequencies on a local basis, advertising on radio and television to a much greater degree than in newspapers reaches a single national audience. In 1967, national advertising accounted for 81 percent of all television advertising revenues, 36 percent of all radio, and only 19 percent of newspaper. Newspapers, maximizing the audience for its 81 percent of local advertising revenues, must stress local news and entertainment features for economic as well as social reasons; television with precisely the opposite ratio of 81 percent national advertising, stresses national, or at least nonlocal, programming.

Thus, the rationale for television: One Big Audience. Ratings of share of audience, to capture advertising, accentuate the single biggest winner. Coming in second even though it may mean reaching millions of households is considered a loss. No newspaper in the country reaches as many as 10 million people, but a prime-time television program that reaches only 10 million is considered a failure.

Stations are placed locally in the 235 major markets with limitations on transmitting power so that they will not interfere with other stations in nearby markets that have similar frequencies. The assumption of public policy that places stations in localities with limited ranges is that broadcasting should serve local purposes. If this were not the case, it would be relatively simple to use a small number of transmitters to reach the whole country at much less cost. But the economics of advertising in broadcasting demands national-scale audiences listening to the same program.

To reach an audience of perhaps fifty million people who will include a vast range of interests, personalities, ages, and social and economic backgrounds, it is necessary to obey two imperatives. One is to find common-denominator interests that span a wide spectrum of people. And it requires highly specialized talent and techniques to maintain attention at a peak over long periods of time, without using the appeal of specialized interests of particular audiences. This extremely high degree of commercial professionalism is expensive, resulting in an estimated cost of $200,000 an hour for national television programming. It is profitable when it achieves top ratings since one minute of commercial time on such a program may sell for $65,000. But it means that national commercial programming must largely ignore collections of minority interests—which is the true nature of the population. Variations of personalities, occupations, hobbies, recreational tastes, and family situation give different groups intense interest in different things. But television is constantly trying to reach One Maximum Audience. Public policy for allocation of transmitters does not permit One Maximum National Transmitter but many local ones, so broadcasting achieves by programming and affiliation contract what it is not permitted to do by electronics.

Thus, networks own programming and their own local stations or negotiate contracts with locally owned stations to commit themselves to carry network programs. For example, in the top fifty markets where 75 percent of the population live, three television networks, NBC, CBS, and ABC, have 94 percent of the audience, as measured in weekly circulation. Thus, three organizations, and sometimes three men, decide what 70 percent of the American population will see on television. The reach for a single audience also takes the form of corporate chains of locally based stations which under common ownership can sell time and transmit programming in large demographic units impossible for a single station. Both have the advantage of using collections of audiences beyond local dimensions and the spreading of the cost of highly professionalized programming over many stations.

In television, chains control 74 percent of all commercial stations.

The FCC forbids any one corporation from owning more than seven stations, of which only five can be VHF. The tendency is to achieve this maximum, as shown in the following table compiled by Bryce Rucker for his book *The First Freedom* (1968).

Growth in Sizes of Television Chains 1956–67[1]

Size of Chain	Number of Chain Owners 1956	1967
Seven Stations	0	2
Six Stations	3	8
Five Stations	4	19
Four Stations	5	21
Three Stations	22	34
Two Stations	46	63
Totals	80	147

Source: Data for 1956 and 1964 are from FCC Public Notice B, December 18, 1964. The total number of chains given here for 1956 and 1964 is one less than figures given in Table 15. The FCC notice did not explain this obvious discrepancy. Data for 1967 are from *Broadcasting Yearbook, 1967,* corrected by cross-checking with an FCC computer print-out of station ownership and revised to reflect station sales through mid-1967. From *The First Freedom*, p. 195.

[1] The column totals for any one year exceed the number of television stations held by chains. Ownership interests in some stations are held by more than one chain.

As Rucker suggests, the FCC rule may be subject to significant evasion by interlocking directors and common ownership of chains by individuals, so that there may be superchains made up of collections of chains that are not subject to the reporting rules of the FCC, which are directed at corporate rather than individual holdings.

The significance of this for news is evident: it militates against local news since this must be locally generated and is of little commercial value elsewhere in a chain or network. And it increases the concentration of control over public information in the hands of a few men and organizations.

This is further accentuated by the heavy newspaper investment in broadcasting properties. Newspapers, for example, own 25 percent of all television stations in the country, and these stations have 34 percent of all revenues (revenues are a rough measure of share of total audience). In the top 25 television markets, where a majority of American households are located, newspapers own 35 percent of all television stations and have 38 percent of revenues. In 16 markets where there are only 2 television stations, newspapers own over half the stations. Newspapers own 249 AM radio stations, which is only 8 percent of all stations, but 97 percent of these are in the top ten markets, where a third of the population lives, and 80 percent are in the top 3 markets.

Newspapers and broadcasters represent separate news and public-affairs systems. In a democracy a large number of distinct voices in public affairs is needed. The existence of chains and of newspaper-broadcasting cross-ownership diminishes the opportunities for both local news and diverse views of information, even though the ecomomics are advantageous.

Diversity of programming is influenced by another corporate development, conglomerates, the common ownership of dissimilar enterprises.

The causes of conglomerate formation are slightly different from those encouraging chains. Conglomerates offer expansion into diversified activities so that the decline of any one kind of business will not strand the parent corporation with a shriveling market. A particular form of conglomerate is organized around the collection and distribution of information in all forms. Many large electronics firms, for example, have acquired book-publishing companies. Having looked ahead at the greatly expanded capacities of information transmission facilities, they realize that control of content will become increasingly profitable, as well as control of the mechanical systems that transmit the content.

For example, the Times-Mirror Co., parent corporation of the Los Angeles *Times,* the third largest daily paper in the country, is a conglomerate that owns over twenty subsidiary firms that had gross revenues of $350 million in 1968, and was engaged in publishing Bibles, dictionaries, medical books, encyclopedias, art books, law books, telephone directories, road maps, flight manuals; was one of the largest publishers of hardcover and paperback books in the world; manufactured slide rules, scientific instruments, filing systems, and plywood; and operated cable-television systems and real-estate holdings.

In broadcasting, NBC is owned by RCA. It is significant that in 1969 the parent firm announced its intention to change its name from Radio Corporation of America to RCA Corporation: radio now represented only 2 percent of its business and the corporation's activities were no longer limited to America. In additon to being in the broadcasting business, a minority part of which is news and public affairs, RCA also sells household appliances and aerospace systems; is a major defense supplier; owns Random House and other book-publishing firms, as well as Arnold Palmer Enterprises and Hertz car and truck rental business; is a leading international telegraph company; owns RCA Victor records; and has extensive foreign investments with just one subsidiary having activities in ninety-three foreign countries.

CBS also has a large number of nonbroadcasting and nonjournalistic enterprises under its control, including Columbia Records, Fender Musical Instruments, the New York Yankees baseball team, Creative Playthings, educational film strips, Holt, Rinehart & Winston book publishing, movie studios, medical textbooks, the magazines *Field & Stream, Popular Gardening, Living Outdoors,* and *Home Modernizing Guide.* It has investments in underwater exploration and control of companies in at least eighteen foreign countries, is an important supplier of the defense and aerospace activities (in 1965 it told its stockholders that it was working hard to increase defense and space orders), and in 1965 had $21 million invested in the credit affiliates of General Motors, Ford, and Chrysler.

The other network, American Broadcasting Company, is rapidly diversifying and in 1968 already had broadcast properties and sales in eleven Latin American and seven other foreign countries, owned 399 movie theaters, was in the movie-producing business, manufactured and sold phonograph records, published some leading farm magazines, and owned tourist resorts in Florida and California.

For every dollar the television networks grossed in their broadcasting activities in the United States, they grossed three in nonbroadcasting activities, and this 75 percent dependence on revenues gave them an intense corporate interest in, among other things, maintaining a high level of defense and space spending by the federal government; which particular books and authors received favorable exposure; the promotion of particular sports like golf and baseball; the growth of rock-'n'-roll and other styles of music using electrical instruments; high sales of automobiles and minimum legal restrictions on consumer loans; which records and songs are played on radio and television and which recording stars get the most profitable exposure;

which movies and therefore which stars are popularized; and which areas of the country are made to look attractive for tourism. Furthermore, each company has a serious financial stake in political developments in a number of foreign regimes and therefore of American policy toward those regimes. These are the natural subject matter of news and public-affairs programming.

In journalism there are daily decisions to select the relatively few items for display from the countless total of potential public events. This gives the news system great discretion in the pattern of subjects brought to the public's attention and the context in which these subjects will be treated. In addition to selection of items from the standard daily news services, there are decisions on which public events will be covered in what depth, like space shots, or which of many congressional hearings will be televised and which will not.

Major journalistic organizations take the initiative to pursue in depth or to make an initial exposé of subjects that do not appear in public spontaneously or are not thrust into view by others. In newspapers this takes the form of special articles, crusades, and exposés. In television it is in the form of documentaries or selections of guests and topics on interview programs.

A corporation in which journalism is merely a by-product has two problems of credibility. One is the question of actual operation so that news selection by its journalistic subsidiary is not influenced by the public relations and political desires of the parent firm. The other is that even if it operates journalistically in good faith, it will suffer from public suspicion. It is normal for corporations to attempt to influence the news in their favor and the public will periodically speculate whether corporations that own journalism firms deny themselves this normal strategy with their own subsidiary.

Corporation A may manufacture a weapons system it truly believes is in the national interest to buy, a belief not lessened by the fact that it may be good for the corporation. In addition to its private dealings with the government, Corporation A also conducts a standard program of public persuasion. This includes a conventional set of public-relations moves: it sends data and photographs to editors and special writers, urging them to use it sympathetically; it holds press conferences to which it invites press representatives; it demonstrates the system for the press in a field exercise that is meaningless unless the press attends, which means that the most important step is to get the reporters assigned to the demonstration; when its spokesmen testify in public or make speeches, it urges editors and reporters to cover the event and, if they should not, the corporation makes its own films and transcripts and delivers them to editors. The more sophisticated corporate public-relations men have recognized the key points at which events enter the news net, the gatekeepers, and they cultivate these men over the years by being genuinely useful and truthful about specialized information in preparation for the crucial time when the corporation has a major stake in getting the gatekeepers to place corporate information into the news system. One of the concerns of ethical journalists and gatekeepers is to prevent the distortion of their professional judgment by this offer of an amiable symbiotic relationship. The journalist also must concern himself with the possibility that under extreme pressure a corporate representative failing to persuade a gatekeeper will go to the gatekeeper's employer.

What if the gatekeeper's employer is Corporation A? Does this Corporation A deny itself the practices its competitor companies use in trying to get their information into the news? But if he uses the same techniques as his competitors it is not really the same: when he attempts to persuade an editor he does so as the editor's employer.

These have not been academic problems in the past nor are they in the present. From 1911 to 1926, the Hearst newspaper, magazine, and movie empire agitated continuously for a declaration of war against Mexico. This campaign included a spectacular series of articles alleging that the Mexican government had attempted to bribe United States Senators with over a million dollars, a charge shown later to have been based on fraudulent documents. During this period, most of the readers of Hearst's newspapers had no way of knowing that Hearst's immediate motivation was to protect his family's holdings of twenty-five hundred square miles of land in Mexico against a series of regimes that toyed with expropriation. There is no doubt that Hearst, like most men, believed that what was good for his financial fortunes was good public policy. The difference was that Hearst, through his control of the mass media, had unique access to the attention and thinking of millions of his fellow citizens, a responsibility that should imply no hidden, self-serving motives.

The late Rafael Trujillo regularly purchased sympathetic news treatment in American media. He paid $2,000 a month to the Hearst-operated International News Service, then one of the three standard American wire agencies, to place Trujillo propaganda masquerading as news into American newsrooms. In 1959 one of Trujillo's agents handed $750,000 in cash to the president of a major American radio broadcasting chain, Mutual Broadcasting System, in return for an agreement to broadcast fourteen minutes a day of news sympathetic to Trujillo. (The network president, Alexander Guterma, later went to jail for a different kind of fraud.)

Less dramatic corporate relations may have a quieter and longer-lasting influence. The staff report of the Subcommittee on Domestic Finance of the House Committee on Banking and Currency on July 8, 1968, noted that banks often have important fiscal holdings in the news media, and at the same time, through holdings in other enter-prises, are in a potential position to influence attitudes: "Several newspaper and magazine publishers have large blocks of stock held by commercial banks covered in the Subcommittee's survey. This included 18 companies publishing 31 newspapers and 17 magazines as well as operating 17 radio and TV stations."

The First National Bank of Chicago, for example, at the time of the committee's survey held 32 percent of the Class A common stock of David McKay book publishers and 6.3 percent of the common stock of Holt, Rinehart & Winston, Inc. (whose majority interest is held by Columbia Broadcasting System); had one director on the board of Time Inc.; and held 100 percent of the common stock and 100 percent of Class B common stock of the Copley Press. The bank, as holders of voting stock or as participating directorships in boards of journalistic companies, has a fiduciary obligation to protect what it conceives to be the financial value of the property. Ethical journalism is frequently called upon to make decisions that are contrary to its property interests and is expected always to make news decisions ignoring its private profit. Thus, corporate partnerships between journalistic and nonjournalistic firms may place in power men who can act properly by ordinary commercial custom, but still compro-mise the integrity of the news.

The extent of direct, cynical orders from above to distort the news is generally exaggerated. It happens occasionally but not normally. Professionalism in news handling is a major protection. But it is not unusual for the news media to protect their corporate interests by using their special access to public attention. A study reported in the spring, 1967, *Journalism Quarterly* by David R. Bowers stated that in measuring the incidence of business-office intervention into the news process among newspapers, "Publisher activity is higher in areas which conceivably might affect the revenue of the newspaper directly or indirectly than in social issues such as politics, race, religion, labor or war." Any issue that affects profits on newspapers receives extraordinary attention in the news. For example, a bill supported by counsel for the American Newspaper Publishers Association that would exempt 3 percent of the 1,752 daily newspapers from antitrust laws has been prominently displayed in the printed news media for three years that it was argued in Congress.

More subtle is the failure to display news that has negative connotations for the journalistic corporation. Though the press in principle places a high value on crusades in the public interest, the American press for years was silent on criticism of automobiles, tobacco, and food supplies, all major sources of advertising revenues for newspapers. Only when criticism of these products by others became overwhelming did the press take notice. Yet, on other subjects, like governmental failings and racketeers, the press has been a consistent initiator of investigation and exposé.

The selection of which informational and cultural areas of American life will be treated by the mass media is a complicated and obscure process. That economic self-interest plays a part is beyond question. But how much of a part when journalism becomes a minority by-product of larger corporations has not yet been sufficiently studied.

All of these considerations could be changed radically by innovations in the technology of news. Newspapers are now typically multi-million-dollar corporations that spend over half their money on the distribution of their information after editorial processing. Broadcasters pay only 10 percent of a much smaller investment for the same step of the process, and as a result there are, despite severe technical limitations on electromagnetic space in the air, five times more broadcasting stations emanating daily information than there are newspapers.

If in the future journalistic firms do not have to maintain expensive manufacturing plants but send their news electronically to the consumer, and if the shortage of space in the air is overcome by sending information through cables to the home, not only will the nature of news corporations change, but the number of them.

The change in economic constraints on news could produce a radically altered market place of political and cultural ideas.

Is Print Dying?

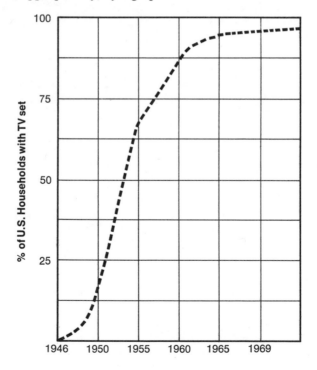

The most rapid change in popular communications and culture the human race has ever experienced is the introduction of television to the American home. The incredible growth of this graphic medium is illustrated, appropriately, by a graph:

In the 1950–1960 decade, the American family reoriented itself around the new activity. Television quickly became more common than flush toilets, running water, bathtubs, showers, electric and gas stoves, telephones, and automobiles. In ten years the electronic box was integrated into the patterns of personal and national life.

The TV set of the average family is now operating more than six hours a day. It communicates to all levels of society. Since the viewer need understand neither printed nor spoken words to be influenced, this includes the very young, to whom it transmits meaning almost before anyone else except, possibly, a mother, though in hours per day the child sees more of television than of his mother. By the time an American child is eighteen years old he has spent twenty thousand hours in front of his television set, more time than he has spent in classrooms, churches, and all other educational and cultural activities. This alters perspectives, values, and habits of communication.

Television gained dominance when, for other reasons, the American family was being transformed. The influence of parents over children diminished as jobs and civic-social activities increasingly took adults farther away from home and neighborhood. Household need for the child dropped almost to the disappearing point as affluence, urbanization, and labor-saving devices in the home made children's work contributions unnecessary. The daily lives of adults and of children became more widely separated as preparation for white-collar careers sent children into long hours of school by day, with lonely homework in the evening. Universality of automobiles gave adults and juveniles separate social lives. Much of the traditional basis for adult influence on the young disappeared but schools, public recreation, and the design of communities largely ignored the profound change. Into the void stepped the new electronic teacher-playmate-babysitter-parent, designed primarily not to educate the mind, develop the personality, or enrich the national culture but to sell the maximum amount of merchandise at minimum cost. In the process it effectively implanted a new way to communicate.

Television's substitution of moving pictures and sounds for cold print, combined with the paperless manipulation of information by that other new electronic presence, the computer, challenged the communications technique that has dominated Western culture for twenty-five hundred years. It raised the question: Is print dying?

According to the doctrine enunciated by Marshall McLuhan and his followers, printed words are an invention contrary to the inherent nature of man. In this view, the one-step-after-another sequence required by the written sentence, and the narrowing of the intake to the highly intellectualized interpretation of abstract symbols, have forced modern man into arbitrary and inhibiting ways of perceiving his world, suppressing other senses and sensitivities. The new electronic media represent a return to a richer and more natural way for man to participate in his environment, engaging more of the senses and more levels of the brain than those used for abstract reasoning. As new generations respond to this multisensory medium, there will be a revival of the dominance of preprint communications—sight, sound, smell, touch, taste—and a disappearance of "the tyranny of print." Some in this school, at least some of the time, insist that the printed document will disappear; at other times it is said that it will survive only as an archaic form unimportant to the average person.

A careful view of the impact of electronic communication is found in the works of men like Harold A. Innis (*The Bias of Communication,* 1951), but most of Innis's work was done before the emergence of the computer and television as mass phenomena. The McLuhan influence has been more dramatic and, in our time, more influential, creating not only a popular dogma but a significant body of belief among some scientists, scholars, academics, and operators of the mass media.

For a civilization that has been called a "paper culture" this is not a small matter. If print is an artificial and inhibiting force in contemporary life, about to be displaced by multisensory, nonsequential experiences, the principal means by which society copes with its environment will be altered.

Most of organized American society is still based on documents. Formal education of the young uses print more than any other medium. So do scholarship and science. Contemporary law, government, and commerce would collapse if they were suddenly denied published paper.

The news system, even with the rapid growth of electronic journalism in the last forty years, is still essentially organized around print, both in the quantity of news delivered and in the human network that collects and processes news. The average American family pays for and receives 26,000 newspaper pages a year. The newspaper industry, whose principal hold on its customers is news, hires 360,000 persons, while television, for which news is a secondary product, employs 53,000 for all purposes.

Yet, the present domination of printed news does not mean it is guaranteed to survive. If the main thrust of the McLuhanite thesis is correct, the intellectual, emotional, and social nature of contemporary man will be so profoundly altered by the electronic media that the dislocations already experienced—the "generation gap," accelerated mobilization of public opinion, and abrupt change in life styles and values—are only a mild preliminary, and in this convulsion printed news would disappear.

At various times McLuhan and some of his collaborators have suggested that the new electronic communications already have started the death throes of publishing, that reading is declining, and the television generation already has begun to reject print.

This thesis is supported by a quite different school, those intellectuals and aesthetes who see a decline in popular values, a deterioration of taste and of intellectuality, brought on by the spread of mass culture. This, they assert, is bringing a decline in reading.

For example, Clifton Fadiman in 1949 wrote: "It seems fairly clear that in our time the attrition of one kind of attention—the ability to read prose and poetry of meaning and substance—is becoming more and more widespread; and that the faculty of attention in general is undergoing a wholesale displacement away from ideas and abstractions toward things and techniques . . . the decline in the ability to read is distressing."

Fadiman's assertion is frequently accepted on its face value, reinforcing the idea that reading and abstract reasoning are declining in the American population. The McLuhanites proclaim this in joy, many intellectuals in despair. But, whether said in celebration or in sadness, it is not true.

Whatever other cultural change this generation has seen, and whatever the growth of electronic media, the ability to read and the power to reason abstractly have never been higher. During the rise of television, more children were educated in the print-oriented intellectual process than ever before.

The percentage of children exposed to systematic education, which today for all practical purposes is synonymous with reading, has steadily increased. The proportion of American children five to seventeen enrolled in school rose from 74 percent in 1910 to 86 percent in 1966.

Of all children formally enrolled, today more actually attend. In 1920 at least 25 percent of children formally enrolled were absent on an average day; today it is 8 percent. The days of required school per year have risen 10 percent since 1920. The number of days actually attended has risen 25 percent.

During this increased schooling, the curriculum has become more difficult, more literary, and more intellectualized.

In the 1960s the average child was superior to his 1950s counterpart in rapid reading, comprehension of material, word recognition, use of words, understanding of mathematical concepts, and solving of mathematical problems—in short, traditional intellectual activity. As reported in *Test Data as Social Indicators,* by William B. Schrader, the 1954 performance that placed a child in the 50th percentile, with half of all children doing better than he, if repeated exactly in 1964 would find 58 percent of all children doing better.

Perhaps the most extensive single program to test what has happened to the intellectuality of American children also brackets the television era. The University of Iowa has conducted statewide testing in the Iowa elementary schools since 1935. In 1965 they gave 38,000 pupils exactly the same test given Iowa public-school children in 1940. The test covered reading, vocabulary, map reading, use of references, use of index, use of dictionaries, reading of graphs and tables, punctuation, capitalization, language usage, spelling, sentence sense, arithmetic concepts, arithmetic computations, and arithmetic problem solving.

In all categories but two there was a significant increase in the 1965 performance. The two exceptions were spelling and arithmetic computation, both mechanical skills. The ability to conceptualize, to handle abstract symbols, to read and comprehend, and to reason were all higher. A. N. Hieronymus, Professor of Education and Psychology at Iowa, said the results are understated in the formal scores. "There were a great many perfect scores in 1965, especially in grades 5 and 8, which attenuated the differences. Tests which were of optimal difficulty in 1940 were found to be too easy in 1965."

In research and study techniques, the 1965 children were almost a full year ahead of the 1940 generation; in use of printed and written language, they were over a full year ahead; and in handling mathematical concepts and problems, they were about a half year ahead.

The evidence is overwhelming that the American child of the 1960s has a more highly trained mind, is capable of reading and writing better, and can handle theories and abstract reasoning more skillfully than any previous generation.

The same applies to higher education and adults. The increase in college enrollments is spectacular, from 1940 to 1964, almost seven times greater than the increase in population. The sale of serious books climbs steadily upward, especially through the period of mass television. From 1950 to 1967, the number of new titles of books increased 380 percent, and these were mainly in subjects that might surprise both the doctrinaire McLuhanites and those who are sure that popular culture is destroying the American mind: art, history, literature, science, and the fastest-rising category, sociology and economics. From 1954 to 1963 money spent on books increased two and a half times. From 1945 to 1965, the average family more than doubled the number of newspaper pages it bought every year.

The McLuhanite claim of the death of print is not only premature but contrary to all the evidence. The elitist proclamation that the American brain is increasingly addled and indiscriminate is not borne out by the best information available on the intellectual activity of the average American.

What convinces the McLuhanites of the decrease in the strength of print is not clear, since none of the objective evidence supports this. What may mislead those who despair at mass culture and education is their own exaggerated view of the past splendor of elite education and intellectualism. The style of Cambridge and Oxford in England and, by extension, Harvard and Yale in the United States, for many years symbolized high culture, intellectualism, and aestheticism. But it was, at best, a symbol: the taste and behavior of the typical university graduates were hardly equal to the symbol of high culture. And, whatever the mental and aesthetic qualities of the average graduate of the elite universities of the pre-World War I era, they represented a tiny fraction of the total population.

Believers in the deterioration of American (and British) culture seem to compare the small educational elite of the past (in 1922 only

9 percent of Americans of college age went to college) with the total population of today, a comparison distorted even further by the romantic view of the former recipients of higher education. This nostalgic view generally forgets that not so long ago a majority of the population was educationally invisible. It is only in this generation that there is a serious attempt to expose the total school-age population to preparation for intellectual competence and higher education. And the best evidence is that the generality of this present population performs intellectual tasks, including reading and handling of abstractions, better than the earlier educated minority.

This is not to say that contemporary education is adequate. It has grievous failures. This is partly because it is attempting a more ambitious task than ever before, since in the past students not committed at an early age to careers in higher education were not given intellectual training. And it is partly because schools and other institutions have not yet adjusted to the shrinkage of the role of family life as training for the future. When most families were on farms and men worked at traditional crafts, children's imitation of adults was adequate preparation for the future, since the young eventually repeated their parents' occupations, place of residence, religion, politics, and style of life. But when each generation evolves a different future imitation of parents is not enough. No institution, including schools has adequately assumed the new role of preparing juveniles for adulthood in a transformed world.

But this is not the same as a general decline in intellectuality among contemporary American youth. It may be deplorable that the young do not receive an education more appropriate to the demand of their own society, but this does not mean that they have les intellectual skill. They plainly have more. And, whatever the evolu tion of culture in the future, higher intellectuality today include greater capacity for reading and abstract reasoning.

Increased use of print and heightened skill in abstract reasoning while disproving the general McLuhanite claim, does not vitiate th McLuhan thesis that there is a new emphasis on nonprinted an nonverbal culture. Much of formal education in the past ignore aesthetic and artistic qualities in personality development and i social life. The new media have stimulated a resurgence. But th same generation that is devoted to rock music, light shows, th psychedelic experience, and other forms of highly subjective emotional expression are also the most skillful readers in history.

Nevertheless, the claim that print is infected with a terminal disease continues to have considerable force, causing large communications corporations to consider a future without printed documents, even though the claim borders on fantasy. It is part of the McLuhan theory that primitive cultures were essentially oral and auditory and therefore superior, while modern society is largely limited to intake by the eyes and therefore narrower. Primitive societies, of course, were intensely visual—the American Indian and the Polynesian sailor were celebrated for being able to interpret the world through acute vision. And the modern American is so dependent on his auditory sense that he sometimes feels trapped: two of the most common communications systems around him, radio and the telephone, are completely auditory. Essential rituals of work and social life are the committee meeting, conference, lecture, cocktail parties, and group sessions by which most of the organizational work of society is consummated. These are so intensely dependent on the ear that the more daring innovations—including those pressed by dedicated McLuhanites—attempt to diminish dependence on the ear by increasing their use of visual techniques.

The quintessence of the McLuhanite thesis is that "the medium is the message," that content of a communication is insignificant compared to the sensation of receiving the communication. Insofar as this means that different methods of communication have different emotional and social effects this is true. Print is a lonely, intellectualized medium and rock-'n'-roll light shows are experiences in group emotion. But these distinctions preceded Gutenberg: Socratic dialogues had a different impact from gladiator fights in the Colosseum. But to accept this, as is commonly done, to mean that the specific content of communication is relatively unimportant so long as it evokes a given level of response is another example of the astonishing willingness of many to suspend critical judgment when confronted with the multimedia dogma, as though messages were roughly equal in such users of the same medium of communications as Matthew, Mark, Luke, and John, Torquemada, Thomas Paine, King George III, King Louis XIV, Sigmund Freud, John Milton, Karl Marx, Adam Smith, Adolf Hitler, and Albert Schweitzer.

It is possible that the conviction that "the medium is the message" has been given added weight because of McLuhan's involvement in commercial advertising. It is closer to the truth that the medium is the message where a million dollars spent on advertising for one detergent is about equally effective if spent for a different detergent. Cynical manipulation of symbols is an ancient trick, and the fact that it sometimes succeeds has been accepted as a universal communications theory that overlooks the fact that it usually doesn't succeed, and that the failures of such manipulations increase as they affect personal lives.

Despite the dogmatic naïveté of McLuhanism, it proclaims a genuinely powerful force: electronics does permit the creation, manipulation, and reproduction of impulses receivable by sight, hearing, touch, smell, and taste. Thus, electronics, combined with refinement of knowledge of the mechanisms by which men think and feel, can produce new modes of communication beyond the printed sentence. It is safe to assume that this multimedia approach has just begun in elementary form with television; the increased use of graphs, charts, three-dimensional constructions sometimes accompanied by sound and color; the rapid flashing of pictures, colors, and forms at almost subliminal speeds; the use of the hand-held movie cameras and tape recorders for the young to "see" and study their environment. The symbolism of the printed word transmits meaning. But so can the symbolism of colors, forms, and sounds, and in ways richer, emotionally broader, and more versatile than anything possible on a static piece of paper. But this, too, is quite different from the assertion that words and sentences expressed in print constitute obsolete artifacts.

Print might very well lose its present share of artificial communication. If it does it will do so because of forces less exotic than a new cult of sensory salvation. The fact is that print, for quite prosaic reasons, may be reaching the upper limits of its usefulness to man: the accumulation of published paper since the invention of printing five hundred years ago has become so massive that it is too difficult to manage.

All the recorded scientific and technical literature in the history of man—omitting, for the moment, literature, law, government, and accounting—reached 2.3 trillion words by 1970. By 1982 it will double to 4.6 trillion words. Twelve years after that, in 1994, if the historic rate continues, it will double again to 9.2 trillion words.

One of print's major advantages is its permanent memory. As long as the type does not fade and the paper does not disintegrate, it is available forever in its original form. This is properly celebrated for what it is, civilization's memory. But in the last twenty years men have become nervously aware that this is also one of print's great disadvantages: it does not go away.

Immediately after Gutenberg in the 1450s, the number of books published remained relatively small. Scholars and scientists, and most others specializing in remote communication, continued for some time to transfer information by written letter or face-to-face conversation. But as systematic science and scholarship changed from a constant restudy of ancient texts to new explorations of the physical and social environment, and as the number of scientists and scholars expanded, the new information grew in quantity. Letters and personal conversations were inadequate to handle the exchange, and in the 1660s the first scientific journal appeared. Just counting scientific periodicals by 1750 there were 10 journals, by 1800 there were 100, by 1850 there were 1,000, by 1900 there were 10,000 and by now there are over 100,000. By 1830 when there were several hundred scientific journals, the individual scientist could no longer read all of the ones relating to his field, so he began to rely on very brief summaries, or abstracts. These could steer him quickly to the full journal articles he wished to see and prevent his spending time reading ones he could dispense with. Since then, numbers of abstracts also have gone up ten times every fifty years.

J. C. R. Licklider has described what this means for the conscientious contemporary scientist. The scientist observes that the existing literature in his particular specialty will be about 1.7 billion words, the equivalent of 11,000 books. If he reads extremely rapidly, about 500 words a minute, which is very fast for scientific literature, and he spends thirteen hours of every day of the year reading, he will have completed his reading at the end of twelve years. At that time he will discover that while he was reading the current literature another 1.7 billion words in his specialty were published.

According to Licklider, a specialist who sixty years ago needed twenty-five minutes a day to read all the current literature in his field eleven years from now will have to read continuously every hour of the day.

For the library, this expanding volume of print is equally unmanageable. The Yale University Library, if it attempts to remain current, by the year 2040 will have 200 million books, occupying over 6,000 miles of shelves, and if it continues to use card catalogues will have 750,000 drawers which alone will require 80 acres of floor space.

The problem is not just money, though that is a formidable requirement for a field that doubles its required volume of purchases every twelve years. Nor is it just space, though that, too, is fearsome, since any building that has to double its area every twelve years soon becomes enormous: a library that was five stories high in 1900 would by now, if it expanded the required amount vertically, be three hundred stories high.

Merely knowing how to look through this enlarging mass has become a major problem. Confronted with the projection for the Yale Library in the year 2040, the reader will start by combing through the eighty acres of card catalogues. Once he has identified the book he is looking for, he or a library aide would then have to scan the six thousand miles of shelves, a formidable physical exploration even with the Dewey decimal system. Once he has reached the proper location, he may find that someone else has the book, and since he must physically hold the book in order to use its contents he must await its return.

The printed news media also have experienced a massive multiplication of published material. In the last twenty years, the number of printed newspaper pages entering each home multiplied $2\frac{1}{2}$ times as individual daily papers have become larger. A Sunday metropolitan newspaper of four hundred pages is not rare. This is printed matter equivalent to more than sixteen three-hundred-page books. It is an example of cultural adaptation: few households would tolerate the idea of sixteen books delivered for perusal every Sunday, but since they have been habituated to it, and have learned to scan and reject getting the sixteen books in the form of four hundred newspaper pages does not seem so forbidding. Even so, the four hundred pages create problems, of disposal, for example. During the heavy advertising seasons, it is not unusual that all the Sunday papers in, for example, Los Angeles County, cost about $22 million to produce, cost the consumers $500,000 to buy, and, the next day, require municipal services to haul away five million pounds of discarded newspapers.

If present techniques are extended, the increased volume of daily print becomes overpowering. In the 1960s newspapers received most of their news by teletype that delivered an average of forty-five words a minute. In the early 1970s they will begin receiving it at the rate first of a thousand words a minute and soon afterward at still higher, and will feed their computers at more than eighty-six thousand words a minute. If the reader were given a proportional printed increase of this added speed, he would receive daily papers averaging thousands of pages. This will not happen, but it does illustrate what the new methods of transmission will mean in potential printed matter if handled in present patterns.

Consequently, there are severe pressures to shift some information from the printed page to a less permanent and bulky form. Electronic communication is the leading alternative.

Conventional contemporary television, for example, has made obvious intrusions on the attention given to printed news. It produces comprehension and involvement through pictures and sounds not easily duplicated by print. Radio has made instant distribution of news commonplace. Both television and radio, far more than print, permit the observer to monitor the news superficially while doing other things. Neither leaves a physical residue. The "off" switch solves the disposal problem.

But there are serious disadvantages to the electronic media today. The recipient is unable to use them at his own speed. He can view the televised image and hear radio words only at the speed of the originator, regardless of his own powers of observation and comprehension. He must listen to the television and radio presentation before he decides that he doesn't want to listen. And, if he decides he doesn't want to listen to one particular segment, he must nevertheless endure it at its own speed if he wishes to hear subsequent items. If he is interested in an item and wishes to compare what he has just heard with what came earlier, he cannot go back except in his own memory. If, after he has seen or heard something on radio, he decides he wants to keep a record of it in its original form, either to present to others or to preserve for his own use, there is no way either to go back, or, with television, to make a permanent record in his home. For the average consumer today, radio and television have no memory.

The requirement to absorb radio and television at their own speed is additionally burdensome for the spoken word: it takes twice as long to speak a thousand words on radio and television as it does for the average person to read a thousand words. When this is combined with the inability to scan and skip, it is a serious reduction in the amount of spoken textual material deliverable by broadcasting.

Reading a whole metropolitan paper over radio or television at normal announcing speeds would take about forty hours. If displayed as text on a television screen, as is done on some CATV stations at the rate of a hundred words a minute, it would take sixty hours. But it is possible to scan such a printed paper—that is, cast the eye on every headline in the paper—and read fifteen thousand words of what is of particular interest in less than an hour.

Much of this can change with new technology. At present, the speed of electronic viewing and hearing cannot be substantially accelerated. But there are other means of giving the consumer more flexibility. One way depends on a large surplus of available channels of broadcast communications, permitting a particular presentation to be broadcast in differing sequences of time. In such a system a program might be presented over ten channels at the same time, each channel five minutes behind the previous one. If a broadcast were being made in real time, as the event was actually taking place, like a Presidential press conference, there would be no way to permit the viewer to look ahead because what lay ahead would not yet have occurred. But, after the first five minutes, the already-completed part could be recycled onto the next channel, and this step duplicated throughout. Thus at every moment the viewer would have the power to switch quickly to any of the earlier five-minute segments. For prerecorded programs, it would be possible to look both ahead and behind.

An unwitting start to this system already exists. The most common radio program for teenage listeners is popular songs that are rated periodically for their popularity and broadcast as "the top forty." A number of radio stations in any large broadcasting market spend most of their broadcasting time playing songs from among the top forty and do so in random sequence in order to hold the attention of an audience waiting for particular songs. Devotees to this kind of program are seldom equally interested in all forty songs. Limited to one station, they would be forced to listen to a large number of songs—the maximum being thirty-nine—before they heard their favorite one. Automobile radios frequently have five tuning buttons which, preset for particular stations, will turn the radio immediately to that station. A teenage listener, if granted one button on the car radio, may tune it to a "top forty" station and at any particular time have one chance in forty of hearing his favorite song. However, granted hegemony over all five of the car radio buttons, he may tune additional buttons to other "top forty" stations. Since all the stations play the top forty in random sequence, but each different from the others, quickly pushing each of the five buttons changes the odds of hearing the favorite song at any given time from one in forty to one in eight. If each song of the top forty required five minutes, including intervening commercials and other station breaks, the listener could listen three hours and twenty minutes before he heard his favorite song on a single station. With five pushbuttons his maximum listening time would be forty minutes. Many teenagers actually do something like this, monitoring enough channels to maximize the chance that they will hear only their favorites and avoid the others.

The unplanned duplication of standard programming on radio helps expand the power of the consumer to "scan" his electronic media, in ways comparable—though at much slower speed—to his scanning of printed information. This primitive form for scanning the top forty songs is in a centralized system, the listener choosing among alternative channels.

There is another possibility, giving the consumer even more efficient control, which many teenagers use. Magnetic tape recorders for audio material have become widespread and inexpensive in a short period of time. In 1960 fewer than 300,000 tape recorders were sold at an average wholesale price of $153. In 1967, 4,580,000 were sold at an average wholesale price of $25. Aided by this growing incidence of tape recorders as a common household device, teenagers tune in their radios for the top forty songs and turn on their tape recorders only for their favorites. After a relatively short period of time they have fixed in a permanent record only those parts of the broadcast they are interested in, with relatively easy playback and selectivity. They have "scanned" and fixed sounds electronically. They have given radio a "memory," a selective one at that, and because the recorders have variable speeds they have made scanning even more efficient.

Video recorders are more expensive. But their cost and versatility will undoubtedly change, as have those of audio tape recorders. When that occurs, making a permanent record of televised presentations will be possible and the playback, slow-motion, and stop-action capabilities, seen now in centralized control in sports events, will be possible under the control of the consumer in his home.

In the long run, the more powerful substitute for print will be the routine storage of information in computers or in the extreme reduction of printed matter and motion pictures into near-microscopic film that can be retrieved and projected onto a screen.

The computer can store enormous quantities of information, including words. If these words, ideas, subject references, paragraphs, and whole documents are indexed and coded as they are introduced into the computer's memory, the memory can be searched for particular parts of its content and they can be extracted quickly. The results of this research by the computer can then be delivered to a human being in a number of ways; onto a magnetic tape that can be "played" at the convenience and in the chosen location of the viewer, flashed in words and graphs on a televisionlike screen, or printed on fast-moving sheets of paper.

The computer can "think" and search its memory much faster than it can "talk." By the end of the 1960s the fastest computers could handle one million characters a second. It could deliver its results onto microfilm at the rate of sixty thousand characters per second, or make a printed document at fifteen thousand characters per second, or flash them onto a TV-like screen. But human beings can read only twenty characters per second.

So, while the speed of the computer is beyond competition in the retrieval of information, and the display of its information is very fast, human reading speed is still a bottleneck.

An average daily newspaper has printing surfaces capable of carrying 600,000 words. Once the information is compiled it may take seven hours to produce and deliver the paper to the consumer. A computer could deliver the 600,000 words through its own printer in seventeen minutes and through a magnetic tape in less than five minutes.

At present there are severe difficulties in taking advantage of the difference between seven hours' production and delivery time for a newspaper and the few minutes for a computer. For one thing, the printing device that handles computer output at that speed costs about $44,000 and leases for $1,000 a month. The printout paper it uses would cost about $1 for the amount needed to carry the information contained in a ten-cent newspaper. The computer printout paper would consist of eighteen thousand lines, one under the other, in a bulky stack. Magnetic tape would be cheaper, about $25 a roll and reusable, but it requires a machine costing several hundred dollars to convert the tape to readable form, and the reader would have to roll through pages in sequence, like the ancient papyrus scroll.

But computer techniques and costs will change. In some cases the computer may produce an image or text on a screen, reducing the need for paper. In others it may produce a facsimile document that the consumer can read at his own speed and convenience.

This disparity between the computer's "thinking" speed and the human reading speed may be bridged in another way. Instead of processing the total output of the computer by eye, the human reader may ask the machine to use its enormous speed to search its memory for those items the reader is interested in and present only selected information for the slow process of human reading. This is already done in conventional use of stored printed matter.

It is possible to imagine the reaction of the scholar of 200 B.C., used to scrolls of papyrus with a maximum extended length of twenty feet, to the suggestion that a modern large library would be practical. When he wanted to refer to a written work, the ancient scholar had to locate the scrolls and then unroll each one and read from the top to find the desired information. If he had been told that he would have to find a particular piece of information in a twentieth-century library consisting of 100 billion words on 300 million pages, in a million-volume library, it would stagger him. To find the desired information could take 690 years of continuous reading. But using the library's card catalogue to locate the one desired book among the million and then using the book's index to find the one desired page might take from a few minutes to an hour. As libraries become larger and men busier, even that is a tedious process, but it effectively overcomes much of the disparity between the masses of available printed information and the ability of the human eye and brain to locate a single item within the mass.

A man can deal with a computer in analogous ways to eliminate what he does not want. The human brain is far richer in its associations and syntheses than any conceivable electronic model of a brain. But a computer does some things better: it can repeat itself exactly when asked to; it will permit itself to be studied meticulously and at length to test its logic, knowledge, and truthfulness; it will do whatever it is instructed to do; and, if its instructor knows what he is doing, it will do it reliably under almost any circumstances.

When a computer places a message onto a TV-like screen, the viewer, if he has a keyboard or other device for querying the computer, can stop it and ask what it means or what basic data support a statement, or ask it to stop for a moment and pursue in depth one point the text made in passing. Or he can tell it to skip this subject and go on to another. Thus, though the eye can process only twenty characters per second of the text the computer presents, the viewer can use the computer's million-characters-per-second speed to search out and present only those characters the eye wishes to behold.

And the computer can do all of this without the use of paper, except for the portions of the total information the viewer wishes recorded and preserved in a document. Instead of multiplying shelves of books or the rising stacks of magazines, or the accumulated sheaves of newspaper, a simple switch dissolves the words on the electronic screen. The information in the computer remains intact, recallable at will, without an inexorable proliferation of paper.

The physical space being occupied by published documents is being reduced by another technique, microfilm, preserving the printed word in miniature on film.

At present microfilms are used in a number of variations. Microfilm is available in most libraries, usually in 35-mm. or 70-mm., often for past files of newspapers and magazines, their reels stored the way books are, read by threading them through a projection machine.

Later contemporary forms are microfiche, a sheet of film, usually four inches by six with sixty images on each sheet; and the aperture card, a computer data card with its rectangular holes bearing frames of microfilm. Recent developments in ultramicroform permit reductions of pages of two hundred to one, permitting thirty-two hundred pages on a four-by-six-inch transparency. If ultramicroform is used, a million-volume library will occupy the space of a small closet. A library of a million printed and bound books would cost about $30 million; the same library in ultramicroform would, if adopted for a large number of locations, cost less than $200,000, including the cost of machines for projecting the miniaturized texts.

Microforms of one kind or another are already in large-scale use, sometimes for business records and sometimes as a substitute for books and periodicals. It is estimated that in 1970 the production and operation of microforms was a $500 million industry. Already one of every five "documents" distributed by the federal government is a microform instead of a printed piece of paper. About 70 percent of all documents published by the Atomic Energy Commission in 1967 were available only in microfiche. The largest user of microfilm in the world is the Social Security system, which puts 30 million documents on film each year and destroys the originals, and handles a total of 168 million accounts through microfilm and magnetic tape. The Internal Revenue Service microfilms revisions of 90 million tax returns and distributes them to regional offices in that form.

The miniaturized text can be produced on film remotely by a cathode ray tube, a highly refined television tube, whose images are produced by a computer. One firm produces such microform at the rate of two thousand frames an hour, each frame indexed so that the computer can, if necessary, revise the information it originally implanted, and can also call it up for rapid display.

In 1969 the National Cash Register Company, which once made machines that did simple addition of dollars and cents, announced that it would begin selling books in ultramicrofiche.

Conceivably books, periodicals, and newspapers could be flashed on demand onto home or neighborhood screens, where a microfilm would be made in a small index-card-sized transparency capable of carrying texts and pictures equivalent to four hundred newspaper pages. High costs and the absence of mass systems make home use of this technique impossible in the near future, but it is a technique that works and could result in future alterations in the ratio between documentary and nondocumentary information in the home.

The commercial use of computers to select and print information at the demand of individual consumers is already at hand. The Encyclopaedia Britannica has stored the entire text of its twenty-volume *Annals of America* series in computer form; articles and data can be revised and brought up to date electronically without the typing-and-printing-and-page-proof routines that now are time-consuming and expensive. The Britannica computer has twenty-two hundred articles stored in it. It will offer school districts abstracts of each article, from which each school will order its desired full articles for its own custom-compiled textbook.

So the accumulation of information in print may very well change radically, including the display of news. There is already a massive intake of daily news through radio and television that uses no document and leaves no permanent record, and this has already conditioned the nature of what is printed in newspapers. There will be growing shifts in what is best displayed momentarily on a screen or some other ephemeral medium and what the consumer wishes to have in a document. But it will not be a simple substitution. If present patterns continue, the wider choice of electronically displayed news will whet the appetite for printed information, and in some cases will intensify the desire for related information reproduced in permanent form. Interest in printed stock-market returns in newspapers seems not to have diminished in those cities where instantaneous stock-market quotations are available on television channels. Before President Kennedy instituted live television press conferences a maximum of three newspapers in the United States printed substantial excerpts of the transcript. One year after the televised conferences had been established, forty-six papers were regularly printing substantial excerpts of the verbatim conference.

Thus, the rise of new electronic media will undoubtedly reduce the ratio of printed to nonprinted information, presenting more images without documents. But the assertion that "the tyranny of print" is ended and that sentences and paragraphs will be displaced almost entirely by nonverbal forms has no basis in present trends or in appreciation of how men think and learn. A permanent record will always be wanted, to permit comparisons with past and present, and to let different individuals interpret for themselves society-wide laws, warnings, instructions, accounting, and speedy comparisons of a wide variety of data. Record keeping, diaries, bookkeeping, mathematics, chronologies, and histories may be adaptable in part to nonverbal images, but for most of them words are quicker and more efficient.

Modern civilization depends on standardized words. It is no accident that the adoption of the Semitic alphabet, reducing all spoken sounds to about twenty-two basic letters, accompanied the rise of Greek logic and philosophy. Using more individualistic symbols makes universal communication almost unmanageable. The oral tradition depends on tone of voice, facial expression, posture of body, personality of the speaker, and attitude of the listener. It is a rich and necessary tradition, but it is ephemeral. Development of the Semitic alphabet was one of the most stunning inventions of man, learnable in a relatively short time and applicable universally without the alterations that come from random personality. The written word gave men a medium that permitted them to express those things that are precise and long-lasting, and that stand apart from unique emotion. It led directly to the growth of logic. If the symbols for an idea or for a body of information remain the same regardless of who prints them or reads them, and if these constant symbols continue to have meaning for a wide variety of people over a period of time, men can judge the universal significance of these abstractions. Without them, history is impossible, because there is no continuous expression that is not substantially altered by the most recent narrator and listener. Nor is there logic, since there is no way to repeat uniformly the steps by which some individual came to a conclusion, and to do this consistently among different persons in widely separated places.

There are, of course, ways of presenting ideas and human situations in graphic form—plays, movies, art—that are transportable and repeatable. Their human meaning is profound. It is inevitable and good that through history sensory and emotional activities should challenge abstractions and universal assumptions. The abstractions do, in fact, have an inherent danger of inhibiting individualism and suppressing that part of the human personality that is not and should not be entirely intellectual. But the fact that electronics has strengthened the power of the nonverbal and that some of this is beneficial has led to a naïve dogma of the manifest destiny of multisensory media. Some of it is not beneficial, since sounds, forms, and other nonverbal sensory reproductions can be used for manipulative evil purposes and can lead to suppression of individuality and personal sensitivity just as print can. And the existence of richer and beneficial sensory activities does not cancel the need for print as a medium peculiarly adept at transmitting precise, rational, and consistent information.

The cult of the nonverbal is not only romantic in its dismissal of words as a basic human communication and in its exaggeration of print's artificial nature. But it also ignores a similar arbitrary restriction in nonprinted expression. The oral tradition has its own severe limitations. The human being can make uncounted thousands of different sounds through the manipulation of his breath drawn in and exhaled, altered by the chest, throat organs, tongue, mouth shape, and lips, plus mechanical sounds in these organs and tongue-and-teeth, plus simultaneous movement of head and body. But nearly all language—including the oral tradition—has reduced these to about forty sounds. The Semitic alphabet created twenty-two symbols (plus or minus a few for variants like English) whose combinations roughly approximate the forty sounds. The oral tradition, like the written, would quickly break down if the several thousand sounds were not standardized down to forty forms in order to let individuals and communities communicate with each other. "The tyranny of print" that turned human expression into visual symbols, has its counterpart in the "tyranny of syllables" by which primitive man became the speaking human being.

Furthermore, facial expressions and bodily gestures are not universal, but vary from culture to culture. These eventually will become standardized as men have widening contact with each other. "Natural" gestures, for example, have different meaning for different cultures. In the United States, pushing the hand, palm outward, forward and down, means "get away from here," while in some European countries and Latin America the same gesture means "come here." As Americans and Europeans increase communications with each other, in person and through electronic media, inevitably there will be standardization of "natural" communications.

Print, while never forgetting, has taught the mind to ignore it when it wants to. In a newspaper-reading test in Des Moines, two facing pages were printed, one having material almost exclusively of interest to women, the other for men. It was impossible to look at one page without being exposed to the other. About 90 percent of the women afterward reported opening the women's page and about 90 percent of the men their page. But 40 percent of the men said they never opened the women's page, though they had to in order to see the men's page. So, though print is cumulative and long-lasting, the human brain has defenses against unwanted print.

Reading continues to be the most intensive method of absorbing formal information.

In the late 1950s, after television had become a nearly universal phenomenon in the United States, Richard L. Meier calculated how much time urbanized Americans spent in various information-absorbing activities. Television clearly occupied more time than any other single method. In millions of person-hours a year he showed this time spent:

Television	6000
Lecture and discussion	4000
Reading	4000
Observation of environment	3000
Radio	1500
Films	160
Miscellaneous	5000

But, if the various methods are calculated not on simple time spent but on the amount of formal information received per minute, the order changes. Meier calculated the number of bits—the smallest unit of meaningful information—received by a single human being. In conventional information theory a bit is counted as one regardless of how many people absorb it, but Meier abandons this in calculating impact, so that each bit is multiplied by the number of individuals who absorb it. His estimated receiving rate of bits per minute received by an urban person for the various media are:

Reading	1,500
Films	800
Television	400
Radio	300
Lecture and discussion	200
Observation of environment	100
Miscellaneous	100

Thus, for every minute spent at information activities, reading is almost double the "efficiency" of the nearest competitor, films, and 3½ times more efficient than its most famous competitor, television. This calculation is solely of formal information, without taking into account the quality or impact of any particular bit. The differing quality of each bit is plainly important in human affairs. Reading is fifteen times more efficient than "observation of the environment" in transmitting specific information, but perceptive observation of human beings can obviously be more informative and more deeply moving than reading a psychology text. The point is not to suggest that information received by reading is always "better" or more significant. Sometimes it is and sometimes it isn't. But it is clear that the printed document is too efficient for some categories of information to be replaced by any medium yet in view. Among these categories of information in which print is superior is systematic, sequential information containing enough detail to make it beneficial for the reader to absorb it at his own speed and make selective visual comparisons between different statements within the adjacent documents. This covers a wide range of contemporary print, including detailed and analytical news stories, as well as more concentrated technical and scholarly work.

New methods of communication usually create new cultures, disrupting old assumptions and causing revolutions. This fact has led many to the conclusion that the electronically transmitted moving picture is peculiar not only in its graphic power but also in its ability to upset traditional ways, as demonstrated in the civil-rights and student rebellions in the United States in the 1960s.

"A great many individuals found . . . so many inconsistencies in the beliefs and categories of understanding handed down to them," we read in one commentary, "that they were impelled to much more conscious, comparative and critical attitudes to the accepted word picture, and notably to the notions of God, the universe, and the past."

This fits the assertion of believers in the uniqueness of the impact of television and other multimedia techniques to produce race riots, student rebellions, and the "generation gap." But the quoted passage is not about television. It describes the introduction of formal written words by abstract alphabets twenty-five hundred years ago, with new ideas and insights overturning the ancient values that had previously been preserved by a strictly oral tradition.

Print is neither dead nor dying. It is being forced to make a place in the family of human communication for a new way of transferring information and emotion, the electronic reproduction of scenes and sensations. The new medium is disrupting and even revolutionary, but it leaves the alphabet and document still indispensable to the efficient use of eye and brain and to the demands of human rationality.

Who Pays for the News?

10

The most innocent view of the economics of news is that the consumer pays his daily dime for his paper and gets broadcast news free.

That is not true, of course. One way or another, the consumer pays more for the systems that bring him his daily news than he does for his telephone service. This is not a small consideration in the future of news. The way Americans will get their public information in the next generation will depend less on the technological question about machines, "Will they work?" but more on "Who pays?"

If it were not for the question of who decides on money spent for news, if the future were determined solely by the ability of new devices to work, the country could start at once installing a far more sophisticated and satisfying system of distributing public information. But that isn't enough. Some of the new machines at present cost too much for ordinary use. Others could be afforded by most families, but they are useful only when part of a large and elaborate network that no one has yet organized.

Innovations will have to appear profitable to those who sell, operate, and buy them. Inventions must convince the public that they will perform old functions more efficiently or will offer new services that are extremely attractive. Electric refrigerators were adopted because in annual costs and performance they were superior substitutes for iceboxes. On the other hand, telephones, radio, and television provided functions the consumer had never experienced before but they looked appealing enough for the average family to make room for them in their budget, their home, and their daily schedule.

Deciding who pays for news is not simple. If news proprietors went to the wholesale market at dawn to buy large quantities of information and retailed it to consumers later in the day, the transaction would be relatively simple. But almost all news is distributed along with unrelated products—merchandising information, entertainment, etc.—that have their own costs and benefits. Today the average consumer cannot select and pay solely for his daily news. In general, no systematic daily news is distributed unless it is associated with other activities whose primary objective is to collect large audiences for the purpose of selling merchandise.

Newspapers get from 70 to 75 percent of their revenues from merchants who buy space in the papers to advertise their goods. Broadcasters get practically 100 percent of their revenue from advertisers. Because the carriers of daily news—newspapers, radio, and television—receive about half of all advertising money spent in the United States, the present and future level of advertising is important.

All advertising expenditures have paralleled general economic activity, at least in this century. In 1867 gross national product was $6.7 billion, of which only $50 million, less than 1 percent, was spent on advertising. But since then both GNP and advertising money have grown substantially, and while the percentage of all money in the country allotted to advertising has declined from a high in the 1920's the great increases in the absolute level of both have meant continuous expansion of advertising money.

Year	GNP ($ billions)	Advertising ($ millions)	Advertising as % of GNP
1920	$ 89	$ 2,935	3.5%
1930	91	2,607	2.8
1940	100.6	2,087	2.0
1950	284.6	5,710	2.0
1960	503.8	11,932	2.4
1969 (est.)	850	18,800	2.1

From *Statistical Abstract of the United States, 1968;* estimated 1969 from U.S. Industrial Outlook, 1969, Department of Commerce, p. 313.

In the 1960s advertising as a percentage of GNP has averaged 2.2 percent. In 1969 this produced $18.8 billion in advertising money, or $306 per household.

Estimates of further GNP for the next 30 years show continuing increases, barring catastrophe. By 1985, according to Wiener and Kahn, GNP should have reached about $1.5 trillion, and by the year 2000 about $2.9 trillion. If the same percent goes into advertising, this would mean that the present expenditure of $306 of advertising per household would rise to $400 by 1985 and to $630 in the year 2000. (There would be about 82 million households in 1985 and 101 million in 2000.)

At present, newspapers get 29 percent of all advertising money, television 17 percent, and radio 6 percent. This means that advertising associated with daily news carriers is spent at the rate of $89 a year per household for newspapers, $52 for television, and $18 for radio. (The news carriers did not receive all of this money, since advertising agencies and others lie between most advertisers and mass outlets.)

Who ultimately benefits from this advertising money is a matter of some contention. Advertisers and media operators like to describe advertising as a "subsidy" that supports the news, since it represents three-quarters of revenues for newspapers and 100 percent for broadcasting. In this view, the citizen gets his printed news at less than a third of its real cost and his broadcast news free.

Money spent on advertising is added to the cost of the product which the consumer pays. Conventional wisdom claims that advertising does not cost the consumer anything and might even save him money, since it stimulates mass sales and mass production which so lower the prices of goods that whatever is spent on advertising is more than made up by the lowered cost of the merchandise.

Many economic authorities on advertising do not agree with this view. They believe that, while advertising can produce increased sales of some items at particular times, and thus influence the flow of cash within the economy, it does not have a significant effect on the overall amount of money spent on goods and services. In this view, if there were no advertising, the gross national product would not change significantly and consumer money now spent in response to ads would be spent on other things. Absence of advertising due to media strikes, for example, does not increase savings. In this view, advertising money is not a "subsidy" for the news but a "hidden tax."

Whether subsidy or hidden tax, it means that "Who pays?" must be refined to "Who handles the money?" The consumer may pay for the advertising in the news media, but he does not control the allocation of the money. Ten billion dollars a year is spent on advertising in newspapers, television, and radio, but neither the news proprietors nor the news consumers have much control over this 90 percent of the economy of the American daily-news media.

Furthermore, allocation of the money is decided by advertising agencies and merchandisers solely on the basis of what they believe will most efficiently sell their goods. Consumers of the end product might make different decisions if they controlled their medium's economy.

The only way the consumer can control the spending of the $10 billion in his news media is to withhold his purchases of advertised goods or of media carrying the advertising. He can refuse to buy a newspaper or to listen to broadcasting. But both newspapers and broadcasting are multifunction media and there are not many consumers who will dismiss an entire medium over dissatisfaction with a part of it.

The consumer has slightly more influence over his printed news since he makes direct payments to the newspaper. But even this is limited. He pays only 25 or 30 percent of the cost. Furthermore, in 96 percent of communities there is only one paper, and the consumer must make the choice between the only local paper or none.

Only a few individuals can completely select and pay for their news, and most of these do it in connection with commercial operations. Stock-market quotations with some general news are available on machines like teletype receivers or on tickers. Newsletters carry no advertising, but they are usually on specialized subjects and are not issued daily. Some cable-television systems use one channel to transmit a continuous picture of a news teletype machine. But even this is only a slight refinement of choice in paying only for news since the cable customer pays a flat amount for connection with the cable system, which produces the usual collection of television programming.

Newspapers receive some money direct from subscribers. Spread among all households in the country (though only about 80 percent actually buy papers) this comes to $25 a year per household. Of the subscriptions paid for papers, the newspaper receives a net of from 60 percent to zero, depending on whether the paper is distributed through neighborhood delivery boys, a news wholesaler, a news-stand operator, or is sold directly by the paper. There are no national data on what consumers in the United States actually pay for their daily and Sunday papers, and none on what part of this eventually reaches the paper.

The usual retail prices of newspapers are 10 cents weekdays and 25 to 30 cents on Sunday. But there are great variations in discounts if the consumer subscribes by the week, month, or year, which over 60 percent do. An estimate based on the RAND study is that the independent deliverers of daily papers receive about one-third of subscriber payments. If this is true nationally, then a calculation of total subscriber payments spread to all households would be $37.

Advertising is the major source of income for daily papers, approximately 72 percent. Using estimates for 1969, daily newspapers received about $4 billion in advertising revenues, but this was the net advertising revenues. The advertisers themselves paid about 20 percent more than this, in advertising-agency fees, production and other costs, or about $5 million for placing ads in daily papers. On the assumption that the consumer ultimately pays for the total cost of these ads, this comes to a cost spread to all 1969 households of $83 per household. Thus, the total ultimate cost of placing daily and Sunday newspapers into homes, spread equally to all households, comes to $37 paid directly by the consumer and $83 via advertising, or about $120 a year.

On the surface it would seem easier to calculate who pays for broadcasting, since all its revenue comes from advertising. This gives the impression, encouraged by commercial broadcast operators, that radio and television are "free."

There is, of course, the cost of advertising, which for television in 1969 was about $3.3 billion (spent by advertisers; broadcasters received less after agency and other processing costs). Spread over every household this comes to $55 per household (97 percent of all households have television sets).

However, unlike newspapers, television cannot be received unless the consumer makes an investment in special equipment. In the last ten years consumer spending on television sets, antennae, and repairs has averaged about $2.6 billion a year. Using the average number of households during this same ten-year period, this comes to about $47 a year paid by each household for the purchase and maintenance of television receiving equipment.

Radio-advertising spending was about $1 billion a year, or $16 per household. In recent years, the cost of car, home, and portable radios, with associated equipment and repairs, has run to about $10 a year per household.

Total direct payments by consumers for radio and television equipment, repairs, and maintenance come to about $57 a year.

Consumers spend much more for equipment to receive broadcasting than producers spend to transmit it. In the 1946–1966 period consumers paid $26.5 billion for television sets, while broadcasters paid $1.2 billion for physical assets in transmitting and studio equipment. Unlike most consumers, broadcasters could deduct their physical investment from taxes. During that period the industry ended with a depreciated value of physical assets of $661 million. So, for every net dollar spent by the television industry in physical equipment to transmit to the consumer, the consumers spent $40 to receive the message.

So advertisers spent $83 per household on newspapers and subscribers about $37, for an annual total of $120. Advertisers spent $55 per household on television, and consumers spent $47 to receive broadcasts, for an annual total of $102. Radio-advertising spending was $16 per household and consumers spent $10 for equipment and repairs, for a total of $26.

This compares with other annual costs for household communications as follows:

Telephone	$225
Newspapers	120
Postal service	116
Television	102
Periodicals	44
Books	42
Radio	26
Phonograph records and tapes	13

(The above figures are not payments made annually by a "typical" or "average" household. They are the total receipts for each activity divided by the total number of households in the country. Most of the activities are organized around household spending; using expenditures on that basis permits projections for future total income and future numbers of households.)

Thus, $688 a year is spent per household for incoming and outgoing communications, of which the primary carriers of daily news represent a third. Disposable personal income is expected to increase by 41 percent by 1985 and by 117 percent by the year 2000. If household communications takes the present proportion of income, it would mean that in fifteen years each home would spend $970 and in thirty years, $1,400.

Families headed by a person with a college degree buy twice as many daily papers as those headed by someone with no high school. By the year 2000 college degrees are expected to be as common as high-school diplomas. Income is another factor in newspaper buying. In 1960 families with less than $6,000 income were 25 percent less likely to buy papers than those with incomes of $10,000 or more. Using 1965 dollars to discount inflation, by the year 2000 families with low-newspaper-buying characteristics will have dropped to one-third of their present incidence in the population, and those with high-newspaper-buying characteristics will have increased by almost three times as a percentage of total families.

Home communications will be influenced by the trend to interconnect different systems. The telegraph and telephone systems at one time were not only competitors but largely separate. Telegrams were sent by the consumer appearing at a local telegraph office, writing out the message by hand, which was transmitted over telegraph wires to the destination, where it was decoded and hand-delivered by a messenger. There is still a separate telegraph system, but most residential messages are called in at the source by telephone and are delivered by telephone at the destination. The fee appears on the telephone bill, though it goes to the telegraph company.

Similarly, as home receiving equipment becomes more versatile it is reasonable to expect it to combine functions. If facsimile becomes practical in the home, and it is possible to switch television transmission from point to point like telephones, the consumer may choose to accept some things electronically that he now pays for in other forms. Some mail, for example, could be displayed as a message on a video screen or be reproduced by home facsimile. The ability to call up articles from publications or parts of books could be borne by some of the present household payments for receiving such information in different form, like mail or whole magazines and books.

In the 1950s Richard Meier estimated that the country spent $12 billion a year on the mass media, another $12 billion on point-to-point communication (like telephone and mail), and $24 billion on face-to-face education. New technology is combining some of these functions. Television, originally a mass medium sending a standard message to large numbers of people, is now used for Picturephone, in which particular sets can be connected with other particular sets to transmit live images in point-to-point communication. Education, traditionally accomplished with the teacher and students physically in the same room, is increasingly being expanded by use of remote communications.

Education expenditures were not included in the home communications costs in the table above, except as books. But there is reason to believe that the coming years will see significant amounts of juvenile and adult education carried out by way of home-communications techniques. But, even without the addition of that spending, the amount of money available for consumer communications systems will be impressive. In 1985 there will be a predicted 82 million households, and if each spends about $1,000 on home communications, it will support an $82-billion system. That is roughly the annual spending on automobiles and automobile repairs, fuels and services, one of the most elaborate consumer systems in existence. Before the automobile and its support networks were established as mass products, it would have seemed fantasy to the average family that a household like theirs could ever pay $3,000 for a complex machine and an annual $400 for its servicing.

Thus, it is not fantasy to project an American home in the next thirty years with a home communications system as expensive and complex as the automobile, serviced by networks of comparable magnitude.

Hopes for reduction in costs through mass production and technological breakthroughs are often frustrated by the harsh realities of beautifully ingenious machines that don't work or well-behaved machines that nobody can afford. But it is similarly unrealistic to ignore the dramatic reductions in cost and improved performance that communications technology and mass production continue to produce.

In twelve years comparable computers went from 5,000 pounds to 50 pounds, from 350 cubic feet in size to $\frac{1}{3}$ of a cubic foot, requiring only $\frac{1}{250}$ the power, and despite these enormous reductions in weight, size, and power could work ten times faster. The trend continues. A set of computations that cost $2,000 in 1955 will cost one cent in 1975.

Between 1950 and 1967, the wholesale price index of all home electronic equipment dropped 20 percent, despite great increases in complexity, capacity, and reliability. Portable radios, considered exotic in the late 1940s, were inexpensive fixtures at almost every level of society by the 1960s.

Payment for household electronic equipment could be altered by leasing rather than purchase. Almost 90 percent of American homes already lease electronic devices: the average residence with a telephone pays an annual bill of more than $100, covering both lease charges and fees for specific services.

There are a number of advantages to large-scale leasing. It permits installation of enough machines to form an interacting system at a faster rate than the period needed to convince enough consumers to make the larger initial payment for purchase of the equipment. It also permits operators of the entire system to integrate and standardize its parts, usually at a lower net cost. Some operators of cable television systems, for example, are convinced that if they had television receivers produced to their specifications for leasing to consumers, they could produce a higher-quality picture at lower overall cost.

The future of advertising and merchandising will be important. The simplest consideration is whether advertising will continue to supply its present share of money going into news systems.

Changing population characteristics and communications techniques could produce radical changes in how advertising money is spent among the various news media. Advertisers deciding that new methods of presenting information are more effective could reduce or eliminate their spending in older media.

There is some experience with this already. In the 1935–1945 period the relationships of the major advertising media did not change radically. There were some changes, many flowing from

World War II when there were massive population changes and limited outlets for consumer spending. After the war there was an enormous increase in money spent on advertising. As the country once more became a consumer-oriented economy, advertising became a growing activity, eclipsing all other single factors as a source of revenue for the media. In the 1945–1950 period all kinds of advertising increased, but in 1950, when television began to grow, there were obvious shifts. Television's electronic cousin, radio, suffered the most, dropping in its absolute revenues as well as its percentage of the market. Magazines benefited only slightly from the added availability of advertising money, with business papers and outdoor advertising even less so. Direct mail and newspapers, along with television, faithfully followed the upward surge in all advertising, which paralleled the gross national product. At no time was the dominance of newspapers as the leading medium of advertising challenged, though television, at a lower absolute level, had a faster rate of growth.

This seems to say two things.

First, the introduction of a new medium may win over attention and money from those most like it, rather than those very different. Radio suffered noticeably with the introduction of television, to a much greater degree than radio was able to affect newspaper revenues when it entered the commercial scene fifteen years earlier. Even more dramatic was the reaction of the motion-picture industry to television. It is not a significant carrier of advertising, but it is an important mass medium. Movie receipts grew significantly even during the Depression and spectacularly in the 1940–1946 period, when it reached the level and growth rate of newspaper advertising receipts. But when television began to be observable in neighborhood bars and other centers in 1947, motion pictures went into a radical decline. They did not begin a recovery until the 1960s and that was chiefly as a supplier to the television industry.

Second, a new actor on the advertising-communications scene seldom enjoys a quick and conclusive triumph over its elders. The new challenger does not stride onto the stage and fling the old stars into the pit. Instead, the stage seems to enlarge, and the old actors remain with the new, all sharing the expanded space, though with changed relationships.

Technology can change the economics of news media in another way. The number of journalistic outlets for daily journalism at present is remarkably stable. Among daily newspapers there is local monopoly in 97 percent of American cities that have papers, and the total number of daily papers has remained almost constant with less than 1 percent variation for twenty-five years. Broadcasting outlets are allocated by the Federal Communications Commission on the basis of available positions on the dial. The number of broadcasting outlets rose rapidly in the post–World War II period, but in recent years, as the available space in the air in major markets has filled, the growth has slowed.

In printed news, new methods could make it less expensive for new papers, and possibly new kinds of papers, to enter the market place. At present, newspapers require a heavy initial investment in plant and equipment, so heavy that it is seldom more profitable for an entrepreneur to start a completely new daily paper than it would be to invest the same amount of money in a different line of business.

A radical change in production methods and costs for newspapers could change its sources of income. Advertising, for example, becomes less important as a share of total revenue as papers become smaller in pages and in circulation. Advertising produces the largest portion of newspaper revenues, but it also requires some of the heaviest costs. Since advertising represents 61 percent of all pages printed in daily papers, it represents the most expensive peak production equipment and labor costs. Advertising is more expensive to handle than news. In a newspaper where it costs $3.23 to process a thousand characters of text matter from typewriter to printed paper, it costs $10.81 for a thousand characters of classified ads.

Paper and ink, which represent 20 percent of total costs for papers of 40,000 circulation and 30 percent for a paper of 400,000 circulation, are directly related to the quantity of ads which normally occupy over 60 percent of the paper. It is not clear what would happen to the economics of daily newspapers if they reduced or even eliminated advertising. It is conceivable under some circumstances that the reduced cost of production might be acceptable to subscribers, who would pay for the entire paper.

Calculations made in the RAND study by Dr. James N. Rosse estimate that if newspapers eliminated all advertising, including the plant and manpower now devoted to the selling, composition, and printing of ads, and instead delivered newspapers consisting solely of the present quantity of news, the subscriber would pay from 65 to 75 percent more for his newspaper than he does today, or about 18 cents.

Using data from the study, Professor Rosse estimated that a paper that now costs subscribers an average of 6.5 cents a copy (when the 10-cent street sale price is averaged with the lower monthly subscription rate) would cost 9.5 cents, and another paper that costs the subscriber 8.5 cents would cost 13 cents. To this about 15 or 25 percent should be added, because the resulting plant of the paper would be much smaller and while this would reduce absolute costs it would increase the percentage of overhead applied to news.

Thus, the adless paper could sell on the street today for seventeen or eighteen cents instead of ten cents. It is not an exorbitant price, considering the change in purchasing power of the dollar plus the rise in real purchasing power over recent decades.

However, advertising is more than a convenient source of cash flow for a newspaper. It is a positive attraction to a large number of readers, as sources of product and price information in daily transactions. In 1940 Marshall Field established an adless paper in New York City, *PM*. It never attracted enough subscribers willing to pay 100 percent of the cost to make it self-supporting. But, just as significant, it discovered that its socially conscious readers demanded merchandising information. *PM* assigned reporters to compile daily listings of bargains in major New York City retail outlets.

Far more likely to change the nature of advertising in the news media is the development of ability by the consumer to do some of his shopping electronically, and to order onto his screen or on his facsimile document the specific information he wants.

Leo Bogart, head of the Bureau of Advertising of the American Newspaper Publishers Association, believes that most advertising of the future may be arranged like classified ads or like a computerized sorting of information in batches of maximum use to the consumer: with characteristics, prices, and locations of competing items next to each other for purposes of comparison.

The enormous increase in available information of all kinds affects merchandising as well as intellectual and technical life. The consumer is confronted with ever larger numbers of items to buy with less time to buy them. Randomized buying is decreasingly attractive. Computers are natural machines for categorizing product information. If, as is already beginning in some areas of commercial life, purchasers of goods are willing to pay a price to get systematic information on comparative prices, styles, and locations of particular items, advertising of all kinds will have to become more useful in giving information in a similar way.

Bogart has said, "Some bright publishing team may some day soon be venturesome enough to produce a newspaper in which display advertising is run as far as possible on a classified basis, with ads for competing products and stores placed next to each other as they are in the real market place, rather than separated to avoid the conflict which most advertisers today assume (without evidence) to be bad."

The householder of the future may be able to call up a "television catalogue" of desired items and with a computer connection order from a store. Standard brands already dominate consumer goods and are readily recognized. Physical presence is not needed to select many of them—boxes of detergent or canned soups are not more intelligently bought through the use of touch or smell. Even fresh vegetables and meat are increasingly packaged, meaning that remote inspection by color television may be as good as personal handling.

Much of advertising may be in the form of computer-stored televised "catalogues" whose storage in a data bank is paid for by the merchandiser, and whose callup on the home screen may be paid for by a unit charge on the consumer's monthly communications bill, as would telephone calls.

If, suddenly, the consumer were asked to pay directly for his full newspaper or for all of television programming that he watches every day, the added conscious cost might produce resistance. He might then become more concerned about one of the characteristics of these media—they contain a great deal of material that no one consumer is interested in. Newspapers especially are collections of minority-appeal materials—foreign news, sports, dress patterns, comic strips, stock-market reports, travel features, pet care, state-house politics, advice to the lovelorn, car ads, lingerie ads, fashion predictions, crossword puzzles, news from Congress, descriptions of local dinner parties, etc. Because the conscious price of this collection is small—

ten cents—there is considerable tolerance and even attraction toward the mixed package whose various parts can be easily scanned and rejected. But if somehow the advertisements were placed free and the consumer paid the whole amount, which would be about thirty cents a day, he might wish to reject some of the things he and his family almost never look at. Or he might reject all the ads, paying for a paper containing only news.

This, in fact, is what new technology might permit him to do. He might scan, through a video index, all the available items but pick only the specific ones he is interested in. On that selected basis he might be willing to pay a small amount to look at the index and a small amount for each story he selects.

If this is applied to advertising, the present $19 billion a year spent in advertising could be shifted to new kinds of merchandising and promotion.

One possibility is computerized product information. A central data bank in each community would contain an inventory of goods for each major retail outlet—sizes, prices, colors, and locations where the items can be ordered. The computer would sort these out so that the consumer could ask for pictures or listings of all items in the same category, regardless of brand or store.

A housewife wishing to buy a raincoat for her child could ask to see pictures or listings of all raincoats in the desired size and price range. These might be listed in textual description or in colored photographs flashed onto the TV screen in sequence, each with a code number like mail-order catalogues. From these the purchase could be made by telephone, or Touch-Tone buttons on the phone, or on some other signaling device in the home. The order would be received on the store's own computer, the amount of the purchase automatically deducted from the consumer's bank account and registered in the store's running inventory.

If such a system should develop, there would be a cost of maintaining the data-bank files. These, in effect, would be a combined catalogue in video form for all the major retail outlets in the community. Since a description in words of each item or a colored display of it would provide for both information and salesmanship, it is likely that the sellers of the goods would want to provide that. It would be a new and more useful form of advertising. It would not necessarily reduce by that amount other forms—like newspapers or broadcasting—but it probably would.

The above is hardly a prediction. Much more predictable is some kind of selection system that will protect the consumer from the increasing overload of unwanted information that taxes his physical and nervous capacity. This is true of scholarly and technical information and it is also true of news and advertising.

At the start of this century, the availability of information about public events and goods for sale was limited. A home might have the Bible, Plutarch's *Lives,* and an occasional small newspaper. Advertising appeared before this average household in the occasional newspaper and magazine that came into the home, perhaps in a mail-order catalogue or farm paper, on the sides of barns, and on the packages of goods. It was an era when the young, discovering the excitement of reading, devoured every word in sight and found that to satisfy this new appetite they had to reread all print in the household many times.

Today the situation is reversed. The average household is inundated with more reading, audio, and video material than it can possibly absorb. Advertising is in the daily papers by scores of pages, in Sunday papers by hundreds of pages. It fills magazines of all kinds, some free and some paid for, some for the young and some for adults. Printed paper that used to be so rare and exciting at the turn of the century is now a problem in disposal. In 1899 there were thirteen pounds of communications-grade paper consumed per capita; in 1966 there were ninety-three pounds. Of the thirteen billion pounds of mail delivered each year, over half is advertising. Ads fill radio and television, penetrate the home by private telephone, appear on billboards along the highway and even in the sky.

The American Association of Advertising Agencies estimates that there are sixteen hundred advertisements aimed at the consumer every day, of which eighty are consciously noticed and twelve provoke some reaction. This overload has changed the strategy of advertisers and of the besieged consumer.

Seventy years ago the primary problem of advertising was physically to intercept the target-citizen's line of sight. Today that—and his range of hearing—are still strategic goals, but the greatest effort now goes toward overcoming the consumer's psychological and sen sory defenses, which must become higher each year as the per-capita assault by advertising increases. Increasingly advertising finds itself pushing against a resistant receiver, and this tendency is not likely to reverse itself as, on one side, the amount of paper and electronic images increases, and, on the other, the education and discrimination of the consumer rises. And as there is no increase in the number of waking hours for the overwhelmed citizen to absorb messages.

Forecasts of the American population for the remainder of the century tell us that the average citizen will be richer, more literate, and busier. He will spend more money, but he will not have any more time to make decisions than he does today. Because he will be better educated and more familiar with the analysis of abstract knowledge, he will be more impatient with unwanted or inadequate information. Having more money and less time, he may be willing to pay for rapid extraction of specific information.

There is no reason to think this will not influence advertising techniques and the news media. It is possible that advertising in the future will place much more emphasis on answering the "pull" of specific consumer interests rather than the "push" of breaking through his wary defenses. A consumer who has already decided on what kind of item he wants would be open to product information and promotion about such items, with a desire to see competing products within that category. He already does this with printed catalogues and newspaper classified ads. Housewives do it regularly with supermarket advertisements, comparing weekend food prices among competing stores.

Home communications of the future will give the individual more control over what he receives from a large inventory of information, including news and advertising. The consumer will continue to pay for it all, as ever, but with increasing control over what he gets.

Today, the average American household pays directly and indirectly about $120 a year for newspapers. Of this, about 69 percent is for advertising, or $83 for daily printed ads, and 31 percent for subscriber payments, or $37. If household income rises as expected, and it is divided among the media the way it is today, then in 1985 each household will pay $121 a year for daily printed advertising information or 34 cents a day, compared to the 23 cents a day each household spends today. For news and other daily nonadvertising, each household would spend $52 a year, or 14 cents a day, compared to the 10 cents paid today. The daily payments in the year 2000 would be 48 cents a day for printed advertising information, and 22 cents for other daily printed information.

Today, each household pays 28 cents a day for all its television programming, including advertising and news. In 1985, if the predictions and shares of market by the media hold, this would become 40 cents a day in 1985 and 61 cents a day in the year 2000.

These are all based on predictions for 1985 and the year 2000. Another prediction that can be made with considerable confidence is that these predictions will not be precisely accurate. The economy and the nature of society will undoubtedly change in ways not known to contemporary prophets. And the mixture of media offered the public and the way the public will respond will not be exactly the present pattern. But households today spend discernible amounts of money for specific informational services. As the consumer is forced to make more discriminating choices, he may pay more attention to how much he pays for each particular service. He already pays a little to publications like *Consumer Reports* that give him objective, systematic product information. What if *Consumer Reports* or an organization like Consumers Union, or a consortium of major advertisers, places this product information, together with government and other test ratings, into central computers available to the public? How much would the public pay? The answer is hinted at when we say that just on newspapers and television the public already pays about fifty cents a day for daily advertising information, most of which it doesn't see or want. If it had a choice, it might spend its fifty cents a day for product information it knows it wants.

Similarly, today, just for daily papers and television, the public pays something a little over ten cents a day for news. (It is difficult to calculate what it pays for televised news since public payments for this are not made and the cost to television is not clear, though it is a relatively small cost.) While the public today is presented with more news than it sees or wants, a greater proportion of the total presentation of news than of advertising is actively intercepted by the public.

The answer to "Who pays?" is, of course, the consumer. But what he pays for indirectly now he may have a choice of paying for directly in the future. He will probably have to do it if for no other reason than to protect himself from the growing avalanche of information. The capacities of future information systems will be so much greater that the selection of what is wanted and what is not will be an absolute necessity. It will probably be through the favorite mechanism of a cash economy, by the consumer paying for what he wants and refusing the rest. That alone will change the nature of daily information as we know it today.

Public Policy, Private Profit,
and the Training of Audiences

All over the world men can be seen performing a calisthenic ritual peculiar to the literate. They unfold their newspapers in a physical act that requires them to raise their arms high enough to permit a free vertical fall of two feet, to hold their hands far enough apart to keep the expanse of paper stretched for two and a half feet, and to extend the whole sheet far enough from the face so that all of the 720 square inches of printed surface is at the proper focal length for the observer's eyeballs.

No careful consideration determined that most newspapers, unlike any other form of printed text, would be large paper blankets, and that this would demand daily human postures that are awkward and tiring. The earliest newspapers were either book size or manuscript size. Nor was it the result of some early realization that such large sheets of print would permit rapid and efficient eye scanning (which they do). Or make possible large illustrations and eye-catching headlines (which were not invented until long after the large sheet size). Or even that the daily exercise of forearm and pectoral muscles would be therapeutic for an otherwise sedentary reading population.

Instead, it was the unintended result of a suggestion in 1711 by an obscure Treasury official in London, who recommended that a tax on newspapers would raise revenues for the government and also inhibit the growth of an increasingly impudent press. The idea delighted the authorities and the next year they imposed the tax which eventually cost 50 percent of the purchase price of the new, inexpensive papers, which were precisely the ones the government wished to suppress. It imposed the tax on the basis of each page printed, which meant that there was the same tax on a small page as on a large page, with consequences nobody thought of at the time. The surviving publishers could sell more print at lower cost if they did it on huge pages, which they proceeded to produce. The tax was imposed in most of Europe for over a century and for a time in colonial America.

By the mid-nineteenth century the tax stamp for newspaper pages had largely disappeared. But by that time the technology of newspapers had been designed around the printing, cutting, and folding of very large pages. And the public had gone through generations of such papers, and, having known nothing else, went through the daily ungainly reflexes under the impression that there was some technical imperative that made the printed blankets normal and necessary. Today newspapers are read in areas of restricted dimensions like private automobiles, buses, subway trains, breakfast tables. In more spacious areas they are subject to wind and water. Yet hardly anyone questions the large newspaper page size, though it may endanger life (a rapidly opened newspaper by the passenger in the front seat of an automobile suddenly obscures the driver's vision of much of the highway), limb (the attempt to turn pages on a wind-swept park bench has been known to cause accidental bruises to other occupants of the bench and dislocate vertebral discs of the reader), and the pursuit of happiness (millions of spouses have grown bitter at breakfast tables where they are separated from their mates by a paper curtain). When these disadvantages are countered by smaller papers, called tabloids, the power of ingrained cultural habit is so great that the public resists the reform.

This is a simple example of how the interplay of technology, public policy, and corporate policy combine to produce public habits that no one foresees, and accidental results that no one wants. Mass communications for the rest of the century are being formed today and it is worth considering how a new world of the media is born, since that history may help us avoid an accidental, unwanted future.

Though an upheaval in mass communications has already started, it is still obscure to the ultimate constituents, the general public. But it is a matter of fierce concern among the business firms involved, each pursuing its self-interest, seeing its own desires as being best for society. In this all the contenders may be wrong. At the very least, they cannot all be right, since some of them are pressing for opposite policies. If history repeats itself, the general public will see the issues clearly only after the corporate and government policies have been committed to a design, money has been invested, and the system is in being. If, at that point, the public dislikes what it gets, or the new media produce undesirable results, it may be too late to uproot and replace an elaborate system. Designs of new public systems could be pernicious to a free and dynamic society in ways more ominous than the eccentricity of two hundred years of huge newspaper pages.

The new media, like the blanket newspaper page, will be the product of large enterprises and remote specialists whose knowledge of alternatives is not known by the public. Once the entrepreneurs and specialists have made their decisions, the general public, seeing a new medium in a particular form, will have no choice but to use it in its original form, or not at all.

There are numerous examples of public perception shaped by public and corporate policy, among them the newspaper page, radio and television programming, and—until television offered an alternative—uniform formats for movies. Millions of motorists must have had an impulse at some time to use a telephone in their cars, to inform home and office of changed plans, and to conduct business during otherwise idle times in traffic. But a mobile phone in an automobile is accepted as an exotic and expensive device reserved to a small professional or status-seeking class. Yet nothing in technology or economics commands that automobile telephones should be any more difficult or expensive than home telephones. But because of the original public and corporate policy that is now a wasteful allocation of the airwaves, the automobile telephone under present practices is an impossible device for normal popular use.

There will be profound social consequences to the choices made in the new media. Involved are such things as the possible deepening of the cultural isolation of portions of the American population, if the new efficiency of mass media are available on strictly class lines; and invasions of personal privacy on a scale unknown to the most efficient police states of the past, in the creation of automatic accumulations of computerized data banks on every aspect of private lives, available not only to government authorities but also to malicious or selfish private parties. Increased numbers of vivid channels into the home will make demagoguery and public deception more effective than ever before. The power to record instant reactions to presentations, and thus conduct an accurately counted poll, could produce irreversible reactions to manipulated public information.

All of these dangers are the negative sides of positive possibilities, of richer and more rewarding information, of substitution of quick transactions in the home for unwanted transportation, of the more effective pursuit of knowledge and experience on an individual basis, of greater diversity in culture, personality development, and social affairs, and of national and local institutions more aware of the needs of their constituents and more responsive to them.

These are conflicting and sometimes parallel possibilities of the same general communications systems. Whichever way the systems are designed, with whatever balance of results for a free society, they involve changed definitions of "news" and more profound interlocks between the news media and their surrounding environment.

It is helpful in looking at the evolving generation of news media to look at the most striking past example—the spectacular growth of television.

Television illustrates a number of forces that will shape future communications, and one of these is a new phenomenon in popular communications: for the first time, the consumer paid most of the direct cost of equipment.

This is a curious development in mass communications. In the past the consumer has paid only for specific messages. Part of this fee, of course, was to pay for the investment and overhead of the total system, but the consumer paid on the basis of each message he received, and the maintenance of the background machinery was the problem of the entrepreneur. The consumer bought a particular book, magazine, newspaper, telephone call, telegram, postage stamp, or movie admission. Before any of these were offered for sale, some-one—a private corporation or the government—had to make a commitment to invest in the whole system and hope that the consumer payments for its products would be profitable.

Newspapers, for example, pay all the direct costs of getting their message into the home. They buy and maintain fleets of trucks, they organize or deal with wholesale operators, and they support elaborate systems of hand delivery to each home. The newspaper reader ultimately pays for this, of course, but only indirectly, and only if he decides he wants a particular paper. If there is trouble with the distribution system it is the newspaper's problem, not his.

Broadcasting is different. It, too, is a mass medium, which means that it must have many participants before it will work, and yet it would never have grown, and certainly not with its remarkable speed, if the consumer for the first time had not become a direct investor in the basic technical equipment.

The consumer's role in the growth of television and its interplay with other forces tells us something of the process that will govern the new technology through which the next generation will receive its public information.

Success of any mass medium is enhanced by rapid adoption. The lone telephone in one house is useless; its potential usefulness increases as additional phones are installed elsewhere, creating a mutually interacting network. If the lone telephone, or only a few telephones, exist too long without stimulating widespread adoption, investing entrepreneurs lose interest. But, once the system begins to grow rapidly, it attracts more investment, which causes even faster growth.

This has always happened with books, magazines, newspapers, and movies. As the audience enlarged or the entrepreneur believed it ready to enlarge, the business produced more of the messages, made them available, and waited for the public to buy them. And as the public bought—as it purchased books or joined book clubs, or subscribed to magazines, or paid for a daily paper, or lined up at the box office of a move house—the entrepreneurs increased their production to meet the demand. The expansion of the system stimulated its own growth. But it was never suggested that the book or magazine reader buy part of the presses, or telephone and telegraph users purchase part of the wire networks, or that moviegoers invest in a studio, or newspaper subscribers pay for the delivery trucks.

With broadcasting there was an important difference: the ordinary consumer, not the producers, made the biggest initial investment. Unlike any other mass medium, it was the users who paid most of the cost of establishing the system.

Broadcasting, like the telephone, will work only if there is a transmitter and a receiver. But in broadcasting, unlike the telephone, the consumer bought the receiver outright. And in the process consumers invested twenty times more money in equipment than did the entrepreneurs. Furthermore, the public had to be convinced to do this before the system would work well.

The average television station has plant and equipment worth less than $2 million. In the average market, consumers have paid more than $40 million in television sets alone, not counting antennae and maintenance. From 1955 to 1968, consumers paid $25.5 billion for home radio and television sets. During that same period, if the 1963 spending was typical, they spent $8 billion more for radio and television repairs. In 1967, for example, the retail value of color and black-and-white television sets bought in the United States was $3.7 billion. That same year the three television networks and the 612 commercial television stations had tangible broadcasting property investments of $1.2 billion in original costs, and $661 million in depreciated value. Thus, after the producers had taken a tax benefit for some of their investment (which consumers could not do), their total investment in plant and equipment for all the years of television was less than 20 percent of what consumers paid in one year for equipment needed to receive their broadcasts.

Despite the need for millions of consumers to make a financial commitment for a relatively unknown device, the growth of television was spectacular, permitting the conversion of a set of machines into an integrated national system.

Sets in use	
1946	10,000
1947	16,000
1948	190,000
1949	1,000,000
1950	4,000,000
1951	10,600,000
1952	15,800,000
1953	21,200,000

This is all the more remarkable because it represented something more than the purchase of a household appliance: it became a new way of life. Educational, cultural, and political patterns changed as the new electronic box moved into homes. Habits of reading, of doing homework and housework, and of eating family meals were rearranged to place the television set into the daily schedule.

What caused this rapid growth?

One simple factor was the price of television sets. The average retail price of sets during these years of initial growth dropped dramatically.

1946	$500
1947	400
1948	350
1949	320
1950	360
1951	370
1952	370
1953	230

This illustrates another self-benefit of rapid growth: as the device succeeds, it is produced in larger numbers, which usually means lower prices from mass production, and, with more companies rushing to meet a growing market, more competition and accumulated production experience.

Even this lowering price underestimates the impact of reduced costs. Sets sold in 1952 for $370 had larger screens and superior quality compared to the ones sold in 1946 for $500. Furthermore, between 1946 and 1952 average family income rose from $3,940 to $5,122, so the 1952 television set was not only larger, less expensive, and superior in performance, but instead of representing 13 percent of average family income, as it did in 1946, it represented 7 percent. In 1967, the average retail value of color television sets was $525, and since average family income by this time was $8,700, a far more complex set cost less than 7 percent of family income.

Popular assumptions about growth of a large-scale consumer system usually stop here: a manufacturer makes the device, the public likes it, causing the manufacturer and his competitors to make larger quantities of the device, which lowers cost through mass production and competition, and through this simple mechanism the device becomes a standard artifact in society.

But the rapid rise of television required more than millions of isolated machines and isolated transmitters. The spectacular growth of the medium was stimulated by the emergence of a "system," and for television this required technical changes that were largely invisible to the public.

A strong appeal of television was not only the novelty of small electronic movies in the home, but the idea that it was showing real events as they occurred. This gave the viewer in his own home the sense of being present elsewhere, and the excitement of knowing that the scenes were not completely predictable.

The most compelling scenes are ones of great national reputation, like a national political convention or a World Series game. But if these are to be seen all over the country at the time of the actual event, it is crucial that everyone be notified that it will be shown at a standard time. This produces the necessary mass audience and the excitement of a sense of mutual observation with its implied sense of mutual participation. This requires unified advertising of the program to the entire country. National programs that go on the air without national notification are in danger of being seen only by accidental audiences. So the ability to show a program at the same time everywhere was a factor in television's rapid growth.

But early television had no capacity for simultaneous distribution of programs nationally. In 1946 when popular television began, the only national network that could connect most homes and be switched from place to place was the telephone system. The amount of electronic information transmitted with simple voice is relatively small, the variations in pitch and volume needed to make words distinguishable. This worked for ordinary telephone lines and for radio when radio wanted to transmit network programs coast to coast. In effect, the radio networks could make a long-distance call over the standard voice telephone system to every distant station in the network.

But television is a richer medium. To the signals it transmits for voice it adds signals that represent the variations in lightness and darkness that make for moving images. The wires that carried television signals required 120 times the electronic capacity of those that carried radio. The existing telephone system could not be used. There was no way to transmit live programs to all national locations.

In 1945, NBC arranged special connections for its stations in New York City, Schenectady, and Philadelphia for a simultaneous telecast of President Harry Truman making a speech in New York. Such connections can be done by massive reservation of telephone lines, which is impractical except on rare occasions; or by use of microwave relays, the parabolic mirrors that are mounted on towers and transmit high-capacity signals through the air to other towers, in line of sight;

or else by a special high-capacity communications cable, called coaxial, able to carry the broadband signals of television.

In the absence of such a national system in the early years of television, programs were filmed and flown, by propeller plane, to each city. The photographic quality of the film was not good and, of course, it did not permit nationwide live programming.

The spread of the coaxial cable coincides with the rise of television-set sales. In 1948 there was little coaxial cable (and there were only 190,000 television sets in use). By July 1, 1949, the cable had reached Chicago and St. Louis, permitting live broadcasting to the eastern third of the country (by then, there were 1 million sets). From there films were flown to Western cities. On September 4, 1951, the coaxial cable having reached the West Coast, there was the first coast-to-coast live television program, the signing of the Japanese Peace Treaty in San Francisco, seen by fifty-two stations simultaneously with the added help of a few microwave links (by then 11 million sets). Though in 1940 there had been no coaxial cable, by 1950 there were 63,000 miles.

The coaxial cable and microwave links permitted national programming of a uniform and widespread kind, which had the effect of stimulating sales of television sets. People buy new communications for the content, not the ingenuity of the machine. National talent shows and intense national promotion of the shows helped fuse the population in a social pattern of viewing that was self-reinforcing. In the late 1940s millions of children left the streets and backyards in the early evening to see *Howdy Doody,* an early popular children's program. They not only knew about it but they were further inclined to watch because other children ended their outdoor play in order to watch the program. Since they all saw it each night, they talked about it the next day, increasing the chances that they would watch again the next night.

The popularity of specific programs publicized the new medium and helped increase sales of television sets. The *Milton Berle Show,* the *Kraft Television Theater,* the *Voice of Firestone,* and *Philco Television Playhouse* were objects of daily conversation and nightly household habits. The showing of the World Series in 1948 and the two national conventions made both the public and the networks eager for the coaxial cable to reach the West Coast. The new device

was cheaper than weekly movies for the whole family, more convenient, and presented a broader range of information.

The speed of the system's growth and the medium's power to shape
national tastes depended then on the conviction of the American
Telephone & Telegraph Company that it would be profitable to install
thousands of miles of coaxial cable and forests of microwave towers.
Growth of a national system was also enhanced by promotion of a
few popular programs at fixed times in all parts of the country; the
urge to buy a television set came not alone from the advertising and
television industries, but also from neighbors and friends who talked
about the new entertainment.

But the evolution of a mass system is more complicated than that,
especially in an industry like broadcasting that is regulated by the
government. Public policy enters the scene. The intertwined forces of
public policy, corporate policy, and induced popular habits shaped
television, as they are about to shape the next generation of public
communications. And here, too, television is a useful example of how
these act on each other.

In the regulated industry, decisions of the Federal Communications
Commission influenced specifications for receiving sets, assigned stations to particular locations, and issued these licenses on the basis of
whatever would "promote public convenience or interest or [would]
serve public necessity." But these were not simple, personal judgments.

To begin with, public policy is reached in a complicated way. It
may depend on a law passed by Congress, which in itself is the result
of many conflicting forces. Or it may be issued by a government
regulatory agency, which, because its members are appointed by the
President and receives its operating funds from Congress, also responds to something more than a theoretical conclusion about the
public welfare based on pure reason and abstract analysis.

Corporations directly involved in public policy decisions do not sit
passively while regulatory agencies reach philosophic conclusions.
They are often in exclusive possession of technical and economic data
which the public, the Congress, and the regulatory agency cannot
easily match. Where decisions are based on these, the corporations
are in the position of both applicants for favored position and
uncontested expert witnesses.

Large corporations are seldom without long and deep associations with influential members of the Congress and of the Executive. Contributions are made to election campaigns. Highly paid and sophisticated lobbyists (or "Washington representatives") work full time for years to establish useful relations with decision makers. Much of the technical language of legislation and of regulatory rules originates with the paid representatives of the industries to be "regulated."

Often there is more than one corporation competing for a favored decision, and the Congress, the White House, or the regulatory agency may find itself in the position of compromiser among competing special interests, rather than enunciator of policy fashioned primarily for benefit of the general public. In all of this, the general public is seldom represented. In the rare cases when it is, its representatives can seldom match the corporate representatives in accumulated technical and economic data and close continuing political associations with decision makers. Nor do public representatives often have the money or the full-time professional expertise of corporate specialists in lobbying, public relations, and advertising.

Consequently, much of public policy is evolved in a relatively closed, specialized proceeding, the results of which the general public sees as an accomplished fact, which it can then either accept totally or reject totally. With telephones, for example, it can decide to use the system with its predetermined characteristics and rates, or it can decide not to use the system. With television, it can buy sets as they are designed, and view programs as they are broadcast, or it can reject them all. It can, of course, complain and petition corporations and government policy-making bodies, and occasionally this is done and on rare occasions it produces results. But this requires large-scale organization and expertise at a time when the implications of the new system are not yet felt by the general public. Only after the new system has been in operation does the consumer see its effects, and by then he has been conditioned by the system to expect only what it already has produced. Communications media create their own audiences, and while they are not immune to independent mass reactions, they establish national tastes as much as they reflect them. If the public, after exposure, comes to an independent judgment against the product of the system, the system by then is so elaborate and committed that it is difficult to alter. Today the original intent of the British Treasury of 1711 in imposing a tax on newspaper pages has long been forgotten, but the resulting large newspaper pages throughout the world endure in the habits of millions of consumers.

Television, in a highly telescoped sequence of events, also was formed of conflicting and unpredictable forces, in which public policy, corporate ambitions, ingrained public habits, and accident played their parts.

The first impulse in television was a corporate one. In the 1930s some entrepreneurs, like David Sarnoff of RCA and Alan DuMont, understood the enormous potential of the new medium and decided to develop it. This was important because many other businessmen either did not understand the new device, or if they did, they decided that the idea of a great national linkage of miniature home movies was an amusing idiocy. This view was especially strong in the movie industry, which saw television as an incredibly inferior fragment of the theater screen.

Men experienced in electronics saw television not as an eccentric form of the cinema, but as an enriched version of an already-successful network of small household boxes, radio. Comprehension of the technological and economic potential of the new device was the first step, and it is not surprising that in the years after World War II it was the radio operators—NBC, CBS, ABC, and DuMont—that became the prime movers in television. This provided an important corporate commitment. In 1946 there were twelve commercial channels that reached from six thousand to ten thousand sets. In mass communications an audience of ten thousand—or of forty thousand if one accepted the estimates of that period of four viewers per set—is no audience at all. Even two years later, in 1948, when there were forty-six stations and one million receivers, the four television networks had revenues of $8 million and expenses of $23 million. In the face of such losses, to stay in the business, as three of them did, required confidence in rapid future growth. It also meant that they were not casual about government rules laid down for their operations.

Some were moved more deeply than others. NBC, like the others, expected that it could make a profit operating television stations and producing programs. But it had the added motivation that its parent corporation, RCA, also manufactured the receivers that consumers would buy if the new medium succeeded. And this was further sweetened by the knowledge that, even if its network competitors produced more attractive programs, they would, whether they liked it or not, be contributing to sales of sets by RCA, which in turn would make it easier for the RCA subsidiary, NBC, to finance more attractive programs.

Public policy entered directly because broadcasting is a regulated industry. The industry was resigned to this because as radio pioneers it had experienced the chaos of radio in the 1920s before government stepped in to assign positions on the dial. They largely accepted FCC power to set minimum standards of transmitting, of location and power of stations, of where each station would be on the dial, of how many stations particular communities would have, and of who would receive the licenses based on a standard of potential public service.

The corporate petitioners in this early public policy understood most of the implications of the government's power to assign locations on the dial, and the early entrepreneurs concentrated on obtaining laws and regulations that would maximize profits. The general public did not see this. Even the technical name, "electro-magnetic spectrum allocation," was forbidding and arcane, and to the lay public seemed an esoteric decision best left to engineers. It was, in fact, a decision that had considerable impact on American culture and politics.

The number of channels in any communications medium has profound consequences. With books and magazines, it means the variety of subjects and, because of mass production and retailing, their availability to a large audience. With newspapers, it decides how many papers a community will have and how many different points of view will be printed. If the number of channels—or flexibility in the market place—is large, then success by the early corporations will attract others who will put out competing products, justifying still more channels. One result of this can be greater diversity of choice for the consumer and lower cost for each channel. If, however, the medium succeeds and the number of channels is limited, there is little room for newcomers. The earliest and most successful entrepreneurs remain in possession of the medium with monopoly or near-monopoly programming and profits, and a rising cost for the scarce channel space.

As early as 1931 technical and manufacturing people in electronics began considering how many television channels there should be and where in the airwaves they should be located. In 1936 there was a recommendation to have channels in the Very High Frequency range. World War II intervened. In 1945 a technical advisory board recommended thirty channels.

Broadcasting corporations had conflicting wishes. NBC wished to place television in the Very High Frequency band. CBS wanted it in the Ultra High Frequencies.

VHF had the advantage of transmitting a strong signal farther, up to forty miles without serious loss, which means that a transmitter in the center of a city could place a strong television picture in homes in the surrounding five thousand square miles, and a fairly good picture in twice that area. But VHF had the disadvantage of being a crowded part of the radio-wave spectrum with room for only thirteen channels interspersed among the frequencies used for radio-telephones, state police cars, aviation radio, and the military. After Channel 1 was put into use it interfered with radio-telephones and was canceled for television, leaving a maximum of twelve channels. But usually only half of the twelve could be used in any one locality, since VHF traveled far enough to interfere with the same channel in the adjacent metropolitan area. So, in general, even-numbered channels were used in one metropolitan area and odd-numbered ones in the one adjacent, which meant a maximum of six channels per market.

UHF was a large and relatively uncrowded part of the radio spectrum, permitting seventy channels of television. But UHF was less successful than VHF in getting beyond obstructions like buildings and hills, and was reliable only for twenty-five miles from the transmitter. This would cover less than two thousand square miles from a midtown tower. The majority of profitable consumers lived in large cities, which is where the largest television entrepreneurs had already established themselves. In a sprawling metropolitan area the difference between five thousand square miles and two thousand square miles translated into numbers of households is enormous. In the largest cities, some of the best customers were in the suburbs, precisely in the area between twenty-five miles and forty miles from downtown, which is where VHF continued strong but UHF began to fade. Furthermore, at the end of World War II, UHF technology was less developed than VHF.

The FCC selected VHF, though it said that someday all of television would end up in UHF. It was a technical, public-policy decision that was to have profound consequences.

As new stations went on the air, what had been considered an advantage of VHF—its ability to send its signal farther—turned into an electronic crisis. On frequent occasions, atmospheric conditions permitted the VHF signals to bounce and skip, so that a Channel 5 in one city would suddenly be received by a Channel 5 in another city five hundred miles away, which in the original plan had been considered far enough away for use of the same channel.

By the middle of 1948 there were forty-six stations on the air, seventy-eight more under construction, three hundred applications pending for additional stations, and still more known to be on the way. Because of the unexpected interference and fast popularity, it was obvious that there would not be enough space under the original VHF plan to satisfy the demand. So on September 30, 1948, the FCC froze all new applications for television stations while it contemplated its dilemma.

The freeze, lengthened by the Korean War, lasted four years. On April 14, 1952, the FCC added the UHF band to television, expanding the potential number of stations from 650 to 2,035. But public policy did not permit the needed growth to the new potential. By the time the freeze ended, there were 17 million home TV sets in use, few of them equipped to receive UHF. UHF stations went on the air and discovered that they were mostly talking to themselves. By 1954 only 8 percent of television sets in use were able to receive UHF, and ten years after that only 10 percent. UHF was, and continues to be, a financial disaster, compared with VHF.

In 1967 the average for all VHF stations was revenues 40 percent higher than expenses—or profit; for all UHF stations it was 20 percent less than expenses—or loss. Again, public policy, with its quiet private influences, was at fault. The VHF broadcasting industry had become established and strong, not only in audience habits, but in political influence in Congress. When the FCC freed the use of the UHF wave lengths, it wished to require all television sets to be made at the factory with UHF built in. But Congress refused. When the FCC granted UHF licenses, it placed most of them in markets where VHF stations were already established and had the only available network affiliations. Network affiliations constitute the most important single factor in making high profits with a television station. And where there were already VHF stations, 90 percent of receivers could not receive the new stations without buying extra converters and antennae. The cycle of more-stations-stimulate-more-receivers-stimulate-more-stations never developed momentum and UHF, admitted late to the game and then with heavy burdens, was ordained to failure.

The mistakes are various and instructive. The false start of the FCC toward all-VHF had its roots partly in technology, the higher confidence in VHF experience, plus the unexpected bounce-and-skip problem. The political influence of the early entrepreneurs in VHF delayed for twelve years the law requiring UHF equipment in television sets, so that seventeen years after UHF stations were permitted to broadcast half the television sets in the country still were not equipped to receive them. The failure to create all-VHF and all-UHF markets further weakened UHF in the competition.

Even if all VHF channels were used and succeeded, there would still be severe limitations on the total number of channels available to the public. The maximum would be six channels in the biggest cities, and four or fewer in 80 percent of all television markets.

The consequences of an unnecessary shortage of television channels during the time of television's formative years and of its most rapid expansion had deeper consequences than the business failures of UHF stations.

As the success of television became clear, and the public began to develop its television tastes and expectations, the usual rush of new competitors into the field did not occur. In the nineteenth century, when newspapers were finally released from the constraints of colonial censorship and wartime shortages, when technology and public tastes supported more printed information, the number of daily and weekly newspapers rose from two hundred in 1800 to sixteen thousand in 1900, or an average of thirty for each urban place of over eight thousand population.

But, in the case of television in an analogous period of growth, there was no such proliferation of alternative channels, and in the shortage of channels, the earliest corporations developed monopoly and near-monopoly domination. With this came standardized programming, with the public presented little choice. Generation One of television accepted the only programming it ever knew as something inherent and unavoidable in the new medium.

The shortage of channels inhibited local programming. The basic Communications Act directed that broadcasting licenses should be distributed in a "fair, efficient and equitable" pattern among communities, and made it plain that this meant studios for originating local programs. This was considered socially important. Otherwise it would have been far cheaper to give every city its present average of six television channels operated by six national studios whose signals are distributed by automatic local relay stations. Instead, almost all local transmitters are part of completely equipped local studios. Yet, at prime time when the main American audience is watching, 95 percent of all programming originates in national network studios.

With a small number of channels, the dominance of national programming was inevitable. The professional polish and access to talent of national organizations could not be matched by individual local stations, and for that reason the national programs would attract a larger audience. Because it could attract a larger audience, it could sell its advertising time for higher prices, which further increased the gap in resources between local and national programs.

Local programming would depend on smaller audiences that would be tolerable only if there were surplus channels after the networks occupied national channels. But in most cities there were no surplus channels after the networks contracted for their time. All of television in its first twenty-five years was fashioned by the idea of One Big National Audience, with advertising, economics, and ratings attuned to audiences in multiples of one million, which in most communities cannot be matched by local programming. At prime time, in the hours after the evening meal, audiences of five million are considered failures, although no newspaper or book ever reaches that many people. A city that at best might squeeze three hundred citizens into a crucial city-council meeting chamber but could televise the same proceedings to an audience of three thousand would be considered unjustified in doing so under the standards for audience size that have been established in commercial television.

The rationale of One Big National Audience inevitably meant that in order to evoke and maintain the interest of so large a single audience all national programming (and, because of its dominance in competition, all local programming) would have to find the lowest common denominator of interest, which is action, conflict, sex, violence, and entertainment of the most general kind.

And, even in the show-business values that inexorably dominated the competition, there was limited variety. Producers of shows and men with new ideas had, in effect, only three networks to bargain with. Even though the new medium presented live performances in real time to the largest audience in the history of man, three organizations decided who would have access to that audience. Since advertisers have one commanding principle, to get their message before the largest possible number of people at the lowest possible cost, the rewards went to the winner in the race for audience. The losers then imitated the winner in programming in order to exploit the formula that brought success.

Ironically, television has the greatest technical reason to be localized—its signals travel in short, straight lines and are blocked by large obstructions. But, because of corporate policy and its influence on regulation, it became a medium dominated by standardized national programming. Local service, to which television's technology and basic national law gives first importance, in fact became a casual afterthought, entered into reluctantly at the least attractive times and at the lowest possible cost.

It would be a mistake to imply that the existence of national programming in news, public affairs, and entertainment is inherently bad or has no value. In any country it is important. In the United States it is a necessity. The richness and creativeness of American society are dependent on intense localism and on the variety of cultural and political sources of its population. But, without some agreement among these diverse elements on the realities of their common environment and on broad national values, the nation would cease to have compatible politics and, ultimately, to be a viable culture. The genius of the federal system, from the start of the nation's history, has been an equilibrium between local diversity and basic national values.

Where this equilibrium has failed there have been tragic consequences. The Deep South, for example, has remained economically, culturally, and politically isolated from the rest of the country. The relationship between its local values and federal ones for 150 years has been unlike that in any other region. Its textbooks, newspapers, and radio stations carried news, information, and social values as distinct from the rest of the country as the United States is from many foreign countries, with only superficial sharing of some of the more important national political and social values—universal suffrage, equal treatment under law, and the ethic of equal opportunity. The fragility of this relationship was revealed when the first powerful national medium, television, penetrated Deep South culture. The rapid rise thereafter of politically suppressed blacks and culturally isolated whites was a reflection of the dangerous chasm that had existed for so long between the values of the Southern caste system and the casteless goals of the rest of the country. This chasm has created the most profound crisis in American unity.

In all regions of the country, television penetrated cultural islands where other media like books and newspapers had been ineffective. In places like big-city ghettos and rural regions, television with its national message found pockets of alienation from the rest of national life. Much of what television has been blamed for—the deliberate use of sex and violence, to maintain large audiences, and the insistent materialism of its commercials—is justified. But some of the social stresses created by the spread of television arose from the medium's power to transmit genuine national values to isolated pockets of parochialism that had resisted all earlier media.

If cohesion in the United States is to be retained, popular national media will be needed to provide commonly available news of reality and social values. But if national media are not to degenerate into rigid conformity and continental bureaucracy, it must have two other characteristics: a wide choice of views and a balance of local mass communications independent of centralized control.

Thus, it is not the idea of national networks that is bad, but the lack of a balance with vigorous and creative local programming. This lack of balance has been the inevitable product not of technology, but of particular corporate and public policies governing the use of the technology.

Future home communications and their offerings of news and public affairs will change in the next generation, probably more radically than television changed the radio and print era. The two most important innovations in technology that will stimulate that change are cable television and the computer, and both of those have already started the process that characterized the swift penetration of the American culture by aerial television.

Cable is the multichanneled wire that carries messages into the home, as a substitute for television that comes through the air. It is more reliable, produces a superior picture, and has a greater capacity for added channels than aerial frequencies now being used. Because the wires go to specific homes, they have the potential for delivering particular messages to particular groups of homes. Cable also has the potential for precisely measuring the size, characteristic, and location of the audience at any given time, which can produce important changes in the economics and programming of the mass media. It has potential far beyond the simple substitution for aerially transmitted radio and television.

The growth curve of cable shows some similarities to that of television—a slow early start that suddenly turns upward in what appears to be the self-speeding phenomenon of rapid spread of a mass medium. But it also shows that this is seriously influenced by rival corporate ambitions and public policy.

Cable Homes

1958	450,000
1959	550,000
1960	650,000
1961	725,000
1962	850,000
1963	950,000
1964	1,085,000
1965	1,600,000
1966	2,500,000
1967	3,000,000
1968	3,500,000

Compared with television's 56 million homes in 1968, cable still had a long way to go. In 1968 television was in 97 percent of all American homes, cable in only 6.4 percent. But cable in the last few years has grown 25 percent a year; this growth if continued will bring it into almost all homes sometime in the late 1970s, and, if the self-feeding intensity of VHF television holds, even earlier.

When cable started twenty years ago, as a rural installation in commercial establishments like motels and saloons, it carried from one to three channels, the usual charge for making the physical installation was $150 per television set, and the continuing monthly charge was from $10 to $15. By 1970, some cable companies were making the initial connection without charge, and the usual monthly fee for twenty channels is $5. What used to be a first-year cost to the consumer of $230 per channel was now $3.

But cable, like other public systems, does not live in a simple world of technology or supply-and-demand. It conflicts with the status and ambitions of other corporate services. They all know that their fates will be conditioned by governmental decisions, and they are not sitting with patient docility while members of Congress and commissioners of the FCC and the courts construct a high-minded philosophy of home communication. The battle, whose sounds are heard only intermittently by the general public, is ferocious, complicated, and full of meaning for American society.

Cable, for example, is a threat to the most highly evolved communications system in the world, the American Telephone & Telegraph Company. AT&T, with its operating subsidiaries, owns the 84 million telephones that are in 87 percent of all American homes, and owns the elaborate $43 billion worth of networks that permit each phone to reach any other phone in a matter of seconds. (There are twenty-two hundred other telephone companies in the United States but none matches AT&T; all two thousand two hundred together have only 16 percent of all telephones and 13 percent of telephone revenues.)

By all accounts, AT&T operates the most effective mass telephone system anywhere, with the exception of those in one or two small countries. It is a legal monopoly, which is to say that it is one of those corporate activities which the public has decided will not benefit from competitive free enterprise in the market place, since duplicated, triplicated, and quadruplicated electric, gas, and telephone services in the same community would be wasteful and expensive to the consuming public. The corporation is regulated by the government to ensure that it delivers maximum public service in return for assurance that wherever it is established it is guaranteed a fair profit and a monopoly. A particular monopoly underlies AT&T's traditional status: no one else had placed a communication wire into the American home. No one, that is, until the appearance of cable television.

Cable is not a duplicate of the telephone system. It is a broadcasting medium, which means that it sends a message outward in only one direction to a large and undifferentiated audience. When the outbound message travels in this novel wire to the home there is no way to send a responsive signal back over the same wire. It is not a switched network, with a mechanism for guiding a particular message to a particular consumer, or connecting one home device with any other home device. Cable does none of these things, which are peculiar to the telephone system.

But, even as a one-way, unswitched wire, cable has some formidable characteristics. The telephone wire into the home carries simple voice signals, which require relatively small electronic capacity. One channel of television, carrying voice and moving images, requires two thousand times more electronic capacity than a telephone voice wire. Most cable systems in the late 1960s were installing twenty-channel wires into homes, and at least one was using forty-two-channel wire. So, where there are two communications lines going into a home, the one for cable television may have eighty-four thousand times more communications capacity than the telephone wire.

This sudden emergence of a high-capacity wire to home and office comes at a particularly unnerving time for AT&T. Until recently, its network was designed solely for sending voice signals, particularly through the elaborate automatic dialing and switching systems that permit connecting each phone with any one of 100 million other phones. Occasionally there was an overload, as there was in the late 1960s in Manhattan's financial district and at a few special periods in residential neighborhoods. But, on the whole, the telephone network evolved at a pace tolerable for a growing population of conversationalists.

But, as communications technology mushroomed, men wished to send more complex messages than simple voice. Television is only one example. Computers, with their mammoth intake and output of information, began adding noticeable burdens to the telephone system, since communication with large computers is usually by telephone line carrying masses of digital signals. By 1975 it is expected that the quantity of computer and data-processing signals will exceed voice. Other commercial operators wished to transmit not only voices but documents such as engineering drawings, blueprints, graphs, tables, and texts in their original form without having to attempt reproduction of them into verbal form for voice or word communication, and this used facsimile, that needed more capacity than telephone lines if it was to be done quickly. Partly as an answer to this, AT&T began introducing its own switched high-capacity system, Picturephone, a small television screen combined with telephone so that men could watch each other as they talked and display documents to each other. But Picturephone, since it sends pictures as well as voices, requires about one hundred times more communications capacity than the normal telephone line. It would be limited for a long time to a few concentrated locations and it would cost about $100 a month. Television uses special coaxial cable and microwave systems because its signals will not fit on telephone lines, and television operators have been increasingly vocal about the $50 million a year they pay AT&T for the special systems that carry programs to the local stations.

Newspapers wishing to escape traffic of large cities have studied the possibility of a scattering of smaller satellite plants in the outskirts, each serving its own area on the rim of the metropolis. The major barrier to transmitting their editorial and advertising information from the central editing locations to the satellite plants is the high cost of transmitting the information electronically through conventional telephone-operated systems.

As the pressure increased for higher-capacity communications lines, so did the complaints of costs, since long-distance communication in the United States is no longer an exotic family holiday exercise but a common commercial transaction. Substantial businesses are more likely than individual families to analyze costs and bargain for their reduction.

At the same time that cable raised its ominous head for the telephone company, so did communications satellites. The normal method of long-distance communications has been wire and microwave towers across continents and undersea cable under water. Until 1956 cables under the Atlantic Ocean were for telegraph service only. The first transatlantic telephone cable was completed in 1956 between the United States and Europe and had only 36 telephone circuits that cost $45 million (until then transatlantic telephone calls went by short-wave radio, whose quality depended on atmospheric conditions). In 1970 a United States–Spain telephone cable had a

720-circuit capacity and cost about $80 million. So cost per telephone circuit from 1956 to 1970 dropped on submarine cables from $1.25 million a circuit to $110,000.

But it could hardly compete with the new satellites. Rocket technology permitted placing them in orbit over a single spot on the earth, rather than letting them wander about like the moon. The fixed position meant that satellites could cover a definite and continuous area of earth, up to a million square miles. Their longevity and effectiveness were higher than expected. The first one, Early Bird, in 1965 had 240 telephone circuits, at a cost for the satellite itself and the cost of rocketing it into orbit of $15,300 per circuit per year. Undersea cables last much longer than space satellites, but the satellites are still cheaper. Intelsat II, put up in 1966, had 240 telephone circuits and cost $8,400 per circuit per year. Intelsat III, in 1968, had 1,200 circuits at a cost of $1,450 per circuit, and Intelsat IV, scheduled for 1971, would have 6,000 circuits at a cost of $500 per circuit per year. Each succeeding satellite has cost less per circuit, has had larger capacity and has had a longer life expectancy. Even though Intelsat IV was expected to live only for seven years, and the latest submarine telephone cable to Spain will last much longer, to match the per-year circuit cost of the Intelsat IV satellite the latest telephone cable would have to work efficiently for 220 years.

These satellites are increasingly used for international television, at rapidly decreasing costs. In three years, for example, the cost of a ten-minute color-television relay by communication satellite went from $2,000 to $660. The impact of this on international relations and global cultural relations will be considerable, since television will effectively overcome many of the language barriers that exist with almost every other medium.

The use of long-distance communications by satellite over the continental United States is no less challenging to conventional land channels. Television network executives have said they used to use a rule of thumb of a-dollar-a-minute-a-mile for AT&T charges for connecting national studios with distant transmitters.

David Sarnoff, chairman of the board of RCA Corporation, in 1965 predicted that by 1975 satellites could transmit three color-TV channels to all of the United States and Canada for the present cost of buying one big-city television station.

Most specialists now believe that satellites will be used in broadcasting for long-distance network transmissions to feed local systems that will distribute the programs by cable to individual homes. Some believe that satellites may broadcast directly to the home, eliminating both local transmitters and local wires. Most likely will be a combination of methods, satellites as the networking device for the long-distance link to local cable systems; but satellites may broadcast direct to individual homes in sparsely populated areas where it is costly to reach each home by wire, or to mobile sets in automobiles, boats, and aircraft where fixed wires are impossible.

It is not just radio and television that might be affected by satellites. In 1969 General Electric filed a study with the Federal Communications Commission in which it said that mail and telegraph messages ought to go by satellite, and that by 1975 it thought a six-hundred-word letter could be transmitted instantly from coast to coast for thirty-three cents, and sometime after that for ten cents.

One profound effect of satellites will be the introduction for the first time in communications history of the idea that the cost of sending a message will not be affected by the distance it has to travel. Postal systems come close to this idea since, in the United States, for example, first-class service costs the same whether a letter is going across the street or across the continent. But, even with the mail, there is an extra cost for airmail, which is generally a function of distance. And, in both instances, the uniform money cost is countered by the cost in added time since in general the farther the distance to be traveled, the longer it takes. For practically all other communications, and certainly for instantaneous ones, the fee charged is directly related to the mileage involved.

In general, this principle has been based on real costs. AT&T maintains a vast complex of real estate, telephone poles, underground cable, microwave towers, and switching stations, all maintained by 700,000 employees, through which long-range messages pass. Western Union has almost one million miles of overhead and underground wires with its system of switching stations and twenty-seven thousand employees, all applied to each message as it travels, mile by mile, over the land system.

Satellites hold the potential for ending the factor of distance in the cost of communication. Parked twenty-two thousand miles above earth, they are like an electronic mirror that accepts the upward-bound message and radiates it back on the twenty-two-thousand-mile downward link, aimed at the destination. The round trip for any message is forty-four thousand miles, with only insignificant variations between different points on earth. It would cost the same to send a message from Boston to its suburb of Stoneham, Massachusetts, an overland distance of ten miles, as it would from Boston to San Francisco, an overland distance of twenty-seven hundred miles. The long-distance mechanism for this forty-four-thousand-mile round trip to any two points is a three-hundred-pound satellite in the sky that cost less than $2 million. Such satellites, along with the $10–$20 million rockets needed to place them into orbit, plus the ground stations that originate and receive their signals, will become a major competitor of the telephone company's earth-bound long distance plant which now has a book value of $7 billion.

Cable and satellites both relate to that great engine of change in human communication, the electronic computer.

The spread of computers has been less visible than that of television, but it has been even more spectacular and may have similarly deep social consequences. In 1955 all the computers in the United States working together could do about 500,000 additions a second; in 1975 they will be able to do 80 billion a second. The 1975 computer will be 1/10,000th the size of the 1955 computer that did comparable work. The same problem that the 1955 computer took eleven hours to solve will take the 1975 computer one second. The computation that cost $200,000 on the 1955 computer will cost $1 on the 1975 model. Though they are only now beginning to realize it, the American public is about to have the electronic computer enter their lives as a mechanism for social change as widespread as the automobile and television set.

The computer is generally understood to be a rapid and obedient servant in making mathematical calculations. The average consumer is less aware of its powers of memory, of its ability to accept anyone's logic to sort out vast masses of information, and its ability to "learn" in the sense that if it is asked to remember the pattern of demands on it by a particular user it can automatically remember the interest of that user and in the future give him the kind of thing he has been asking for in the past. It stores not only numbers and logic, but enormous quantities of printed and graphic material, and if this is indexed properly it can sort through and select out only those parts that are of interest to the questioner. If, for example, all the issues of the *New York Times* in its history are committed to a computer memory, as the *Times* plans to do, and these are indexed properly, as the *Times* also plans to do, it will be possible for a questioner to learn in seconds the answer to a question like "Since 1851 [the founding of the original *New York Times*] which presidential Cabinet members and other prominent advisers have resigned over policy differences with the White House?" Or "Please print out with its date and place of delivery every paragraph spoken or written that Politician X has made on the issue of race relations since 1946. And please follow this with all his recorded votes on race-related issues before Congress."

Computerized libraries and specialized journals are already developing this kind of capacity, some with the ability to reproduce requested documents in distant places.

As a household device, the computer can record all the utility meters, automatically instruct the householder's bank computer to "pay" the utility based on the meter readings, keep a record of this with an automatic item for all tax-deductible portions, and when income tax time comes, deliver all the other tax-related information the consumer needs.

It can be connected with thermostats so that an ominous pattern of high temperatures can automatically notify the fire department. It can do the same with sensing devices on door locks and windows, for burglaries. It can operate ovens in complicated patterns. It could even release fresh food and water for pets left at home for a long period, "know" when the animal has not eaten the food, and notify the veterinarian to check the home.

Libraries, and other central collections of information, will eventually have their material in computerized form, for queries to and from other locations like schools and, eventually, from the home.

Credit bureaus, government agencies, and other information establishments will have interconnected computers so that massive data about each individual and about the total population will be known and, what is more important, inexpensively searched. Already where many people eat in restaurants, fly in airplanes, stay in hotels, and drive cars is known in computer form through their credit-card companies. The inventories of their household belongings will be known to insurance companies and moving-van operators. Precise and useful studies of society can come from this, but also an invasion of privacy and the possibility of malicious use beyond anything previously known.

Computers as switching mechanisms will affect the mass media. They can receive messages for an individual—mail, news, published texts—find the home communication line belonging to the individual, and send the message into his home, to appear either on a Xerox-like facsimile device, or on a television screen, or onto a magnetic tape to be played on the home screen at the convenience of the individual.

If cable television is connected to a computer, it will be possible to record who is listening to what program for how long. If, in addition, the cable has two-way capacity, with the consumer in his home able to signal back to the computer, this will permit, among other things, an instant public-opinion poll on a variety of subjects, commercial and political. Or, if positive electronic identification of each person is developed, citizens may be able to vote from their homes.

Social reaction and responsiveness will reach greater precision and sensitivity than ever before. But the same technique also poses the danger of massive manipulation and deception. A powerful public leader on television could present a picture of national crisis and ask for an immediate response, and use the response to his unfiltered and unexamined warning as justification for drastic and irreversible action.

Cable connected to computers has two less dramatic possibilities that could change the basic forms of the mass media. One is advertising. The other is the measuring of audiences.

Today advertising provides almost 100 percent of all commercial broadcasting operations and 75 percent of newspaper revenues. This is all "push" advertising in the sense that the merchant "pushes" a uniform message to a total audience in the expectation that in the exposure to the total audience he will find the minority—on national television 2 percent is enough—who will buy his product. Because in most media, either national or local, he is pushing his message before the total audience, he provides most of the revenues for the total medium he uses.

There are a few departures from this. One is a catalogue in which the merchant provides product information to a narrower audience he considers the most likely customers, and these customers take the initiative to select the particular items they want to order.

In some cases, the area for choice is even more precise. A customer can ask for a list of particular classes of goods. A book collector can ask a dealer for his list on comparative anthropology. Or a housewife can call the department store on the telephone and ask for the prices of the one item she knows she wants. This is the "pull" phenomenon in merchandising, in which the customer already knows what he wants and "pulls" information about it from the merchant.

Cable holds the possibility of the color-television catalogue. If there is a two-way communication, the customer in his home can ask to see a colored photograph, or moving-picture demonstration, of a particular item or class of item, along with text describing its specifications and price and its availability in nearby stores. On the basis of that presentation, he may make his decision on the spot. This would seriously undercut the present advertising basis for the news media, especially if such a televised, computerized catalogue was operated independently of the media. Merchants, instead of blanketing the entire audience by paying the broadcasting stations and newspapers, would put their money into the film and texts on the central shopping computer. Instead of the advertiser "pushing" information at a general audience, individual consumers would "pull" the information from the data bank. The "push" strategy of advertising represents about $5 billion a year in newspaper revenues, $3 billion for television, $1 billion for radio, and $1 billion for magazines. Some of this $10 billion, or its future equivalent, probably will be diverted to "pull" advertising responding to consumer initiative.

The other basic change that cable-connected-to-computers would make in the mass media would be in the measurement of audiences. This would affect broadcasting more than newspapers, since there is more precision in measuring newspaper audiences. But if the "pull" pattern also applied to news—with the consumer asking for specific classes of information—this would influence the nature of all future news organizations.

The $4 billion a year that supports almost all of broadcasting is allocated on the basis of ratings of the size of audience for particular programs on particular stations. The ratings that measure the audience are based on meters attached to a sample of the nation's radio and television sets, or on diaries that a different sample of listeners are asked to keep of programs they actually listen to.

There have been many criticisms of the ratings. An extensive hearing by a House of Representatives subcommittee in 1964–1965 inquired into rating procedures. The Nielsen television ratings were based on twelve hundred meters attached to a carefully selected twelve hundred home TV sets that would represent a sample of all the sets in the country, and a thousand meters on radio sets. The meter had a continuous film that recorded which station was tuned in at every minute the set was turned on. The American Research Bureau used diaries kept by a sample of families.

The theory of sampling fifty million television sets by twelve hundred meters is sound statistically, just as public-opinion polling of seventy million voters by sixteen hundred questionnaires is sound, so long as care is taken to be sure that the sample is not biased in any direction different from the total population.

For national and major local television programs, where there are relatively few competitors on the air, and the audiences are large, such sampling, with all its flaws, is tolerably accurate. And this determines what the American public sees on television: the ratings point to the most popular programs, and nonrated programs tend to follow the leader because advertisers allocate their money on the basis of the ratings.

If a rating service shows that a prime-time television program has forty million listeners all over the country, an advertiser is fairly safe in assuming that among the forty million listeners there are people who may buy his product. In the absence of more accurate information, he depends on the supposition that scattered through the forty million are the people with characteristics good for his business.

But there is no present way in which local programs for small audiences can be measured economically. It is possible that, in a city of forty thousand households that has twenty radio and television stations, one of the smaller radio stations at 9 P.M. might have all four thousand of the richest families in town, or five thousand of the strongest buyers of books, or ten thousand of the families most likely to buy a foreign car, or any of the numberless permutations of commercially profitable special audiences. But small local audiences are not measured because the sampling would have to be so elaborate to catch that particular audience at that particular time on one particular radio channel that the cost of the survey would be exorbitant.

There is much complaint about the lack of specialized programming on television and particularly on radio. And, though there are a number of factors involved, the most important single one is the high cost of measuring anything but a mass audience. And in the absence of more precise measurements, advertisers have spent their broadcasting money on the national mass programs for which there are reliable statistics.

The result has been the reverse in broadcasting of what has happened in magazine publishing. Where once large popular national magazines were dominant—the *Saturday Evening Post, Colliers, Liberty, Look,* and *Life*—today the general popular magazine is dying. Its advertising revenue is being drained away to the smaller, specialized magazines, whose audiences are carefully separated by subject matter—an "automatic" measurement of specialized audiences through subscription lists.

The audience for boating, flying, sewing, home decorating, cooking, stamp collecting, and sportscar driving, and consumer groups identified in many other ways are reachable by magazines directed at that specialty. The advertiser is able to pay lower rates because he can focus tightly on his maximum buyers, and not waste money on a magazine that goes to a far larger audience than the advertiser wishes to reach. The nature of that small audience is implied by the subject matter of the magazine, and the success in reaching that audience is measured by the magazine's audited circulation. The audience is even more attractive because its interest is proven by its paying for the magazine.

Broadcasting has no similar identification of special audiences or easy measurement of the intensity of interest in any particular field. The large, undifferentiated mass broadcasting ratings have obliterated the special smaller audiences of which every mass audience is composed.

Numerous stations have argued that their subject matter—classical music, or sophisticated talk shows, or policy debates—attracts a small but highly selective audience peculiarly attractive for some advertisers. But the advertisers have to accept this on faith. It does not pay to measure an audience of ten thousand by sampling, especially if you must show that (1) they are listening to something, (2) they are listening to one of twenty-five possible stations, and (3) they are listening to one of those twenty-five stations during a particular fifteen-minute segment. For a large city this measurement of local, special audiences would take a sample numbering in the several thousands. In the 1963 House hearings, it was said that some New York City broadcast audiences for national programs were measured by thirty-six responses.

Cable television connected to computers could change this. The present broadcasting industry is less worried about cable's superior picture than they are that cable will fragment the audience, permitting the measuring of specialized groups that will bring the same impact on networks as specialized magazines did on the *Saturday Evening Post, Colliers,* and *Liberty.* With cable it will be possible to know when each set is turned on, to what channel, and at what time. The connection with computers will permit the recording and analysis of this, so that the audience, far from being sampled, will be counted, set by set, continuously and instantly. Furthermore, it will not be difficult to feed into the computer data about each household connected to the cable, so that among other things the computer will show the economic, educational, occupational and other characteristics of households listening to each program.

Under these conditions, it will be possible for the first time in broadcasting history to direct programs at special small audiences, and to prove that the audience is listening. When that happens the specialized broadcast program will be as viable economically as the specialized magazine.

This could change the content of standard broadcasting faster than all the agitation of cultural critics. With, for example, most of the upper-income families probably watching a specialized program, the large mass program will lose some of its attractiveness for advertisers. If, furthermore, the seriousness of the special audience is documented by the fact that they are paying an extra fee to see their program, this further increases the attractiveness of that segment of the audience as an advertising target. This, rather than a passionate devotion to providing "free TV" underlies the battle of aerial television against cable.

The home cable with its large number of channels will fragment the audience in still other ways. Its large number of channels capable of being localized means that for the first time broadcasting can be narrowed to particular neighborhoods or small communities. It will be possible to monitor routinely all public meetings in a locality, since the cost of the time for the channel will be determined by the cost of maintaining the multiple-channel wire, which is already paid by the consumer, rather than by the competition of mass advertisers for limited aerial channels.

The local school will be able to use broadcasting routinely, which it cannot do now because it has to compete with commercial programming, and even if it succeeds or finds the money, most of the audience it reaches live outside the school district. Local candidates will find the same identifiable local audience. And so will local residents, who can use the idle channels for local announcements, for amateur performances, and for the communications cohesion that has been lost to modern communities during this century.

If cables are connected to home facsimile machines they will be capable of producing a newspaper, but it will be a very different newspaper from today's.

The intense localization of programming through cable and identifying of audience precisely by computer will not be an unmixed blessing. Fragmenting the audience has some dangers. It would encourage a semipermanent cultural separation of the population, since it would diminish the dominance of the present few leading news and entertainment programs. The cultural and intellectual level of mass programming would probably decline, since the existence of One Big Audience forces television to prevent too low an intellectual quality since they might lose a commercially valuable part of the audience. The country requires a national level of news, and the more attractive the strictly local channels, the more these new channels will drain away national audiences.

But national news and national-level programming of all kinds would undoubtedly continue to be mutually attractive and common. The primary attraction of localized programming will be its relevance to strictly local matters, a desperately needed addition to the present mass media. But there has been a demonstrable commitment of the public to national and world news, which would not disappear. On cultural and entertainment programs, local talent cannot compete with national talent, except in familiarity of personality and interest of friends and neighbors, which is also needed. There is no reason to expect obliteration of national programming, but rather a new and necessary balance.

Even the wisest decisions about communications policy cannot work unless other basic institutions are changed to recognize the unmet needs in contemporary society. For example, some of the tensions between whites and blacks, the educated and the uneducated, intellectuals and nonintellectuals, ghetto and suburb, long-haired youth and hard-hat laborer are the result of loss of community contact, the separation of classes brought about by the automobile. This is exacerbated by increasing specialization of education—highly specialized schools in which different social classes see different textbooks and think ahead to different careers. While some of this took place in earlier times, the individuals developing their differing perceptions were nonetheless members of the same primary community, practically all went to school together in their formative years and, outside of occupational specialization, shared community experiences.

The multiclass town and public school of the last century were crucial to the development of American democracy; the one-class community and public school developing in this century could be the end of it. Highly localized television could further the present cultural separation if neighborhoods and communities themselves were sharply separated, as they tend to be. If mass communications serve only their own withdrawn segments of society, it will increase national alienation and aggression. National and regional mass media will help overcome this sense of separation, but they will not be enough, as they are not enough to overcome today's mutual isolation of special groups.

Pathologies created by the continued formation of towns and neighborhoods on the basis of the fastest possible profit for the most aggressive real-estate entrepreneurs, now the primary designers of American community life, will never be overcome by any conceivable artificial communications. The intensification of alienation by public schools that reflect these residential patterns of separation by race, income level, educational attainment, and occupational status, will be more influential than any combination of new electronic techniques.

Communications policy, like all public policy, cannot be made in a social vacuum.

Whatever the ultimate pattern of home communications, if it follows past history it will be the result of corporate rivalry among traditional companies protecting their own interests. This rivalry is a useful source of energy in the building of systems, but such companies have seldom been sensitive to those social needs that do not happen to fit their momentary corporate ambitions.

Needed now is a public communications policy designed to fill the informational needs of the American public for the rest of this century, and regulatory rules that reward those corporations that play a role in filling these needs. This will be the reverse of the usual order of things. But, to have a chance of succeeding, the makers of public policy must examine what the next generation is most likely to need, they must know what new technology can contribute, and they will need an informed public to support new policies in the ultimate arena of politics.

There are a number of communications goals that seem clear. One is that there should be a surplus of communications channels, probably for color television since that is technically feasible. It is a rich medium for transmitting information, and the public is attracted by it. A plenitude of channels for color television almost guarantees the capacity also needed for other kinds of communication—facsimile, computer use, and other modern methods of exchanging thoughts and images from one place to another.

The practical use of such rich channels will require the efficient use of computers, but communication with computers ought to be inexpensive enough to let the electronic thinkers do what they can to relieve human beings of drudgery or unwanted guesswork. Here, too, plentiful channels are important, whether in the telephone system or in cable.

But the general-information computer containing personal information must be protected against harmful invasion of privacy and malicious manipulation. This can be done now, while the computer industry is in its adolescence, but it will be much more difficult a few years from now when it may be so intricately evolved that protections are impossible.

Each individual, for example, should have unlimited access to his own personal information of all kinds. The accumulation of false, mistaken, and trivial but harmful information in FBI and credit-bureau files has already been documented, and the experience of the government security system has been that the most reliable method of judging raw information is to let the individual involved examine the material about himself.

Each query about a person should automatically record the origin of the inquiry, and when the inquiries form a particular pattern approaching private and potentially harmful information—on medical and psychiatric history, for example—the file should be locked automatically and notification sent to the subject that someone is asking these questions of the computer, identifying the inquirer.

Computer programmers and file keepers for data banks containing highly personal information should be licensed, and random queries of files should be made to detect cheating by the professionals.

These and other techniques that have been suggested for computer privacy are urgently needed because even with them the extraordinary capacities of the computer will provide opportunities for mischief. It will be possible, for example, with cable connected to a computer, to know who did and did not listen to a speech by the President, and of those who listened at what particular point a particular family turned off the speech. That kind of information is necessary for measuring audience and designing programs for public tastes, but it could also be used by unscrupulous authorities to embarrass or coerce individuals.

The building of plentiful channels is feasible. But the question of regulation, intensified by corporate rivalries, could prevent optimum development. The wisest policy would seem to be establishment of cable television as a common carrier, like the telephone and telegraph system, the owners and operators guaranteed a local monopoly on condition that they meet minimum standards of service, which would include a large number of channels usable at reasonable rates. It would also require that they make channels available to all members of the public on an equitable basis. With twenty or forty or a hundred channels, a number could be reserved for national programming, others for regional and metropolitan program origination, providing the channels for present commercial broadcasters that are now transmitting through the air.

Other channels would be reserved for educational, instructional, and noncommercial use. The tradition in the United States for commercial programming, and its economic power even under highly developed local cable, will continue. But it cannot fulfill all needs. Commercial programming will always be under pressure to maximize its audience all the time, and this will push it always, as it does today, toward a narrow spectrum of themes and a short attention span. Consequently, there is a need for programming designed for smaller audiences than is possible under commercial pressures. In England, this is satisfied by the BBC and in Japan by the NHK, which are noncommercial, directed by nongovernmental public boards, and financed from the license fees charged in those countries for receiving sets.

In the United States the Corporation for Public Broadcasting is already in existence but it needs a reliable and adequate source of funds that is not dependent on the whims of any particular political administration. Annual appropriations by Congress would be fatal to independent professionalism if the annual experience of the United States Information Agency is any measure.

A proposal by the Ford Foundation is more suitable, providing a percentage of the revenues gained by commercial use of the new communications satellites. Thus, with a fixed percentage established, income would be adequate and free from political pressures. An alternative is a new excise tax on the sale of radio and television sets, the proceeds to go to noncommercial broadcasting.

This kind of funding would permit quality presentations not required to compete for commercial audiences. If five million people are unacceptable as a prime-time commercial audience, they are a significant audience nevertheless.

The creation of surplus local cable channels would permit access to a color television presentation for anyone who could pay the nominal costs. Once channels are localized and in surplus, their cost would be nominal, in the tens of dollars per hour, compared to the thousands on present metropolitan air channels. The freedom of channels could be comparable to freedom of speech in a public place with about the same rules. There would be no guarantee of an audience—except, possibly the use of one channel for a continuous listing of all channel programs—but then there is no guarantee of an audience for a speaker in a public park.

The separation of the ownership of the mechanical channel from the ownership of the program would solve both the problem of monopoly-like programming and the lack of diversity that now characterize commercial broadcasting. Channel operators would be selling time on an equal basis to all, the way the telephone company does. They would have no more concern or control over the use of the channel time than the electric company has over the appliances plugged into household outlets. They would profit by having a maximum of users, rather than being tempted to create an artificial shortage in order to raise prices.

Organized producers or syndicates of producers undoubtedly would form, to exploit continuity of programming. But their competitors would be guaranteed channels without having to build and buy the hardware for studios and transmission, and buy licenses, as they must now.

Separating operation of the channel hardware from the content would have another advantage. In the next twenty years there will probably be a proliferation of sophisticated home communications devices—facsimile machines, high-resolution screens for the display of texts, and teletype keyboards for communication with computers and with TV-like screens in other homes. Their success will depend on their rapid increase, so that the benefits of an interacting system will be evident to the users. They will require standardization of design so that they will be compatible with each other and with the communications links between them. This will be aided if such devices are leased to the householder for a monthly charge, as the telephone now is (and as future, more sophisticated telephones undoubtedly will be). Without making a large financial commitment in permanent purchases, millions of householders can install such machines quickly. This could be done by an independent business, but a natural corporation to do this would be the cable and the telephone companies, since such devices would be attached to both lines in various ways. Present cable companies, for example, say they could improve the quality of television reception more cheaply if they designed both the cable and the set. Today it is more expensive to change the cable to make up for shortcomings in contemporary sets than it would be to redesign the sets being made in the factories.

As the 1970s began, the FCC was moving toward such a plan of common-carrier cable, but it was not clear that each community would have plentiful and inexpensive channels, nor was it yet clear that the final result would be something other than a private compromise by the corporations protecting their interests while the consuming public is not yet aware of its stake in the struggle.

The Future Content of News

12

Vernon Parrington has written that it is impossible to understand the significance of theological disputes in colonial America unless the references to "theology" are seen as really meaning political philosophy. This is not because Cotton Mather and Roger Williams used sly code words but because these were the only terms most people knew with which to describe the relationship of the individual to authority. The Reformation idea of each man acting as his own priest stimulated the radical idea of democracy; if the automatic authority of so traditional a mediator with the supernatural as a clergyman could be doubted, then even more dubious was the infallibility of political leaders. The conceptions that men have in their heads—in this case of the relationship of man to God—and the methods used to express themselves—in this case, through theological disputes uttered in church pulpits by clergymen—determine the content and style of political and social discourse.

The content of news and the terms in which it is written are undergoing changes similar to the old theological upheavals. The style of news also reflects the conceptions men have of their relationship to authority: is the average consumer of news to be treated as an independent decision maker or as an obedient follower? News reflects the terms people are familiar with: is the political process to be presented solely as a titillating conflict of personalities or as social issues that transcend personalities? The political evolution of society is influenced by the methods used to communicate information: does the system routinely offer full information to the whole population, or only to a selected elite?

If thirty years from now men live in different kinds of communities with different social and political values, they will read and watch a different kind of news. But if they do live differently one reason will be that they have been exposed to a particular kind of news.

Changes in the future content and form of news will reflect changes in its technology.

When a natural disaster like a flood or hurricane eliminates all electricity, newspapers and broadcasting stations discover that they cannot speak; when it cuts off all incoming telephone calls, they discover that they have nothing to say: news cannot be separated from the total communications environment.

Today information pours into a general news organization through a number of systems: mail; telephone; ground and air express; packets on buses, planes, and trains; telegraph; leased wires to teletype machines; microwave towers and coaxial cable; international communications satellites; transoceanic cable; direct monitoring of events publicly broadcast by television or radio; hand delivery by couriers who walk, take subways, drive cars, or ride motorcycles; and the transportation by plane, helicopter, or private car of the reporter who has the information stored in his notebook and brain and will convert these to typewritten accounts when he is able to reach a news headquarters or a communications terminal.

Once the news is compiled, it is distributed through networks that are somewhat less dependent on public systems, but far from untouched by them. Weekly and small daily papers still use the U.S. mails for a significant part of their distribution, subsidized by special low rates. Most dailies are delivered through a combination of private truck fleets and neighborhood hand carriers, but these require the use of public highways, sometimes at their most congested periods. Some outgoing bundles of newspapers are sent to local distribution points by way of common carriers like trains, buses, and airplanes.

Distribution of broadcasting is much simpler. As long as the local station has its own electricity, it can deliver the news. But to receive television the consumer also must have electricity, and unlike many broadcasting stations, the consumer is not prepared to meet a power failure with his private generators. Radio is less dependent on central electricity, since portable transistor radios operate on batteries and during power blackouts become the primary mass communication.

A serious change in any of these techniques of compiling and distributing the news will change the nature of the news and its impact. And changes are clearly on the way.

In the eighteenth century, most American papers received news from beyond their communities by slow and expensive stagecoach and postriders carrying newspapers from the capital, which smaller papers clipped and reprinted. Today they may have an array of teletype machines typing out news supplied by networks of news handlers who are in turn fed by thousands of originating points in the United States and abroad. All such wire service news must pass through regional headquarters that have to eliminate much of the available information in order to fit it into the restricted capacity of the main circuits. This capacity at present is limited to an average of 45 words a minute, which means that in the twelve hours before a daily paper goes to press a teletype machine can deliver a maximum of 32,400 words. But this is over a period of twelve hours. If, fifteen minutes before deadline, a major event occurs, the most the one machine handling major news can deliver the local news headquarters is 675 words, which is not very much on a major event.

Consequently the system produces a product that has been severely edited at many points in order to fit the limited capacity of each succeeding link. The local editor has already had his choices narrowed by men whom he usually never knows or sees, or whose decisions he cannot often review since he can't know what the system has eliminated. Finally, the information receives another winnowing by the local editor, in most cases elimination of 80 percent of what was received in the local news office, and for larger papers, elimination of over 90 percent.

Most of this has a useful social function as well as a necessary mechanical one. No reader and no local editor could possibly review the total available news; the editing down at each step will always occur simply to produce a manageable body of information. But the more limited the capacity of the system, the greater the dependence of the reader on the decisions of unknown men who exercise this crucial function. The decisions on selecting news are made on the basis of mixed motivations—the intense time pressure for fast decisions which makes the quantity of decisions more important than the quality; the social values of the individual and his superiors; the perceived social values of the local editor who buys the service; the perceived social values of the reader to whom the local editor presumably will be sensitive; and, finally, professional judgment of what is important regardless of all the above.

The more restricted the capacity of each link in the process, the greater the chance that the surviving items will be compatible with conventional wisdom, since each gatekeeper in the system is scored on how successfully he guesses the acceptance of his selections by the next decision point. The more severely the incoming items have to be cut to fit the capacity of the next link in the system, the more the system will reject those items that seem to be contrary to prevailing ideas.

The capacity of the present news system, in its totality and in each link, is vastly greater than anything in the past. Yet this is no cause for complacency. The interdependency of societies, and of communities and individuals within societies, is greater than ever before in history. As communications make distant events relevant and make clear that they are relevant, more information is needed from more distant places. As the historic trend in governments continues toward more popular electoral forms, the significance of all public events increases, and the appetite of the public for such news expands.

As fast communications accelerate social reaction times, all parties in the process need faster information. Leaders need it because they must make policy decisions to meet the challenge of their constituents who have the same information and react spontaneously to it. Because electorates have the power to act, they know they can influence their leadership by their reactions. All of this increases the public appetite for news that seems to affect their lives.

As the originating sources of news are expanded, globally and within the United States, the movement of this enlarged mass of news through the system depends on the capacity of the local reporters of information, on the capacity of the channels that link these originating sources with various switching points in the news system, on the capacity of the local news headquarters to receive information, on the capacity of the news medium issued by the local organization, and, finally, on the capacity of the consumer to absorb news, all influenced by new technology.

But the relationship of technology to the news is not a simple one.

The telegraph revolutionized the news by delivering first-hand accounts direct to local editors, eliminating the dependence on remote and semiofficial accounts. But its greatest impact on the news was what it did to the rest of society.

Before the railroads of the 1830s and the telegraph of the 1850s, Americans typically lived in small, isolated communities. Their towns and villages were self-sufficient, self-centered, and detached from the outer world. Because the communities were small, information passed efficiently by word-of-mouth. A newspaper could not often report a local public (or private) event that was not known already. And, in a community where all the members regularly met each other and expected to continue to do so all the days of their lives, codes of courtesy and social propriety prevented the easy outbreak of outward acrimony that would have made continued face-to-face contact intolerable.

The content of news reflected this life. News of local events tended to be ritualistic, recording as history what everyone already knew. There was little critical judgment by the editor on local personalities and local issues because the editor met all the participants on the street. He was not likely to be any more belligerent or contentious in print than he was in his daily social contacts. There were exceptions, in the tradition of the local fighting editor, but these were rare, made historic by legend and melodrama. Where there were local fighting editors there were also public fist fights, duels, and lynchings which increased the pressure for prudence on the part of the editor, who lived as a member of a small, tightly knit community that could not stand public acrimony. Small local papers, to this day, tend to be perfunctory and to avoid local controversy.

Urbanization and rapid communications changed all that. Cities have become so large that it is impossible to meet or to know every other inhabitant. Word-of-mouth is no longer a reliable medium of communication. In fact, because it must travel so far through so many unknown links, at such a geographic and psychological distance from the original event, word-of-mouth in modern cities is quickly converted into rumor and panic. A newspaper or broadcasting station reporting most civic events can safely assume that almost none of its consumers knows the news ahead of time at first hand, or even by rumor.

The modern city is not detached and self-sufficient. It is dependent on the outside world, and except for pockets of political paranoia, it is conscious that it is dependent on the outside. The city must maintain connections with the outside to get its food, fuel, shelter, and occupational income. And news.

The status of the individual within the city is changed. He is dependent on others within his city whom he never sees. Policy-making bodies for which he may or may not vote decide what his children will learn in school, the route of highways where he will drive his car, and where and how he may build his own house, and with what subsequent tax rates. He cannot do this by personal participation because there is no longer a town meeting but a remote process of impersonal information broadcast outward to the population. An occasional vote is taken in which the individual may express his generalized feelings about the multitude of decisions that have been made in his absence.

Where the isolated small town made formal courteous relations between all individuals a condition for survival, the cities make anonymity and impersonality necessary for survival. In 1790 there were fewer than five Americans per square mile, and while they gathered in villages they tended to be dispersed, so that to meet another individual was an event to be welcomed and pondered. In 1960 there were fifty people per square mile, but they were clustered in cities like Chicago where there might be ten thousand per square mile. One cannot "meet" ten thousand people a day and certainly one cannot ponder each contact. If individuals in the city are to focus their intelligence and their emotions on those who mean the most to them, they are forced to learn to ignore most of the rest.

The growth of the city changed the nature of news. It made the reporting of immediate public events a primary activity instead of a marginal ritual. Anonymity, the lack of personal contact among all the residents of the city, and the physical and psychological separation of the editor from the source of news, made the news more critical, judgmental, and contentious. If a councilman was found guilty of stealing city money, the paper that ignored this or treated it with vague euphemisms would not be counted a benefactor of community strength but a corrupt observer that failed its mission.

The evolution of journalism also has been shaped by the growth of specialization. The early foundations of journalistic freedom were laid down by participants in the social struggle who fought not for the freedom of "objective" reporting but for the opposite, the freedom of advocacy. John Milton's *Areopagitica,* considered the primary proclamation of freedom of the press in the English language, was subtitled "A Speech of Mr. John Milton, for the Liberty of Unlicensed Printing." He wrote it in connection with his arguments in favor of divorce, an issue he pressed because, among other reasons, he wanted a divorce. To have suggested to the early journalists like Daniel Defoe and Jonathan Swift that they should write in calm and balanced tones giving a fair argument for both sides would have struck them as bizarre. Early journalism was the propagation of personal causes. There were, in the beginning, no professional journalists in the modern sense. There were official printers and there were pamphleteers. The content of news reflected their separate roles.

The early American newspaper was a printer's product, an organ of merchandising and reprinted safe articles from afar, extensions of community bulletin boards. The idea of independent reporting or judgment was not encouraged. The first newspaper in America, *Publick Occurrences Both Foreign and Domestick,* issued on September 25, 1690, in Boston, appears to the modern eye to be innocuous. Its pages are about the size of a book's, three of them printed and the fourth left blank so that subscribers who forwarded the paper to friends and relatives could use the last page for personal messages written by hand. But the paper was suppressed by the colonial governor for printing "reflections of a very high nature," probably because of some reprinted gossip about the King of France (an enemy, but nevertheless an Authority) and about Canadian Indians (then the allies of the British) torturing captured French soldiers. It was almost 50 years before the courts in the John Peter Zenger case affirmed the right of a newspaper to print material critical of the ruling governor. For the next 150 years newspaper content and style were more contentious, partisan, violent, and scurrilous.

The standard historians of American journalism seldom omit the quotation of Thomas Jefferson in his letter of 1787 to Edward Carrington when he wrote that if he had to take his choice he would prefer newspapers without a government rather than a government without newspapers. They almost never quote a letter Jefferson wrote to John Norvell twenty years later, after he had been President of the United States: "The man who never looks into a newspaper is better informed than he who reads them, inasmuch as he who knows nothing is nearer to truth than he whose mind is filled with false-hoods. . . . Nothing can now be believed which is seen in a news-paper."

The successful editor was often the one with the most solid reputation for ingenious lies. Some of the early giants of American journalism—James Gordon Bennett, William Randolph Hearst—were gigantic inventors of melodramatic fiction masquerading as news. As late as the 1920s, some of the most prominent journalists—Damon Runyon, H. L. Mencken—were praised for the clever stories they invented and printed as though they were factual news.

Great tides of change maintained this long stretch of wild jour-nalism.

One was the development of a technology that lowered the cost of printing so that newspapers began to be a popular commodity instead of an elitist one. The decade of the 1830s, for example, began with the typical cost of a city newspaper, sixpence. A year's subscription cost the average householder more than two full weeks' pay. But in that same decade prices went down to one cent, immediately expand-ing the audience. The new audience included those who were reading daily information for the first time and who therefore were relatively innocent in political and social affairs. Being innocent, they were more easily enticed by oversimplified, spectacular news, and this is what they received.

Because it was cheap to print small papers, there were thousands of new papers started when candidates and causes wanted to further themselves. In 1800 there were 200 daily and weekly papers in the United States; in 1900 there were 16,000. In 1900 there were 547 urban places of 8,000 population or more, so that if the 16,000 daily and weekly papers had been evenly distributed, which they were not, there would have been 30 papers per urban place. Among these 16,000 there were 2,200 dailies, which was 4 daily papers per urban place. Today there are approximately 2,700 urban places of 8,000 population or more, and fewer than one daily paper per urban place. The large number of papers in the nineteenth century and the volatil-ity of their coming and going are understated. There were uncounted thousands of papers that were started and later suspended, and not numbered among the 16,000. The fact that they were started for specific personal or ideological reasons influenced their style and content. They were contentious and partisan, and after they had served their purpose—their sponsor either was elected to office or not, the special cause succeeded or it did not, the political enemy the paper was created to destroy either lost position or held it—these papers were dropped. This was something like the market place of contending forces that the Founding Fathers had in mind when they wrote the First Amendment guaranteeing freedom of the press, a field of special pleaders battling in public, with the citizen exposed to them all and able to take his pick.

Rising education and affluence affected news content. Reading during the nineteenth century shifted from being a skill possessed by a minority to one held by a majority. Family income shifted from a farm subsistence to an urban cash economy, making the purchase of newspapers possible for additional millions. Quite beyond the lowered cost of newspapers, the increased incomes of families brought new populations into daily reading, and they, of course, tended to be newcomers to such information and susceptible to glittering oversimplifications.

Despite the rapidly enlarging audience for newspapers—758,000 average daily circulation in 1850; 20 million in 1904—as the new readers increased their collective levels of education and political knowledge, the new sophistication was diminished by immigration of 24 million Europeans to the United States between 1880 and 1920, usually illiterate in English, renewing the large audience for relatively primitive and sensational news.

But something else was happening that changed the nature of news. News, which had gone from a by-product of a commercial printer to the special pleading of a small enterprise, was becoming a big business. As advertising revenue became more important to the economics of newspapers, and as functional literacy began to approach 100 percent, the engine of monopoly drove each newspaper organization to become the dominant publication in its own community.

Changes in the news that came with local monopoly were a mixed blessing. Monopoly ended the daily competition for the unwary eye, the screaming headlines over falsified or sensationalized news. It moderated narrow partisanship. It strengthened the doctrine of objectivity that dominated American reportage for two generations. "Objectivity" in the news means different things to different people, and all thoughtful journalists are aware that there is no such thing as total objectivity in describing human affairs. But in general it means that the reporter and his editor should not bias an account with their own opinions. Adolph Ochs, buying the failing *New York Times* in 1896, produced a factual and careful paper as a relief from the sensational and partisan journalism of the late nineteenth century. His approach was a success financially and journalistically, one of the most important events in determining the style of early twentieth-century American journalism.

This tendency to objectivity was further deepened by the growth of news networks, the wire services that distribute their news to a wide variety of papers. Their growth was rapid during this same period. In 1914 there were about one hundred members of the AP and five hundred of United Press, the two leading services, but by 1940 they each had about fourteen hundred clients. This meant that the same news report would be written for an ultra-conservative segregationist paper in the South as for a liberal integrationist paper in the North, for a Republican paper in the Midwest and a Democratic one in New England. The same account of social, political, and economic affairs had to satisfy editors and publishers of varying tastes in news. Objectivity became as much a commercial imperative as an intellectual one.

What was happening with national news distributed to newspapers was also happening to news distributed in the paper's own community. Since the paper either had a monopoly or was working toward one, it wished to sell a newspaper to every household in the town. And these households varied in tastes and social values. The same newspaper went to Irish Catholics and to Yankee Protestants, liquor drinkers and teetotalers, Democrats and Republicans, rich and poor. Here, too, objectivity—the withholding of explicit personal values in a news account—became a commercial need.

This kind of objectivity was not a complete blessing. What is objective can also be bland; what is a desire not to offend partisans can also be a withdrawal from important controversy. A retreat into the mechanically factual can produce meaningless prose. It is possible to describe a tax bill in Congress with every name spelled correctly, all the quotations of the participants in the debate recorded accurately, and a fair balance of space given the contending forces, and still fail to discriminate between what is more important and what is less so. A competent and fair journalist should test surface assertions with background information, but in doing so he has made value judgments, and he may offend partisans. It is not always a dispute over the accuracy of facts that is at stake, but a dispute over which facts are most important. And here the doctrine of objectivity in its most stringent form usually fails.

Nevertheless, the idea of objectivity grew at a crucial time. A newspaper in the twentieth century was no longer the work of an itinerant printer, or a random partisan, or a group of varying small entrepreneurs, but of a single man who was one of the most powerful industrialists in the community. Given the size and cost of investment of the modern daily newspaper, the publisher usually has the special point of view of substantial industrialists: he is antagonistic toward labor unionism, with which he fights regularly; he is opposed to most public-sector spending, since the amount of his corporate taxes impresses him deeply; and unless he is an unusual industrialist, he has a circle of friends and associates who reinforce these attitudes and tend to divorce him further from the perspectives of most of his subscribers. It is no accident that, with the exception of 1964, from 1936 to 1968 no Republican presidential candidate ever received less than 75 percent of those daily-newspaper endorsements making a Republican-Democratic choice. And yet, during this same period, the majority of the American people, including most daily newspaper subscribers, were registering and voting pro-Democratic. Objectivity in the news was one defense against the latent suspicion, frequently confirmed, that the men who control news organizations would like to use them to promote their own political and social values.

The same doctrine protected the publisher from his own reportorial staff. Working journalists tend to be pro-Democratic, like most Americans of their education, income, and social background. The publisher has the power to hire, fire, and promote, and can control the content of his paper in ways that range from direct intervention to subtle social pressures. And there are many instances in which modern monopoly newspapers are run as polemic advocates for the publisher's point of view, including in the selection, writing, and display of news. But the reporters were the men on the scene, who controlled the information to the point of editing. As professionalism increased after the 1900's, traditional conformity to the wishes of superiors as a condition of work diminished. Public disclosure of distorted news became increasingly embarrassing. As publishers became local monopolists, they inherited some of the public suspicion of all monopolists, and as larger segments of the working population voted and became engaged in politics, sensitivity to special pleading in the news increased. Some publishers developed a genuine dedication to the principle of fairness in the news. Objectivity that held strictly to the recitation of publicly provable facts diminished these conflicts.

Consequently, the standard style of news was meticulous attribution of all facts to real people in order to avoid the suspicion that they were really sentiments of the writer or his publisher. The news services tended to report only what could be supported by an official record recently made public, which is not the same thing as a perceptive view of the environment. But it was safer for a mass system.

Technology influenced how the news was written. When fourteen hundred newspapers all get the same account at approximately the same time, the standard story finds itself in a variety of circumstances. Papers will have varying degrees of interest in the story, so that one paper might want twenty paragraphs and another only two. Different papers will have differing amounts of time to process the story, since they will have varying deadlines, so one paper might be able to include ten paragraphs of the story in its next edition, while another only one paragraph. As they all handle the story as rapidly as possible, the account is fitted into available space that is not precisely predictable, and at the last moment varying amounts of the story may have to be cut summarily. Consequently, an inverted style prevailed: the most important and most recent facts were in the first paragraph, which included a conglomeration of the who-what-when-where. After that came the next most recent event in the episode, and this continued with each subsequent paragraph containing less timely information. This permitted the mechanical cutting of stories from the bottom with the assurance that wherever the cut was made the story would not require rewriting and the cut would not sacrifice the latest information. But it also meant that many stories were told backward—what happened first in an episode was told last—and coherent narrative and explanation were subordinated to an inventory of the physical facts listed in reverse order of their occurrence.

Combined with the policy of repeating only official facts, the inverted style was increasingly frustrating to those desiring a more human and explanatory style. As public affairs became more complex, and as the public became more sophisticated in the causes and effects of social forces, the simplified recital of physical acts and official quotations was plainly inadequate. The emphasizing of the latest physical act and official statement was not the same thing as an intelligent view of the social and political realities. Police statistics and official pronouncements by spokesmen for conflicting forces seldom explained the heart of the matter.

Furthermore, "objectivity" did not apply to the single most important act in journalism—the initial decision of what to report. Under the strictest versions of the doctrine of objectivity, it would have been possible for a first-century reporter to describe accurately and at length the plight of lions being starved in the Roman Colosseum, together with official data on the decalcification of lion bones and other evidences of metabolic harm to the animals, and if all the facts were accurate and properly attributed to the responsible officials, to meet the requirements of strict objectivity. But it would still omit the more important fact that the lions were being starved in order to increase their appetites for human martyrs, whose deaths might never be reported.

The lion-bones syndrome of objective reporting reached a crisis in the career of the late Senator Joseph McCarthy, after which American journalism expanded its content and style. The Senator had a five-year career of wild charges of communism among the highest officials of the United States government, and though he seldom documented his charges and often lied or distorted, newspapers continued to report him without dispute in news stories because he was a United States Senator (and because initially many publishers believed him to be a conservative performing a useful service). The Senator came close to paralyzing the United States government. It was an episode from which traditional objectivity never recovered.

But, had it not been the destructiveness of Joseph McCarthy, some other important event would have dramatized the fact that the American public had developed too much skill finding alternative sources of information to be satisfied with mechanical recitations of official facts. Analysis of causes, identification of underlying social forces, and assigning of priorities among competing facts became necessary in the news. They have resulted in less superficial and more enterprising reportage.

This was accelerated by television, which ended the citizen's dependence on the interpretation of his local paper. He saw many public events directly. And, since it was an exciting, vivid medium that periodically reported news, and since it required the listener to be exposed to each segment of programming if he wished to reach the next, many people were exposed to public-affairs information through television who had been untouched by newspapers. Or whose interest in newspapers had been limited to something other than news.

President Kennedy's live television press conferences constituted the most effective single popular demonstration of the governmental process in this generation. President Eisenhower in the 1950s had permitted taped televised conferences for later airing, and this was the beginning of direct presentation of this partly symbolic and partly real governmental policy making. But the realization that the Eisenhower sessions were taped and edited removed some of the excitement of the unpredictability of live conferences; the Kennedy conferences had this excitement plus an involvement with new issues that affected personal lives.

Even the most active presidential press conferences are hardly representative of the workings of public policy, but if they are not completely prefabricated they impart a sense of issues and decision making to an enormous audience. Most of this audience was never before acquainted with the interplay of conflicting forces in policy making. The effect on printed journalism was clear: after presidential conferences were televised, many more newspapers printed the full texts of the questions and answers, accompanied by more interpretive and analytical stories on the meaning of the sessions. This was because the audience for print was already interested in the subject and, being interested and knowing the basic facts, were more interested in a discussion of what it meant.

The impact of the televised presidential press conference is a useful hint of the future content of electronic and printed news. It is expected that before the end of the 1970s most American homes will have cable connections for their television sets, and it is likely that most of these cables will have more than twenty channels, perhaps more than forty. Among other things, this means that it will not cost as much to enter the television system as it does now, and that will permit the transmission of programming that ordinarily would not be shown because it could not guarantee a very large audience.

If the new cable system is operated under public policy that encourages a healthy balance among national, regional, and local channels, it could transform the nature of public-affairs reporting in the news by permitting a direct televising of many governmental and other public proceedings that are now limited to those who can be physically present. Because most of the potential audience for meetings of public bodies cannot be present, they now depend almost entirely on news of these events. But the press, too, is limited in what it can cover directly. So the majority of important national, regional, and local policy-making meetings are semiprivate proceedings even though most of them are, in fact, open to the public.

On the national level, this means that the sessions of both the House and Senate, though open to the public that is able to be in Washington and wait in line for a seat in the galleries, is not seen by those who cannot personally visit the chambers. The majority of congressional committee hearings each day are open and most are not covered by the press or visited by any but the witnesses and their friends. There are dozens of press conferences below the presidential level that are often significant—by the Secretary of State, Secretary of Defense, and other cabinet and agency leaders, and while these are covered by the press, in the limitations of time and channels of information only the most dramatic and immediate results are broadcast or printed.

The same pattern of proceedings exists in statehouses, where sessions of state legislatures and their committees unfold in dreary obscurity. It is an obscurity that is often deserved, but that is mainly because they are unattended activities of government: dreary and desultory though the sessions may be, they reach decisions that make a difference to people's lives and, when this impact is felt, there is a significant level of public attention, but too late.

On the local level the same pattern exists, except that this is usually even more obscure, though even more influential in the life of the community. Meetings of the city council and its committees, of school boards, PTAs, zoning boards, highway commissions, city planning agencies, and dozens of other policy-making and future-planning groups are now conducted in semi-private, partly because there has only recently been a public realization of their importance, but partly because there are so many of them that the conscientious citizen, if he felt impelled to attend all of them, could spend all of his nonworking hours trying to be personally present. And fail because of conflicts of dates and places.

The most widespread and vivid news medium for such public-policy reporting is television, but its reportage of this is limited only to the most melodramatic, physically interesting, and predictable portions of the sessions, and only tiny fragments even of those. Sixty seconds of film of such a session on an evening television newscast is considered long.

With the existence of channels of television reserved for non-commercial purposes, it will be possible to monitor many public bodies routinely. The expense of televising crews—correspondent, cameraman, soundman, and maybe a chauffeur—would not be necessary. The recording on videotape with the editing to select seconds out of minutes, and the mechanical processing and splicing into a formal newscast would no longer establish the limits of reporting. Instead, a fixed camera or two, with no more supervision than is now given public-address microphones, could give a continuous view of the scene. It would lack some of the dramatic variations in camera-work needed to maximize attention and catch the most compelling moments, but with a multitude of open channels such professionalism to maximize audiences will not be necessary. The audience would watch not for entertainment or excitement but because they have an intense personal interest in the proceedings.

The usual response of television-educated newsmen to such proposals is that most people would not watch most of such sessions. That is undoubtedly true. But the proceedings would be there for those who wished it, and because each channel would not have to justify itself by proving a mass audience, it could settle for a 1 percent or 10 percent audience, which present commercial standards reject.

At noon, when sessions of the House and Senate usually open, there are 12 million television sets and 57 million radios turned on in continental United States. If the owners of only one out of each 100 sets decided to watch Congress in action, this would be 120,000 American households watching, and over half a million listening to radio sets. If such numbers appeared in Washington to enter the galleries of the Congress, it would be a national phenomenon. Yet, in present thinking about the mass media, those numbers are considered unviable.

The effect of this on reporting would be parallel to the effect of the live presidential press conferences: a heightened public awareness of the events would evoke more reporting that goes beyond the physical facts.

Furthermore, the expansion of electronic channels will permit journalistic monitoring of many public sessions that are not able to reach the general public. There are often more than twenty congressional committee hearings in Washington during the day and not all of them will be televised, at least not until the time when available channels number in the hundreds (which is technically quite feasible). But those that are not channeled to the general public might very well be transmitted to newsrooms and other editing points. This will permit the kind of monitoring now reserved for high politicians and professionals who have multiple television sets in order to watch every channel transmitting a public event, or the news directors of television at dramatic times who watch monitors being fed from perhaps twenty cameras to decide which one will be switched to the public.

With the development of inexpensive videotaping (which may come faster than American predictions because of Japanese enterprise), the journalistic monitors of multiple hearings could scan constantly as proceedings unfold, noting which ones seem to be developing newsworthy episodes. Videotape reproducing those segments would be available for later reporting purposes and selected portions could be broadcast to the public.

Reporting on the scene will continue to be important and demanding. Fixed-camera monitoring of sessions provides a vastly expanded dissemination of basic physical events. But monitoring alone can produce a delusion that watching a public scene is synonymous with understanding issues. After the general public has been provided with a general view of the scene, the analysis and interpretation of significance will become all the more important. Critical and relevant questions must be asked in private if they are not asked in public. A knowledge of what has preceded an event is necessary if public affairs are not to become a superficial series of tableaux. In order to decrease the dangers of fragmentary knowledge, the competent and critical observer will be needed more than ever.

Editors will become more important than they are today. The growth in total information that will become available to them in the next ten years will be phenomenal. Where their machines today place forty-five words a minute onto their desks, machines will be able to place millions into their computers. Even though their computers will help sort these out and offer up manageable clues to the total contents, the editors will have two new pressures to face. They will have an audience more knowledgeable and, because of added channels of information, more varied in its specialized interests. And they will have a greatly enlarged number of possibilities from which to choose, requiring greater selectivity. The standard package of news is not likely to expand much in words and video time, so the same quantity of information will have to be selected from a much larger reservoir, and presented in a way compatible with a more knowledgeable audience.

This pressure will be somewhat relieved by another likely development. Today almost all unused daily news dies in the newspaper wastebasket and the television studio cutting-room floor. What the editor discards is lost. There is small survival in such things as Sunday magazine articles and surveys that permit more detail and interpretation than could be fitted into the daily package, but this is a small percentage of all observed and transmitted news.

In the future, thanks to computers and additional channels to the home, the citizen will be able to pursue subjects beyond the standard daily news package. So the decisions of the editor and his computer selecting a few items for immediate use will leave the remainder alive. This could be subjects that may not have appeared at all in the standard package, but which will be listed in an inventory of available video and text items running on an index channel. Or it may be further detail and interpretation on items that did appear in the standard package. The editor will have available not only the product of daily reporting and monitoring, but more specialized articles that appear only in periodicals and books. These, too, will be computerized and in microforms, and will be available to the reporter and editor for reference in compiling the daily package of news, and to the consumer who wishes to see them or portions of them.

This suggests a new role, the editor as research librarian, in addition to the man or woman who will select which of the daily journalistic reports will appear in the standard package.

The daily packages will probably continue to be available in both video and print, reflecting the different inherent advantages of each. But after newspapers have been delivered quickly and in constantly updated form by facsimile in the home, video news will probably take the shape of footage of significant public events with graphic, lecture-like demonstrations of background and commentary.

The predictions for home newspaper facsimile do not see this as widespread until the 1990s. But these predictions are based on the present newspaper and, perhaps, present communications channels.

One can suppose a change in newspapers, a change not suggested to the panel that was asked predictions. Home cable attached to central computers could permit electronic shopping. "Pull" advertising, concentrating on answering consumers' questions about products instead of giving answers to those who have no questions, would reduce the quantity of advertising to stimulate impulse buying. This would reduce the size of newspapers, 60 percent of whose present pages are devoted entirely to advertising. Transmitting a physically smaller newspaper into the home by facsimile avoids the inconvenience of masses of unpackaged paper spewing onto the living-room floor, or even into a container during the night. And it also reduces the time needed for transmission and its cost.

The high-capacity cable is important to this, because it makes electronic capacity cheaper by mass installation, and it also permits a proportionate reduction in time of production. Dr. Kenneth H. Fischbeck, of RCA Graphic Systems Applied Research Laboratories, has written that new communications channels are so cheap and efficient that time and distance may be unimportant to cost. He notes that the contents of a newspaper can now be delivered in three days by second-class mail, in one day by first-class mail, in forty minutes if transmitted by electronic signals over an ordinary telephone line, but two seconds over coaxial cable of the kind in home cable installations. Presumably, the newspaper would take more than two seconds to emerge from the mechanical reproduction process in the home, but a reduced-page paper would take a relatively short time, and if constantly updated could be asked for at many times of day.

The consumer, if his disposable income continues to rise while competition for his free time increases, will be willing to pay for commercial information. It will be worth some money to find out exactly what he wants, precisely what its characteristics and costs are, and how best to obtain it quickly, none of which is done well in ordinary mass advertising. Hc will probably be able to augment this with color display on a TV-like screen or a full-color document printed inside his home.

Furthermore, he will have, either close by in his neighborhood or in his own home, a machine that will make fast and inexpensive facsimile documents on the basis of cable-transmitted electronic signals. Since the cost and convenience of getting his news this way will punish huge, bulky newspapers and reward smaller ones, there will be a new emphasis on the unique product of newspapers unavailable elsewhere—organized processing and presentation of social and political intelligence.

Today newspapers print a square foot of information at remarkably low cost and this sustains daily metropolitan papers of enormous bulk. But the reader has decreasing time for reading news. He is increasingly irritated at the failure to get precise product information from advertising (note the growth of "consumerism"), and at having to handle masses of unwanted information. He is likely to become less tolerant of metropolitan newspaper bulk as he develops alternative ways to get most of its content.

What will emerge is a more carefully selected daily package that concentrates on unique products unavailable elsewhere. Many present ads will be more quickly and rationally presented by other means, though not necessarily all. There will always be some advantage to seeing a printed document giving the reader the ability to compare adjacent characteristics, prices, and designs. Headline news will become even less important, as it has already begun to be, since in a few years there will probably be a television channel exclusively devoted to a fast-moving succession of leading headlines and one-paragraph summaries, as there are already all-news radio stations. Scanning of these will be even faster since there may be separate channels for sports, financial news, and other major categories of popular daily information. Even illustrations will become less important in newspapers, since their original introduction to entice the semiliterate has already begun to lose its basis, and the choice of high-quality color television with many channels will satisfy some of the demand now met by printed photographs.

In both news and graphics, there will be a need for knowledgeable and discriminating presentation that will not be easily duplicated in other daily channels. Background and analysis of news will dominate, a tendency already begun. The printed document offers the most attractive setting for such information, compared with voice alone or film or moving words on a screen. It is this kind of journalism that is least perishable in hour-by-hour competition with the faster broadcasting media.

Newspapers will have to decide whether they are printing factories or analysts of daily political and social information. This will not be easy. Though most managements would deny it, today they operate as though they believed themselves to be essentially industrial manufacturers. They do this not only in the proportion of money they spend on their corporations, which is unavoidable in traditional production techniques, but also in how they select their leadership, reward their corporate hierarchies, and how they plan or do not plan for the future. They would do well to plan for the future by asking how appropriate their present leadership and plans would be if editorial operations instead of taking 10 percent of their budgets as they do today took 90 percent. This is only a slight exaggeration of the probable shift in emphasis in newspaper corporations in the coming generation, but it is one that only a few newspapers take seriously.

If existing journalistic corporations do not take this change of emphasis seriously, new ones will. If cable becomes a common carrier, hundreds of small information-gathering organizations will be able to afford to buy time to compete for the consumer's attention. It will be as though each household had its choice of a dozen televised newsletters at any given time.

If present newspapers do not prepare to become research libraries for political and social information, then the inevitable demand by the consumer for a few subjects pursued in depth will be met by other kinds of organizations. A few journalistic organizations recognize today that some of the information that they cannot use each day because of the limitations of the standard printed package is nevertheless valuable and even marketable in different forms. Within the next two decades the standard package will be expandable on demand by the reader in his home and he may get the extended information from a library, a newspaper, or some new clearinghouse of public-affairs news and analysis.

The distinction between printed and broadcast news will become even more blurred as time passes. A standard package of broadcast news will continue to have attractions, even as the printed package will. But, beyond that, broadcasters will begin to feel the lack of depth in professional journalism talents from which they now suffer. The source of news for broadcasting today is essentially the printed news system. Widespread televised monitoring of public meetings will call for more detail and analysis than is presently permitted on the short attention span of commercial television. As the consumer calls for more information in depth, he will get it from whichever organization has the best talent most effectively organized. At present this is the printed news, but whoever reaches the market place first will also attract the talent.

Whether or not the home-produced newspaper is produced before the 1990s, the standard package, using national, regional, and highly professionalized talent, will prevail, but the smaller processors of information will add to the total menu available to the citizen in his home.

The social benefits of strictly local information will be important. The present lack of neighborhood and community cohesiveness would be diminished. Small local enterprises would have an information outlet that would help sustain them in the face of massive regional merchandisers. Local groups with special pleading and debates would not have to enter the ad hoc publishing business or obtain time in metropolitan channels to air their ideas. Neighborhood and community amateur youth and adult activities would have an outlet that would be less expensive than hiring a small hall.

These would compete with the standard news for the citizen's time but it would also create information that the metropolitan news would have to acknowledge from time to time. Perhaps instead of daily scanning the list of scheduled meetings in a community, the future editor will scan a list of scheduled neighborhood and community cablecasts.

The existence of small-area cablecasting and text facsimile will reduce the dangers of centralization that come with highly organized electronic systems. Today it is difficult to address any community without obtaining access to the limited space and time on news media that cover very large geographical areas and therefore are limited in what they can admit from any one part of it.

But this will raise another danger which already haunts television: will public affairs be reduced to a series of performances researched by psychological warriors, contrived by scenario writers, and enacted by public figures who are trained to create artificial scenes before the camera? Will "news" become even more what the historian Daniel Boorstin has popularized as the "pseudo-event," the consciously planned act—press conference, demonstration, speech—designed entirely for coverage by the mass media and meaningless unless cameras and reporters are present?

The reality of conscious planning to make a desired impression on the public has led to a widespread assumption that the more mass the media, the more fraudulent their public-affairs coverage will be.

There are arguments against televising the proceedings of Congress, for example, on grounds that it will increase the tendency to play to the cameras instead of to the issues. The fact that Senators and Congressmen behave differently at hearings that are televised than at hearings that are not is seen as evidence that projecting such events routinely on the mass media will degrade the quality of public discourse and judgment.

The presence of cameras, especially cameras known to be presenting a picture to a potential audience of millions, does change men's behavior. The performance of a public figure at a press conference is different because there are reporters there. But this really goes to the heart of democratic politics, for the only way to insulate policy makers from the consciousness of public observance is to place them beyond the power of the public. It is a necessary cost of doing business in an open society.

Fear of the "pseudo-event" is exaggerated. First, political figures doing business in public, as they do on the floor of Congress, are already adjusting to the public impression they give. Playing to the galleries is part of the consciousness of every intelligent person who communicates to a large audience, whether he is a member of Congress, a corporation president at a stockholders' meeting, a university president at a meeting of the American Council on Education, a professor giving a lecture, or a general briefing the National Security Council. It is also true of politicians running for office.

The argument against routine televising of public events is, at heart, an argument against the democratic process except for one thing: television increases the real and psychological distance between the public figure and the audience. The politician addressing a rally in a meeting hall is "playing to the gallery" but the gallery is able to make itself heard, and the speaker cannot completely control the program. Television in controllable, and the audience can do little except turn it off. This difference between live and televised events is real enough and dangerous enough. But it is exaggerated as a new phenomenon. The careful planning of the use of television to project a preconceived image has been cited constantly as the determining factor in the elections of men like John Kennedy in 1960 and Richard Nixon in 1968. But these were all close races in which a number of marginal factors could have represented the difference between victory and defeat. And if television was a factor it was as a more efficient projection of the kind of image the candidate would have produced if he had made only personal appearances. The managers of William McKinley and Warren G. Harding contrived to control their campaign appearances as rigidly as Richard Nixon's, and, it might be said, with more decisive results.

Furthermore, as television is increasingly used in presenting the full spectrum of public affairs, the impact of short, contrived performances is diluted. If a member of Congress appears on national television for one three-minute segment a year, he will do his utmost to project his highest-priority impact during that time. If he is on the screen almost every day, artificial behavior becomes less viable and less convincing. The greatest fears of the stage managers of candidates is extended, uncontrolled exposure to the cameras.

The mass media as one-way communications will not last forever

When audiences can respond immediately in an expression of recorded opinion on what they are watching, the fear of passivity changes to a fear of overreaction. But this, too, is a legitimate cost of doing democratic business. Men have adjusted to the sensitivity of a fast-reacting political system, and there is no evidence of more epidemics of panic after the advent of the mass media.

Against any loss of quality in public proceedings because the persons involved will be self-conscious at being on television must be placed the gain that this brings. Whatever gallery playing and insincere performance a live camera might stimulate, it cannot possibly be worse than the effects of, for example, public boards making decisions in private. The existence of corruption, the cynical disregard of established policy, the pursuit of private advantage to the damage of public welfare are endemic among various local boards and a powerful reason for this is that their proceedings are conducted without much public observance. For every civic agency that is more honest and responsible because of an exposé of a careful journalist, there are hundreds which are restrained in corruption and irresponsibility for fear of that publicity.

Most of the routine proceedings of public bodies are boring. Yet nothing ordains that governmental processes be melodramatic all the time. Neither is it true that what is boring to most people is boring to all. On each issue that is boring to a majority there is an audience for which it is intensely important. That, too, is inevitable in an open and specialized society. It is not an argument for restricting the record of proceedings. When channels are available, boredom of the majority is unimportant.

What makes the argument of boredom persuasive today is commercial television patterns that force each minute of television to compete against the most skilled stimulation of quick attention the world has ever known. The most highly paid writers, actors, musicians, and producers in the world are not those that create education for the young, or drama for adults, or political programs for the voters. They are the men and women who create television commercials. This is a serious distortion of the uses of national talent for a society struggling with dangerous social tensions. The attention of the American population is one of the most valuable commodities in history. The United States produces more than $785 billion worth of goods and services each year. Almost two-thirds of that, $492 billion, is in consumer spending. To capture a larger share of that almost half-trillion-dollar annual prize, various corporations spend $17 billion a year in advertising. This bombards the population with daily assaults of sophistry, with incalculable effects on the creation of cynicism and propagation of insistent materialism.

There are deeper psychic losses. The American Association of Advertising Agencies has estimated that sixteen hundred advertisements daily are aimed at the public. They say that eighty are noticed and twelve provoke some specific reaction. This attempt to gain attention is made on top of the natural level of multiple signals that urban man must normally live with. He drives on highways and walks on sidewalks with more human beings and objects within his vision than he can possibly register and think about, so he has to learn to ignore most of them. He is confronted with more print than he wants, so he learns to ignore most and focus on what is important to him. There is an absolute need to detect quickly the existence of many things and reject most before they take too much attention, permitting the individual to dwell on what means a great deal to him. This requirement is the source of the lonely crowd, the men and women who live in cities to take advantage of its multiple contacts and communications but, in order to select what is significant for them, protect themselves from most of the contacts and communications that surround them.

Urban man walks around with a selective shield around him, sensitive enough to detect incoming signals and fast enough to reject the majority that are not wanted. One of the remarkable achievements of urbanized life is the rapidity with which individuals learn to perform this with intelligence and skill.

The $17 billion in advertising a year is designed to deceive this shield. Its chief weapon is novelty, since the individual has learned how to identify and reject older cues. New words, new ideas, new faces, new pictures are like new weapons—they are capable of surprise attack and of penetrating old defenses. Because of the rewards of surprise attack on the American consciousness—the $492 billion in personal expenditures a year—the most costly talent in the society is put to work designing the new weapons, creating novelty for which the individual is unprepared, to penetrate his defenses with an endless succession of unidentified lying objects. Nothing is too exotic or remote. Advertising quickly adopted the psychedelic style, making standard in two years what might have taken a generation. It uses sexuality in ways that are forbidden on the stage, in schools, and in the nonadvertising parts of television, but that are accepted because they are commercial. It even uses unexpected truth when it is needed to seize attention, like advertising that a car is ugly but . . .

The exploitation of symbols for the sake of merchandising has had a severe attrition rate on language, ideas, and styles. The existence of the mass media and of urban life has already created and spread new symbols quickly and efficiently, but advertising uses them so intensely and ingeniously that the rate is accelerated even more. Intense promotion of songs kills them in three weeks despite enormous popularity. Language has always changed as new phenomena created new words that displaced older ones. There were 150,000 words in the English language in 1600 and there are probably about 600,000 now. But the mass media have destroyed words by repetition and conversion to merchandising purposes.

Standards of boredom and novelty have been so altered by the advertising industry that although all the objective measurements of this generation show more knowledge and more intellectual acuity, the most persuasive communication they know, television, trains them to receive intensely only the thirty-second and sixty-second messages of highly contrived methods of selling. The 30-second message is not an ancient inheritance; educated and uneducated people used to listen together to four-hour speeches and sermons.

Against the ingenuity, novelty, and polish of sixty-second commercials, other programming seems to pall. And if the gross national product and the mass media continue to grow with the same level of intense merchandising, there will always be a built-in influence against programs that appeal to smaller audiences, that depend on calm observation, and that do not require melodramatic novelty.

The conversion of advertising to providing product information will reduce some of the sensory attack on the population. It will tend to concentrate mass advertising to its most useful function, product information and those "impulse" ads that notify the public of goods and services that it might not otherwise know about.

If substantial advertising money is diverted from the news media to data banks it will remove a force that has had a useful, though unintended, social impact. Most advertising is concentrated in news and newslike media; 65 percent of the $17 billion a year goes to newspapers, television, magazines, radio, and business papers, in that order. And, because almost all of this is directed at mass audiences, it has impelled the news media to design themselves for the widest possible spectrum of the American population. It has meant that advertising on television helped spread television to its present 97 percent of American homes, and to place newspapers in 80 percent of households. It did this partly by supporting the initial investment in the medium but also by rewarding those media that had popular content, which meant a great deal of light entertainment.

One has to consider what would happen if the consumer were more in control of his own information system, if he knew he was paying for the advertisement, and if he could decide to take television with the news or without, or the newspaper with or without the interpretive articles. Might a man decide to buy only the comic and sports page? And if he were not waiting for a comedy show might he skip the television news? Whatever the answer, there should not be enforced exposure to any kind of programming. If the consumer has a free choice and if he makes an "unenlightened" decision, that, too, is a cost of doing democratic business. But the data on audiences for public-affairs information show that the demand for serious news is widespread.

What is more concrete in the coming years is the problem of who will own home communications centers that have high efficiency in receiving and sending information. There is already a social problem in the difference between the poor and the affluent in coping with their environment. In addition to other factors, the poor are further burdened by lower ownership of telephones and automobiles, which makes it more expensive for them to find work, to shop, and to conduct personal business. If the information machines of the future will have easy access to all the best libraries, will they be available mainly to the schoolchildren whose parents are affluent? And will this further deepen the cultural division in American society?

It is conceivable that there will be a day when basic communications devices will be required in all dwellings the way running water and electricity are required in all urban homes. Tax-supported education could be the basis for this. New machines will be useful for preschool, adolescent, and adult education, often as a scheduled part of normal schooling. It may be less expensive for a community to install certain kinds of computer-assisted televised teaching systems in homes than to attempt to expand conventional systems of classrooms and teachers for all subjects for all students.

The spread of high-capacity home communications may be further encouraged by the very real possibility of electronic mail received in the home, which would allocate some of the money now used for the physical system of trains, airplanes, sorting stations, and pedestrian carriers to tax-supported cable-delivered postal messages.

Merchants, instead of placing all their retail advertising in the news media, might instead find ways of subsidizing home devices on which the televised catalogue or the video and text ad could be displayed on call. Some pharmaceutical companies have already calculated that it would be profitable for them to support special color television by cable to doctors' offices as a substitute for their drug salesmen, who now make laborious visits to individual doctors' offices. Mass merchandising will probably convert much of its present energies toward electronic outlets in the average home.

The home cable connected with a computer eventually will be as important to urban man as the telephone. In many instances it will be a substitute for an automobile, since it will permit him to avoid unwanted personal travel by doing his impersonal transactions by home communications. It will be a tool of such spectacular capacity and efficiency that homes that do not have it will be hampered in their educational and household efficiency.

Consequently, public policy needs to encourage the spreading of new devices with equity throughout the population, as educational devices and as methods of dealing effectively with the outside environment. Otherwise, the new information machines could create semipermanent class divisions and widen an already dangerous chasm between social groups who see the same environment in incompatible ways.

The professionally packaged news seems likely to survive for the same reason it is so widespread today: it is a useful way for busy people to make sure that they are exposed briefly to the most urgent information from the outside world. It will continue to provide a common view of the social environment. It will undoubtedly be more analytical and have capacity for pursuit in depth, since many of the physical events will have been seen, or will be retrievable on tape as they originally unfolded. The citizen will want explanation rather than simple description. But the nature of future politics will depend on how evenly this new power to pursue information is distributed throughout society.

Beyond the standard "news package" there will be more diversity. More independent channels of communication to each information corporation and into each home will end the homogenizing of news that now occurs because it must be prepared for such a wide spectrum of consumers. To the intellectually satisfying power to pursue in depth there will also be the power to pursue doctrinaire and extreme values. The carefully balanced account of a Supreme Court decision on racial integration may be augmented by a racist interpretation of the same thing. Not all the new information will be sweetness and light. But, unless the foundation of the open society and the democratic state is false, it will ultimately enrich and strengthen the body politic.

Future News and Future Society

13

In 1635 Cardinal Richelieu created the French Academy to decide the proper forms of French speech, grammar, and spelling. Its work has never been finished. During the intervening three centuries, millions of Frenchmen failed to await the completed verdict of the Academy, continuing to speak, write, and spell the language however seemed best at the time.

There is no way of knowing if future events will confirm the guesses expressed in this book. In any case, life will not wait in respectful suspense for the verdict, men will continue to deal with each other in whatever way seems best at the time, and their interactions will create new relationships that will be reported: the news will go on.

Unless the weaknesses and dangers of the present media are clear, the emergence of new technological systems will bring no miraculous improvement in how men use their information machines. Nor will complex machines change the human impulses of those who understand and exploit them. There are growing numbers of men who understand how news is generated, organized, and transmitted, and it would be unintelligent of them if they did not use it to their own advantage. It is natural that with this knowledge they should try to control not only their own behavior in public events, but the news of those events, which they perceive correctly as almost as important as the event itself.

The new technology will provide the most awesome capacity for creating ideas and images that civilization has ever dealt with. Interconnected computers and vivid displays of information will select from the universe the world picture that the individual will carry in his head. This is already happening. But in the future the quantity of available information and the breadth of its variety will be far greater, giving those who have control of the system more selectivity in creating the ultimate picture the public will see.

Present news systems already are highly selective. Daily newspapers in the United States are almost all local monopolies, so that the printed picture of the community is under control of one man or a small group of men. This is intensified by the fact that half of these papers are also owned by men who control other monopoly papers as well, so that if they wish to exercise a bias, each proprietor has this power over many cities. This power is moderated by many things, including the possibility of presenting many ideas at once in printed form, the desire to keep as many readers as possible, the dedication of some proprietors to the idea of equitable access to their columns, and the growth of journalistic professionalism that attempts to ignore corporate pressures.

But nothing in the world matches the communication power of American television networks. There are three national systems that place vivid pictures and sounds simultaneously into more homes and a greater percentage of national households than any other method in existence. Because they are centralized, they can use the most expensive talents in the country to create programming, and because their economic drive presses them inexorably to achieve the largest possible audiences, they produce a nationalized culture even though the networks are operated as private, unregulated private enterprises.

In fact, because they are private enterprises and are in such fierce competition, they tend to imitate each other in trying to achieve the same goal, making for a duplication of content that culturally is the equivalent of having one system. A highly popular comedy program on one network is duplicated on another by a comedy program as similar as possible. A successful late-night talk show on one network is quickly imitated as closely as possible by the other two. The scheduling of football games on Sunday afternoon by one network guarantees an attempt by the other two to do exactly the same thing. So, despite the vastness of the system and its separation into three entities, it has presented a minimum of real diversity, a contradiction of the conventional wisdom that holds that commercial competition guarantees a maximum of choice.

Another result of the nationalization of television content is the overwhelming of local information and culture, even though the United States has more local television studios than any other country, and they all hold their licenses on condition that they must determine and meet the "needs, tastes and interests" of the communities they serve. The failure of local broadcasting comes largely from the rewards of the commercial network system that go to the collectors of the largest audiences, making smaller audiences noncompetitive. And, since networks offer highly professionalized talent of a national caliber, and have always done so, the idea of less-polished though more homely programming has never been established in commercial broadcasting.

There are many thoughtful men in television broadcasting who worry about this centralized power, and it is fair to say that were it up to some of the leaders of television they would democratize access to their prime time—so long as it did not damage profits. But they are responsible to stockholders and directors, to whom ratings are crucial. So the men who run networks are trapped between the need to maintain maximum audiences a maximum amount of time, and their recognition that they ought to be more responsive to social need.

So, whatever the good intentions of network leaders or their often ingenious attempts to compromise the two different goals, they operate centralized systems that speak with almost one voice to most of the public. At times of drama and concern, the networks can speak to almost every American home. The events following President Kennedy's assassination were seen by 96 percent of all homes and they watched an average of thirty-one hours and thirty-eight minutes. When President Johnson announced his decision not to run for re-election, he was seen by 77 million people, under conditions of sight and sound completely under his control. No individual human beings in history have ever held such communications power, not Alexander the Great, nor Caesar, nor Napoleon, nor Hitler, nor Stalin. The projection of the personal, moving image into the presence of each citizen at the same time is unprecedented.

Who has access to this system? Who controls what so many people will experience in so lifelike a way?

The greatest access is by national corporations that manufacture mass-consumption goods. Together such corporations paid $609 million in 1967 to control most of television content, including 95 percent of all prime-time access to American households. A whole generation's cultural values have sprung from that access. Ten corporations paid 78 percent of all advertising on television networks, with a proportionate impact on what enters the American brain while its owner is watching television: in a real sense, major educators of the American population have been Procter & Gamble, Bristol-Myers, General Foods, R. J. Reynolds Industries, American Home Products, Colgate-Palmolive, General Motors, Gillette, Sterling Drug, and Lever Brothers. These ten corporations control more time in the American consciousness than schools and churches.

The goal of the corporations that advertise is understandable, to sell their goods. For the most part they have not been interested in selling political ideas or ideologies. But in the process of maximizing their sales by television they have unwittingly propagated social ideas, like the glorification of violence on their entertainment programs in order to hold attention, and then when the attention is fixed they have celebrated materialism in the most talented and insistent creations of American culture, the commercials to sell goods.

The pitfall of political and social indoctrination, except for such persistent themes as violence and materialism, has been largely avoided because of economic competition and the desire to please the audience for the purpose of selling goods. If anything, there has been a tendency to withdraw from explicit indoctrination because it would interfere with maximum sales.

The second most influential access to the communications power of networks is by the network corporations themselves. They sign the contracts that allot time to the corporations that advertise and in this they exercise a measure of control. But the practical application of that control is minimal because of the need to maintain large audiences and maximize sales; the three networks consistently award access to the audience to the same large advertisers.

Networks do exercise more control over news and public affairs. Their own staffs compile the news and their own executives decide which public affairs will be broadcast. But, even here, they must take into account a number of factors: the need to convince local stations to carry their programming since that will decide the size of the total audience they have to sell or hand on to the next, sponsored program; the requirement by the FCC that local stations must carry some public-service programs; and pressures from the networks' own journalistic professionals, who attempt to enlarge their share of content against commercial pressures.

Networks presenting their own public-affairs programming do have power in propagating social values and ideas. They obviously favored racial integration, as measured in documentaries and commentaries. But they are constrained even here by national and local pressures, since too explicit a dedication to particular ideas will hurt them with corporations which do not wish to alienate parts of the audience, with local stations that are closer to public reaction, and with national political leaders who, through the FCC regulation of local stations may express their displeasure with the content of network public-affairs programming.

The third most powerful access to the centralized television system is national leadership, particularly the President of the United States. In some ways, this exceeds the power of even corporations and networks themselves, since it is almost unthinkable that a President would be denied control of the entire system for periodic addresses to the total audience. And, when the President goes on the air, unlike the advertising corporations, he is dealing explicitly and completely with political, social, and ideological matters of national policy.

This enormous power presents a democracy with a threat that was first felt with the rise of radio: the use of simultaneous, controlled access to the total audience in order to sway an entire population. The authoritarian regimes of Mussolini, Hitler, and Stalin were the first to recognize and exploit electronics for this, and they used radio for that purpose. They worked to produce mass conformity, to make dissent dangerous, and to produce pressures on foreign societies by using the appearance of total conformity at home.

The use of the mass media to produce mass conformity was a natural activity for authoritarian regimes, since these are governed by an ideology that assumes that it knows the nature of the ideal state and a fixed blueprint of achieving it and therefore knows how to shape individuals to reach those goals.

It was not shrewdness or malice that led the dictators to use radio as a manipulative device. It was a positive obligation under their philosophy. When "truth" is fixed and specific, to true believers its propagation appears to be mandatory. To leaders with total power who are committed to a faith in fixed, religious goals, dissent is not a method of testing truth, but treason to the perfect society. So dictators need not be cynical in using centralized communications to manipulate their audiences toward fixed goals. They are often cynical in the sense that they consciously lie, but they believe that since they are lying for "good purposes"—that is, the achievement of ultimate "truth"—their lying promotes "truthfulness."

There have always been leaders in democracies who chided their societies for failing to match the skill of the dictators in the use of mass media to achieve officially approved goals. Open societies are painted as less shrewd, less unified, less rational, less manipulative, less competitive than the authoritarians, as though the mass-media access to the national mind were a neglected weapons system. This longing for unified manipulation is encouraged by the fact that the systems have the capacity for marshaling the immediate attention of almost everyone in the country at the same time. To fail to use this instrument in ideological struggles seems to some to be like failing to use a machine gun against an enemy who himself has a gun.

The impulse to use the mass media as a unified instrument of official power reveals an endemic failure in American education, a lapse that jeopardizes the best uses of the mass media. This is the inadequate grounding of children in the pragmatic and philosophic basis for a free society. In the longing many people have for a fixed ideology for the United States, sometimes for their own assurance and sometimes to match the rigidities of other nations, they seldom go to the historic justification for the *process* of freedom. There is teaching of the Declaration of Independence and the Bill of Rights of the Constitution, and repeated references to individual freedom, and "the free world." Conservatives and liberals agree on the need for maximum freedom for themselves, but few children are taught in a clear and historical way what led the writers of the Declaration and of the Bill of Rights to their conclusions, and how their judgment has been confirmed by two hundred years of experience in the United States and by centuries of previous history.

No individual and no group can foresee all the consequences of every human act. Not even identical twins brought up in identical households emerge with identical personalities. Each individual, being different in important ways from every other individual, creates a unique interaction with others. The accumulated interactions of individuals and of groups give them needs that no distant observer can completely predict or, for that matter, record. To find relevant ideas to meet the unending turbulence of human affairs, a society needs a maximum flow of reactions and information from its constituents. When social policy is established, no policy maker can be sure what the ultimate effects will be. To judge how well policies are meeting the needs of human groups, a society must hear from its constituents freely and in their own terms.

Rigid societies are constantly confronted with crises because they lack the free flow of ideas that keep official policies in adjustment with reality. Errors, maladjustments, irrelevancies, corruptions, and inefficiencies in the working of high policy accumulate to dangerous levels before they make themselves felt. In a free society, mechanisms of citizen complaint, expression of opinion, and unfettered speculation provide knowledge with which to meet new situations and to avoid dangerous accumulations of error. Wherever free societies have suppressed freedom of action and expression, as the United States did in the racial caste system for 150 years, they have faced the social pathology inherent in closed societies.

It is difficult to predict the ultimate value of any idea. What may seem eccentric or dangerous in one time or place may become an absolute necessity in another. The free society assumes that an idea will live or die on the basis of how relevant it seems to how many people after it has been enunciated, not on the basis of approval or disapproval before it is expressed. Certainly not on the basis of approval by authorities, since authorities, committed as they are to policies that they wish to make effective, are hardly the best judges of differing ideas.

In a small village the dissenter, the eccentric, the nay sayer is heard if he wishes to be. He is often punished, since he is faced personally by those who disagree with him. But, if he wishes to pay the penalty, the eccentric and the heretic has available to him the prevailing communications medium—face-to-face contact.

In urbanized society the medium is no longer face-to-face contact but a technological apparatus. If the mass media are not put to use in achieving a maximum flow of ideas, there is no other effective alternative for public discourse. Mass communication is then expressed in melodramatic acts like men who burn their draft cards, or their neighborhoods or themselves. The narrow standards of televised debate is one reason the physical demonstration has emerged as a medium of communication of officially disapproved ideas.

Because the electronic media are centralized, and their control is necessarily left to relatively few men, the possibility of using them as instruments of official policy is a constant temptation. But the arguments against it are not just the slogans of diversity and freedom of expression as pieties of American history; such freedom is a practical necessity. Diversity and openness are not luxuries granted by an indulgent social system: they are the difference between that system's living and dying.

Consequently, the almost automatic access to the central television system available to national leaders is both a need in the country—there is no better way for constituents to be reached by their elected officials—and a threat—no one else in the world has so much power as a President of the United States when he pre-empts prime time on television networks. Many countries, including the United States, have had mad or malicious or stupid leaders who have tried to use their power to push their societies into disaster. By marshaling so much attention of so much of the electorate on so vivid and live a medium as television, it would be possible to commit the country to irreversible action, or to mislead it on a historic scale.

This has not happened in the electronic era because Presidents have restrained themselves, though each has chafed under the pressure of disagreement from others who also use the media of newspapers, radio, and television. President Franklin Roosevelt devised the radio Fireside Chat to bypass hostile newspapers and reach the audience directly. But in a letter to a friend he said privately he must use this powerful instrument sparingly. President Eisenhower's press secretary, James Hagerty, recognized the new power of television but Dwight Eisenhower was by nature moderate and cautious in its use. President Kennedy recognized the enormous strength he had at his television podium when in five minutes of strong language he forced the most powerful steel companies in the country to rescind a price increase. But afterward both he and the networks were awed and worried about the exercise of such power.

In November, 1969, Vice President Spiro T. Agnew attacked the television networks because after a presidential speech on Vietnam a "majority" of television commentators criticized it (the word "majority" was underlined in the official text of the Vice President's speech). As the Vice President said in his criticism, the problem of centralized power in television is real. But this centralization is at its most extreme when the highest national leader has access to most of the country, as President Nixon did when he had thirty-two uninterrupted minutes of prime time to speak to seventy million Americans, in a time, place, and circumstance under his complete control. It is ironic that Mr. Agnew attacked one of the few practices that exist for diminishing the dangers that flow from such power.

In the future, the mass media, including those that concentrate on the news, will not be less efficient. They will collect ever larger reservoirs of information, to select from this what view of the world will be seen by the citizen, and to spread it more convincingly to larger audiences. If they are centralized, whoever has access to the system will have ever larger powers.

If this is not to lead to the paralysis of the free flow of ideas and information from all levels of society, the new technology must be put to uses that support the process of freedom rather than some single goal of monetary profit, or mechanical efficiency, or indoctrination.

One way to do this with the news is to increase professionalism, to separate more than now the compiling and dissemination of political and social information from the pressures of the private corporations that own the medium, and from officialdom that licenses broadcasting stations. Professionalism is already growing, but it must increase further.

But journalistic professionals are not more perfect prophets than Presidents of the United States or network executives, nor are they immune to the temptations of pride, self-righteousness, and moral certitude. The answer is not a platonic judgment by a panel of professional journalists but a great many competing groups of journalists. Today that means competing journalistic corporations, and there are not many such corporations that compete in the same place. And one reason for this is the dependence of present-day news on the existence of a maximum audience for advertising, which is best served by a monopoly corporation.

In the future, news will not be manufactured and distributed by today's expensive and cumbersome methods. If it is delivered by cable to the home, for example, a news organization could consist of a small group that buys a small amount of cable transmission time each day, which could cost a few thousand dollars a year for distribution instead of a few million. There would undoubtedly be a few major organizations in each city, since the selection and compilation of comprehensive local and national news is a substantial operation requiring high skill. But smaller groups with interests in special kinds of news, or in small geographical areas, could disseminate their news without becoming major industrialists, increasing the flow of ideas and the range of choices for the citizen.

This will require many channels of cable available at low cost, which is technically feasible. It will also require maximum freedom of access to those who wish to buy cable time. Cable systems ought to be operated as common carriers, selling time rather than controlling content. There are laws against libel and obscenity, and except for these, all should be free to present what they wish.

If cable is not to become organized into an even more centralized national system, provision must be made for its use as a major medium for the neighborhood and community, as well as for the metropolis and the nation. If it is designed to follow present imperatives of maximum audiences for the purposes of merchandising, there will be no local channels, and the nationalization of television content will continue.

On the other hand, if it is recognized that television presence at civic meetings and public events is important, and that people live not only as citizens of a nation but as neighbors and townspeople, and that they communicate on this basis only with the help of the instruments of information, cable channels will help promote identity and citizen decision making that once made the small town a satisfying place to live.

The need for national communications will always exist, if for no other reason than to provide some view of the outside world. It will always have appeal. People who wish to hear a PTA debate on their children's local curriculum are often the same ones interested in a presidential speech. The need for using the new communications for neighborhood and community purposes does not require the elimination of national information. Local cable channels can bring the news more nearly into balance with the way people actually live.

If the new communications are designed to serve people in their family and community life, as well as national life, and if these local channels are to be truly open to all who wish to speak, it will require more than the new machines.

Electrons have no morals. They serve free men and dictators with equal fervor. Their use in transmitting human ideas depends on those who design the machines and control their use, and in the United States this ultimately will depend on the general public. If the designers of the new machines and the policy makers who enunciate the rules for their use commit them to narrow and restrictive goals, it will be because this is what the public accepts. The public in every country, including the United States, desperately needs to know the nature of the information machines and how much they will influence lives. It needs to know more clearly than it now learns in schools, the reason why individual freedom of expression on the new machines as well as in person is central to the survival of a creative democracy.

The information machines will do what they are instructed by their human masters. But from then on the roles will be reversed and the machines in their impersonal efficiency will thenceforth become the teachers of a generation of human beings.

Station	News Items				Words				Longest Item	News Time	Total Broadcast Day [a]	% News
	New	Repeated	(%)	Total	New	Repeated	(%)	Total				
TV Stations												
1. WOOD-TV	83	49	(37)	132	8,910	4,540	(34)	13,450	700	1:29	18:33	8
2. WKZO-TV	56	4	(7)	60	5,550	610	(10)	6,160	420	0:41	22:47	3
3. WZZM-TV	35	29	(45)	64	3,450	2,440	(41)	5,890	380	0:39	21:40	3
Total	174	82	(32)	256	17,910	7,590	(30)	25,500	1,500	2:49	63:00	4
Average	58	27	(32)	85	5,970	2,530	(30)	8,500	500	0:56	21:00	4
FM Stations												
4. WOOD-FM	64	66	(51)	130	3,550	3,330	(48)	6,880	200	0:47	19:35	4
5. WLAV-FM	92	55	(37)	147	4,900	2,750	(36)	7,650	190	0:53	22:05	4
6. WJBL-FM	72	78	(52)	150	5,100	2,920	(36)	8,020	200	0:55	22:55	4
7. WJFM-FM	99	94	(49)	193	9,610	9,440	(50)	19,050	420	2:12	22:00	10
8. WYON-FM	84	107	(56)	191	6,020	6,260	(51)	12,280	180	1:25	20:14	7
9. WXTO-FM	83	64	(44)	147	6,090	4,040	(40)	10,130	240	1:10	19:27	6
10. WVGR-FM	128	75	(37)	203	12,070	5,410	(31)	17,480	780	2:10	12:45	17
11. WFUR-FM	78	133	(63)	211	7,160	7,580	(51)	14,740	310	1:42	18:53	9
Total	700	672	(49)	1,372	54,500	41,730	(43)	96,230	2,520	11:14	157:54	7
Average	88	84	(49)	172	6,813	5,216	(43)	12,029	315	1:24	19:44	7
AM Stations												
12. WOOD-AM	112	221	(66)	333	7,420	9,490	(56)	16,910	240	1:57	17:44	11
13. WKZO-AM	124	132	(52)	256	10,720	10,940	(51)	21,660	290	2:29	19:06	13
14. WALV-AM	153	372	(71)	525	9,240	16,940	(65)	26,180	200	3:00	23:05	13
15. WGRD-AM	45	60	(57)	105	1,770	2,040	(54)	3,810	180	0:26	14:27	3
16. WJET-AM	130	124	(49)	254	9,550	8,870	(48)	18,420	330	2:07	17:38	12
17. WFUR-AM	79	129	(62)	208	5,390	7,780	(59)	13,170	260	1:31	15:10	10
18. WAOP-AM	103	123	(54)	226	7,473	7,130	(49)	14,603	380	1:40	13:53	12
19. WJBZ-AM	79	130	(62)	209	6,101	7,344	(55)	13,445	216	1:33	14:05	11
20. WHTC-AM	121	233	(66)	354	6,964	12,158	(64)	19,122	170	2:12	18:20	12
21. WAFT-AM	76	96	(56)	172	4,360	5,070	(54)	9,430	160	1:05	15:29	7
22. WLS-AM	158	294	(65)	452	8,840	16,150	(65)	24,990	200	2:53	24:00	12
23. WGN-AM	70	83	(54)	153	5,130	5,690	(53)	10,820	230	1:25	23:37	6
24. WERX-AM	97	197	(67)	294	6,400	8,920	(58)	15,320	270	1:46	14:43	12
Total	1,347	2,194	(62)	3,541	89,358	118,522	(57)	207,880	3,126	24:04	231:17	10
Average	104	169	(62)	272	6,874	9,117	(57)	15,991	240	1:51	17:47	10
Grand Total	2,221	2,948	(57)	5,169	161,768	167,842	(51)	329,610	7,146	38:07	452:11	8
Average	93	123	(57)	215	6,740	6,993	(51)	13,734	298	1:36	18:50	8

[a] Times are expressed in hours:minutes. These are actual newscasting times and do not include commercials, promotionals, or station identifications that were part of the newscast. Nor do they include sports and weather if they were broadcast separately.

Appendix. Predictions of New Devices

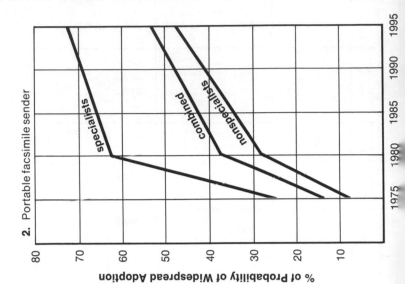

1. Reporter's portable keyboard for direct input to local news headquarters with transmission via acoustic coupler or portable radio

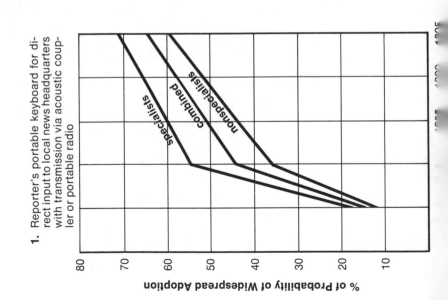

2. Portable facsimile sender

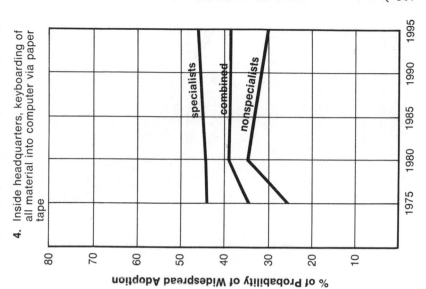

4. Inside headquarters, keyboarding of all material into computer via paper tape

% of Probability of Widespread Adoption

specialists
combined
nonspecialists

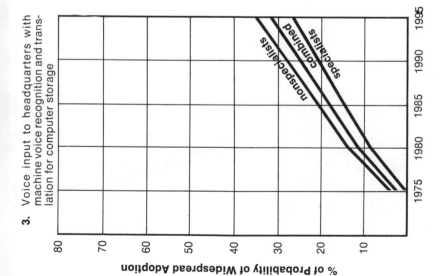

3. Voice input to headquarters with machine voice recognition and translation for computer storage

% of Probability of Widespread Adoption

nonspecialists
combined
specialists

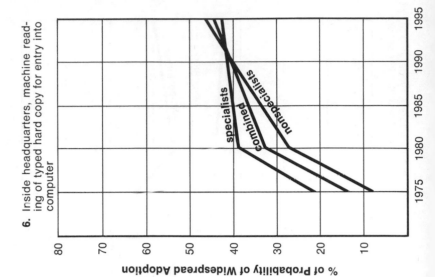

6. Inside headquarters, machine reading of typed hard copy for entry into computer

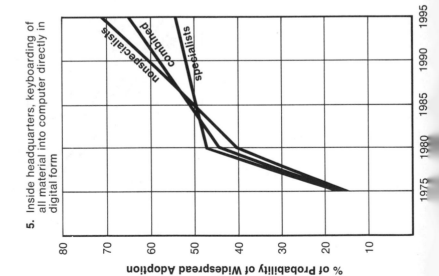

5. Inside headquarters, keyboarding of all material into computer directly in digital form

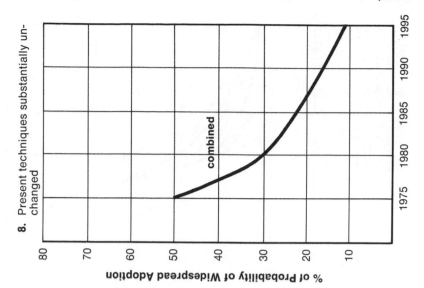

8. Present techniques substantially unchanged

% of Probability of Widespread Adoption

combined

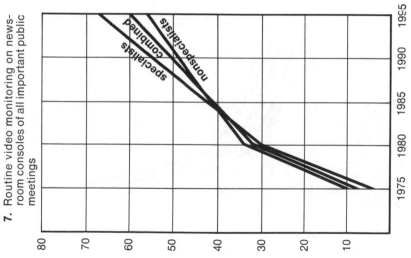

7. Routine video monitoring on newsroom consoles of all important public meetings

% of Probability of Widespread Adoption

nonspecialists

specialists

combined

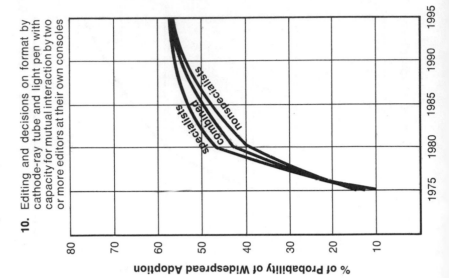

10. Editing and decisions on format by cathode-ray tube and light pen with capacity for mutual interaction by two or more editors at their own consoles

% of Probability of Widespread Adoption

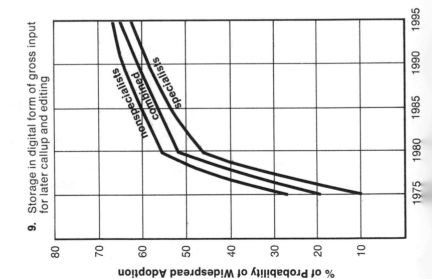

9. Storage in digital form of gross input for later callup and editing

% of Probability of Widespread Adoption

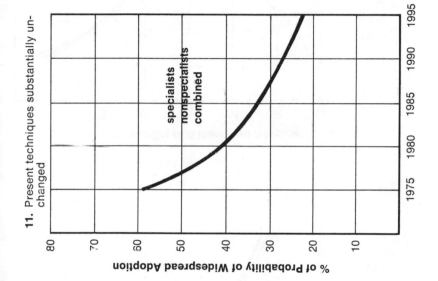

11. Present techniques substantially unchanged

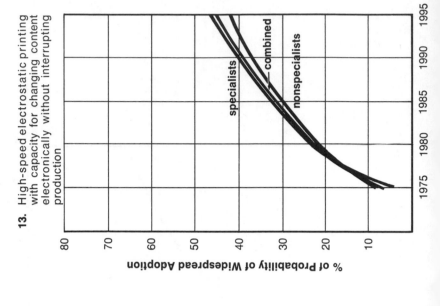

13. High-speed electrostatic printing with capacity for changing content electronically without interrupting production

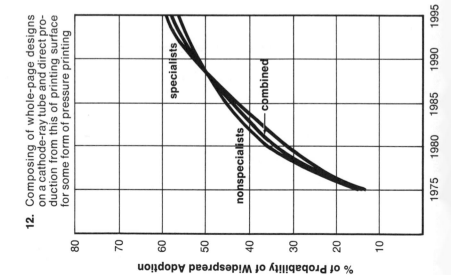

12. Composing of whole-page designs on a cathode-ray tube and direct production from this of printing surface for some form of pressure printing

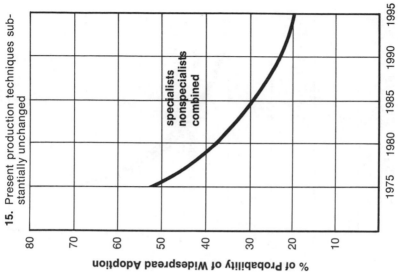

15. Present production techniques substantially unchanged

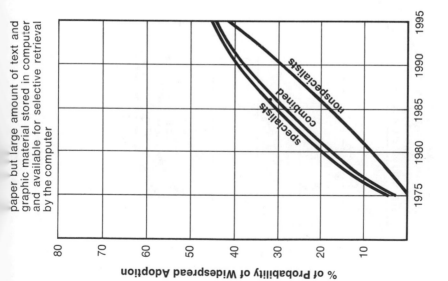

paper but large amount of text and graphic material stored in computer and available for selective retrieval by the computer

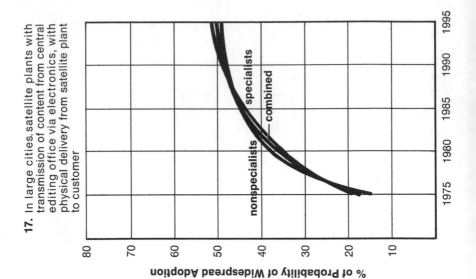

17. In large cities, satellite plants with transmission of content from central editing office via electronics, with physical delivery from satellite plant to customer

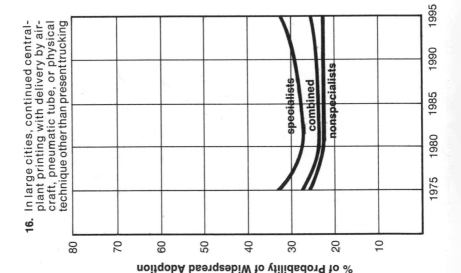

16. In large cities, continued central-plant printing with delivery by aircraft, pneumatic tube, or physical technique other than present trucking

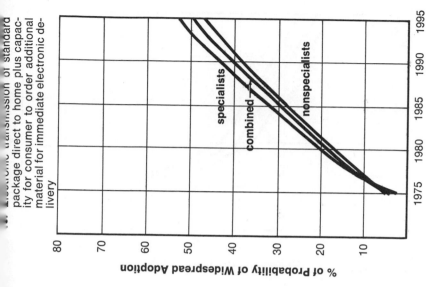

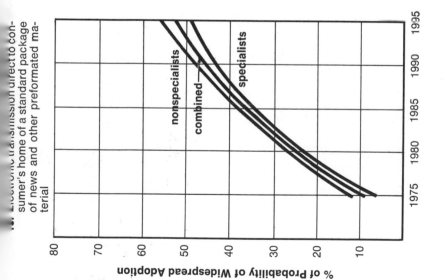

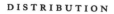

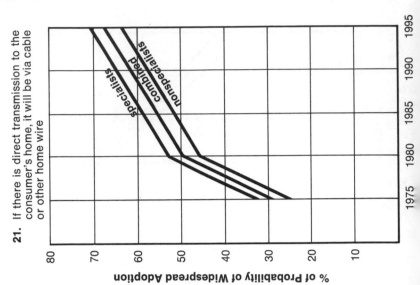

21. If there is direct transmission to the consumer's home, it will be via cable or other home wire

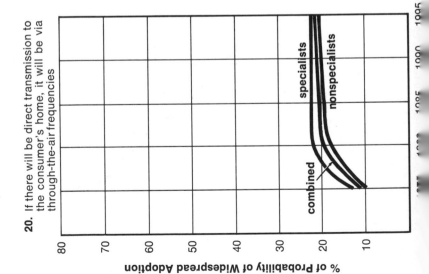

20. If there will be direct transmission to the consumer's home, it will be via through-the-air frequencies

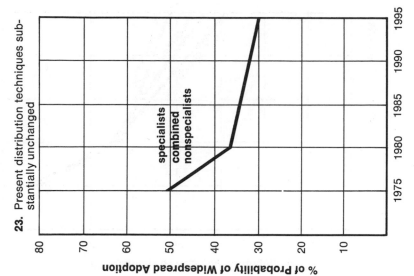

23. Present distribution techniques substantially unchanged

% of Probability of Widespread Adoption

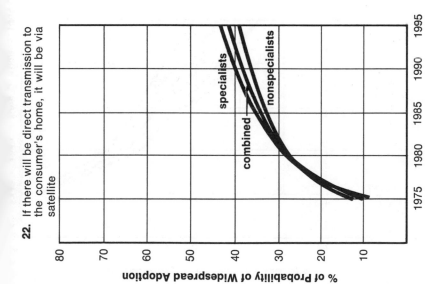

22. If there will be direct transmission to the consumer's home, it will be via satellite

% of Probability of Widespread Adoption

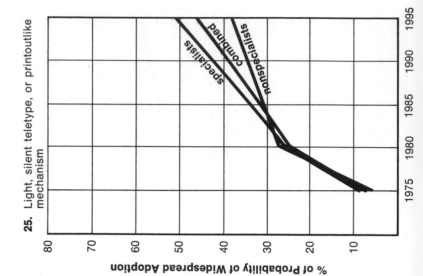

25. Light, silent teletype, or printoutlike mechanism

24. Facsimile capable of rapid production of newspaperlike content

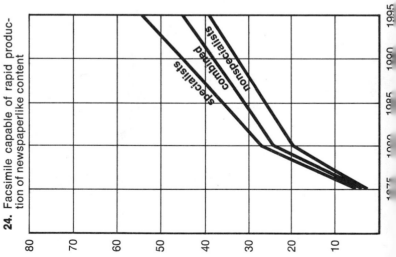

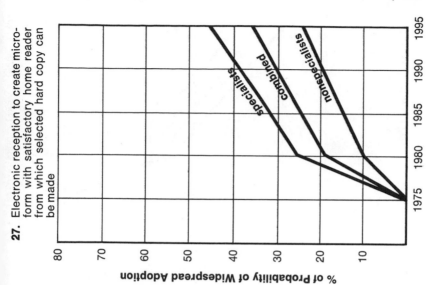

27. Electronic reception to create microform with satisfactory home reader from which selected hard copy can be made

% of Probability of Widespread Adoption

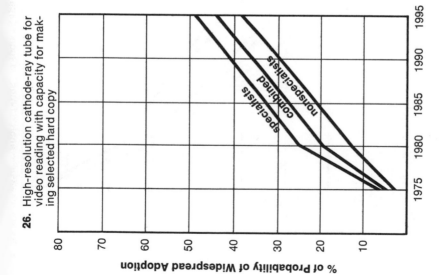

26. High-resolution cathode-ray tube for video reading with capacity for making selected hard copy

% of Probability of Widespread Adoption

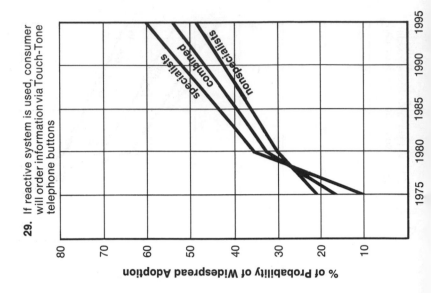

29. If reactive system is used, consumer will order information via Touch-Tone telephone buttons

% of Probability of Widespread Adoption

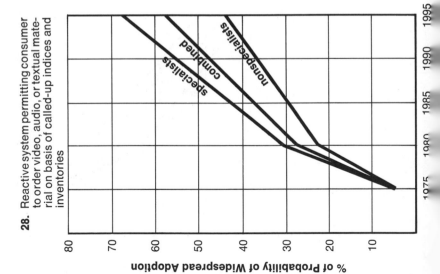

28. Reactive system permitting consumer to order video, audio, or textual material on basis of called-up indices and inventories

% of Probability of Widespread Adoption

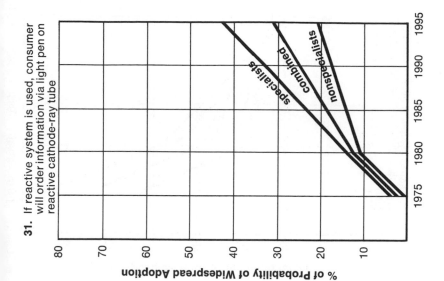

31. If reactive system is used, consumer will order information via light pen on reactive cathode-ray tube

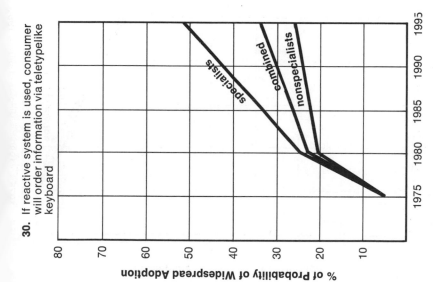

30. If reactive system is used, consumer will order information via teletypelike keyboard

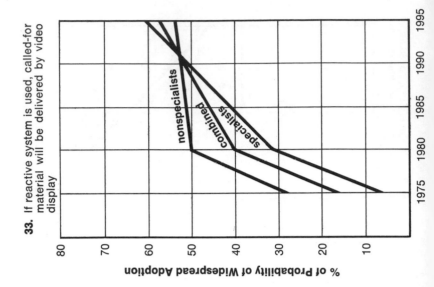

33. If reactive system is used, called-for material will be delivered by video display

% of Probability of Widespread Adoption

nonspecialists

combined

specialists

1975 1980 1985 1990 1995

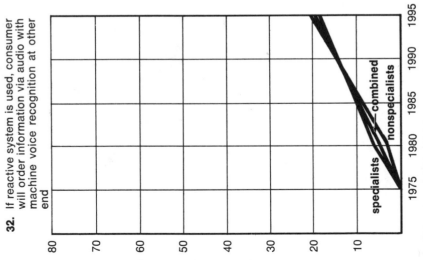

32. If reactive system is used, consumer will order information via audio with machine voice recognition at other end

% of Probability of Widespread Adoption

specialists

combined

nonspecialists

1975 1980 1985 1990 1995

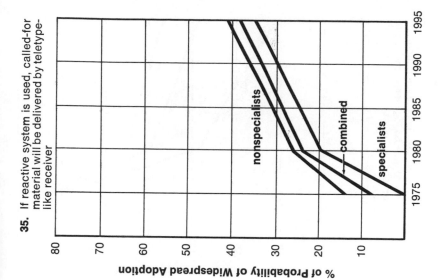

35. If reactive system is used, called-for material will be delivered by teletype-like receiver

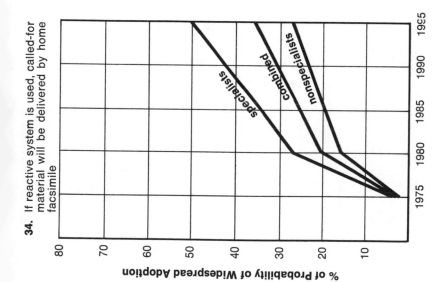

34. If reactive system is used, called-for material will be delivered by home facsimile

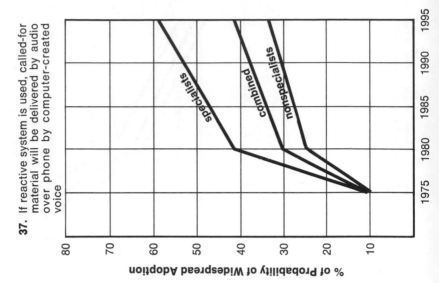

37. If reactive system is used, called-for material will be delivered by audio over phone by computer-created voice

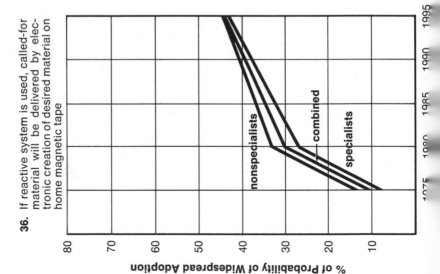

36. If reactive system is used, called-for material will be delivered by electronic creation of desired material on home magnetic tape

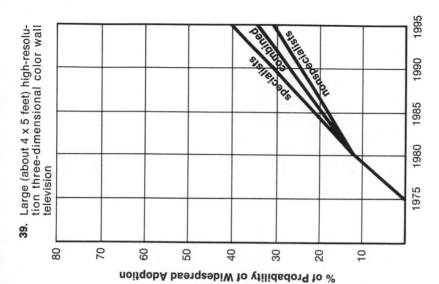

39. Large (about 4 x 5 feet) high-resolution three-dimensional color wall television

% of Probability of Widespread Adoption

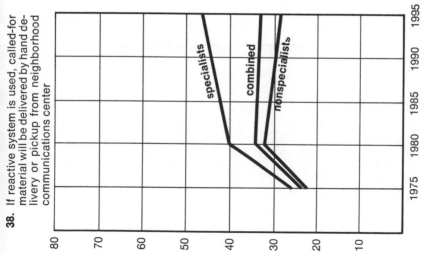

38. If reactive system is used, called-for material will be delivered by hand delivery or pickup from neighborhood communications center

% of Probability of Widespread Adoption

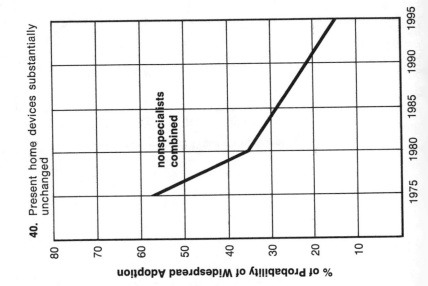

40. Present home devices substantially unchanged

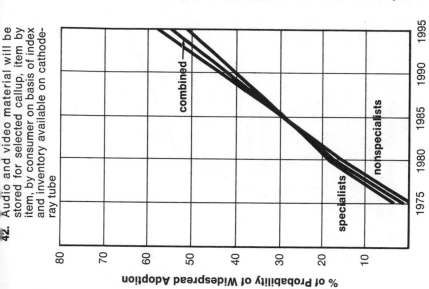

42. Audio and video material will be stored for selected callup, item by item, by consumer on basis of index and inventory available on cathode-ray tube

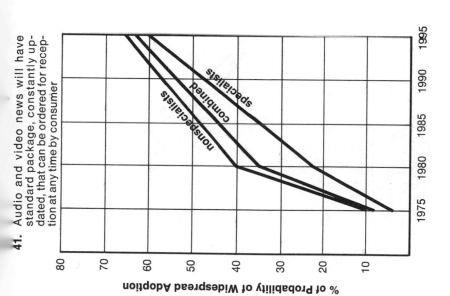

41. Audio and video news will have standard package, constantly updated, that can be ordered for reception at any time by consumer

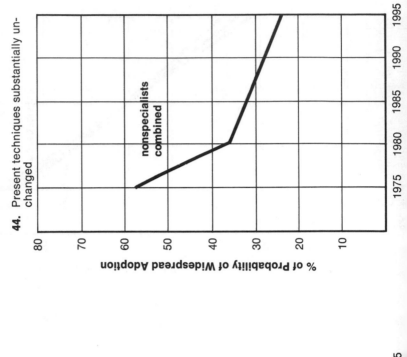

44. Present techniques substantially un-changed

% of Probability of Widespread Adoption

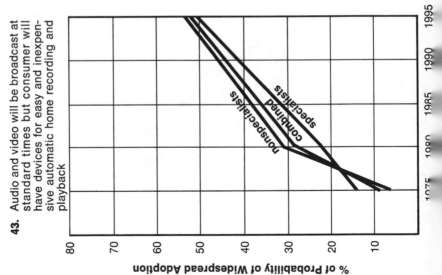

43. Audio and video will be broadcast at standard times but consumer will have devices for easy and inexpensive automatic home recording and playback

% of Probability of Widespread Adoption

References

Introduction

The early experiments of Philo Farnsworth in television are described in *The Golden Web: A History of Broadcasting in the United States*, Vol. 2, by Erik Barnouw, Oxford University Press, 1968, pages 39 and 40.

The incidence of television sets compared with electric lights comes from *The Statistical Abstract of the United States, 1968*, page 710, which shows that there were 60,100,000 homes with electricity and 58,900,000 with television.

The use of radar at Pearl Harbor is described in *Pearl Harbor: Warning and Decision* by Roberta Wohlstetter, Stanford University Press, 1962, pages 6–10.

The quotation from Ralph Waldo Emerson is from *Society and Solitude*, 1870.

Extent of absorption by the American public of printed and broadcast news is indicated in television industry tabulations of audience for news and Bureau of the Census surveys of household delivery of newspapers in notes cited in detail in notes for Chapter 4.

The quotation from Hedley Donovan appears in the journal *Daedalus* of the American Academy of Arts and Sciences, special issue entitled *Toward the Year 2000*, published in 1967, containing the proceedings of a conference on the future held on February 11 and 12, 1966.

Errors in forecasting are taken from *Profiles of the Future*, by Arthur C. Clarke, 1962.

Response to the 1938 prediction of David Sarnoff is described in *The Age of Television* by Leo Bogart, page 8. Ungar Publishing, 1956.

Average family weekly income for 1940 is based on the data given in the *Historical Statistics of the United States,* page 166, table G99–117, in which the average family personal income for 1941, the closest year cited, is given in current dollars as $2,209. Average family income for 1970 is based on data in *The Statistical Abstract of the United States, 1968,* page 325, extrapolating from the 1960 and 1965 median incomes to 1970 and assuming average and median to be sufficiently close for this particular calculation.

The Adolf Berle passage is from "What GNP Doesn't Tell Us," in the *Saturday Review,* August 31, 1968, page 12.

The evolution of writing on early writing surfaces from papyrus to parchment is from the books *A History of Libraries* by Ruben Peiss, page 1, The Scarecrow Press, New Brunswick, New Jersey, 1955; *The Hand Produced Book,* by David Diringer, page 170, Philosophical Library, New York City, 1953; and *On the Origins of Paper,* by A. Blum, Whitaker, 1934.

The California railroad episode is described in *The Fragmented Metropolis,* by Robert M. Fogelson, page 11, Harvard University Press, 1967.

The attempted suppression of radio news is described in "The Collapse of the Press-Radio News Bureau," in *Journalism Quarterly,* Volume 44, No. 3, page 549.

Inhibitions placed on pay television are described in *The First Freedom* by Bryce W. Rucker, pages 171–174, Southern Illinois University Press, 1968.

The forecasting technique used in this book is based on the general idea of Delphi, which was evolved at the RAND Corporation and is described in RAND publications, including, among others, "A Report on a Long-Range Forecasting Study," by T. J. Gordon and Olaf Helmer, September, 1964, P-2982, RAND Corporation, Santa Monica, California.

The average of six channels of television available in most cities is based on data included in "A Study of Distribution Methods for Telecommunications," COMPLAN Associates, May, 1968.

The rapid transmission of stock-market quotations to the Los Angeles *Times* is described in *Editor and Publisher* for June 7, 1969, page 78.

Contemporary cost for newspapers is based on original research done for this book, sponsored by the RAND Corporation and conducted in its economic phase by Dr. James N. Rosse, Department of Economics, Stanford University, and published in detail in a RAND monograph.

Square footage of Sunday newspapers is based on average pages of newspapers as given in *The Statistical Abstract of the United States, 1968,* page 505, and the square feet of printed surface in the newspaper page of 2.1 square feet per page.

Television investment in tangible broadcasting properties is drawn from the document "News," by the Federal Communications Commission, December 31, 1968, No. 26097, entitled "TV Broadcast Financial Data—

1967," table 9, labeled "Investment in Tangible Broadcast Property of Television Networks and 612 TV Stations as of December 31, 1967." This table shows investment in tangible broadcasting property for the three networks and their fifteen owned and operated stations, original cost $237,636,000 minus depreciation listed at $147,334,000. The 597 non-network-owned stations when added to this bring a total original cost of $1,184,759,000, with a depreciated cost of $661,067,000.

The amount of money invested by consumers in television receiving equipment is calculated from data given in *The Statistical Abstract of the United States, 1968*, page 753, which shows the retail value of television sets sold in 1967 to be, for color TV sets $3,033,000,000 and for black-and-white sets $678,000,000 for a total of $3,711,000,000. The cost per household is based on the households in the United States calculated at 58,845,000.

The amount of money paid by subscribers for daily and Sunday newspapers in the United States is based on two sources. The first is *The Statistical Abstract of the United States, 1968*, page 506, showing receipts for daily and Sunday newspapers from subscribers at $1,064,000,000; and the RAND economic studies of newspapers conducted by Professor Rosse, which suggests that the billion dollars received by newspapers from subscribers represented approximately two-thirds of the amounts paid by subscribers. Delivery boys and other independent distributors received the other third. The approximate total of subscription payments in that case was $1,414,000,000. Divided by total households, this provides a calculation of average amount spent for newspapers per household, assuming that all households shared in these costs. It is recognized that not all households share since only approximately 80 percent receive daily papers regularly, but since this is a calculation which attempts to describe the payments made for new media of all kinds it is being spread to all households for purposes of comparison. The above figure for newspaper distribution costs is based on the figures for 1963, which are the latest published by the Bureau of the Census in its Census of Manufacturers. It is raised by extrapolation to cover more recent years for purposes of comparison with broadcasting payments. For newspapers the figures for more recent advertising receipts were used with an assumption of a ratio between advertising and subscription receipts of three to one throughout the 1960s.

Total production costs for all newspapers is based on total revenues of papers as given in *The Statistical Abstract of the United States, 1968*, and brought up to date by the more recent figures on advertising expenditures for newspapers in the United States, plus the production costs calculated in the RAND field studies.

The period in which half the households in the United States purchased telephone services is based on the table in *The Statistical Abstract of the United States, 1968,* page 497, showing that 39 percent of households had telephones in 1940 and 62 percent had telephones in 1950.

The proportion of daily newspapers in the United States using the offset printing process is from *U.S. Industrial Outlook,* 1969, page 49, U.S. Department of Commerce, Business and Defense Services Administration, Government Printing Office, Washington, D.C., December, 1968.

1. Information Machines and Political Man

Information on line-of-sight visual communication in the nineteenth century is from the chapter on communications in the *Encyclopedia Americana,* Volume 14, page 344.

Data on mid-nineteenth-century revolutions is from the *International Encyclopedia of the Social Sciences,* Volume 13, page 501.

Growth in use of steamships and railroads also is from the *International Encyclopedia of the Social Sciences,* Volumes 9–10, page 511 and following.

Use of newsprint in the United States in the early nineteenth century is from *The Daily Newspaper in America* by A. M. Lee, Macmillan, 1937, appendix.

Taxes on newspaper pages are described in the *Encyclopaedia Britannica,* 1943, Volume 16, page 335.

Early communications for colonial American papers are described in *The Daily Newspaper in America* by A. M. Lee, cited above.

Worldwide illiteracy is described in the *UNESCO Statistical Yearbook, 1965.*

Differences in illiteracy between whites and nonwhites in the United States are given in *The Statistical Abstract of the United States, 1968.*

Book production and sales throughout the world come from information in *The UNESCO Statistical Yearbook, 1965.*

Use of communications-grade paper in the United States from 1900 on is described in *A Communications Theory of Urban Growth* by R. L. Meier, M.I.T. Press, 1962, page 17.

Change in use of communications media by Americans between 1955 and 1965 was tabulated on the basis of data provided in *The Statistical Abstract of the United States, 1967,* pages 888 and 889, table 1280, and from *The Statistical Abstract of the United States, 1960,* pages 945 and 946, table 1234.

Television use by class is drawn from *Social Stratification: Class in America* by Harold M. Hodges, Jr., Schenkman Publishing Company, Cambridge, Mass., 1964.

The quotation from Father Hurley is from the article, "Tele-Culture and the Third World," *Commonweal,* April 19, 1968, pages 131–133.

The procedure by which George Washington disseminated news of his decision not to run for re-election is described in *The Daily Newspaper in America* by A. M. Lee, cited previously.

The use of mass media during the student rebellion in Paris in 1968 is described in, among other places, *Broadcasting Magazine*, June 3, 1968, page 60.

Size of the television audience for the 1968 announcement by President Johnson that he would not run for re-election is from the *New York Times* for April 2, 1968.

Comparisons of use of the communications media by the United States and the rest of the world are drawn from *The Statistical Abstracts* for 1968 and 1960, previously cited.

The change in use of radio receivers per 1,000 population comes from *The UNESCO Statistical Yearbook for 1965*.

American factory sales of transistors is drawn from the *Electronic Industry's Yearbook*, 1968, issued by the Electronic Industry Association, Washington, D.C.

Number of radio and television receivers and radio and television transmitters are described in *The UNESCO Statistical Yearbook, 1965*.

The number of shortwave radio operators in Russia was estimated by the Advanced Research Projects Agency of the Department of Defense in *Newsweek*, June 13, 1966, page 27.

The growth of television viewing in the slums of Mexico is described in the book *Five Families* by Oscar Lewis.

The use of television in Saudi Arabia is described in the *New York Times* for March 19, 1968, page 10.

The use of television in Buenos Aires is described in the *New York Times* for January 28, 1968, page 7.

The number of radio transmitters in the world 1952–1964 is described in *The UNESCO Statistical Yearbook, 1965*.

The citation from Father Hurley is given previously.

Czechoslovakian tourism in Europe before the rebellion of Prague in 1968 is described in the *New York Times* for June 2, 1968, page 14.

The growth of international air passenger miles flown over the years is from *The Statistical Abstract of the United States, 1968*, page 586.

2. How Good Is Fast?

Events surrounding the War of 1812 are drawn from the following books: *The Diplomacy of the War of 1812* by Frank A. Updyke, Johns Hopkins Press, Baltimore, 1915: *The War of 1812* by Francis F. Beirne, E. P. Dutton and Company, 1949; *The War of 1812*, by Harry L. Coles, University of Chicago Press, 1965; *History of the Political and Military Events of the Late War Between the U.S. and Great Britain*, by Samuel Perkins, S. Converse, New Haven, 1825; *Annals of the Congress of the United States*, 13th Congress, 3rd Session; and *A Nation on Trial*, by Patrick C. T. White, John Wiley and Sons, 1965.

The airplane hijacking episode is described on the basis of the following sources: the *New York Times,* August 5, 1961; *The Congressional Record,* August 3, 1961; *Editor & Publisher,* August 12, 1961; Washington *Daily News,* August 4, 1961; Washington *Daily News,* August 3, 1961; and a personal letter to the author from William C. Payette.

The quotation from John Foster Dulles is found in *International Communications and the New Diplomacy,* pages 51, 52, and 53.

A description of public opinion in Cuba toward Fidel Castro prior to the Bay of Pigs invasion is found in the article "The Role of Perception in U.S.–Cuban Relations," by Alfred Charles Stepan, in *Selected Essays in Foreign Policy* by the International Fellows of 1964–1965, page 20 in particular.

Data on the speed of the spreading of news of the assassination of President John Kennedy are found in the article "Diffusion of News of the Kennedy Assassination," by Bradley Greenberg, *Public Opinion Quarterly,* Volume 28, pages 225–232.

The percentage of the population regularly exposed to a daily newspaper and the proportion of the population regularly exposed to radio and television will be described in notes for Chapter 4.

An account of the Orson Welles radio program simulating an invasion from Mars is found in *The Golden Web: A History of Broadcasting in the United States,* Volume 2, 1933–1953, by Erik Barnouw, cited previously. Pages 85 and following.

3. The Audience for News

Population of the United States in 1790 is from *The Statistical Abtract of the United States, 1968,* page 5, table 1.

Votes cast in the election of Andrew Jackson are cited in *Historical Statistics of the United States, Colonial Times to 1957,* pages 683, table Y–27–31.

Present popular-vote proportion is from *The Statistical Abstract of the United States, 1968,* page 372, table 534.

Characteristics of voters are given in *The Statistical Abstract of the United States, 1968,* page 372, table 535.

Percent of illiteracy in the United States is from *The Statistical Abstract of the United States, 1968,* page 866. Note that functional illiteracy is higher.

The number of daily newspapers in the world is given in the *Encyclopaedia Britannica,* volume 16, page 382, which cites UNESCO statistics. The United States' share is given in *The Statistical Abstract of the United States, 1968.*

Early newspaper circulation in the United States is given in *The Daily Newspaper in America* by A. M. Lee, previously cited, page 725. Circulations for intermediate years are in the *Historical Statistics of the United*

States, page 500, table R–173–186. Nineteen sixty-eight data from the *Editor & Publisher Yearbook*, 1969, page 15.

Formation of the Audit Bureau of Circulation is described in A. M. Lee, cited previously.

Survey of household delivery of papers is given in the *Current Population Reports, Population Characteristics*, June 3, 1960, Series P–20, No. 102, "Household Delivery of Daily and Sunday Newspapers: 1959."

Data on readership of newspapers are from "When People Want To Know . . . Where Do They Go to Find Out?" undated, based on data collected November 11–23, 1966. This study was sponsored by the Newsprint Information Committee, an organization created by the Abitibi Paper Company, Anglo-Canadian Pulp and Paper Mills, British Columbia Forest Products, Domtar Newsprint, The Great Lakes Paper Company, James Maclaren Company, and Macmillan Bloedel. The study was fielded and tabulated by the Opinion Research Corporation of Princeton, New Jersey, under the general guidance of the Bureau of Advertising of the American Newspaper Publishers Association. Its explanatory note states, "The study design was developed by Opinion Research Corporation and Bureau of Advertising jointly, following an overall plan devised by the latter." A national probability sample of 2,470 individuals was used, of whom 1,991 were adults 21 years old and older, and 479 were aged 12 to 20. The report is based primarily on the adult sample.

Population changes since World War II are described on the basis of data in *The Statistical Abstract of the United States, 1968*, page 11, on educational attainment; page 226, on occupational patterns; page 463, on income; page 369, on voting-age population; and page 18, on urbanization.

The average circulation of dying papers as opposed to that of new papers in 1963 is based on the list of papers with their circulations given in the *A.N.P.A. General Bulletin*, No. 5, January 29, 1964. Size of papers involved is drawn from *Editor & Publisher Yearbook*, for 1963 and 1966.

Data on U.S. families with radio sets are given in *The Statistical Abstract of the United States, 1968*.

Reduction in numbers of daily papers sold per family is described in *The Statistical Abstract of the United States, 1968*, page 505, table 744.

Television ownership by United States families is described in *The Statistical Abstract of the United States, 1968*.

Characteristics of families with television sets is from *Current Housing Reports, Housing Characteristics*, January, 1968, Series H–121, No. 14, "Household with Television Sets in the United States, June 1967."

Extent of television viewing from 1966 is from "Dimensions of Television," 1966, National Association of Broadcasters, Washington, D.C., page 12.

Median hours of viewing by individuals is from "A Ten-Year View of Public Attitudes Toward Television and Other Mass Media, 1959–1968," a report by Roper Research Associates, March 26, 1969, issued by Television Information Office, New York City.

Wording of the newspaper survey is from the above-cited pamphlet, "When People Want To Know . . . ," page 12.

Prediction of future population characteristics is drawn from *The Year 2000* by Herman Kahn and Anthony Wiener, Macmillan, 1967; *This U.S.A.* by Ben J. Wattenberg and Richard M. Scammon, Doubleday, 1965; and *The Statistical Abstract of the United States, 1968*.

The quotation from Wattenberg and Scammon is found on page 301 of *This U.S.A.*

New transmission speeds expected for new wire services is from a paper by William L. Rivers from the RAND News Media Project.

Advertising revenues for the United States in 1967 is from *The Statistical Abstract of the United States, 1968*, page 782, table 1190.

Differences in viewing by social class are from the book, *Social Stratification*, by Harold M. Hodges, Jr., previously cited.

Quotes and class preferences of television programs are from *Social Stratification* by Hodges, previously cited, pages 161–162.

4. Some Peculiarities of American News

Data on concentration of newspaper circulation in capital cities of countries are drawn from *Editor & Publisher Yearbook*, 1969, page 451 and following.

The reference to station WLW is from Rucker, *The First Freedom*, page 90, cited previously.

Numbers of state and local governments is from *The Statistical Abstract of the United States, 1968*, pages 405 and 406.

Change in American family income is from *Historical Statistics of the United States, Colonial Times to 1957*, page 165, and from *Historical Statistics of the United States, Continuation to 1962 and Revisions*, page 23.

Information on retail trade establishments is from *The Statistical Abstract of the United States, 1968*, pages 762 and 763.

Data on the distribution of households by broadcasting markets are from *Broadcasting Yearbook*, 1969.

Advertising revenues in the Pittsburgh and New York markets is drawn from the FCC document "News," No. 26097, dated December 31, 1968, "TV Broadcast Financial Data—1967," table 13, entitled, "Individual TV Market Data, 1967."

Material on the growth of early American newspapers is drawn from *The Daily Newspaper in America* by A. M. Lee, previously cited, and from *American Journalism, A History: 1690–1960* by Frank Luther Mott, Macmillan, 1962.

Growth of circulation of individual daily newspapers with national circulation is drawn from *The Editor and Publisher Yearbook*, for appropriate years. Circulation of publications within their home cities compared with their national circulations from the circulation departments of the newspapers cited.

News magazine and other national periodical circulations are from the document "Rates and Circulation Changes, Newsweek and Competitors, 1969," *Newsweek*.

Growth in the use of supplementary news services is based on data supplied by the individual news services.

Comparative growth of circulation between weekly and daily papers is drawn from *U.S. Industrial Outlook, 1969*, U.S. Department of Commerce, Business and Defense Services Administration, Washington, D.C., December, 1968, page 47.

Change in number of average pages in U.S. dailies is drawn from *The Statistical Abstract of the United States, 1968*, page 505.

Data from a survey taken by the Bureau of Advertising of the A.N.P.A. are based on material which is cited in the reference notes for Chapter 4.

Data on television broadcasting markets for Delaware, Maryland, and Pennsylvania are taken from *Television Factbook*, Stations Volume, 1967 edition, Washington, D.C. This includes data on markets for each station and fees charged by each station as listed in their formal rate cards.

5. The Printed News System

Statistics for numbers of associations, governmental units, schools and colleges, churches and business firms, are from *The Statistical Abstract of the United States, 1968*.

Circulation and news services of the Washington *Post* come from the *Editor & Publisher Yearbook*, 1969.

Information on the quantity of news and decisions by gatekeepers on newspapers is from data collected during the RAND news-media study by the study team headed by Professor William L. Rivers of Stanford University.

Description of the change in typesetting and other basic production processes used in newspapers is drawn from *The Daily Newspaper in the United States* by A. M. Lee, cited previously, and from the pamphlet "Technological Developments in Newspaper Publishing," by William D. Rinehart, American Newspaper Publishers Association Research Institute, Inc., 1967.

Requirements for high-speed castings in large newspapers compared for letter press and offset printing are made on the estimate of Hy Shannon, production specialist in the RAND news-media study team.

Estimates of the amount of money invested in machinery by newspapers of various sizes is made by Professor Jame N. Rosse, of Stanford University, and Hy Shannon, both of the RAND news-media study team.

Use of Associated Press wire copy as a function of time of reception in Wisconsin is from "Analysis of AP News on Trunk and Wisconsin State Wires," by George A. Van Horn, *Journalism Quarterly*, Volume 29, pages 426–432.

Calculations of words of teletype copy received in newsrooms by hour of day were made on the basis of observations by Daniel Garvey and John Mayo in the RAND news-media study team.

The quotation from the David Manning White study of gatekeepers is from the article "The Gate Keeper," by David M. White, *Journalism Quarterly*, Volume 27, pages 383–390.

The Warren Breed findings are found in "Social Control in the News Room: A Functional Analysis," in *Social Forces*, Volume 23, pages 326–335, May 1955.

Characteristics of gatekeepers observed in the RAND field study of newspapers were analyzed by Dr. William L. Rivers of Stanford University.

The Republicanism of newspaper proprietors as manifested in endorsements for President is based on surveys in presidential years by the trade publication *Editor & Publisher*, which shows the following percentages for presidential years for Democrats as follows, 1936, 36%; 1940, 23%; 1944, 22%; 1948, 15%; 1952, 14%; 1956, 15%; 1960, 16%; 1964, 42%; and 1968, 19%. Earlier election endorsements can be found in *American Journalism* by Frank Luther Mott, previously cited, page 858 and following.

Reading of newspapers by income and education level is drawn from data cited in the notes for Chapter 4.

6. Printed News as a Corporate Enterprise

Numbers of newspapers of all kinds is from the 1963 Census of Manufacturers, Major Group 27, Newspapers, Periodicals, Books, and Miscellaneous Publishing. U.S. Bureau of the Census, Cenus of Manufacturers Industry Statistics, U.S. Government Printing Office, Washington, D.C., 1966. Publication MC 63(2)27A.

Size of establishments for newspapers is from *The Statistical Abstract of the United States, 1968*, page 480, table 697, and from *Industrial Outlook 1969*, page 45.

Number of newspaper corporations offering stock for public sale is from *Editor & Publisher* for May 10, 1969, page 84.

Size of daily newspaper chains is from *Editor & Publisher* for June 1, 1969, page 17.

Quotation from John Kenneth Galbraith is from *The New Industrial*

State by John Kenneth Galbraith, Houghton Mifflin, 1967, pages 60 and 61.

Past circulation of U.S. newspapers is from the appendix of the book *The Daily Newspaper in the United States* by A. M. Lee, previously cited.

Contemporary circulations of American papers is from the *Editor & Publisher Yearbook*, 1969, page 15.

Data on *Average Medium Daily* are based on field studies of the RAND news-media project.

Circulation of the largest dailies in the United States is from *Editor & Publisher Yearbook* 1969.

Quotations from The Economist Intelligence Unit is from the printed report "The National Newspaper Industry, A Survey," 1966, The Economist Intelligence Unit, November 1966, London.

Quotations from Elmer Brown are from a personal interview with the author, August 1967.

The number of American cities with daily newspapers in 1910 is based on data given in Part 6, page 2842, of the *Hearings of the Sub-Committee on Anti-Trust and Monopoly of the Committee on the Judiciary of the United States Senate,* 90th Congress, 2nd Session, entitled "The Failing Newspaper Act," Part 6.

Data on chains in the United States are from *Editor & Publisher Yearbook,* previously cited.

The obituary of Frank Munsey is taken from the Emporia *Gazette,* Emporia, Kansas, for December 23, 1925, and is quoted in *The Autobiography of William Allen White,* page 629.

The statement made at the time of sale of the Orlando newspapers to the Chicago Tribune Company is quoted in *Editor & Publisher* in September 4, 1965, page 53.

The Du Pont policy on the possible sale of its newspapers is from a 1962 memorandum from Charles L. Reese, Jr., editor-publisher of the Wilmington *News* and *Journal* to Lammot Du Pont Copeland, president of the Du Pont Company.

The exclusion of newspaper data from standard industrial information is seen in *The Statistical Abstract of the United States, 1968,* on, among other places, pages 733 and 480.

The statement that the American Newspaper Publishers Association had no estimate of the value of newspaper physical assets was made in a personal interview with the general manager of th ANPA, Stanford Smith.

Industrial profits that omit newspapers are found in *The Statistical Abstract of the United States, 1968,* pages 482 and 483.

Testimony of Paul Rand Dixon is found on pages 3096 and 3097 of Part 7 of the *Hearings of the Sub-Committee on Anti-Trust and Monopoly,* previously cited.

Testimony of William Farson is found on page 206 of Part 1 of the *Hearings of the Sub-Committee on Anti-Trust and Monopoly*, previously cited.

Largest industrial corporations are found listed in *The Statistical Abstract of the United States, 1968*, page 480, table 697.

Return on equity for industries in the United States is found in *The Statistical Abstract of the United States, 1968*, page 483, table 703.

7. The Broadcast News System

Monopoly patterns in American daily newspapers is drawn from *Hearings of the Sub-Committee on Anti-Trust and Monopoly of the Committee on the Judiciary of the United States Senate*, 90th Congress, 2nd Session, entitled "The Failing Newspaper Act," page 2842, Part 6.

Total number of radio and television stations on the air at the end of 1969 is taken from *Broadcasting Magazine*, December 8, 1969.

Statements on the degree of duplication of timing and of content in broadcasting are drawn from the analysis of radio stations heard in the Grand Rapids–Kalamazoo market area, recorded by the Department of Journalism of the University of Michigan in cooperation with RAND news-media study project. Results of the transcriptions were analyzed at RAND.

Standard types of radio-station programs are found in a number of conventional listings, including trade sources and newspapers as given by stations themselves. For example, in the Washington *Post* of October 25, 1969, page C–8, one finds the listings of seven categories of AM and FM stations as described by the stations themselves.

Information on employees and editorial departments of medium-size papers is drawn from the RAND field studies of newspapers, as cited previously.

The observations of news operations in a smaller radio station and in a larger television station are real observations of real stations. The AM station in the text is called XYZ, the television PQR–TV for purposes of anonymity. The observations were made by Frank Allen Philpot.

Size of the television market in the Grand Rapids–Kalamazoo area is drawn from *Broadcasting Yearbook, 1969*.

Financial data for broadcasting stations in the Grand Rapids–Kalamazoo area are from FCC sources, "News," previously cited.

Data on the content of the Kalamazoo *Gazette* and the Grand Rapids *Press* are drawn from an examination of the papers for the dates bracketing the news events which were displayed in broadcasting June 2–3, 1969.

The geographical area covered by the broadcasting stations in the Grand Rapids–Kalamazoo area is drawn from market maps in *Television Factbook*, Stations Volume, 1967.

The number of counties and governmental units covered in the market areas of the broadcasting stations is taken from *The Statistical Abstract of the United States, 1968,* page 406, showing the numbers and kinds of local governments in the state of Michigan.

Descriptions of the entries in logs submitted to the Federal Communications Commission for license renewal are based on examination of a large number of such logs.

Numbers of people and procedures in reviewing logs submitted for license renewal to the Federal Communications are described in a letter to the author from the FCC, November 30, 1967.

Content survey of the Western states of the United States showing strong conservative concentration in local broadcasting programming usually presented as public service is in the document issued by the Office of Communication of the United Church of Christ, dated January 25, 1968, by Dr. Gordon G. Henderson.

The $65,000 cost of one minute of air time on the best commercial programming is taken from *Broadcasting Magazine,* March 10, 1969, which reports that a one-minute commercial on the television programs "Laugh-In," "Mission Impossible," and "Mayberry RFD" is $65,000. The lowest cost per minute on other network prime-time shows was $33,000.

Expenses for average television stations is based on the financial data given in the FCC document, "News," entitled "TV Broadcast Financial Data—1967," cited previously.

The market value of television stations in the top 50 markets is estimated in *Broadcasting Magazine,* February 3, 1969, pages 20 and 21.

8. Broadcast News as a Corporate Enterprise

Material on the early days of radio is drawn from the *The First Freedom* by Rucker, previously cited, and from *The Golden Web* by Barnouw, also previously cited.

Numbers of current radio stations is taken from the pamphlet "Dimensions of Radio, 1967," National Association of Broadcasters, Washington, D.C. The citation of 25 million people beyond the range of local night broadcasting is taken from Rucker, previously cited.

Data on the assets and cost of equipment of newspapers are found in the notes for Chapter 7.

The value of assets for radio stations is taken from the FCC document "News—AM–FM Broadcast Data—1967," dated February 7, 1969.

Material on the early newscasters on radio is taken from *The Golden Web* by Barnouw, previously cited.

Information on radio chains and networks is taken from Rucker, pages 189–195, previously cited.

Data on the number of television stations over the years are taken from the pamphlet "Dimensions of TV, 1966," National Association of Broadcasters, Washington, D.C.

Financial data for television stations is taken from the FCC document

"News" entitled "TV Broadcast Financial Data—1967" dated December 31, 1968.

The current market value of television stations in the top markets is taken from *Broadcasting Magazine*, February 3, 1969, page 21.

The proportion of network programming appearing on local stations is taken from a speech by E. William Henry, former chairman of the FCC, given before the National Association of Broadcasters in Washington, D.C., on March 23, 1965.

Earnings per employee for television stations is derived from the FCC document "News" entitled "TV Broadcast Financial Data," previously cited.

The division between local advertising and national advertising revenues is also taken from "TV Broadcast Financial Data."

Network access to 94 percent of the audience in the 50 top markets is taken from testimony of FCC Commissioner Bartley, as given on page 2886, Part 7 of *Hearings Before the Sub-Committee on Anti-Trust and Monopoly of the Committee on the Judiciary of the United States Senate,* 90th Congress, 2nd Session, entitled "The Failing Newspaper Act," held in 1968.

Newspaper ownership of television stations is described on page 3410, Part 7 of the Senate hearing cited above.

Newspaper ownership of radio stations is cited on page 3411 of the same hearings cited above.

Corporate interests of the Times Mirror Company are taken from *Moody's Industrial Manual,* July, 1969, page 894.

Corporate interests of RCA are taken from *Moody's Industrial Manual,* page 1483.

Corporate interests of CBS are taken from *Moody's Manual,* page 2248. Additional information is from *Columbia Journalism Review,* spring, 1967, in the article "News As a By-Product" by B. H. Bagdikian.

Material on Hearst involvement in Mexican affairs is taken from *Citizen Hearst,* by W. A. Swanberg.

Material on the involvement of Rafael Trujillo in American broadcasting is drawn from the hearings of the Senate Foreign Relations Committee, entitled, "Activities of Non-Diplomatic Representatives of Foreign Principals in the United States," 1963.

Data on bank investments in the mass media are from a staff report for the Sub-Committee on Domestic Finance of the Committee on Banking and Currency of the House of Representatives, 90th Congress, 2nd Session, entitled, "Commercial Banks and Their Trust Activities: A Merging Influence on the American Economy," Volume 1, page 503.

9. Is Print Dying?

Numbers of television sets in the United States comes from *The Statistical Abstract of the United States, 1968,* page 505.

Percentage of homes in the United States with television sets comes from the pamphlet "Dimensions of TV, 1966," National Association of Broadcasters, Washington, D.C.

The incidence of common appliances in American homes comes from *The Statistical Abstract of the United States, 1968*, page 555. These data show that in the late 1960s, 95 percent of American homes had television sets, 95 percent had electric or gas stoves, 93 percent had running water, 90 percent had flush toilets, 88 percent had a bathtub or shower, 88 percent had telephones, and 78 percent had automobiles.

The amount of time the average American television set was on each day was 6 hours and 38 minutes during 1968 as measured by the Nielsen Television Index cited in *The Broadcasting Yearbook*, 1969, page 26.

The average number of newspaper pages paid for and received by the American family is based on data in *The Statistical Abstract of the United States, 1968*, page 505.

Employment of persons in newspapers is from the *Industrial Outlook for 1969*, page 45, and television industry from the FCC document "News," cited previously.

The quotation from Clifton Fadiman comes from the article "The Decline of Attention," in the *Saturday Review*, August 6, 1949, pages 20–24.

Numbers of children aged five to seventeen enrolled in school over periods of time is from *Historical Statistics of the United States*, page 207. The figure for 1966 comes from *The Statistical Abstract of the United States, 1968*, page 109. Data on average daily attendance in school comes from *Historical Statistics of the United States* and from *The Statistical Abstract of the United States, 1968*, page 115.

The University of Iowa student test data are from unpublished findings furnished to the author by Professor A. N. Hieronymus, University of Iowa.

Historical data on college enrollments is from *Historical Statistics of the United States*, page 210.

Sales of books in the United States over time is drawn from data in *The Statistical Abstract of the United States, 1968*, page 59.

Increase in newspaper buying is from *The Statistical Abstract of the United States, 1968*, page 505.

Increases in the rate of production of scientific and technical literature is given in the article "A Crisis in Scientific and Technical Communications," J. C. R. Licklider, in *The American Psychologist*, for November, 1966.

Growth in numbers of scientific journals and abstracts of journals is cited in a special issue of *The Johns Hopkins Magazine*, entitled "Information Explosion," fall, 1967.

The theoretical growth of the Yale Library is cited in the publication above.

The cost and weight of Sunday newspapers in Los Angeles County is based on Sunday circulations as given in page A–25 of "Newspaper Circulation Analysis," 1969–70, issued by Standard Rate and Data Service, Inc., Skokie, Illinois.

Receiving rate of teletypes in American newspaper offices is based on field studies in the RAND news-media study project conducted by Dr. William L. Rivers.

Data on the increase in tape-recorder sales and decrease in price are from the *Electronic Industry Yearbook,* 1968, page 32.

Speed of modern computers is from the monograph, "Future Computer Technology and Its Impact," by Willis H. Ware, March, 1966, RAND Corporation, P–3279.

Suggestions on microform are from "A Billion Books for Education in America and the World: A Proposal," by David G. Hays and others, RM–5574–RC, April, 1968, RAND Corporation.

Data on the growth of the use of microforms are from "Microform, A Growth Industry," U.S. Department of Commerce, Business and Defense Services Administration, February, 1969.

Plans for book sales by the National Cash Register Company are from *The Graphic Communications Weekly,* page 3, July 8, 1969.

Plans for computerized information by the *Encyclopaedia Britannica* are described in "The Printed Word Goes Electronic," by Lawrence Lessing, *Fortune Magazine,* September, 1969, Volume 80, Number 4, page 119.

Evolution of human sounds into alphabet is described in *Literacy in Traditional Societies,* Jack Goody, editor, Cambridge University Press, 1968.

Receiving rate of information in urban populations is described by R. L. Meier in *A Communications Theory of Urban Growth,* M.I.T. Press, 1962, pages 43 and 130.

The quotation beginning, "A great many individuals found . . ." comes from the book, *Literacy in Traditional Societies,* cited previously, in the chapter, "The Consequences of Literacy" by Jack Goody and Ian Watt, page 48.

10. Who Pays for News?

Percentage of revenues from advertising for newspapers is from *The Statistical Abstract of the United States, 1968,* page 506, table 745.

Broadcasting revenues from advertising constitute almost, but not quite, 100 percent. The insignificant percentage that makes it less than 100 percent represents revenues from such activities as resale of copyrighted material.

Data on gross national product by year and advertising expenditures by year are from the *Historical Statistics of the United States* and *The Statistical Abstract of the United States, 1968,* with percentages added by the author.

The references to Wiener and Kahn are to the book *The Year 2000,* previously cited.

The share of advertising revenues for various media is from *The Statistical Abstract of the United States, 1968,* page 783, table 1191.

Estimates for 1969 daily newspaper revenues is from the *Industrial Outlook, U.S.,* 1969, page 45, previously cited.

Advertising expenditures for television are cited in the above source.

Estimates of money spent by American households on television sets, antennas, and repairs are based on the total receipts of radio and television repair services as listed in *The Statistical Abstract of the United States, 1968,* page 777, table 1183; and the retail value of consumer electronic products, specifically for radio and television sets, as listed in *The Statistical Abstract of the United States, 1968,* page 753, table 1158.

Expenditures of advertising money by medium are listed in *The Statistical Abstract of the United States, 1968,* page 783, table 1191. It should be noted that money spent by the advertisers is not the same as money received by the advertising medium, since there are middleman charges, including advertising-agency fees and the cost of producing ad material. However, since the consumer is assumed ultimately to pay for all advertising including the costs of agencies and of productions, the total cost is allocated to the consumer.

Investment by broadcasters in tangible properties for television operation is from the FCC publication "News" entitled "TV Broadcast Financial Data—1967," dated December 31, 1968, table 9.

In the table listing money spent per household for various types of communications, ranging from telephones to phonograph records, it should be noted, as listed under the table, that this is not a survey of how much households actually spend. It is a compilation of total consumer spending for those activities in the United States divided by the total number of households. It is recognized that not all households spend equally for all these media, and that in some cases, such as in the postal service, part of postal expenditures are for commercial services. But the main body of these is related to consumer activities. In all instances the expenditures are spread among total households for purposes of comparison with future household income and for a uniform comparison of how much is spent on each kind of activity in the present.

Estimates of characteristics of the future American population are from Wiener and Kahn, previously cited.

Reference to Meier is to *A Communications Theory of Urban Growth,* by R. L. Meier, previously cited.

Changes in the characteristics of computers from 1955 to 1965 and projected to 1975 are from the work of Willis Ware, RAND Corporation, previously cited.

Change in wholesale price index for home electronic equipment is from *The Statistical Abstract of the United States, 1968,* page 343, table

500, listed under furniture and household durables with the subtitle "Home Electronic Equipment," which uses 1957–1959 as a base period to equal 100 and lists 1950 at 103.2 and 1967 at 82.5.

Estimates of average residence telephone bills is based on national data on residential telephone use and specific estimates for the Pacific Telephone and Telegraph Company, which calculates that average residential telephone bills in California are $12.50 a month.

Data on the cost of handling advertising as compared with non-advertising material in newspapers are based on information compiled by Publishing Systems, IBM, entitled "Summary of Newspaper Production, Functions and Cost." This was a study of processing costs per character. The RAND study estimated cost of major functions of newspaper production on the basis of total costs from the beginning and end of the basic operations of papers, rather than reduced to a per-character basis. Both are useful but for different purposes.

Cost of paper and ink in papers of various sizes is based on the RAND field studies.

The reference to proposals by Dr. Leo Bogart are from his speech entitled "Newspaper Advertising: Moving Toward the Year 2000." Dr. Bogart is executive vice-president and general manager of the Bureau of Advertising of the American Newspaper Publishers Association. His speech was delivered to the International Newspaper Advertising Executives, meeting in New Orleans, Louisiana, January 17, 1968.

The estimate by the American Association of Advertising Agencies that 1,600 advertisements are aimed daily at the public, that 80 are noticed, and only 12 provoke some reaction, is quoted in *Broadcasting Magazine,* January 1, 1968, in the article "A Message Is Much More Than Words and Pictures," by Ernest A. Jones, of MacManus, John and Adams, of Bloomfield Hills, Michigan.

11. Public Policy, Private Profit, and the Training of Audiences

The ease by which automobiles could have telephone service is based on the availability of radio spectrum if available airways are used in different ways than at present. Present policy allocates blocks of frequency to particular classes of users, without regard to how often they use them. Consequently, there are large parts of the airways that are idle while other parts are intensely crowded. Changing of policy on allocating parts of the radio spectrum plus changes in the regulatory policies on mobile telephones would make it relatively easy for each car to have a telephone.

The problem of privacy and computers is well described in *The Computer and Invasion of Privacy, The Controversial United States Government Hearings on the Proposed National Data Center,* a reprinting of the hearings before the Sub-Committee on Government Operations, 89th Congress, 2nd Session, 1966. Particularly useful is the testimony of Paul Baran, formerly of Rand, now of the Institute for the Future.

Sources for investments of television stations and of consumers in tangible physical property are cited previously.

Information on home television sets in use from 1946 to 1953 are drawn from "Dimensions of Television, 1966," National Association of Broadcasters, Washington, D.C.

The retail value of television sets 1946–1953 is calculated from the table "U.S. TV Set Production—1946–1968," which lists, by year, the number of TV sets produced and their retail value, page 24, *Broadcasting Yearbook, 1969*.

The data on average family income are from *Historical Statistics of the United States*, and *The Statistical Abstract of the United States, 1968*.

Average retail value of color television sets in 1967 is from *The Statistical Abstract of the United States, 1968*, page 753.

Comparative electronic capacity needed for various media communications are from *McGraw-Hill Encyclopedia of Science and Technology*, Volume 2, page 94.

Accounts of the early networking of television are from *The First Freedom* by Rucker, pages 131 and following, cited previously.

The financial losses of television networks in 1948 is drawn from the article "TV: The Money Rolls Out," in *Fortune Magazine*, Volume 40, No. 1, July, 1949.

On the early history of VHF and UHF television-channel allocations, I am indebted to Edward Bedrosian of the RAND Corporation, reports of the Institute of Radio Engineers, and the Ad Hoc Committee on Propagation, and the FCC Sixth Report and Order.

Losses by UHF stations are listed in the FCC document "News" entitled "TV Broadcast—1967," financial data previously cited.

Maximum channels per market if all UHF channels were used is cited by Leland Johnson of RAND.

The number of daily newspapers in the nineteenth century is cited in A. M. Lee, previously cited, and Mott, previously cited.

Growth in number of cable-connected homes 1958–1968 is from *Broadcasting Yearbook, 1969*, page 22.

Early costs of cable connections is described in the article "1969 Promises More CATV," *Broadcasting Yearbook, 1969*, page 20 and following.

Characteristics of telephone companies, including AT&T, are given in *The Statistical Abstract of the United States, 1968*, pages 497 and 498.

A 42-channel cable system was being installed in San Jose as cited in the RAND document by Leland Johnson entitled "Cable Television and Over-the-Air Broadcasting."

Comparative capacities of undersea cables and of communications satellites is given in the RAND paper by Leland Johnson "The Promise and Problems of New Communications Technology," and from the *EBU. Review* of June, 1969, pages 137 and 138.

Plans of the *New York Times* to establish a data bank that includes its newspaper editions and its annual index are described in *Editor & Publisher,* April 5, 1969, page 9 and following.

Hearings on broadcast ratings are found in *Report of the House Subcommittee of the Committee on Interstate and Foreign Commerce,* 88th Congress, 1st Session, "Broadcast Ratings."

12. The Future Content of News

An interesting discussion of the influences on newspaper style in the eighteenth century is found in the article "The Influence of Social Change on Newspaper Style," by Malcolm M. Willey, in *Sociology and Social Research,* Volume 13, pages 30–37, 1928.

Density of American population historically is found in *The Statistical Abstract of the United States, 1968,* page 5, table 1.

A description of the suppression of the first newspaper in America is found in *American Journalism* by Mott, pages 9 and following, previously cited.

Cost of early newspapers in America is found in *The Daily Newspaper in America* by A. M. Lee, previously cited. Numbers of papers in the United States over a period of years is found in the appendix to the same book.

The estimate of 2,700 urban places of 8,000 population or more in the United States today is reached by interpolating between present population size categories given in *The Statistical Abstract of the United States, 1968.*

Statistics on immigration into the United States in the nineteenth and twentieth centuries is from the *Historical Statistics of the United States.*

Size of the membership of the Associated Press and United Press in their early history is found in *The Daily Newspaper in America* by A. M. Lee, previously cited, and in *American Journalism* by F. L. Mott, previously cited.

Endorsements of Republican candidates for president by newspapers is developed from the quadrennial information published by *Editor & Publisher* magazine on presidential endorsements. These figures are also discussed in *American Journalism* by Mott, previously cited.

The number of television and radio sets turned on at various times of day, used to approximate sets turned on at noontime, is drawn from data published in the *Broadcasting Yearbook, 1969.*

The estimates of transmission time for newspaper facsimile is from an article by Dr. Fischbeck in *Printing Magazine/National Lithographer* and quoted in *Graphic Communications Weekly,* page 9, for August 6, 1968.

Gross national product in 1967 is found in *The Statistical Abstract of the United States, 1968,* page 313. This same table gives personal consumption expenditures.

Total advertising expenditures in 1967 are found in *The Statistical Abstract of the United States, 1968,* page 782.

The amount of advertising allocated to each medium is found in *The Statistical Abstract of the United States, 1968,* page 783.

13. Future News and Future Society

The proportion of households watching certain kinds of programs is drawn from the Television Information Office, New York City, which bases its estimates on ratings by Nielsen.

The amount of commercial time bought from networks in 1967 is based on the FCC document "News," entitled "TV Broadcast Financial Data—1967," table 1, previously cited.

The leading commercial buyers of time on national television are listed in *Broadcasting Magazine,* for February 5, 1968, page 22.

The reference to Franklin Roosevelt and the Fireside Chats is found in the collected letters of FDR, *F.D.R., His Personal Letters, 1928–1945,* Volume II, Duell, Sloan and Pearce, 1950.

Index

Selected R A N D Books

Dole, Stephen H. and Isaac Asimov, *Planets for Man*. New York: Random House, Inc., 1964.

Downs, Anthony, *Inside Bureaucracy*. Boston, Massachusetts: Little, Brown and Company, 1967.

George, Alexander L., *Propaganda Analysis: A Study of Inferences Made from Nazi Propaganda in World War II*. Evanston, Illinois: Row, Peterson and Company, 1959.

Goldhamer, Herbert and Andrew W. Marshall, *Psychosis and Civilization*. Glencoe, Illinois: The Free Press, 1953.

Hitch, Charles J., and Roland McKean, *The Economics of Defense in the Nuclear Age*. Cambridge, Massachusetts: Harvard University Press, 1960.

Kershaw, Joseph A., and Roland N. McKean, *Teacher Shortages and Salary Schedules*. New York: McGraw-Hill Book Company, Inc., 1962.

McKinsey, J. C. C., *Introduction to the Theory of Games*. New York: McGraw-Hill Book Company, Inc., 1952.

Mead, Margaret, *Soviet Attitudes Toward Authority: An Inter-disciplinary Approach to Problems of Soviet Character*. New York: McGraw-Hill Book Company, Inc., 1951.

Meyer, John R., Martin Wohl, and John F. Kain, *The Urban Transportation Problem*. Cambridge, Massachusetts: Harvard University Press, 1965.

Nelson, Richard R., Merton J. Peck and Edward D. Kalachek, *Technology Economic Growth and Public Policy*. Washington, D.C.: The Brookings Institution, 1967.

Novick, David (ed.), *Program Budgeting: Program Analysis and the Federal Budget,* Cambridge, Massachusetts: Harvard University Press, 1965.

Pascal, Anthony, *Thinking About Cities: New Perspectives on Urban Problems.* Belmont, California: Dickenson Publishing Company, 1970.

Sharpe, William F., *The Economics of Computers.* New York: Columbia University Press, 1969.

Sheppard, Joseph J., *Human Color Perception.* New York: American Elsevier Publishing Company, 1968.

Smith, Bruce L., and Chitra M. Smith, *International Communication and Political Opinion: A Guide to the Literature.* Princeton, New Jersey: Princeton University Press, 1956.

The RAND Corporation, *A Million Random Digits with 100,000 Normal Deviates.* Glencoe, Illinois: The Free Press, 1955.

Williams, John D., *The Compleat Strategyst: Being a Primer on the Theory of Games of Strategy.* New York: McGraw-Hill Book Company, Inc., 1954.

71 72 73 10 9 8 7 6 5 4 3 2 1